Explaining One's Self to Others: Reason-Giving in a Social Context

COMMUNICATION

A series of volumes edited by
Dolf Zillmann and Jennings Bryant

Explaining One's Self to Others:
Reason-Giving in a Social Context

Edited by

Margaret L. McLaughlin
Michael J. Cody
Stephen J. Read
University of Southern California

LEA LAWRENCE ERLBAUM ASSOCIATES, PUBLISHERS
1992 Hillsdale, New Jersey   Hove and London

Lawrence Erlbaum Associates, Inc., Publishers
365 Broadway
Hillsdale, New Jersey 07642

Library of Congress Cataloging-in-Publication Data

Explaining one's self to others : reason-giving in a social context /
   edited by Margaret L. McLaughlin, Michael J. Cody, and Stephen J. Read.
      p.   cm.
   ISBN 0-8058-0799-3
   1. Attribution (Social psychology) 2. Explanation.
   3. Interpersonal relations. I. McLaughlin, Margaret L. II. Cody,
   Michael J. III. Read, Stephen J.
   HM132.E963 1992
   302'.12—dc20   91-27122
                                                              CIP

Printed in the United States of America
10 9 8 7 6 5 4 3 2 1

Contents

Contributors

KARIN ARONSSON is Professor, Department of Child Studies, Linkoping University, Sweden. She received her PhD in Psychology from the University of Lund. Her major research is in language acquisition, bilingualism, and language and social interaction. Several recent publications concern institutional discourse, including pediatric interviews and courtroom interaction.

LANCE BENNETT is Professor of Political Science, University of Washington. He is interested in the study of narrative discourse in the courtroom. His books include *News: The Politics of Illusion* and *Reconstructing Reality in the Courtroom: Justice and Judgment in American Culture.*

ROBERT J. BIES (PhD, Stanford University) is Associate Professor of Management, School of Business Administration, Georgetown University. His research focuses on the delivery of bad news, account-giving, procedural justice, and legalistic influences in organizations. His research has appeared in *Communication Research, Academy of Management Journal, Academy of Management Review, Research in Organizational Behavior,* and *Research on Negotiations in Organizations.*

DAVID O. BRAATEN (PhD, University of Southern California) is Associate Professor of Cross Cultural Communication, Thunderbird American Graduate School of International Management. He studies conflict and communication problems in international corporations.

MICHAEL J. CODY (PhD, Michigan State University) is Professor of Communication Arts and Sciences, University of Southern California. He studies social influence processes.

RISA DICKSON (PhD, University of Southern California) is Assistant Professor of Communication Studies, California State University, San Bernardino. Her interests include attribution processes, attachment styles, and communication among the aging.

PHILOMENA ESSED, Center for Race and Ethnic Studies, University of Amsterdam, has published articles in the fields of race relations theory, social psychology, discourse studies, and feminist theory. Her research interests include the development of interdisciplinary and cross-cultural perspectives on the experience of Black women. She is the author of *Everyday Racism* and *Understanding Everyday Racism.*

FRANK D. FINCHAM was a Rhodes Scholar at the University of Oxford, where he obtained his PhD. Since then he has conducted research on marital dysfunction and on the relationship between marital and child problems. His work has resulted in career awards from the British Psychological Society and the International Network on Personal Relationships.

ADRIAN FURNHAM was educated at the London School of Economics and Oxford University and is currently Reader in Psychology at University College, London. His interests lie mainly in applied, occupational, personality and social psychology. He has published ten books and about 250 papers on these topics. His most current interests include lay theories of psychotherapy and of occupational success.

JOHN H. HARVEY is Professor of Psychology at the University of Iowa. His primary area of interest is attribution theory, especially as applied to the dynamics of close relationships. His books include (with W. J. Ickes and R. F. Kidd) the *New Directions in Attribution Research* series, (with G. Weary) *Perspectives on Attributional Processes,* (with H. H. Kelley et al.) *Close Relationships,* and the forthcoming *Attribution, Accounts, and Close Relationships* (with T. L. Orbuch and A. L. Weber).

DENIS HILTON was an Alexander von Humboldt Research Fellow at ZUMA, Mannheim and the Universität Mannheim during the period of the research reported in this volume. He has also taught and researched at universities in Great Britain and the United States, and is interested in processes of causal explanation.

MANSUR LALLJEE obtained a degree in Philosophy at Bombay University, and then studied Psychology and Philosophy at Oxford University, where he went on to complete his PhD in Psychology. He is currently in the Department of Applied Social Studies and Social Research at Oxford, where he is a Fellow of Jesus College. He has held visiting appointments at Trinity College, Dublin; the University of New South Wales, Sydney; and Yale University. His current research interests lie mainly in the area of attributions and attitudes.

ROGER LAMB has Oxford University degrees in Philosophy and Classics as well as Psychology. He has published primarily on communication and social cognition, and is an editor of several books including *The Encyclopedic Dictionary of Psychology* and the *Dictionary of Personality and Social Psychology*. He teaches at Oxford University and Oxford Polytechnic.

VALERIE MANUSOV (PhD, University of Southern California) is Assistant Professor of Communication, Rutgers. Her interests include attribution processes and nonverbal communication in interpersonal relationships.

RAINER MATHES is Director of the Department for Text Analysis, Media Analysis and Coding at ZUMA (Center for Survey and Methodology) in Mannheim, Germany. He is a communication researcher, mainly interested in the analysis of mass media content and media effects.

JOHN McCLURE is lecturer in Psychology at Victoria University, Wellington, New Zealand. He received his PhD at the University of Oxford and is author of the book, *Explanations, Accounts, and Illusions*. His research interests focus on explanations, causal reasoning, and helplessness; he also has an interest in theories in social psychology.

MARGARET L. McLAUGHLIN (PhD, University of Illinois) is Professor of Communication Arts and Sciences, University of Southern California. Her interests include conversation analysis, communication and the sexes, and explanations in social contexts.

CLAES NILHOLM is a doctoral student in the Department of Communication Studies at the University of Linkoping, Sweden. He is completing his dissertation about mother–child interaction and he is working in a project concerning communication with severely brain-injured adults.

TERRI L. ORBUCH is Assistant Professor of Sociology at the University of Michigan. She recently completed a postdoctoral fellowship in the Department of Psychology at the University of Iowa. She is editor of the forthcoming, *Close Relationship Loss: Theoretical Approaches*.

STEPHEN J. READ (PhD, University of Texas) is Associate Professor of Psychology at the University of Southern California. His primary interests are in models of social explanation and the cognitive processes involved in close relationships. He has published several articles on a knowledge structure approach to explanation, and with Lynn C. Miller has published several chapters on their Interpersonalism Model, a goal-based model of the cognitive and behavioral processes underlying dyadic interactions.

SIM B. SITKIN (PhD, Stanford University) is Assistant Professor of Management, Graduate School of Business, University of Texas at Austin. His research focuses on secrecy in organizations, the rising influence of legal concerns in organizations, mergers and acquisitions, and how organizations learn from failure. His research has appeared in *Administrative Science Quarterly, Academy of Management Review, Research in Organizational Behavior,* and *Research in the Sociology of Organizations.*

TOM TRABASSO is head of the Department of Psychology at the University of Chicago. His main interests are in cognitive and developmental psychology, and he has worked on concept learning, inference processes, and memory for stories.

WILLIAM TURNBULL is an Associate Professor of Psychology at Simon Graser University. His main research interests are psychological pragmatics and the social psychology of counterfactual worlds.

ANN L. WEBER is Professor of Psychology at the University of North Carolina at Asheville. She is co-author (with Harvey and Orbuch) of *Interpersonal Accounts: A Social Psychological Perspective.* She is the author of chapters in *Accounting for Relationships, The State of Social Psychology,* and *Intimacy.* In addition to her work on accounts, she is interested in social psychology and the psychology of close relationships.

BERNARD WEINER is Professor of Psychology at the University of California, Los Angeles. His major research is in the areas of motivation and emotion from an attributional perspective. He is the 1990 recipient of the Donald Campbell Distinguished Research in Social Psychology Award from the American Psychological Association.

Introduction

The study of communicated explanations has been, at best, unsystematic. Researchers in that aspect of social psychology, ordinarily referred to as attribution theory, have, historically, studied the process of explanation strictly as an intrapsychic phenomenon. That is, there has been very little recognition that many, if not most, explanations will eventually be delivered to a hearer or hearers, and that this potential audience constitutes a source of constraint on the ultimate way the explanation is shaped. Similarly, researchers who have devoted themselves to the study of "accounts," a tradition found largely within the confines of sociology, organizational behavior, and communication studies, have, for the most part, examined only the discourse manifestations of explanation, without a concomitant interest in the fundamental processes of event comprehension. This volume is devoted to bridging the gap between the two traditions.

The chapters in the first section, "The Nature of Social Explanation," examine general issues of social explanation, in particular, the cognitive processes and knowledge involved in the construction of accounts. In fact, several of the chapters present general models of the cognitive processes underlying account-giving. Many of these chapters also deal with general aspects of the social context that affect the kind of explanation people offer. However, they do not focus on the impact of concrete social contexts or on specific kinds of accounts (despite the use of concrete examples to illustrate their general concerns). In contrast, chapters in the second section of the book deal more concretely with accounts. They examine the role of accounts in specific kinds of settings, such as organizations, or the courts; or they deal with specific kinds of accounts, such as accounts of racism or accounts of relationship breakdowns.

Read (chapter 1) has previously presented a general model of how people comprehend and explain social interaction (Miller & Read, in press; Read, 1987; Read & Collins, in press). The emphasis in these writings was on how people make sense of social behavior. Here he outlines how this model, with appropriate modifications, can also be used to explicate the process by which people construct accounts to try to repair a social failure. The model integrates Schank and Abelson's (1977) work on a knowledge structure approach and other work on text comprehension (e.g., Kintsch, 1988), with recent work on connectionist modeling (e.g., Rumelhart, McClelland, and the PDP Research Group, 1986; Thagard, 1989). A central part of the model is the argument that judgments of the coherence of an account and of the way in which it hangs together will play major roles in how the account is constructed and will subsequently play a major role in whether it is honored. Based on Thagard's (1989) model of explanatory coherence, Read outlines specific principles that underlie coherence judgments.

In presenting the model, Read also analyzes many of the other factors that go into the construction of a successful account. For example, an effective accounter needs to assess what the recipient knows and believes because this can place important constraints on the nature of the account that one can construct. In addition, an accounter must pay attention to his or her goals in constructing the account and to whether the account, as constructed, is likely to achieve those goals. Further, in constructing the account, it is useful to try to take the recipient's perspective and try to evaluate whether he or she is likely to find the account to be coherent.

Read outlines how these and additional factors can all be integrated in a general model for constructing accounts. He also, as just noted, indicates how the construction of accounts depends on many of the same processes that are involved in the understanding of social interaction.

Lamb and Lalljee (chapter 2) start with the question of how people generate causal hypotheses in trying to explain actions. They argue that actions are typically represented in terms of prototypes, with a set of typical explanations associated with these actions. Thus, when an action is categorized, the associated typical explanations give a range of possible explanations from which people may select. The choice from among this range may be affected by self-presentational concerns, as well as by the plausibility of the explanation given the evidence. Only rarely will people go beyond this set of typical explanations.

They present two studies that support this model. In the first, they show that schoolgirls' explanations of their own aggressive behavior were drawn from the same set of explanations identified by a separate sample as typical explanations of aggression. However, there was some evidence that the nature of the selection was consistent with a self-enhancing or self-protective motivation. In a second study, they demonstrated that subjects' categorizations of an ambiguous story as being about a particular type of crime was strongly related to subjects' tendencies to explain that story in terms of typical explanations for that type of crime. Interestingly, in both studies they found that people often use a chain of several interrelated causes to explain an action; this is in contrast to a typical assumption in the attribution literature that people tend to give only one explanation for an event. This finding is related to McClure's discussion in this volume, that contrary to the received wisdom in attribution theory, discounting of explanations is often not evident. Instead people often show a preference for multiple causation of actions.

Hilton, Mathes, and Trabasso (chapter 3) present an interesting alternative to the typical theoretical and methodological approaches to the study of attributions in social psychology. They do this in two ways: by elaborating on Hilton's conversation model of explanation and by presenting a detailed coding scheme for the analysis of naturally occurring explanations.

Hilton's conversation model of explanations relies on work on ordinary language philosophy and conversational maxims (Grice, 1975) to explicate how people construct explanations and present them to others. The model has two stages: First, people diagnose the cause of an event, typically starting with an initial, vague hypothesis and then, by a process of elaboration and specification, try to develop an explanation they believe to be true. Second, people use this diagnosis to answer specific "why" questions about the event. In answering the why questions, subjects may "tune" their answers based on their assumptions about what would be an informative answer for their audience.

Hilton, Mathes, and Trabasso present their detailed coding system as an antidote to methodological shortcomings in much standard attribution research. They note that most work in attribution has focused on fairly simple events in laboratory settings. They argue that if we wish to understand how explanations are actually constructed in real world settings, then we need to study spontaneous explanations of complex [real-world] events. They present a detailed model for coding such explanations in terms of quantitative content analysis, along with an initial application of this coding system to accounts of the Challenger shuttle disaster printed by *The New York Times*. This method looks to be extremely promising for the study of naturally occurring complex explanations.

McClure (chapter 4) attacks one of the sacred cows of the attribution literature, the principle of discounting. In a careful review of the literature on discounting effects in attribution and on people's use of conjunctive explanations (explanations involving multiple causes), he shows that, in contrast to the usual assumption that there is strong support for discounting, in fact ". . . people systematically deviate from the discounting rule, and frequently make attributions consistent with multiple causation."

After establishing this, McClure then analyzes the factors that influence when people do and do not discount. One factor that appears to be central is the structure and content of the possible causes for the particular event being explained. For example, the structure of a situation is often such that a given action will achieve multiple goals or there are several factors that impact on any given outcome. In such situations, all the factors may be jointly responsible for the outcome and it would be unlikely that people would discount alternative causes. To take McClure's example: "When a person is violent, for example, the fact that the individual is drunk does not entail that provocation was absent." In fact, drunkenness and provocation together undoubtedly provide a more satisfying explanation than either one alone. McClure suggests that we are most likely to get discounting when the alternative causes are mutually exclusive or incompatible.

He also proposes that we may sometimes get what looks like discounting in conversations because of people's conversational goals. McClure argues, as have others, that people often selectively recount only parts of what they consider to be the complete explanation, because they believe that some of the factors in the explanation can be presupposed. Parenthetically, Thagard's principles of explanatory coherence (discussed in Read's chapter) such as parsimony, breadth, and being explained by higher-order explanations, may also be relevant to an understanding as to when we should and should not expect discounting.

Furnham (chapter 5) focuses on the lay theories that people possess about most aspects of social life and on the implications of these lay theories for people's explanations of social behavior. He identifies a number of different facets of lay theories, such as their etiology, structure, and function, that need to be much more extensively studied. Following this, he reviews examples of research on lay theories, such as lay theories of child development and the impact of contextual factors on people's expression of their lay theories. He closes by reviewing the literature on the Barnum effect.

Turnbull (chapter 6) investigates the impact of social structure on explanation in social interaction. His particular focus is accounters' concerns with their own or the other's image or face and the impact this has on explanations. He uses Brown and Levinson's (1987) politeness model as a framework for investigating the impact of one kind of social structure and relative status on the use of politeness strategies when refusing to comply with a request. Turnbull argues that individuals who refuse a request will rarely do so directly, but will, instead, use various politeness strategies. Further, the higher the relative status of the one making the request, the greater should be the use of such strategies.

Turnbull manipulated the status of an individual requesting undergraduates to participate in an experiment at a very inconvenient time. As expected, individuals who refused this request (as all did) rarely used direct refusals, but instead used various politeness strategies such as delaying and mitigating their refusal, and offering excuses for why they could not accede to the request. Contrary to predictions, there was no impact of the status of the requester on the use of politeness strategies. Turnbull discusses the implications of this latter finding for the politeness model.

Weiner (chapter 7) applies his work on the dimensions underlying explanations to understanding both the characteristics of people's excuses and what makes for an effective excuse. First, he compares the dimensional structure of what people said were the real reasons various transgressions occurred, with the dimensional structure of the accounts they actually gave. He found that "causes that are with-held are internal to the transgressor, under that person's control, and stable." In contrast, the actual causes that were communicated were "external to the offender, not controllable by that person, and quite unstable." The largest difference be-tween withheld (true) explanations and communicated explanations is on control-lability. Weiner demonstrates that these characteristics of excuses are related to their effectiveness. Excuses in terms of external, uncontrollable, and unstable causes "enhance the personal relationship, maintain the self-image of the excuse-giver, lessen that person's responsibility, and reduce the anger of the listener toward the excuse-giver, when compared with the estimates of the effects of the with-held cause."

Interestingly, Weiner presents evidence that an understanding of the charac-teristics of effective excuses might be related to social competence in children. He found that at-risk, aggressive children do not seem to understand the charac-teristics of effective excuses as well as normal children. At-risk children expect-ed higher levels of aggression following an explanation for a transgression in terms of uncontrollable causes, and they were more likely to give controllable causes and less likely to give uncontrollable causes than were normal children.

In Part II, "Explanations and Social Contexts," the volume moves more nar-rowly into the examination of explanations in social contexts. Contributors con-sider the limiting effects of a variety of extra-cognitive factors such as institutional traditions and practices, relationship history, social and political inequalities, and interactional constraints.

Bennett (chapter 8) argues that jurors' verdicts are shaped by the attorney's narratives of evidence and testimony. Jurors reach their decisions by assembling a coherent narrative of events in the face of (or with the assistance of) competing "stories" from defense and prosecution. Bennett explicates the process by which lawyers develop and support a narrative that fits their case theory, guiding it through the obstacle course posed by conflicting testimony, unsatisfactory wit-nesses, opposition challenges, and other distracting factors. Of crucial impor-tance to jurors' acceptance of a narrative, Bennett argues, is that the jurors be able to accept the structure of assumptions that underlie the story; that is, that they accept the accounts of the defendant's motives and behavior as plausible. Much of the attorney's work may lie, Bennett reports, in educating the jury to the ways of life in the world of the defendant. The defendant receives a just hear-ing only if the lawyer can develop a theory of the facts that fits with the most favorable legal theory, and can provide the background knowledge necessary for jurors to comprehend and accept the factual theory as it unfolds in courtroom narrative.

Fincham (chapter 9) analyzes four factors in accounting episodes: the antece-dent conditions that instigate the account, the reproach that calls for the account, the account itself, and its evaluation. For each factor, he develops postulates that might be explored in future research. In considering account episodes in close relationships, Fincham considers the effects of enduring personality variables (self-esteem level, optimism/pessimism) on interpretation of minor relational infractions, including immediate evaluation of accounts for the violation and subsequent reappraisals. Fincham also argues for the importance of relationship satisfaction and spouses' goals to the interpretation and evaluation of failure events in close relationships.

Bies and Sitkin (chapter 10) review their own and others' research on excuses for failure events in organizational settings, such as poor employee performance, budget cuts, unethical behavior, and so forth. Bies and Sitkin consider the content of excuses (e.g., formal company policy, the political environment, coordination needs), as well as the use of multiple reasons and the timing of excuses. The authors review research on the mitigating effects of excuses as well as such factors as perceived sincerity, outcome negativity, and audience characteristics that influence the effectiveness of excuse-making.

Essed's chapter (chapter 11), in something of a departure from others in this section, examines the effects of knowledge of racism in victims' accounts for episodes of sexual harrassment. Essed reconstructs the process by which women come to recognize their experiences as manifestations of sexual racism.

Essed develops a flow diagram of interpretive steps, in which the initial steps in interpretation of questionable behavior depend on the effective use of situation knowledge: (a) is the behavior acceptable or not? (b) if not, are there acceptable excuses for the unacceptable behavior? Subsequent steps in the diagram invoke general knowledge of racism: (c) is it because I am Black? (d) is the specific event excusable? (e) is the event socially significant? (f) where does the event fit within the historical and social context of sexual racism? Essed demonstrates relationships between her model and Kelley's covariation principle.

Cody and Braaten (chapter 12) consider the relationship between reproaches for failure events, the accounts that they elicit, and the evaluation of those accounts. Of particular interest is a rather consistently obtained relationship between severely negative reproaching, defensive accounts, and negative evaluation or rejection of accounts as offered. Cody and Braaten review the basic structure of account episodes and survey the considerable variety of negative reproach forms, including anger expressions, threats, and attacks on self-esteem.

Cody and Braaten call for researchers to give renewed attention to attribution theory in their pursuit of knowledge about accounts. Especially needed, the authors argue, is an understanding of how account-givers attribute the causes of a reproacher's behavior and how reproachers deal with impression management issues.

Aronsson and Nilholm (chapter 13) demonstrate, through an ingenious experiment, that lay judges in a child custody case distort the temporal order of events in a sequence to coincide with a preferred version or story. The authors demonstrate that such reconstructions can occur collaboratively in interacting groups, with co-participants actually ratifying invented temporal sequences to support a colleague's preferred story ordering or to disambiguate task complexities.

Weber, Harvey, and Orbuch (chapter 14) review their considerable research on the topic of explanations for relationship dissolution. The authors consider the variety of roles played by the process of developing, refining, and communicating accounts among those who have experienced a relationship loss. Accounts can contribute to the ability to make sense of the loss and constitute a major portion of the "obsessive review" that some persons go through following dissolution. Accounts provide a vehicle through which the need to disclose, unburden, or confess may be implemented. For those who epitomize what has been called the "triumph of hope over experience," a coherent and face-preserving account of the reasons for the relationship break-up can be an invaluable tool in the process of dating and re-mating.

In the final chapter, McLaughlin, Cody, Dickson, and Manusov (chapter 15) report on their study of explanations for failure to follow advice. Like Weiner, McLaughlin et al. were interested in the differences between communicated explanations and "real reasons." The authors adopt the Leddo and Abelson premise that a good place to look for explanations for a failure event is in the sequence of actions required for the successful performance of that act.

McLaughlin et al. report that, in accounting for one's hypothetical failure to follow a friend's advice, most respondents did indeed regard script-based accounts (preparation failure, entry failure, doing failure, etc.) as good excuses, but tended to regard goal-based explanations such as forgetting or lack of will as more likely candidates for "real reasons."

ACKNOWLEDGMENTS

Many of the chapters in this volume began as papers presented at a session on "Communicated Explanations" presented at the 40th annual meeting of the International Communication Association at Trinity College, Dublin, Ireland, in June of 1990. The editors would like to express their gratitude here to Sylvester Whitaker, Dean, College of Social Sciences and Communication, for his support of our efforts in organizing and presenting the program of papers.

REFERENCES

Brown, P., & Levinson, S. (1987). *Politeness: Some universals in language usage*. Cambridge, England: Cambridge University Press.

Grice, H. P. (1975). Logic and conversation. In P. Cole & J. L. Morgan (Eds.), *Syntax and semantics: Vol 3. Speech acts* (pp. 41–58). New York: Academic.

Kintsch, W. (1988). The role of knowledge in discourse comprehension: A construction-integration model. *Psychological Review, 95*, 163–182.

Miller, L. C., & Read, S. J. (1991). On the coherence of mental models of persons and relationships: A knowledge structure approach. In G. J. O. Fletcher & F. Fincham (Eds.), *Cognition in close relationships* (pp. 69–99). Hillsdale, NJ: Lawrence Erlbaum Associates.

Read, S. J. (1987). Constructing causal scenarios: A knowledge structure approach to causal reasoning. *Journal of Personality and Social Psychology, 52,* 288–302.

Read, S. J., & Collins, N. L. (in press). Accounting for relationships: A knowledge structure approach. In J. Harvey, T. Orbuch, & A. Weber (Eds.), *Attributions, accounts, and close relationships.* New York: Springer-Verlag.

Rumelhart, D. E., McClelland, J. L., and the PDP Research Group (1986). *Parallel distributed processing. Explorations in the microstructure of cognition. Vol. 1: Foundations.* Cambridge, MA: MIT Press.

Schank, R. C., & Abelson, R. P. (1977). *Scripts, plans, goals, and understanding.* Hillsdale, NJ: Lawrence Erlbaum Associates.

Thagard, P. (1989). Explanatory coherence. *Behavioral and Brain Sciences, 12,* 435–467.

The Nature of
Social Explanations

1
▼▼▼▼▼▼▼

Constructing Accounts: The Role of Explanatory Coherence

Stephen J. Read
University of Southern California

When we are reproached for some social failure, such as harming someone or violating important social rules, how do we construct an account for that failure so that it will be honored? Although considerable research has focused on the nature of different kinds of accounts and their function in interpersonal situations, little work has examined how people actually construct their accounts (for a partial exception see Cody & McLaughlin, 1990). Yet clearly when we construct our accounts we want them to be honored by the recipient. What is the process by which we do this?

In this chapter we outline a model of how people construct accounts, based on recent work on a knowledge structure approach to explanation and causal reasoning (Miller & Read, in press; Read, 1987; Read & Miller, 1989). This model is based on Schank and Abelson's (1977) knowledge structure approach and other recent work in text comprehension and cognitive science (Kintsch, 1988; Thagard, 1989; for related accounts see Abelson & Lalljee, 1988; Lalljee & Abelson, 1983).

Central to this model is the argument that judgments of the coherence of an account, of whether and to what extent it "hangs together," play a major role both in its construction and in its evaluation by others. Thus, when people construct accounts they strive to construct a coherent account in which everything "fits together." And when people receive an account, their judgments of its coherence will play a large part in whether they honor it. In this model the coherence of an account is strongly based on goal-based and causal links among the elements composing it. Our discussion of coherence relies heavily on Thagard's (1989)

3

model of explanatory coherence. A further feature of the present model is the claim that in order to construct accounts that will be honored, we must take the perspective of our reproachers in constructing our accounts and evaluate how coherent they are likely to find them to be.

Researchers on *accounts* have applied the term to somewhat different phenomena (see Antaki, 1987, for a discussion). Some have used account to refer to the narratives or stories that we use to explain and make sense of social interaction. Others have meant by account the way in which people try to affect a repair of a social failure. Here we focus on this second sense. Nevertheless, although the functions of these kinds of accounts differ, both rely on many of the same cognitive processes for their construction.

In examining how people construct accounts it is helpful to first consider the canonical form of the account sequence as discussed by Cody and McLaughlin (1985, 1988) and Schonbach (1990). It begins with the failure event for which an account must be given. This failure typically involves a violation of social norms or expectations or an apparent injury to another. This then leads to a reproach or request for repair. This reproach typically identifies what needs to be accounted for and thereby tells the accounter to what things he or she needs to attend.

In response, the accounter must give an account. It is this step on which this chapter focuses. Once the account is offered, the reproacher then evaluates the account for its adequacy in effecting repair. Some of what is said about how accounts are constructed is also relevant to how the adequacy of accounts is evaluated.

Work on accounts (e.g., Cody & McLaughlin, 1990; Schonbach, 1990) has identified four major types. Each tries to do a different thing, and, thus, each has its own unique implications for how that type of account will be constructed.

In giving an *excuse*, offenders deny their responsibility for the failure and thus attempt to avoid blame and punishment. The offender admits that a harmful act occurred but argues that he or she is not responsible for the harm. Possible excuses include the claim that the negative consequences were not foreseen or were not foreseeable, or that the individual was under a considerable amount of outside pressure. Perhaps the most effective way to deny responsibility for an event is to claim that one had no causal impact on the outcome. In line with this, Weiner (this volume) argues that effective excuses displace causality from the offender to some other source. He finds that an effective excuse refers to causes that are external to the offender, uncontrollable by the offender and unstable.

In providing a *justification*, the offender admits responsibility for the offense but tries to show why no reproach is warranted. For example, the offender may claim that the behavior was justified because no harm was actually done or because the action had positive consequences that outweighed any negative consequences.

A third type of account is the *concession*, in which the offender simply admits to the claimed offense, although often to the accompaniment of apologies, expressions of remorse, or offers to make restitution. Interestingly, when individuals apologize or make offers of restitution they may still be seeking to deflect censure and blame, but they are not using an account of the failure event to do so.

The fourth category of account is the *refusal*. One type of refusal is to deny that the action for which one is being reproached even occurred. This is essentially to claim that the reproacher's version of the facts is wrong. For example: "How can you say that I insulted David? That wasn't an insult. This is just part of a certain kind of verbal game playing in which many men engage. I didn't intend it as an insult and he didn't take it that way." Or in Cody and McLaughlin's (1988) work on accounting for traffic violations, a refusal would be a denial that the claimed traffic violation, such as speeding or parking illegally, had actually occurred. Or in a murder trial one might try to argue that the alleged victim was not murdered, either because no body has been found or because the victim died of natural causes.

Another type of refusal is to deny that the other party has the right of reproach. For example, one could claim that because the reproacher was not the party that was supposedly offended then the reproacher has no grounds for making the reproach. For instance, "This has nothing to do with you. If Bob is so upset let him tell me himself."

HOW ACCOUNTS ARE CONSTRUCTED

The Role of Goals in Constructing Accounts

Accounts are shaped by goals in social interaction, and different goals may shape accounts in different ways. For example, one important goal is to represent the world as accurately as possible. However, other possible goals are to avoid blame and censure, which often lead us to try to excuse or justify our behavior.

If we are fortunate, all these goals are consistent. Unfortunately, the goals of truthfulness and avoiding blame frequently conflict. Many times presenting an accurate account will neither excuse nor justify our behavior, but instead will simply confirm that the reproacher was right to reproach us. Here, we must decide which goals take precedence.

If our primary goal is truth, then our focus is to develop the most accurate account possible. However, if our primary goal is to justify or excuse our behavior we must focus on how to do this. And, if in constructing such an account, we must be less than faithful to the facts, we must ensure that the reproacher does not find out. As we discuss in more detail later, this suggests that often we may be quite concerned with what the reproacher knows so that we can know whether and how the facts constrain us.

However, there is an additional, more general goal when we construct accounts.

This is to have our account be honored. After all, it is pointless to construct an account of the proper form if it is not honored.

Thus, our accounts are shaped by two major purposes: (a) to construct an account that, if honored, would achieve the purpose of that kind of account, whether it be to excuse one's behavior, justify it, or to accept reproach from others; and (b) to have the account be honored.

Preliminary Steps in Constructing an Account

How do we construct accounts so that they achieve both of these purposes? Central to this process is trying to take the perspective of the reproacher to whom we will offer it. Ideally, we should figure out what the reproacher knows about the failure event (Schlenker, 1980), how he or she interprets the situation, and what his or her theories are about the social and physical worlds (Schlenker). Then, guided by the purpose for which we are constructing the account, we must combine our knowledge about the other with our own knowledge and beliefs to construct a tentative account. We must then look at the account from the reproacher's perspective and evaluate whether he or she is likely to find the account coherent and thus honor it. In addition, we must also evaluate whether, if it is honored, it will have the impact we desire. For example, if we are trying to give an excuse in which we deflect causality away from ourselves does the reproacher interpret the account that way and honor it? Many times the accounter may mentally try out several alternative accounts and try to evaluate which one is most likely to be honored by the reproacher.

Let us look at this process in more detail.

We (Miller & Read, 1991; Read, 1987; Read & Collins, 1991) and others (Bennett, this volume; Weber, Harvey, & Orbuch, this volume) have argued that accounts can be viewed as stories or narratives that present a particular version of the events at issue. Consistent with work on story comprehension (e.g., Mandler, 1978; Mandler & Johnson, 1977; Rumelhart, 1977; Schank & Abelson, 1977; Stein & Glenn, 1979) and on the structure of social episodes (e.g., Argyle, Furnham, & Graham, 1981; Barker, 1963; Forgas, 1979), we argue that such narratives have a typical form consisting of:

1. the goals of the actor(s),
2. factors that instigated those goals, such as the actions of others, environmental occurrences, or personal characteristics of the actor(s),
3. a behavioral sequence composed of the plans and strategies that are being enacted to achieve those goals,
4. what happened to the goals. Are the goals satisfied or blocked?, and
5. the physical and social situation in which the actions occurred.

The reproacher, either explicitly or implicitly, projects a narrative having this general form in which the accounter's actions have had negative consequences either for the reproacher or for others. The reproacher typically identifies these negative consequences as intended outcomes of the accounter's behavior, as clearly foreseen, or as due to the carelessness or lack of foresight of the accounter.

In response to the reproach, the accounter responds with his or her own story. Its form depends on the kind of account being offered. In the concession the accounter's story is basically the same as the reproacher's and simply affirms the reproacher's account of the events. However, in excuses, justifications, and refusals the accounter seeks to "tell" a story that is different from the reproacher's. Moreover, each of these three types of accounts seeks to tell a different kind of story. In providing an excuse, the accounter tries to present a story in which the occurrence of the negative consequences was essentially outside the control of the accounter. For instance, they were due to external forces over which the accounter has no control. Thus, there is no relation between the intentional behavior of the accounter and the negative consequences.

In providing a justification, the accounter admits that he or she intentionally committed the alleged offense but claims that the behavior was justified given the consequences. For instance, the accounter may claim that contrary to what the reproacher says, there were no negative consequences to the accounter's actions. Alternatively, the accounter may admit that there were negative consequences but claim that the negative consequences were actually minor or were outweighed by the positive consequences.

Finally, in a refusal, the accounter argues that there is no basis for reproach, that the offense did not occur. Here the accounter is essentially claiming that the reproacher's story is completely wrong, that the accounter did not behave as claimed. For example, "I did not park in a no parking zone," "I was not speeding," or "I did not murder Jonathan. There is no body."

Now how does the accounter construct such narratives. First, the accounter must assess the facts of the case. This is clearly important if we want our account to accurately reflect what really happened. However, this is also very important if we intend to be "creative" with the facts. Any account should be constructed with the facts in mind, although the relation of the facts to the account may be quite loose, depending on various factors, such as our goals in giving the account, the actual facts, and what the reproacher knows of the facts of the case.

Second, the accounter must ascertain what the reproacher knows (or is likely to learn) of the facts (Schlenker, 1980). One reason for this is that we may be being reproached because the other is unaware of certain facts that, if known, would change his or her interpretation of the event. For example, a complete accounting of the facts may indicate that no offense was committed.

However, information about what the reproacher knows also tells us how tightly constrained we are by what actually happened and how "creative" we can be in giving our account. If the reproacher has all the facts then if we wish our account to be honored it must stick to them. Here, most of our work in creating our account is focused on what the facts mean and how they can be explained. After all, frequently a set of facts has multiple interpretations. The reproacher's interpretation is not the only one.

The importance of determining what the reproacher knows depends on the kind of account being constructed. Presumably, individuals who are trying to excuse or justify their behavior are very concerned with determining how creative they can be. However, individuals interested in giving an accurate accounting should be less concerned with determining the reproacher's knowledge. Although, even these individuals will have some interest in what the reproacher knows simply because of the pragmatics of successful communication (Clark, 1985).

Assessment of what the reproacher knows may also have a major impact on the kind of account that is given. For instance, an accounter may initially wish to excuse his or her behavior. However, if the reproacher is thought to know the facts and the facts admit of only one interpretation, that the reproach is indeed justified, then the accounter may decide that the only recourse is to give an accurate account and to throw oneself on the mercy of the court.

Third, it is also helpful to know the reproacher's interpretation of the facts, because it is this that led to the reproach. The interpretation is often revealed by the reproach, in conjunction with the failure event. Frequently, the interpretation is explicit: "Why do you always forget my birthday? Don't you love me?" However, other times the interpretation will be left implicit because there are widely accepted default explanations of which both parties are aware.

One reason it is so important to understand the reproacher's interpretation of the facts is that in most kinds of accounts the accounter is disputing that version of events. In disputing another's version of events we need to know what that version is.

Fourth, it can be of great importance to assess the reproachers' theories of social and physical causality (Schlenker, 1980), because these theories provide the basis for the kinds of explanations the reproacher is likely to accept. For example, an individual who strongly believes in a God who takes a hand in human affairs, or who believes in the paranormal or UFOs will be willing to accept classes of explanations that others would not. More mundanely, different beliefs about such things as roles and responsibilities can lead to important differences in what are viewed as acceptable accounts. In assessing the reproacher's theories we can rely on: (a) our assumptions about the beliefs they are likely to hold simply as human beings, (b) our assumptions about an individual's beliefs as a member of a particular class or group of people, and (c) our knowledge of them as individuals developed through our interactions with them and from information provided by others.

Fifth, if we have not already done so, we must decide what kind of account we wish to construct, and what constraints or guidance this places on the account we can build.

Thus, when we construct our account we must bear in mind:

1. the kind of account we wish to construct (excuse, justification, concession, or refusal),
2. our desire to have the account honored,
3. what we know of the facts of the case,
4. what the reproacher knows of the facts (or is likely to learn),
5. the reproacher's beliefs about social and physical causality, and
6. our own beliefs about physical and social causality.

Keeping all this in mind we must then construct one or several accounts that we hope will achieve the desired goal of that type of account. In doing this, we must try to evaluate the account we construct from the perspective of the reproacher so that we can judge the likelihood that the account will be honored.

As is argued in more detail shortly, one major criterion for whether an account is honored is the extent to which the reproacher finds the account to be explanatorily coherent and to be more coherent than alternative accounts that the reproacher is likely to entertain. To accurately assess its coherence from the perspective of the recipient, we must have a good idea of what facts the recipient knows and what social and physical theories they hold.

Bennett (this volume) argues that in some situations, if we wish to have our account honored, we must provide to our recipient certain facts and the social theories that make these facts intelligible. For instance, he argues that one problem lower-class defendants may have in court is that the jury is often composed of individuals who do not have the same social class background, and thus may not share the theories and knowledge that make the defendant's actions intelligible.

Bringing It All Together: Constructing the Account

As is obvious from the foregoing, constructing an account requires the integration of a tremendous amount of information into a coherent package. Now, how do we do this? One possibility is the following model proposed by Miller and Read (1991) and based on work in text comprehension (e.g., Kintsch, 1988; Schank & Abelson, 1977) and connectionist modeling (e.g., Rumelhart, McClelland, and the PDP research group, 1986; Thagard, 1989. See Miller & Read, 1991, for further discussion of the model). The model includes two major steps. First, concepts associated with input information are activated and organized into a loose, heterogeneous network. Doing this necessitates the making of numerous inferences about social and physical causality, based on extensive knowledge of the social and physical worlds. The nature of this knowledge has been extensively analyzed previously (Galambos, Abelson, & Black, 1986; Schank & Abelson, 1977; see also Miller & Read, 1991; Read & Miller, 1989) so we do not say much about it here. Second, this heterogeneous network of concepts is organized into a coherent representation of the input by the application of parallel constraint satisfaction processes that act to evaluate the explanatory coherence of the network. Some of the work on which this model is based has been explicitly modeled in various computer simulations (Kintsch, 1988; Thagard, 1989), although it can be understood on its own conceptual merits, apart from these simulations.

Step 1: Activation of Related Concepts.   Concepts are activated through something like a spreading activation process (e.g., Anderson, 1983; Collins & Loftus, 1975) in which activation spreads from an activated concept to those that are linked to it. The greater the activation of a structure, the more likely it is to be used to interpret information. Structures that are used in comprehension receive additional activation, but those that are not used decay.

Now, what kinds of things activate concepts, and what kinds of concepts are likely to be activated? Three primary sources of activated concepts are probably the failure for which we are being asked to account; the facts surrounding the failure, including events and situations leading up to the failure; and our goals in giving our account.

First, the failure event should activate a wide range of associated concepts. For example, if we are late for an appointment, this may activate a variety of potential explanations for being late, such as forgetting, getting stuck in traffic, having a previous appointment run over time, or having some kind of emergency. Abelson and Lalljee (1988) and Schank (1986) (see also Lamb & Lalljee, this volume) have suggested that many kinds of unexpected events (such as deaths or loss of valuables) nevertheless occur frequently enough that stereotyped explanations have been developed and stored for these events. Cody and McLaughlin (1990) argued that such explanation prototypes are an easily accessible, primary source of interpersonal accounts.

The activation of an explanation pattern may also activate various pieces of evidence or "facts" that are typically associated with that pattern. For instance, the family emergency explanation pattern might activate the concept of a sick child, or a spouse who had to go to the emergency ward. Or activation of the traffic jam explanation will probably lead to the activation of various reasons for traffic jams: stalled car, accident, or highway work. This suggests that these explanation patterns, in addition to providing potential explanations for known facts, would also be useful starting points for the fabrication of facts that can be used to further elaborate a false account.

The facts of the case should also activate associated concepts. For example, if we drove to our appointment then the concept of driving on the freeway should activate a whole host of related concepts including information about freeways (accidents, shootings on the freeway, couches in the freeway) and cars (stalled car, flat tire, etc.). Further, those things we actually observed on our drive, such as a freeway shooting or someone shaving while they are driving, would also be active concepts and should also activate related concepts.

On the other hand, if we walked down the hallway to the appointment, or came from another building, there are different concepts activated, such as running into someone who had an urgent question, forgetting, having a previous appointment, and so forth. And again, concepts will be activated by our actual experiences during the walk.

Finally, our goals in constructing the account should also affect which concepts are activated, as these goals shape the kind of account we try to build (e.g., concession, excuse, justification, and refusal). Because different kinds of accounts have quite different characteristics, different accounting goals should lead to the activation of different concepts. For example, people know that if they want to excuse an event the most effective way is to shift causality away from themselves (Weiner, this volume). Thus, this goal should tend to activate explanations that are external and uncontrollable. The goal of providing a justification should tend to activate concepts and explanations that demonstrate the unexpected benefits of the action or that show that the negative consequences are not as severe as the reproacher suggests. And the goal of refusing to account should lead the individual to search for concepts that provide interpretations of the event in which no failure occurred.

Clearly, a large number of concepts may be activated. Kintsch (1988) argued that at first concepts are activated somewhat indiscriminately, with little check on their consistency with other activated concepts. One can think of this stage in constructing the account as resulting in a "cloud" or "swarm" of concepts, facts, and explanations, some consistent, some contradictory, and some unrelated. All are connected in a loose network that is not yet a coherent account. In forming this network, items that initially activated each other will be connected, with a bias toward linking concepts that have causal and goal-based links with each other (Galambos, Abelson, & Black, 1986). Concepts that support each other, such as a fact and its potential explanation or a concept that further explains another explanation, will have positive links to each other and so will positively activate each other, whereas concepts that contradict each other, such as a fact that is inconsistent with an explanation, will have negative links, so that the activation of a concept will decrease the activation of concepts to which it has a negative link. Explanations are positively linked to facts they explain and negatively linked to facts that contradict the explanation. Further, explanations are positively linked to other explanations that support them and negatively linked to explanations that contradict them.

At first, this network includes an assortment of concepts that are relevant, irrelevant, or even inconsistent with the eventual representation of the event. Further, this network may include potential explanations of the input that are inconsistent with one another. However, during the second stage, by the application of a parallel constraint satisfaction process, a coherent account is arrived at.

Step 2: Arriving at a Coherent Representation. How do we move to a coherent representation? We propose a process in which activation is propagated through the links and concepts in parallel to arrive at the resulting level of activation for the concepts (e.g., Kintsch, 1988; Rumelhart, McClelland, and the PDP research group, 1986; Thagard, 1989). This process determines which of the activated concepts best characterizes the event and allows one to arrive at a coherent, consistent representation. The activation of a concept can be thought of as an indication of how strongly supported it is by other concepts as part of the representation. The greater the number of excitatory links to a concept and the greater the strength of the links, the higher the activation of that concept. Conversely, the greater the number of negative links and the greater their strength, the lower the activation of that concept. By this process, concepts that are not supported by other concepts in the network or that are strongly contradicted by other concepts "die out," and concepts that are supported are strengthened. For example, suppose two possible explanations for missing an appointment were activated during the first stage of processing: a family emergency and forgetting the appointment. If the family emergency successfully explains a variety of different aspects of the event then this explanation will receive a great deal of activation from those facts. Conversely, if forgetting explains few of the facts then it will receive little activation and will die out. Further, because the two explanations are somewhat inconsistent with each other they will send negative activation to each other. But because the family emergency explanation gets more activation from its supporting facts than does the forgetting explanation, the family emergency explanation will send more negative activation to the forgetting explanation, than vice versa. As a result, the forgetting explanation has an even lower level of activation and "dies out."

Concepts that are highly activated are taken as the representation of the interaction. Thus, if an individual originally entertained several alternative accounts for a failure, the account that is best supported by other concepts and data will be accepted.

This is an example of a parallel constraint satisfaction process that is a fundamental part of recent work on connectionist modeling or parallel distributed processing (e.g., Kintsch, 1988; Rumelhart, McClelland, and the PDP research group, 1986; Thagard, 1989). Such a process evaluates, in parallel and simultaneously, the extent to which concepts in the network are consistent with and supported by other concepts in the network. This is in contrast to a serial process where each concept would be evaluated, one at a time.

This is a quite general characterization of a parallel constraint satisfaction process, which, in practice, has been implemented in a variety of ways. One particularly useful implementation for a model of accounting is Thagard's (1989) model of explanatory coherence, which seeks to simulate what makes a set of data and the hypotheses that explain them explanatorily coherent. Thagard's model is particularly applicable, because the goals of individuals and the causes of behavior and outcomes are central in accounts of social behavior. Thus, the evaluation of the causal and explanatory structure of the network of concepts that make up a potential account should be central in the construction and choice of accounts.

Thagard proposed several principles for the evaluation of the coherence of the network of data and hypothesized explanations. Although these principles are implemented in a computer simulation, the model is quite useful apart from its connectionist implementation. However, it is important to note that the connectionist implementation allows for the application of all the principles simultaneously, rather than serially, one at a time.

The principles are the following. First, the explanation that requires the fewest assumptions will be more coherent. This is the well known principle of *parsimony* or *simplicity*. For example, an excuse for being late for a meeting that requires a detailed, complicated scenario with lots of different explanatory hypotheses will be far less coherent than a simple, "I got stuck behind a major accident on the freeway." This is implemented in the actual model by assuming that the activation from a fact to its potential explanatory hypotheses is divided among them. Thus, the greater the number of explanations needed to explain a single fact, the smaller the amount of activation from that fact to each explanation.

Second, an explanation that explains more facts, that has greater *breadth*, will be more coherent. Further, any given explanation becomes more coherent as more facts are introduced that support it. This occurs because an explanatory hypothesis receives activation from the facts it explains. As an explanatory hypothesis explains more facts it receives more activation.

This principle suggests that individuals can often make an account more coherent by "manufacturing" or "making up" facts that one's account explains. By doing so one can increase the breadth of one's explanation.

Third, any given explanation is less coherent to the extent that some facts actively contradict it. Facts that contradict an explanatory hypothesis have a negative relationship to it and thus send negative activation to that hypothesis and so reduce its activation.

This suggests one way in which an accounter may try to deal with a reproach. The accounter may attempt to show the reproacher that the reproach is not plausible because it is not consistent with some of the facts. In doing this, the accounter may either try to make salient facts that the reproacher has ignored or acquaint the reproacher with facts of which he or she was unaware. However, the accounter may not restrict this tactic to the use of actual facts, but may actually try to fabricate "facts" that if believed by the reproacher will reduce the plausibility of the narrative underlying the reproach.

Fourth, explanations are more coherent if they are explained by higher order explanations. For example, an explanation that we were late because of a traffic jam becomes more coherent if we can explain why the traffic jam occurred. For instance: "I got caught in a massive traffic jam caused by everyone leaving the football game." Or an explanation that we were abrupt in a phone conversation because we had a lot of work to do becomes more coherent if we also point out that our boss has really been on our back lately about getting behind.

Fifth, explanations are more coherent if they are supported by an analogy to another system with the same causal structure (Read & Cesa, 1991). Bennett (this volume) essentially suggests that in a jury trial one can make a defendant's account of his or her behavior more coherent and more understandable to the jury if one can present an analogy that is within the jurors' own experience.

In addition to these principles, Thagard's model assumes that the evaluation of explanations is often comparative. Instead of evaluating each explanation individually for whether it is coherent, one often evaluates several explanations at the same time to see which is more coherent. Alternative explanations can compete with each other, that is, send negative activation to each other. This means that an explanation that is viewed as reasonably coherent when evaluated in isolation will be viewed as much less coherent if another more coherent explanation is introduced, because the more coherent explanation sends more negative activation to the other explanation than vice versa.

One implication of this is that one way to defeat a reproacher's account of a failure event is to introduce your own version that is more coherent. Obviously, to do this successfully one must be able to evaluate whether one's own account is more coherent than the reproacher's. As indicated earlier, one way to make one's account more coherent is to introduce "made up" facts that the reproacher's account cannot deal with but that your account can handle nicely.

The current model assumes that when accounting for an event there are typically multiple knowledge structures active at the same time and that oftentimes interpreting a sequence requires people to integrate these multiple sources of knowledge. Further, there are often multiple interpretations of the same behaviors active at the same time. Thagard's model provides an elegant approach to understanding how people might choose among alternative interpretations of an individual's actions. Which knowledge structures are chosen and which scenario is constructed depends on which is more explanatorily coherent. What makes Thagard's model particularly useful is that it is based explicitly on a set of assumptions about how higher-order, causal, and goal-based theories are used to explain "data" and other inferences.

The primary emphasis in the preceding has been on how people would construct relatively accurate accounts for a social failure (although the possibility of fabricating accounts was alluded to). Here there should be a strong emphasis on the observed facts in building the account. In fact, in Thagard's (1989) model observed facts are given a special status compared to explanatory hypotheses. Facts are given extra activation simply by virtue of being observed rather than hypothesized. As a result, facts strongly constrain any possible explanation.

Unfortunately, fidelity to the facts is not always the primary goal of an account. Sometimes people's desire to excuse or justify their behavior or to refuse a reproach might override any interest in accuracy.

What does the accounting process look like when accuracy goes by the board? Individuals should still strive to create a coherent account, because that is a major criterion by which it will be evaluated. But it will be an account that excuses or justifies the failure rather than one that accurately deals with the facts known to the accounter.

Thus, the goals of excusing or justifying the failure will play a major role in how the explanation is constructed. In contrast, the facts should be much less important here than they are when the primary goal is to create an accurate account. Therefore, when the primary emphasis is on constructing an accurate account, we should work from the facts to the explanations. However, when the primary goal is to excuse or justify, then we may often work from potential explanations to the "facts."

The goals of excusing and justifying should have three effects on the explanation, two of which occur during the first stage of the model, when concepts are activated. First, they should affect which kinds of possible explanations are activated. Second, when they activate potential explanations, they may also activate aspects of those explanations that may lead to the fabrication of facts that make one's account more coherent. For example, if the "traffic jam" explanation is activated as a potential explanation for being late, aspects of this explanation, such as a stalled car or an accident, might also be activated, thereby suggesting potential "facts" that can become part of one's account. A third effect of the goals occurs during the second stage of the model when parallel constraint satisfaction processes are applied to create a coherent account. Here, an individual's goals should send positive activation to explanations that are consistent with it and negative activation to explanations that are inconsistent.

Let us consider what happens when an individual tries to fabricate an account that will be accepted by the reproacher. First, the goals of the account will activate potential explanations and these explanations may activate additional concepts that may become "potential facts." Second, the accounter knows what failure has to be accounted for. This failure will also activate potential explanations and associated concepts that also provide the basis for "potential facts." Third, the accounter should ascertain what facts the reproacher knows or is likely to know. These "known" facts should become part of any plausible account and they should also activate a variety of related concepts, including potential explanations. Moreover, facts that are known to the reproacher place strong constraints on the explanation and on any attempt to fabricate "facts." Fourth, the accounter should figure out what social and physical theories are believed by the reproacher. These theories provide potential explanations for the failure event.

It is perhaps useful here to think of two kinds of "facts." Some are known by the reproacher and should thereby be given greater weight by the accounter when constructing the account. Others are hypothesized, or "made up," and should therefore receive less weight. If a fact known to the reproacher and an "hypothesized" fact contradict each other, then the known fact should have the advantage. However, the "hypothesized" fact gains greater plausibility if it is explained by an explanation and is not contradicted by other facts or explanations.

One part of Thagard's model that is important here is that the transmission of activation is symmetric. Not only do facts send activation to their explanations, but explanations send activation to the facts they explain. Thus, a coherent explanation can provide support for "hypothesized" facts that it explains and help make these "facts" believable. One can see good examples of this in murder mysteries, where the plausibility of inferences about certain actions and motives of the suspect (for which there is no directly observed evidence) are bolstered by a coherent narrative.

Once the potential explanations and "facts" are activated to form the loose network, or "cloud," of concepts, parallel constraint satisfaction processes are then executed. At this point, the accounter must keep a considerable amount of information in mind, including what the reproacher knows and what the reproacher believes about social and physical causality. The accounter must try to evaluate the explanatory coherence of the account from the perspective of the reproacher. This task requires a certain amount of meta-cognitive processing. Individuals must "step back" and analyze their accounts from the perspective of another and try to judge how coherent the other will find the account to be and whether they will honor it.

Clearly, such a task can strain one's cognitive capacities. One way an individual can simplify this task is to assume, either deliberately or else unconsciously, that the reproacher has the same facts at his or her disposal and has the same beliefs as the accounter. Thus, the accounter can simply evaluate the account from his or her own perspective, drastically simplifying the cognitive task. Unfortunately, this reduces the probability that the accounter will arrive at an account that will be accepted by the reproacher.

Honoring the Account

Considerable research has focused on the consequences of honoring or not honoring an account (Bies & Sitkin, this volume; Cody & Braaten, this volume; Cody & McLaughlin, 1990; Schonbach, 1990). However, little attention has been paid to the issue of how the reproacher decides whether or not to honor the account. The current model provides some insight into this question. Just as the accounter evaluates the coherence of the account as he or she constructs it, we would argue that key to the reproacher's decision as to whether to accept the account is the reproacher's judgment of its coherence. And the reproacher's judgment of coherence will depend on exactly the same principles as are used by the accounter in constructing the account. However, this does not mean that reproacher and accounter will find the same account to be equally coherent. After all, the coherence of an account depends on the facts and explanatory theories held by the individual judging coherence. If reproacher and accounter differ on these things, they may well differ radically in their perceptions of the coherence of an account. This provides potential insights into why a reproacher may refuse to honor an account that the accounter thinks is quite convincing.

SUMMARY AND CONCLUSION

Constructing an account so that it will be both honored and successful is a daunting enterprise. It demands of accounters that they integrate numerous sources of information and constraint. They must bring together their theories about the world and what they know of the facts, as well as what they believe are the reproacher's theories and what the reproacher knows of the facts. Moreover, this must all be brought together under the control of the accounters' goals. And to complicate their task even further, if they are to be successful they must often try to take the perspective of the reproacher and judge whether the reproacher will accept their account. Finally, in the midst of all this, accounters often "create" certain facts as part of their accounts. How is all this done? We have suggested a two-stage process. First, the various sources of information and the accounter's goals activate a cloud of concepts that are arrayed in a loose network. Second, this loose network is organized into a coherent account using a parallel constraint satisfaction process based on principles of explanatory coherence.

The complexity of this process has several implications for the nature of people's accounts. First, it may provide some insight into why people's accounts are often unsuccessful. Creating a successful account requires the integration of considerable information and often requires taking the other's perspective while doing so. Moreover, creating a successful account may take a reasonable amount of time as we consider alternatives. If we then add factors such as time pressure or high levels of anxiety, which often seem to characterize accounting episodes, the task becomes even more difficult and less likely to be carried out satisfactorily. And not only does time pressure make the task more difficult, it may also mean that people have to terminate their attempt to construct an account before they have arrived at a satisfactory one.

The current model provides a general approach to understanding how people create the wide variety of stories or narratives about their social world that are so much a part of everyday social commerce. First, rather than focusing on one or two factors, it shows how a variety of different factors can be brought together into a single, integrated model. Second, it provides a single model that can account for a variety of apparently different kinds of social judgments. For example, it shows how the accounter's construction of an account and the reproacher's decision about accepting it rely on many of the same cognitive processes and are part of the same cognitive system.

Further, although this chapter focuses on accounts for social failures, this model can be applied more widely. It has already been used to explicate how people form impressions and models of others in social interactions, such as first encounters (Miller & Read, 1991), as well as to analyze how individuals explain problems in long-term, close relationships (Read & Collins, 1991). This suggests that fundamental to all of these different tasks, and indeed to much of social interaction, is the creation of coherent mental models of our social worlds.

REFERENCES

Abelson, R. P., & Lalljee, M. (1988). Knowledge structures and causal explanation. In D. Hilton (Ed.), *Contemporary science and natural explanation: Commonsense conceptions of causality* (pp. 175–203). London: Harvester Press.

Anderson, J. R. (1983). *The architecture of cognition.* Cambridge, MA: Harvard University Press.

Antaki, C. (1987). Performed and unperformable: A guide to accounts of relationships. In R. Burnett, P. McGhee, & D. Clarke (Eds.), *Accounting for relationships: Explanation, representation, and knowledge.* London: Methuen.

Argyle, M., Furnham, A., & Graham, J. A. (1981). *Social situations.* Cambridge, England: Cambridge University Press.

Barker, R. G. (Ed.). (1963). *The stream of behavior.* New York: Appleton-Century-Crofts.

Clark, H. H. (1985). Language use and language users. In G. Lindzey & E. Aronson (Eds.), *The Handbook of social psychology* (Vol. 2, pp. 179–231). New York: Random House.

Cody, M. J., & McLaughlin, M. L. (1985). Models for the sequential construction of accounting episodes: Situational and interactional constraints on message selection and evaluation. In R. L. Street & J. N. Cappella (Eds.), *Sequence and pattern in communicative behavior* (pp. 50–69). London: Edward Arnold.

Cody, M. J., & McLaughlin, M. L. (1988). Accounts on trial: Oral arguments in traffic court. In C. Antaki (Ed.), *Analyzing everyday explanation: A casebook of methods* (pp. 113–126). London: Sage.

Cody, M. J., & McLaughlin, M. L. (1990). Interpersonal accounting. In H. Giles & P. Robinson (Eds.), *Handbook of language and social psychology* (pp. 227–255). London: Wiley.

Collins, A. M., & Loftus, E. F. (1975). A spreading activation theory of semantic processing. *Psychological Review, 82,* 407–428.

Forgas, J. (1979). *Social episodes: The study of interaction routines.* London: Academic Press.

Galambos, J. A., Abelson, R. P., & Black, J. B. (Eds.). (1986). *Knowledge structures.* Hillsdale, NJ: Lawrence Erlbaum Associates.

Kintsch, W. (1988). The role of knowledge in discourse comprehension: A construction-integration model. *Psychological Review, 95,* 163–182.

Lalljee, M., & Abelson, R. P. (1983). The organization of explanations. In M. Hewstone (Ed.), *Attribution theory: Social and functional extensions* (pp. 65–80). Oxford, England: Blackwell.

Mandler, J. M. (1978). A code in the node: The use of a story schema in retrieval. *Discourse Processes, 1,* 14–35.

Mandler, J. M., & Johnson, N. S. (1977). Remembrance of things parsed: Story structure and recall. *Cognitive Psychology, 9,* 111–151.

Miller, L. C., & Read, S. J. (1991). On the coherence of mental models of persons and relationships: A knowledge structure approach. In G. J. O. Fletcher & F. Fincham (Eds.), *Cognition in close relationships* (pp. 69–100). Hillsdale, NJ: Lawrence Erlbaum Associates.

Read, S. J. (1987). Constructing causal scenarios: A knowledge structure approach to causal reasoning. *Journal of Personality and Social Psychology, 52,* 288–302.

Read, S. J., & Cesa, I. L. (1991). This reminds me of the time when. . . : Expectation failures in reminding and explanation. *Journal of Experimental Social Psychology, 27,* 1–25.

Read, S. J., & Collins, N. L. (1991). Accounting for relationships: A knowledge structure approach. In J. H. Harvey, T. L. Orbuch, & A. L. Weber (Eds.), *Attributions, Accounts and Close Relationships* (pp. 116–143). New York: Springer-Verlag.

Read, S. J., & Miller, L. C. (1989). Inter-personalism: Toward a goal-based theory of persons in relationships. In L. Pervin (Ed.), *Goal concepts in personality and social psychology* (pp. 413–472). Hillsdale, NJ: Lawrence Erlbaum Associates.

Rumelhart, D. E. (1977). Understanding and summarizing brief stories. In D. LaBerge & J. Samuels (Eds.), *Basic processes in reading and comprehension* (pp. 265–303). Hillsdale, NJ: Lawrence Erlbaum Associates.

Rumelhart, D. E., McClelland, J. L., and the PDP research group. (1986). *Parallel distributed processing. Explorations in the microstructure of cognition. Vol. 1: Foundations.* Cambridge: MIT Press.

Schank, R. C. (1986). *Explanation patterns: Understanding mechanically and creatively.* Hillsdale, NJ: Lawrence Erlbaum Associates.

Schank, R. C., & Abelson, R. P. (1977). *Scripts, plans, goals and understanding.* Hillsdale, NJ: Lawrence Erlbaum Associates.

Schlenker, B. R. (1980). *Impression management: The self-concept, social identity, and interpersonal relations.* Monterey, CA: Brooks/Cole.

Schonbach, P. (1990). *Account episodes: The management or escalation of conflict.* Cambridge, England: Cambridge University Press.

Stein, N. L., & Glenn, C. G. (1979). An analysis of story comprehension in elementary school children. In R. O. Freedle (Ed.), *New directions in discourse processing* (Vol. 2, pp. 83–107). Norwood, NJ: Ablex.

Thagard, P. (1989). Explanatory coherence. *Behavioral and Brain Sciences, 12,* 435–467.

2

▼▼▼▼▼▼▼

The Use of Prototypical
Explanations in First- and
Third-Person Accounts

Roger Lamb
Mansur Lalljee
Oxford University

KELLEY AND HIS CRITICS

The model of the attribution process that Kelley developed between 1967 and 1973 still stands as the most thoroughgoing attempt to systematize findings about the manner in which people arrive at explanations of their own and others' behavior. But Kelley (1967) himself could only list the ways in which real explanations might deviate from his idealized model and did not try to integrate the various biases that he and Heider (1958) before him had recognized as important aspects of the explanations that people actually give. Apart from its inability to do the job for which it was designed, Kelley's model has certain fundamental internal weaknesses. It is extremely vague on crucial points. One omission that has attracted criticism is the failure to address the question of hypothesis generation.

The model sets out only to cover an exhaustive or, in the schema version (Kelley, 1972), a somewhat less exhaustive process of hypothesis testing. Kelley said that we generate "plausible causes" for events that we wish to explain, and he seems to envisage our listing such candidate causes and then deciding between them. But he had nothing to say about how we generate these explanatory hypotheses for particular events. Critics such as Lalljee and Abelson (1983) have pointed out that both the testing process and, more obviously, the generation of these plausible causes require that we make use of stored knowledge about the behavior or event to be explained. This is not merely an adjunct to Kelley's model because such knowledge would presumably affect the attributer's need or willingness to search for the sort of information the model claims people use.

Despite problems with schema concepts in research on memory (see e.g., Alba & Hasher, 1983; McKoon, Ratcliff, & Seifert, 1989), more recent approaches to attribution have openly embraced schema theories in an attempt to explicate when and how people frame explanations. The most commonly invoked schema model has been Schank and Abelson's (1977) script-plan-goal approach. This and similar, more flexible models have been used with success in elucidating story understanding (e.g., Abbott, Black, & Smith, 1985; Wilensky, 1983), but they have not been without their critics (e.g., Kintsch, 1988). There have been a number of papers showing how a script model could work when people are explaining events (e.g., Abelson & Lalljee, 1988; Lalljee & Abelson, 1983; Read, 1987), but there has been comparatively little empirical work to test these claims (e.g., Leddo & Abelson, 1986). In this chapter we shall discuss a simple model of the generation of explanatory hypotheses from memory and present some data that suggests that both first- and third-person accounts rely on people's beliefs about typical sequences of events.

CATEGORIZATION AND EXPLANATION

Our view of the basic process involved in explanation derives ultimately from the work of Schank and Abelson (1977) and from work on categorization (e.g., Mervis & Rosch, 1981; Smith & Medin, 1981). Work on scripts has shown the stereotypical nature of people's concepts of many everyday events (e.g., Bower, Black, & Turner, 1979). But Schank and Abelson saw that not many events consist of inflexible sequences. People must therefore be able to recognize actions by fitting them into much looser structures. Schank and Abelson paid particular attention to the means-end relationship in people's plans, and the story-understanding literature has shown the importance of *initiating events*, which cause protagonists to desire a goal (e.g., Mandler, 1984; Rumelhart, 1977). Such waysta-tions of before and after are obviously part of everyday explanations and appear in philosophical discussions of reasons and causes. They are also closely bound up with our categorization of an action or event. They are defining features of some actions. Cause and intent, for instance, distinguish murder from manslaugh-ter. But even when there is a less determinate relationship between the category of event and its causal antecedents or goals there will usually be a set of causes or goals that are *typical* of that sort of event. For instance, hitting someone or playing tennis may each have many possible causes and goals, but there is only a limited set that would strike people as typical.

Studies of categorization of people and objects have shown that putting some-one or something in one category rather than another may affect recall (Brewer & Treyens, 1981; Carmichael, Hogan, & Walter, 1932), recognition (Cantor &

Mischel, 1977), inference (Asch, 1946), attitude (Tajfel, 1982), and behavior (Kelley, 1950; Snyder, Tanke, & Berscheid, 1977). The inferences people make from categorization may include attributions for behavior and achievement. For example, Duncan (1976) found that U.S. Whites interpreted a shove from a Black as more aggressive than a shove from a White. Stevens and DeNisi (1980) found that males' success was attributed to ability and effort, whereas females' success was more likely to be attributed to luck.

Categorization is a basic cognitive process. We are constantly "seeing things" as clouds or mountains, snakes or hosepipes, and we use these labels to make predictions and to decide on our own course of action. The idea that we can use scripts or plans to understand the world rests on the assumption that we can access the appropriate script or plan in memory. To do this we must categorize events as, for example, games or violent assaults. We can assimilate many events in human life to sequences with which we are familiar even where there is no recognizable plan or script. Bartlett's (1932) pioneering work on schemata in memory showed how English readers interpreted a short American-Indian tale as a story of fighting, injury, and death. This led them to remember obscure detail such as "something black" that came from the protagonist's mouth as blood or his soul.

When we categorize we infer from visible features to other invisible features, and categorization gives us access to a much wider range of features that are typically associated with the category. If we categorize an event, episode, or action one way rather than another we can think of it as part of one sequence with one set of causes rather than another. We decide it is a fight rather than a reunion because of the demeanor of the participants. We may not know why they are fighting, but we can easily think of a set of typical reasons. These are the plausible causes, that Kelley (1967, 1972) took for granted. Lists of them come readily to mind. Kelley worked on this (correct) assumption without bothering to consider that the generation of such lists is an interesting part of the process of attribution. It is hardly surprising that people have this causal information ready at hand. Causal inference does seem to underlie our comprehension of the world. Piaget (e.g., 1954) based a great deal of his theorizing about cognitive development on his perception of the child's development of causal schemata from primitive sensori-motor operations such as "pulling a string in order to shake a rattle." Some of our causal beliefs are learned firsthand from our attempts to manipulate our environment. But much is learned by observation and from what we are told. Piaget (1959) found that a 6-year-old's "why" questions addressed human motivation far more than the cause-and-effect relations he might have learned from (literally) pulling strings.

In adult life, we are constantly regaled with implicit psychological theories in newspapers, films, novels, and the gossip we pass around at parties. We are also bombarded with causal information about medicine, astronomy, economics, crime, and the military activity in the Middle East. It follows that we are acquainted with theories about the causes of innumerable categories of everyday events, particularly of human actions and emotions. Most people can, therefore, think of answers to questions about why various kinds of actions and events occur. The explanations of categories of actions may be seen as features that we associate with those actions, just as we associate flight and song with small birds. In that sense they belong to the prototype of the action. (There are difficulties with the prototype theory of categories, e.g., Medin, 1989. We are not making claims in favor of a particular theory of the psychological representation of categories. But our method is related to prototype research.)

We assume that a good guide to the set of causal factors that people associate with any event or action is to ask them why it typically occurs. Work on people's explanations of success and failure (e.g., Weiner, 1980) has relied on the ease with which people can generate lists of plausible causes. In our own work (e.g., Lalljee, Lamb, Furnham, & Jaspars, 1984) we have found that they can generate explanations for a wide range of different events.

People who are asked to list the attributes of a category most commonly write down those that other subjects consider the most typical features (Dahlgren, 1985). So the list of explanations common to a number of subjects who say why an event typically occurs may be regarded as the typical causes of that category of event. (*Cause* is used generically and includes goals and other kinds of explanatory factors.)

We also assume that the factors that appear in explanations of particular instances of any action will generally be ones that belong to the set of typical causal factors. This relation between the typical factors and the explanations given for particular events is itself causal. The set of typical factors determines what people say, for these are the factors that come to mind when people are searching for an explanation. People will only find an explanation among the factors that they recognize as plausible causes of the event. Of course they will not always opt for the most typical explanation, for the most typical is only the one that applies most frequently or in the prototypical case. If someone believes that the prototypical or the most frequently appropriate explanation for success is hard work, he or she may still acknowledge that success is sometimes due to luck. The set of typical causal factors constrains the range of plausible explanations, but the most typical is only most plausible in the absence of any information apart from the category of event. Factors such as the abilities and aims of the person whose actions or success one is explaining determine which member of the set of typical explanations one selects.

Anderson (1983, 1985) produced evidence that gives some support to this model, although his theoretical orientation was not ours. In 1983 he asked participants to think of plausible causal candidates for 20 success and failure contexts. This is exactly what we mean by the elicitation of a set of typical causal factors. In 1985 he asked other respondents to imagine either themselves or an "average student" in each of these contexts and to explain their success or failure.

Eighty-five percent of the explanations given in the 1985 study were the same or of the same type as those listed as plausible causal candidates in the 1983 study. Anderson argued that this showed the influence of what he called "the causal structure of the situations" on the attributions made in the second study. The weakness of this finding is that the participants in the second study were only accounting for hypothetical events, so they had only their prototypes of these events to determine what they said.

THE PROPOSED MODEL
AND IMPRESSION MANAGEMENT

Other researchers interested in explanations stress that people often may not have primarily cognitive concerns. Tetlock (1985) pointed out that "attributions serve, in the most general sense, identity maintenance and enhancement functions" (p. 208). Views like this have led to a great deal of work on attributions that appear in people's accounts of their own behavior. The interest is in how people construct such accounts, particularly in remedial interchanges after doing something wrong. Recent work with this interactional, self-presentational approach has drawn on the classic interactional ideas of the 1960s (e.g., Goffman 1959, 1967; Scott & Lyman, 1968) but has often gone into great detail based on more solid empirical data than those writers had available. Authors such as Backman (1976) and Schonbach (1980) have produced typologies of accounts, detailing the kinds of moves open to people describing and explaining their own behavior. More recently there have been examinations of sequences of moves that may be made by different parties in episodes involving such accounts (e.g., Cody & McLaughlin, 1985) or other self-presentations (e.g., Deaux & Major, 1987).

Deaux and Major's paper makes it clear how individuals' self-presentational tactics are dictated by their interpretation of other people's reactions to their earlier moves. In this sense, cognitive processes underlie self-presentation. As Goffman (1983) said, "our activity, behavioral and verbal, could not be meaningfully organized" unless we had such a "cognitive relation" with others (p. 4). But the question is not whether self-presentation depends on the beliefs and processes with which the cognitively oriented attribution researchers have been concerned. Clearly it does. The question is whether self-presentational motives affect the content of people's accounts of their own behavior and, if so, how.

In Anderson's 1985 study, participants who imagined themselves in the 20 contexts gave explanations that were significantly less like the "plausible candidates" than those given by participants who imagined an average student. A possible reason why first-person accounts might deviate from the typical is self-serving bias. But Anderson's respondents who imagined themselves were actually less biased in their own favor than the other respondents were in favor of the average student. Nevertheless our model is perfectly compatible with the view that people's accounts of their own behavior (or successes and failures) are influenced by self-enhancing motives. We definitely assume that the set of typical explanations for an action will constrain first-person accounts just as much as third-person accounts. People will not offer atypical or outlandish explanations for their own behavior. But the set of typical explanations gives a range of alternatives. One criterion for selecting one rather than another member of the set would be plausibility in the light of background information. Luck might be a plausible explanation for a particular candidate's success if he did not seem very bright and had done no work. But another criterion might be to justify or praise someone's behavior or results. This might be an important criterion when accounting for one's own aggression or success.

If our model is correct, people's accounts will rarely cite causal factors beyond a comparatively small set that are generally regarded as plausible causes of whatever they are explaining. Within this set, however, the accounter has room for choice. It is a repertoire from which people can select a "line" (to use Goffman's word) that they can sell. The fact that they must sell the line to justify themselves in their own or others' eyes makes it all the more likely that they will generally work with the typical explanations; to gain a payoff from impression management or self-deception, the line must be credible. Explanations that stick to typical causal factors are presumably those that most audiences will find most credible most often.

This model fits approaches to accounting like Backman's (1976, 1988). He spoke of "defining situations in such a manner as to alter the meaning and evaluation of one's behavior" (1988, p. 232). In our model this would be an attempt to place one's action in one category rather than another exactly because each category is associated with a different set of causes or intentions. These in turn lead to different evaluations of the action. Backman (1976) used the example of calling embezzling "borrowing." This he called a "conventionalization." Backman also pointed out that when people accept a bad label (category) for their action (e.g., assault) they often attempt to justify it by citing a reasonable cause, such as self-defense. This is the kind of selection from the set of typical explanations that we envisage in our model.

We are therefore proposing a model of explanation that holds that any action (and many other events) will have an associated set of typical, plausible explanatory factors. When explaining an instance of this kind of action, people draw on this set. Rather than use the most typical explanation, they may select another from the set. One criterion of selection is how well the explanation fits the available circumstantial information. Another criterion may be that one of the set of explanations shows the action in a better (or worse) light than others. Both the aim for plausibility and the aim to show the action in a good light will probably operate when people are giving accounts of their own behavior.

There have, of course, been attempts to explain away phenomena that appear to show self-enhancing motives. Psychologists such as L. Ross (1977; also Miller

& M. Ross, 1975) have demonstrated that people's apparent tendency to take credit for success and deny responsibility for failure may not be due to a self-serving bias but to the information and beliefs they have about the events. This dispute may be undecidable, as Tetlock and Levi (1982) have argued, but it will not go away. Papers such as those by Anderson and Slusher (1986) and Pyszczynski and Greenberg (1987) continue to address the issue and look for evidence that might decide it one way or the other.

Both these papers suggest models in which motivational factors determine the content of cognitive processes. Our model suggests that motivational factors are secondary, operating only on the process of selection from the accessible set of typical causal factors. But our primary concern here is with the role of categorization and the constraining effect of the set of typical explanations.

We wish to describe three kinds of data of our own, namely, (a) people's views of typical factors that explain various actions, (b) first-person accounts of behavior, and (c) explanations of the behavior of characters in stories. We have data on theft and aggression from 315 respondents whose ages ranged from 15 to 69. Because we have people's accounts of their own behavior and their interpretations of fairly complex and detailed stories, we can investigate the relations between the typical and the particular more thoroughly than a study like Anderson's (1985), which used only hypothetical events.

There are two relationships that we want to consider. The first is between one sample's accounts of their own aggression and another sample's answers to questions about why aggression typically occurs. The second is between third-person accounts of different thefts and answers to questions about why such thefts typically occur. In both cases our principal concern was whether the accounts of particular incidents would employ explanations from the typical set. If our model is correct the typical set will constrain both first- and third-person accounts.

RELATIONSHIP BETWEEN TYPICAL EXPLANATIONS AND FIRST PERSON ACCOUNTS OF AGGRESSION

Twenty students (5 male, 15 female) at Oxford Polytechnic filled out a questionnaire that contained 11 questions about the typical features of aggression. The questions included "What sort of person typically does this?" "Why do people typically do this?" "Who are the typical victims?" and covered other features such as when, where and how. The answers to "how" showed that the typical aggressions were physical, sometimes more precisely hitting or punching, and verbal, sometimes more precisely shouting or being sarcastic. Sixteen of the 20 cited verbal or physical types of aggression, 11 giving both.

All the first-person accounts were given by 109 schoolgirls (average age 16) from Birmingham, England. We asked each to "describe an occasion when you were nice to another person" and "an occasion when you were unpleasant to another

TABLE 2.1
Typical Explanations of Aggression and Their Use in the First-Person Accounts

		First Person Accounts	
	Typical	Aggression	Other
Negative Emotion	17	22	19
Victim's Behavior	4	37	43
Power/Status	3	1	2
State/Trait	2	11	4
Circumstances	2	5	4
None	1	3	2
Number of Respondents	20	52	52

person." In each case they were also asked to say why they acted as they did. One hundred four girls gave complete descriptions and explanations of unpleasant actions. Fifty-two of them gave accounts of verbal or physical aggression; 52 others gave accounts of unpleasant behavior such as ignoring or rejecting friendly overtures from someone. Their aggressions were clearly comparable to those mentioned as typical by the students.

Table 2.1 shows the typical explanations and the girls' most common explanations for their own aggression and their other unpleasant actions. Detailed comparisons were made between the girls' 52 accounts of aggression and the 20 typical accounts, but we have included the other 52 girls' unpleasant actions to demonstrate that some of the points we make about aggression are probably equally applicable to the other actions as well.

In Table 2.1, the figures in each category of explanation are the number of participants who mentioned that factor but not necessarily as their complete explanation. So the column totals are greater than the number of respondents, as many cited more than one explanatory factor. The "none" category includes all respondents who did not use any of the five named categories of explanation.

The 20 students showed consensus about the typical cause of aggression. In answer to *why,* 17 students (85%) cited such factors as anger, annoyance, frustration, upset, tension, and "feelings" in expressions like "to relieve feelings." We regarded all these as emotional reaction and labeled them *negative emotion.* The only other explanatory factors mentioned in answer to *why* by more than one student were provocation or the *victim's behavior,* given by four, goals of *power or status* (e.g., "to prove themselves"), *state or trait* (e.g., "feelings of inadequacy"), and *circumstances* (e.g., "can't cope with life situation"). We shall refer to these five categories as the *typical explanations* of aggression, and to the most commonly given, *negative emotion,* as the *modal typical* explanation. (Only one of the 20 students used none of these. She said "often for small reasons." Three of the other 19 gave additional replies that did not fit the five categories, namely, "drunk," "loss of self-control," and "to get a kick.")

Table 2.1 makes it clear that the schoolgirls' accounts of their own actions seldom used any explanation not in the five typical categories. Only three (5.8%) used atypical explanations for aggression. The data therefore supported our hypothesis. There was no evidence that first-person accounts import atypical explanations to show the accounter in a good light. There was, however, some evidence of selection, which implied a self-enhancing motive.

Among the typical explanations, negative emotion was by far the most common. In contrast, the girls' accounts most commonly cited the victim's behavior. Thirty-seven of the 52 (71.2%) girls who explained their aggression mentioned the victim's behavior. Examples were: "because she said things about me," "she had hit me," "because she wouldn't let me show my point of view," and "because she had been seeing my boyfriend." Negative emotion was the girls' second most common explanation, but they cited it less often than the students who were giving typical explanations. Twenty-two girls (42.3%) explained their aggression by such feelings as anger (the most frequent), upset, and jealousy. (As Table 2.1 shows, the figures were very similar for the 52 girls who recounted aggressions and the 52 who recounted other unpleasant behavior.)

Relative to typical *why* answers, only the frequencies of negative emotion and provocation differed. The girls' references to negative emotion were significantly less: typical 17 out of 20, girls 22 out of 52: $\chi^2 = 10.705$, $p < .002$. They made considerably more references to provocation: typical 4 out of 20, girls 37 out of 52: $\chi^2 = 15.466$, $p < .000$, 2-tailed.

As predicted, therefore, the girls did not go beyond the set of typical explanations, but they selected among them rather than merely going for the most typical: They played down the modal typical negative emotion and correspondingly played up the victim's behavior. These two tendencies might both result in less blame attaching to the agent, for there was not so much anger and loss of control. There was retaliation due to the actions of the victim. We cannot determine whether the girls' selection was an effort to show themselves in a good light, but such selection among the typical explanations was in line with the model.

CAUSAL CHAINS

The model envisages a selection process in which there is a set of typical explanatory factors, such as anger or provocation. The accounter accesses this set and selects from it. As we have seen, our respondents did select from the set of typical explanations of aggression. Not all of them however selected only one member of the set. For although some of them gave simple, one element explanations such as "I was angry" or "She was naughty," many of them mentioned more than one factor. They did not, of course, offer these factors disjunctively ("either . . . or") or in a list like some of the typical answers. They used conjunctions such as "because she was being silly and I was in a bad mood" or causal chains that sometimes included conjunctions. One girl said, "because he teased me. This made me angry." Another said, "because he was really getting on my nerves (by) acting really immature." Both of these explanations suggest that the respondents' aggression was the result of irritation, but they also added that the victim's behavior caused the irritation. Multielement explanations that combined conjunctions and chains commonly cited two factors as the cause of a third that itself explained the aggression. One example was, "I was angry (because) they were unpleasant to me and I didn't like (them)."

Table 2.2 shows the numbers of girls who gave conjunction, chain, and mixed conjunction plus chain explanations, as well as those who used simple, one-element ones. Overall, multielement explanations outnumbered simple ones 59 to 45, indicating that the girls tended to use more than one explanatory factor. They also used explanations that involved causal chains more than they used plain conjunctions, for there were only 19 of the latter among the 59 multielement explanations.

The common pattern of chain joined together negative emotion and the victim's behavior as in the aforementioned examples. Table 2.2 shows that 20 out of 52 explanations of aggression contained chains (10 chains, 10 mixed). Nineteen of these had chains that explained negative emotion, that is, respondents gave anger or jealousy as the proximal cause of the aggression but cited other factors as the cause of the anger or jealousy. Eighteen of these 19 had the victim's behavior alone (9) or in conjunction with other factors (9) as the explanation for the negative emotion.

Chains also appeared in 20 of the 52 explanations of other unpleasant actions. These also mentioned emotion caused by the victim's behavior. A chain-explanation could therefore serve to place a negative act in a better light. For it could justify a possibly negative cause, such as anger, by claiming that the anger was itself caused by the victim's blameworthy behavior. Chains however were not confined to explanations of negative acts. The girls were asked for accounts of their prosocial as well as their antisocial actions. Forty-nine of their 106 accounts (46%) of nice behavior included causal chains. These chains also involved feelings caused by some aspect of the person toward whom the prosocial action was directed. The use of such chains did not therefore appear to be a self-enhancing ploy.

TABLE 2.2
Simple and Multi-Element Explanations in First-Person
Accounts of Aggression and Other Unpleasant Actions

	Aggression	*Other*	*Total*
Simple	24	21	45
Conjunction	8	11	19
Chain	10	18	28
Mixed (chain plus conjunction)	10	2	12
Total	52	52	104

The general conclusion that can be drawn about the construction of first-person accounts is very important, for the girls' accounts show that people may often explain their own behavior as the end product of a set of causes. Read (1987; Read, Druian, & Miller, 1989) made much of the fact that we may often wish to explain sequences rather than individual actions or events. The use of chains in 42% of these girls' accounts points up the fact that we may explain individual actions by locating them in a sequence.

This is a more complex process than simple selection from the set of typical explanations. It also fits in perfectly with the idea on which our model is based, namely that people understand, categorize, and explain actions and events by placing them in typical sequences of the kinds discussed in research on scripts and story understanding. The chains strongly suggest that the typical explanatory factors for aggression (negative emotion and provocation) are themselves linked elements in the typical sequence of events that culminates in an act of aggression. It is by reference to this sequence or some part of it that the girls explained what they had done.

We did not have any third-person accounts of particular aggressive incidents, so we could not complete our comparisons by seeing if such accounts have a similar structure to first-person ones. But Wright and Mischel (1988) found that adult observers mentioned both negative internal (e.g., feels angry) and negative interpersonal (e.g., was teased) antecedents for children's observed aggression. The degree of association between each of these two factors and aggression was high and very similar, with the interpersonal events slightly higher. This is not very different from the girls' accounts but does differ from our typical *why* answers. Wright and Mischel's data did not come from an explanations study and are not directly comparable with ours. But they do suggest that first- and third-person accounts of aggression may be similar. This would be a blow to the theory that bias plays a large part in the selection among typical explanations.

RELATIONSHIP BETWEEN TYPICAL EXPLANATIONS AND THIRD-PERSON ACCOUNTS OF THEFTS

It might be argued that the similarities between the typical accounts and the accounts of particular incidents cannot be evidence that the prototype or set of typical explanations causes the accounts to take the form they do. To assume that they can is an unjustified inference from correlation to causation. The typical accounts could be as they are because they are accurate summaries of particular incidents that people have encountered. This is true. But the correlational evidence suggests that people's beliefs about the causes of aggression may determine what they say in their accounts of particular incidents. In fact, we have clear evidence of a set of typical explanations determining accounts in another study.

In this study, respondents read ambiguous stories about particular incidents. Different interpretations of the same story produced radically different explanations. This suggests that the way in which the actions in the story were categorized determined how they were explained. In this case we were concerned with typical explanations and third-person accounts of thefts. Comparisons between these typical and third-person explanations produced similar findings to the comparison between the typical aggression explanations and the girls' accounts.

We elicited typical features in the same way as with aggression. But we asked about four thefts that previous respondents had judged to be very different from each other. The four were purse snatching, bank robbery, embezzling, and hijacking. For each we asked 20 respondents to answer questions like those for aggression, for example, "What sort of person typically does this?" and "Why do people typically do this?" We used the answers to the *how, when,* and *where* questions to construct brief, ambiguous stories about each of the four. We aimed for ambiguity because we wanted stories that could be interpreted in more than one way. This allowed comparison between the explanations given for different interpretations of the same story, which showed whether exactly the same information resulted in very different explanations if the action was differently categorized. This is what we should expect if the categorization of an event determines how it is explained.

We also constructed descriptions of four agents based on the typical thieves for the four thefts. The features in these descriptions derived from the answers to the *who* and *why* questions, but we fleshed these details out with much more information about their personalities and circumstances to give sketches of 250 to 300 words. For example, answers to the *who* and *why* questions depicted the typical purse snatcher as a socially disadvantaged young male who needed money. We added invented information about his family life and his frail widowed mother. Similar invented information was added for each thief. The embezzler, for instance, had a difficult marriage to a wife who was chronically sick.

Each of the four profiles was paired with each of the four ambiguous descriptions of the actions in a 4 × 4 design. Eighty-five respondents, mainly students from Oxford University and Oxford Polytechnic, were each given four of these stories to read. Respondents received all four events, but each in one version only. They were asked to say what the main character was doing and to explain why he was doing it. There were similar patterns of interpretation and explanations across the four stories and across their different versions. So for current purposes, the results have been collapsed.

Overall the four events were interpreted as the relevant crimes in 47.3% of the cases, so the stories were satisfactorily ambiguous. The other 52.7% of interpretations were largely neutral or benign: making a legitimate withdrawal rather than robbing a bank, helping someone with her shopping rather than snatching her purse, working late rather than embezzling, and informing the stewardess that a fellow passenger was ill.

TABLE 2.3
Typical Explanations of Four Crimes

	Purse snatching	Bank robbery	Embezzlement	Hijacking
Material Gain	20	17	17	6
Political Aims				16
Greed		2	4	
Desperation		1	2	2
Pleasure	1	2		
It's easy	2	1		
Economic Problems	1	1	1	
Challenge		1	1	
Character		1	1	
Number of Respondents	20	20	20	20

Table 2.3 shows the explanations given by the twenty respondents who were asked "Why do people typically do this?" for each of the four thefts. (There were three other explanations, each given by only one person, that are not shown in the table.) The figures refer to the number of respondents who gave each explanation as all or part of their answer. The column totals are therefore greater than the number of respondents. Material gain was the modal typical explanation for embezzling, purse snatching, and bank robbery. It was also the second most typical explanation for hijacking. But political aims were modal for that. There were other, far less frequent, typical explanations, such as pleasure, desperation, and greed.

Table 2.4 shows the number of respondents who interpreted the ambiguous stories as thefts or benign actions, omitting those who offered no explanation for the protagonists' behavior. It gives the numbers who used the modal typical theft explanations (politics for the airplane story, material gain for the other three). Table 2.4 also shows the number of respondents who did not use the modal typical but did use one of the other typical explanations in Table 2.3 (i.e., those who used material gain or desperation for hijacking, pleasure, economic problems, or "it's easy" for purse snatching, etc.). The third row shows the number of respondents whose explanations did not fit any of the typical categories of explanation for the relevant thefts.

Eighty-eight (59.1%) of the 149 respondents who interpreted the stories as thefts offered the appropriate modal typical theft explanations such as "He is robbing the bank for gain" or "hijacking for attention for his cause." In contrast, only 32 (19.2%) of the 167 who gave benign interpretations offered either of these types of explanation. There was a similar contrast for the complete set of typical explanations. One hundred seventeen (78.5%) used typical theft explanations for the thefts, but only 51 (30.5%) used any explanations from this set for the benign actions. Analyses of the theft/benign differences in the use of typical theft explanations were performed story by story. The least significant of the four was on the embezzling/overtime story: $\chi^2(1) = 10.009$, $p < .001$, 1-tailed.

TABLE 2.4
Modal and Other Typical Explanations for Theft and for Benign
Interpretations of the Ambiguous Stories

	Theft	Benign	Total
Modal	88	32	120
Other Typical	29	19	48
Not Typical	32	116	148
Total	149	167	316

This demonstrates that categorization can determine explanation. Given that some of the background information in the stories was derived from features of the typical thieves, including their typical motives, it is hardly surprising that respondents used it in explaining the events when they interpreted them as thefts. One might even argue that they read off the explanations that were given to them or that were implied in the stories. But this argument turns out to be false, for they did not read it off when they gave noncriminal interpretations. So the information in the stories about the protagonists' financial or political motives did not force respondents to refer to these motives when they were inappropriate or not typically appropriate for the interpretation of the relevant event.

PARALLELS BETWEEN THE FIRST- AND THIRD-PERSON ACCOUNTS

There were two important comparisons between the accounts of the actions in these stories and the girls' accounts of their aggression: (a) preference for typical and modal typical explanations; and (b) the use of chains.

Preference for Typical and Modal Typical Explanations

Fifty-two girls gave accounts of their own aggression: of these, 22 (42.3%) cited the modal typical explanation, negative emotion, and a further 26 cited other typical explanations, notably provocation. In total, 48 (92.3%) gave typical causal factors. Eighty-eight (59.1%) of the third-person accounts of theft cited the modal typical explanations. A further 29 used nonmodal typical explanations. In total, therefore, 117 (78.5%) of the 149 cited typical causal factors. These were available in most versions of the four stories because the background details were based in part on the typical features of the four thefts, including the *why* answers.

The girls' accounts were therefore less likely than the third-person accounts to provide the modal typical explanation. This implies more selection in first-person accounts, but might simply be a matter of the salience of various explanatory factors in the ambiguous stories used in the third-person study. The more important point is that the girls' accounts of their own real-life aggression stuck more thoroughly to the set of typical explanations than did the third-person accounts of events in stories, even though the stories actually mentioned typical factors. We should not expect this if first-person accounts followed the dictates of self-enhancement rather than being constrained by assumptions about the typical plausible explanations for aggression.

The Use of Chains

Forty of the girls' 104 accounts of antisocial behavior placed the action as a last link in a causal chain. Forty-nine of their 106 accounts of prosocial behavior also used such causal chains. The third-person accounts of theft and benign actions cited chains in very similar numbers: 75 (51%) of the 147 theft accounts and 74 (45.1%) of the 164 benign accounts placed the action in a causal chain.

This shows that descriptions of chains of factors are not confined to first-person accounts. Most chains in the third-person accounts were simply descriptive (e.g., "for money for a better homelife with his wife," or "to raise cash for his political activities"). These examples illustrate how the chains integrated the action into the framework of background information about the protagonists' characters and problems. They therefore seemed designed to make the action comprehensible. In fact they frequently seem to have followed Wilensky's (1983) principles of parsimony and exhaustion in story comprehension, for they integrated the maximum amount of the information in the stories (exhaustion) into a single coherent form (parsimony).

Chains, therefore, seem to be a way of constructing coherent circumstantial explanations. Both first- and third-person accounts included such chains of causally linked factors. They explained the action but also took the story further by placing the immediate proximal explanation in the context of other causal factors, thereby outlining the action's history.

CONCLUSIONS

Our original model proposed that the prototype of an action would encapsulate a set of typical possible explanations. These explanations would constitute the set of plausible causes, and this set would constrain people's accounts of actions of that kind. We argued, however, that the relative plausibility of different explanations within the set is not fixed but would be affected by how the explanations fitted in with other available information; for instance, about the actor's character, aims in life, or general relationship to the victim. We also suggested that even if actors are influenced by a self-enhancing motive, their accounts of their own behavior will still be constrained by the set of plausible causes. Their motivation will only lead them to select among the members of this set, because anyone who strays beyond the set will diminish the plausibility of the account.

The girls' first-person accounts fitted the model perfectly. They did not stray beyond the typical explanations, but they did appear to play up the role of the victim and play down their own anger.

The third-person accounts of events in the ambiguous stories allowed us to go further in supporting the constraining effect of the prototypical set of explanations:

1. There was clear evidence that the categorization of an action determines its explanation because the theft and benign interpretations of the same stories were given quite different explanations.

2. The typical theft explanations were used to explain particular thefts, but slightly less often than the girls used the typical aggression explanations to explain their own aggression. Together these two points suggest that the set of typical explanations of aggression determined the content of the girls' accounts.

3. Causal chains were used to give a circumstantial history of how the action came about, just as they were in the girls' accounts.

None of this means that motivational bias never carries people beyond the constraints of the typical explanations. It is clear that the sample who gave our corpus of first-person accounts may not be representative and that the circumstances in which they gave them were not parallel to those in which someone is "put on the spot" and has to excuse her behavior. The girls wrote their accounts retrospectively. This was a case of aggression recollected in tranquility. Accounts given in the immediate aftermath might be different. (The direction of difference is not wholly predictable. Burger, 1986, found that attributions for success and failure showed *more* apparent self-serving bias after a lapse of time.) First-person accounts generated in the heat of the moment would certainly be useful additional data. There is also an obvious need for more comparisons between typical explanations and both first- and third-person accounts of many different types of action.

More first-person accounts are also needed from males and from older people. It is hard to believe that teenage girls are not concerned about the impression they make, but there is evidence that male college students are more self-serving than female students when accounting for success and failure (e.g., Forsyth & Schlenker, 1977). We can interpret that modesty as being due to gender role. But anger and aggression are presumably more taboo for females than males (Eagly & Steffen, 1986). We should therefore expect more denial of responsibility for aggression from girls.

The evidence from both the third-person and the first-person accounts has supported the model's proposal that categorization of an action determines the available set of plausible explanations. This still fits in well with the idea that people may try to *redefine* their behavior to escape blame (Backman, 1976, 1985, 1988).

This is just what the model leads us to expect, because the redefinition of the action immediately allows it a different range of attributions. We should expect people generally to relabel an action rather than to accept a label and offer an explanation that is atypical for actions of that category. Thus, self-enhancing motives should lead to accounts filled with typical explanations.

Given that the way in which the act is defined or categorized constrains the range of plausible explanations, there is the intriguing possibility that first-person accounts might be more constrained than third-person accounts, exactly because of self-presentational concerns. Someone accounting for his or her own behavior must try to give a credible explanation. One that is not drawn from among the more typical will not make a good impression on the average audience. So we may smuggle self-presentational motivation back in as a reason why first-person accounts should be close to the typical! This would not be a matter of the accounter's belief about the true causes of his or her behavior, nor necessarily of his or her belief about what generally causes such behavior. One need only know what the typical explanations are and then give a mundane account, because this would be one he or she could "sell" to an audience without seeming eccentric.

All this, however, is speculative. The solid conclusion from the data presented here is that both first- and third-person accounts do stick to the set of typical explanations of the actions they cover. This is as our original model proposed. The other important finding was people's use of causal chains to give a circumstantial story about the antecedents and goals of the actions that they were explaining. Such chains of linked explanatory factors were equally common in first-person (42.4%) and third-person accounts (47.9%). Their frequency in both reveals that people may often explain their own and others' actions by explicitly placing them in a typical sequence. This of course fits the original insights of Schank and Abelson's (1977) script theory very well.

ACKNOWLEDGMENT

The research reported in this chapter was supported by ESRC Grant No. RC/00/23/2325.

REFERENCES

Abbott, V., Black, J. B., & Smith, E. E. (1985). The representation of scripts in memory. *Journal of Memory and Language, 24,* 179–199.

Abelson, R. P., & Lalljee, M. (1988). Knowledge structures and causal explanation. In D. J. Hilton (Ed.), *Contemporary science and natural explanation* (pp. 175–203). Brighton: Harvester.

Alba, J. W., & Hasher, L. (1983). Is memory schematic? *Psychological Bulletin, 93,* 203–231.

Anderson, C. A. (1983). The causal structure of situations: The generation of plausible causal attributions as a function of type of event situation. *Journal of Experimental Social Psychology, 19,* 185–203.

Anderson, C. A. (1985). Actor and observer attributions for different types of situations: Causal structure effects, individual differences, and the dimensionality of causes. *Social Cognition, 3,* 323-340.

Anderson, C. A., & Slusher, M. P. (1986). Relocating motivational effects: A synthesis of cognitive and motivational effects on attributions for success and failure. *Social Cognition, 4,* 270-292.

Asch, S. E. (1946). Forming impressions of personality. *Journal of Abnormal and Social Psychology, 41,* 258-290.

Backman, C. W. (1976). Explorations in psycho-ethics: The warranting of judgments. In R. Harre (Ed.), *Life sentences: Aspects of the social role of language* (pp. 98-108). London: Wiley.

Backman, C. W. (1985). Identity, self-presentation, and the resolution of moral dilemmas: Towards a social psychological theory of moral behavior. In B. R. Schlenker (Ed.), *The self and social life* (pp. 261-289). New York: McGraw-Hill.

Backman, C. W. (1988). The self: A dialectical approach. *Advances in Experimental Social Psychology, 21,* 229-260.

Bartlett, F. C. (1932). *Remembering: A study in experimental and social psychology.* New York: Cambridge University Press.

Bower, G. H., Black, J. B., & Turner, T. J. (1979). Scripts in memory for text. *Cognitive Psychology, 11,* 177-220.

Brewer, W. F., & Treyens, J. C. (1981). Role of schemata in memory for places. *Cognitive Psychology, 13,* 207-230.

Burger, J. M. (1986). Temporal effects on attributions: Actor and observer differences. *Social Cognition, 4,* 377-387.

Cantor, N., & Mischel, W. (1977). Traits as prototypes: Effects on recognition memory. *Journal of Personality and Social Psychology, 35,* 38-48.

Carmichael, L., Hogan, H. P., & Walter, A. (1932). An experimental study of the effect of language on the reproduction of visually perceived form. *Journal of Experimental Psychology, 15,* 73-86.

Cody, M. J., & McLaughlin, M. L. (1985). Models for the sequential construction of accounting episodes: Situational and interactional constraints on message selection and evaluation. In R. L. Street & J. N. Cappella (Eds.), *Sequence and pattern in communicative behaviour* (pp. 50–69). London: Edward Arnold.

Dahlgren, K. (1985). The cognitive structure of social categories. *Cognitive Science, 9,* 379-398.

Deaux, K., & Major, B. (1987). Putting gender into context: An interactive model of gender-related behavior. *Psychological Review, 94,* 369-389.

Duncan, B. L. (1976). Differential social perception and attribution of intergroup violence: Testing the lower limits of stereotyping blacks. *Journal of Personality and Social Psychology, 34,* 590-598.

Eagly, A. H., & Steffen, V. J. (1986). Gender and aggressive behavior: A meta-analytic review of the social psychological literature. *Psychological Bulletin, 100,* 309-330.

Forsyth, D. R., & Schlenker, B. R. (1977). Attributional egocentrism following performance of a competitive task. *Journal of Social Psychology, 102,* 215-222.

Goffman, E. (1959). *The presentation of self in everyday life.* New York: Doubleday.

Goffman, E. (1967). *Interaction ritual.* New York: Doubleday.

Goffman, E. (1983). The interaction order. *American Sociological Review, 48,* 1-17.

Heider, F. (1958). *The psychology of interpersonal relations.* New York: Wiley.

Kelley, H. H. (1950). The warm-cold variable in first impressions of persons. *Journal of Personality, 18,* 431-439.

Kelley, H. H. (1967). Attribution theory in social psychology. In D. Levine (Ed.), *Nebraska Symposium on Motivation* (pp. 192-240). Lincoln, NE: University of Nebraska Press.

Kelley, H. H. (1972). Causal schemata and the attribution process. In E. E. Jones, D. E. Kanouse, H. H. Kelley, R. E. Nisbett, S. Valins, & B. Weiner (Eds.), *Attribution: Perceiving the causes of behavior* (pp. 151-174). Morristown, NJ: General Learning Press.

Kintsch, W. (1988). The role of knowledge in discourse comprehension: A construction-integration model. *Psychological Review, 95,* 163-182.

Lalljee, M., & Abelson, R. P. (1983). The organization of explanations. In M. Hewstone (Ed.), *Attribution theory: Social and functional extensions* (pp. 65-80). Oxford: Basil Blackwell.

Lalljee, M., Lamb, R., Furnham, A., & Jaspars, J. (1984). Explanations and information search: Inductive and hypothesis-testing approaches to arriving at an explanation. *British Journal of Social Psychology, 23,* 201-212.

Leddo, J., & Abelson, R. P. (1986). The nature of explanations. In J. A. Galambos, R. P. Abelson, & J. B. Black (Eds.), *Knowledge structures.* Hillsdale, NJ: Lawrence Erlbaum Associates.

Mandler, J. M. (1984). *Stories, scripts and scenes: Aspects of a schema theory.* Hillsdale, NJ: Lawrence Erlbaum Associates.

McKoon, G., Ratcliff, R., & Seifert, C. (1989). Making the connection: Generalized knowledge-structures in story understanding. *Journal of Memory and Language, 28,* 711-734.

Medin, D. L. (1989). Concepts and conceptual structure. *American Psychologist, 44,* 1469-1481.

Mervis, C. B., & Rosch, E. (1981). Categorization of natural objects. *Annual Review of Psychology, 32,* 89-115.

Miller, D. T., & Ross, M. (1975). Self-serving biases in attribution of causality: Fact or fiction? *Psychological Bulletin, 82,* 213-225.

Piaget, J. (1954). *The construction of reality in the child.* New York: Basic Books.

Piaget, J. (1959). *Language and thought of the child.* New York: Humanities Press.

Pyszczynski, T., & Greenberg, J. (1987). Toward an integration of cognitive and motivational perspectives on social inference: A biased hypothesis-testing model. *Advances in Experimental Social Psychology, 20,* 297-340.

Read, S. J. (1987). Constructing causal scenarios: A knowledge-structure approach to causal reasoning. *Journal of Personality and Social Psychology, 52,* 288-302.

Read, S. J., Druian, P. R., & Miller, L. C. (1989). The role of causal sequence in the meaning of actions. *British Journal of Social Psychology, 28,* 341-351.

Ross, L. (1977). The intuitive psychologist and his (sic) shortcomings: Distortions in the attribution process. *Advances in Experimental Social Psychology, 10,* 173-219.

Rumelhart, D. E. (1977). Understanding and summarizing brief stories. In D. Laberge & S. J. Samuels (Eds.), *Basic processes in reading* (pp. 265-303). Hillsdale, NJ: Lawrence Erlbaum Associates.

Schank, R. C., & Abelson, R. P. (1977). *Scripts, plans, goals and understanding: An inquiry into human knowledge structures.* Hillsdale, NJ: Lawrence Erlbaum Associates.

Schonbach, P. (1980). A category system for account phases. *European Journal of Social Psychology, 10,* 195-200.

Scott, M. B., & Lyman, S. (1968). Accounts. *American Sociological Review, 33,* 46-62.

Smith, E. E., & Medin, D. L. (1981). *Categories and concepts.* Cambridge, MA: Harvard University Press.

Snyder, M., Tanke, E., & Berscheid, E. (1977). Social perception and interpersonal behavior: On the self-fulfilling nature of social stereotypes. *Journal of Personality and Social Psychology, 35,* 103-122.

Stevens, G. E., & DeNisi, A. S. (1980). Women as managers: Attitudes and attributions for performance by men and women. *Academy of Management Journal, 23,* 355-361.

Tajfel, H. (1982). Social psychology of intergroup relations. *Annual Review of Psychology, 33,* 1-39.

Tetlock, P. E. (1985). Toward an intuitive politician model of attribution processes. In B. R. Schlenker (Ed.), *The self and social life* (pp. 203-234). New York: McGraw-Hill.

Tetlock, P. E., & Levi, A. (1982). Attribution bias: On the inconclusiveness of the cognition-motivation debate. *Journal of Experimental Social Psychology, 18,* 68-88.

Weiner, B. (1980). *Human motivation.* New York: Holt, Rinehart & Winston.

Wilensky, R. (1983). *Planning and understanding: A computational approach to human reasoning.* Reading, MA: Addison-Wesley.

Wright, J. C., & Mischel, W. (1988). Conditional hedges and the intuitive psychology of traits. *Journal of Personality and Social Psychology, 55,* 454-469.

3

▼▼▼▼▼▼▼

The Study of Causal Explanation in Natural Language: Analysing Reports of the Challenger Disaster in *The New York Times*

Denis J. Hilton
Ecole Supérieure de Commerce, Toulouse

Rainer H. Mathes
Zentrum fuer Umfragen, Methoden und Analysen, Mannheim

Thomas R. Trabasso
University of Chicago

CAUSAL EXPLANATION AND ATTRIBUTION THEORY

Causal explanation is central to our understanding of the world we live in. We seek to know not only what happens and when and where it happens, but how and why an event happened the way it did. The study of causal attribution processes has thus become a major topic of study for social psychologists interested in how people understand their own and others' behavior (Heider, 1958; Jones & Davis, 1965; Kelley, 1967). Research in this area, known as attribution theory, has been prolific (see Harvey & Weary, 1984; Kelley & Michela, 1980; Ross & Fletcher, 1985 for relevant reviews).

The dominant model of the attribution process has been the "man the scientist" model proposed by Heider (1958), who suggested that causal attribution proceeds through a process similar to Mill's (1872/1973) method of difference. Kelley proposed a particular version of this analogy in his ANOVA model, in which he compared lay causal attribution to the scientific analysis of variance. According to this analogy, the layperson analyzes covariation information to determine which factors caused the event in question. Although it took some time for the ANOVA model to be formulated and tested properly (Hilton, 1990), results show that respondents can use covariation information to arrive at causal judgments much as would be predicted by an analysis of variance (Cheng & Novick, 1990; Försterling, 1989).

Despite its successes, critics have argued that the ANOVA model has limitations. For example, following research on "explanation-based" story understand-

41

ing in artificial intelligence (Schank & Abelson, 1977; Wilensky, 1978, 1983), it has been objected that the ANOVA model does not describe the role of knowledge structures in the causal comprehension of events (Hilton, 1985; Lalljee & Abelson, 1983; Newcombe & Rutter, 1982; Read, 1987). Another source of alternative models of causal explanation has come from philosophical analyses of causal reasoning (Hart & Honoré, 1985; Mackie, 1974). Models derived from ordinary language philosophy have been applied with some success to the study of causal attribution (Hilton & Slugoski, 1986), responsibility attribution (Fincham & Jaspars, 1980), and story comprehension (Trabasso & Sperry, 1985; Trabasso & van den Broek, 1985).

Psychologists have sought support for the above positions through traditional experimental methods. When presented with suitably structured experimental tasks, respondents are indeed able to use covariation information to make causal attributions (Cheng & Novick, 1990; Försterling, 1989) as would be predicted by proper formulations of Kelley's (1967) ANOVA model. As well as covariation information, respondents also appear to use information activated by knowledge-structures in causal attribution (Hilton & Knibbs, 1988), and the kind studied by Schank and Abelson (1977). They are also able to use world knowledge about what normally occurs to define abnormal conditions (Hilton & Slugoski, 1986), which are then identified as causes, as would be predicted by Hart and Honoré's (1985) analysis of causal attribution. Again consistent with Hart and Honoré's analysis, respondents are also able to differentiate between judgments of causation, responsibility, and blame (Fincham & Jaspars, 1980). Finally, respondents' representations of simple stories correspond to causal networks constructed using an adaptation of Mackie's (1974) analysis of counterfactual reasoning (Trabasso and Sperry, 1985; Trabasso & van den Broek, 1985).

Although encouraging, the question arises as to what extent these processes of causal explanation spontaneously occur. The question of spontaneous causal reasoning has recently been raised (Weiner, 1985), but there has been greater concern with the question of when causal reasoning occurs rather than with what *kind* of causal reasoning processes spontaneously occur. Furthermore, studies that have content-analyzed causal explanations have for the most part used very simple events as stems (e.g., Garland, Hardy, & Stephenson, 1975; Lalljee, Lamb, Furnham, & Jaspars, 1984) and have prompted respondents to explain these events without waiting for spontaneous explanations.

Consequently, theories of causal attribution have been tested with a limited range of methods. The before mentioned studies usually use experimental research. Although experimental methods allow strict control of variables, they run the risk of presenting respondents with impoverished information sets that are not representative of real-world reasoning tasks. Consequently, models tested using these methods may lack external validity.

In this chapter, we describe a new method for studying natural attribution processes. We think that it is important to study spontaneous explanations of complex events in order to broaden our understanding of attribution processes. To do this we study newspaper reports of major disasters. Our approach draws heavily on ideas in ordinary language philosophy (Grice, 1975; Hart & Honoré, 1985; Mackie, 1974) in an attempt to represent the complexities of natural language in a systematic way. In particular, we discuss the implications of the conversational model of causal explanation (Hilton, 1990, 1991) for the study of newspaper explanations. We show what kind of content-analytic categories and techniques are necessary to study the kinds of processes we are interested in. Finally, we present a preliminary analysis that illustrates what our approach can reveal and discuss directions for future research using these methods.

THE APPROACH OF THE PRESENT INVESTIGATION

Our aim in the present research is to test models of causal explanation in a natural context, namely, media reports of major disasters. We picked media reports for both methodological and substantive reasons. First, they are spontaneous productions that do not suffer from experimental demand characteristics. Second, they are sequential in nature; day-by-day newspaper reports offer "snapshots" of how an explanation develops that enable us to study the sequential structure of causal explanation. Third, and more substantively, mass media are an important means of communication and social influence and worthy of study in their own right. The explanation of topical events is one of the major tasks of journalism. The audience is expecting not only to learn who did what, where, and when, but also to be informed why, what the consequences are, and who is responsible for them. Thus the mass media are an important source of social influence because they shape public knowledge of and opinion about an event.

In particular, we picked disasters as news topics that are likely to generate causal explanations. Unexpected and unwanted events are already known to be likely to stimulate explanations (Bohner, Bless, Schwarz, & Strack, 1988; Hastie, 1984; Weiner, 1985). We decided to begin by analyzing *The New York Times* reports of the explosion of the space shuttle Challenger because this was likely to be a particularly rich example. The explosion of Challenger 78 seconds after liftoff on January 26th, 1986, caused widespread shock and disbelief. It also prompted a Pulitzer prize-winning investigation of the story behind the disaster by the staff of *The New York Times*. We felt optimistic that a model and content analysis system that was adequate to describe these reports would readily be able to generalize to other reports of disasters.

The method that we have developed has the potential to test a wide range of questions about processes of causal explanation in a natural context. Here we illustrate this potential in a general way, with some examples. We distinguish between different types of causal reasoning and show what kinds of content-analytic measures are necessary to represent these types of reasoning.

TYPES OF CAUSAL REASONING

Following Hart and Honoré (1985), we distinguish between three main types of causal reasoning. The first, *assessment of consequences,* involves forward chaining from the target event to determine what further events it, in turn, causes. For example, the explosion of the space shuttle Challenger had consequences that were both immediate (e.g., the death of the astronauts) and long term (e.g., the indefinite grounding of the space shuttle program). In legal reasoning, assessment of consequences is often important to determine the extent of damage for which the person who is considered responsible will be held liable.

The second kind of causal reasoning we term *generation of causal explanations.* This involves backward chaining from the event in question to determine which events caused it. Sometimes it will be initially unclear what the causes are, and extensive causal investigations will be required. For example, in the case of Challenger, the explosion was quite unexpected and, at first, seemingly inexplicable. Numerous hypotheses were proposed, considered, and eliminated before the accident was finally thought to be explained. At first, it was thought that some fault in the external fuel tank of the Challenger may have caused the accident. After much accumulation and sifting of evidence, it was decided that the probable cause of the accident was a fault in the booster rocket, specifically in its seals.

The third type of inquiry we term *responsibility attribution.* Here there is no real puzzle as to what the cause of the accident is. It is accepted, say, that a fault in the seals caused the disaster. The question is then who should be held responsible for the problem, blamed, and punished? It may be that the designers of the rocket should be held responsible for an inadequate design. Alternatively, mission control might be held responsible for going ahead with the launch despite advice that the seals might not hold in cold weather.

These three types of causal reasoning are distinct, corresponding to what Hart and Honoré (1985) term *tracing of consequences, explanatory inquiries,* and *attributive inquiries,* respectively. They are dissociable and may occur at different stages in the causal comprehension of an event. For example, responsibility attribution is normally likely to commence when the cause of an event has been established. Previous studies have demonstrated that reasoning about causes and consequences involves different processes (e.g., Graesser, Robertson, & Anderson, 1981; Graesser, Robertson, Lovelace, & Swinehart, 1980) or that causal and responsibility attribution are not the same thing (Fincham & Jaspars, 1980). However, the sequential nature of our method enables us to study the onset of offset of each type of causal reasoning.

Here, we cannot give full descriptions of how we model and code each type of causal reasoning. Instead, we focus primarily on how we model and code the explanation generation stage and show how our method may enable a fuller understanding of this process than has been allowed by previous experimental approaches to the problem.

MAXIMS OF CAUSAL EXPLANATION

Our approach extends previous work applying ordinary language philosophy to the study of causal explanation (Hilton 1990). Grice (1975) proposed that utterances made in normal co-operative conversation should follow four maxims. The *maxim of quality* states that an utterance should be true, or reasonably likely to be true. The *maxim of quantity* states that an utterance should be informative. The *maxim of relation* states that an utterance should be relevant and to the point. Finally, the *maxim of manner* states that the utterance should be clear. Good explanations should satisfy these four maxims (Hilton, 1990). Moreover the maxims provide constraints that need to be satisfied by any process of explanation generation.

This can be demonstrated with reference to explanations of the Challenger disaster. Suppose a completely uninitiated observer, unaware of the workings of space rocketry or of the history of the Challenger disaster, were to ask why the accident happened and received the answer, "Because the spaceship was launched in cold weather." Without further information of various types, the truth, informativeness, relevance, and clarity of this explanation would remain to be established.

Perhaps the first question to be answered is, how could cold weather possibly be connected to the final explosion? To understand the relevance of the answer to the causal question, the hearer needs to have background information about the rocket's structure (e.g., that rubber O-rings were used to seal the booster rockets) and some knowledge of the relevant physics (e.g., that cold weather causes rubber to lose its flexibility, hence hindering the seal's efficiency). Consequently, for a given explanation to satisfy the maxim of relation, the hearer must have appropriate background knowledge.

Coherent explanations show how a number of relevant facts are combined into a single, underlying "story" through some hypothesized process. Part of the final explanation of the Challenger disaster runs along the following lines. Cold weather made the rubber O-rings inflexible, which impeded the efficiency of the seals, thus leading to a burnthrough of one of the lower seals in the left-hand booster rocket. This explains the puff of smoke that emerged by the seal during liftoff and why the final disaster was sparked by an explosion in this area some 70 seconds later. It also explains the complete failure to receive warnings of the disaster due to the absence of sensors in this area of the rocket, other than the loss of power in the left-hand booster 4 seconds before the final catastrophe.

Note that in order to satisfy the maxim of quality, the explanation itself must not only be true but also consistent with background knowledge. Thus it is not enough to know that it was cold on the day of liftoff, we must also be confident that the other, implied parts of the explanation are true. For example, if we explained the disaster in terms of cold weather on the understanding that the intervening cause was that the liftoff blast blew ice onto the space shuttle orbiter, which then caused disaster, then we would consider the explanation untrue if we considered the underlying hypothesis to be untrue. In fact, cold weather was cited as a possible cause under a "blasted ice" hypothesis, which was then discarded, only to be resurrected again as a possible cause under the "faulty seal" hypothesis.

Finally, explanations should satisfy the maxim of quantity. If the hearer already knows that the cold weather is part of the explanation, then it would be more informative to cite parts of the explanation that the hearer does not yet know about, for example, the flawed performance of the rubber seals in cold weather. Likewise, explanations should avoid unclarity. Thus, an explanation should not use jargon such as "O-rings" if the hearer does not know that this refers to the rubber seals.

Grice's (1975) maxims specify an idealized model of the relationship between logic and conversation. However, they appear to be built into the expectations that people have about most normal forms of discourse to such an extent that we can take them seriously as a general model of communication that can be applied to a variety of forms of discourse.

For example, daily newspaper reports about a long-running story such as the Challenger disaster cannot rely on readers either knowing or remembering previous reports. Consequently, a substantial amount of space is often devoted to summarizing "the story so far" to enable the reader to see the significance of the new information being reported that day. More generally, the writers of *The New York Times* appear to have had an idealized reader in mind who had an intelligent interest in the causes of the disaster but no detailed knowledge of space rocketry and physics. Consequently, especially in early phases of reporting, much space was devoted to explanation of these topics for the lay reader in the form of background information and cutaway diagrams of the workings of the space shuttle and its launching system. Although not part of the Challenger story itself, this information was necessary to "set the scene," much as characters and settings are introduced in archetypal narrative forms (e.g., Propp, 1968). However, what the Gricean approach allows us to do, that a purely structuralist approach such as Propp's cannot, is to predict what kind of background information will be included as a function of the audience. So, for example, we could predict that quite different background information about the disaster would be presented in an astronautics publication with a specialist audience than in a general publication such as *The New York Times*.

We also claim that the Gricean approach has important implications for understanding cognitive processes. It is, after all, a theory about the relationship between logic and conversation. So, although information seeking and hypothesis generation are cognitive activities, it is important to recognize that they are often driven by interpersonal and communicational goals, rather than simple curiosity of the mind. For example, analysis of legal proceedings suggests that causal and responsibility inquiries are most likely initiated when a question of liability has to be settled in order for a plaintiff to recover damages (Lloyd-Bostock, 1983). Likewise, the goals of establishing responsibility and of producing an accurate, informative, relevant, and readable report drove the inquiries of the presidential commission appointed to investigate the disaster. If the presidential committee, under William Rogers, had not succeeded in its brief in establishing the causes of the accident in an accurate and readable form, it would have been judged a failure, resulting in a concomitant loss of face for its members.

More specifically, the Gricean maxims of truth, informativeness, relevance, and clarity have much in common with principles of scenario construction that have been enunciated in cognitive science. Read (1987), following Wilensky (1983), stipulated that scenarios should be coherent, as concrete as possible, use as few extra assumptions as possible, be exhaustive, and be parsimonious. Both sets of precepts emphasize trade-offs between accuracy, completeness, relevance, and economy and may be thought of as complementary. Communicational constraints such as consideration of the intended audience can influence both scenario construction and explanation tuning.

A nice example of audience effects on scenario construction comes in the *Management Case Studies* article published on the causes of the Challenger disaster (Marx, Stubbart, Traub, & Cavanaugh, 1987). In this article, a detailed representation of the decisionmaking system at NASA is built up, with nothing but the most rudimentary information about the engineering problems that led to the disaster. Clearly, the drive to be informative and relevant for a specialized audience constrained what was investigated, which details were concretized, and which causal links were exhaustively spelled out. Here, conversational maxims constrain hypothesis generation.

Consideration of the audience may also determine the process of causal selection (Hesslow, 1983, 1988; Hilton, 1990, 1991; Mackie, 1974; Turnbull, 1986; Turnbull & Slugoski, 1988). When constructed, a scenario specifies a plethora of necessary conditions but for which the target event would not have happened. Had the weather not been so cold, or had the O-rings sealed properly, or had the recommendation of Thiokol engineers not to launch been accepted, or had there not been oxygen in the air when the hydrogen leaked, to mention but a few conditions, the explosion would never have happened. However, in everyday conversation, we typically mention just one or two factors as "the" cause. Which one we select may depend on our audience. For example, it may seem more relevant to answer an engineer's enquiry as the causes of the accident by reference to the faulty design of the O-rings. However, on the basis of the same scenario, we might prefer to mention the decision making failures in response to an identical enquiry from a management consultant. Here, conversational maxims constrain what part of the constructed scenario is "tuned" to meet the inquirer's needs and interests.

A MODEL OF THE PROCESS
OF EXPLANATION GENERATION

Below we outline a two-stage model of explanation generation that satisfies general constraints of conversation and apply it to the analysis of newspaper reports of the Challenger disaster. The first stage we term *hypothesis generation* and the second we term *explanation tuning*. Hypothesis generation corresponds to the process whereby we diagnose what the cause of an event is, whereas explanation tuning refers to the process whereby we use our diagnosis to answer some specific *why* question (cf. Hilton, 1990).

In the first stage of hypothesis generation the aim is to find the causal explanation of the target event that is most probably true. In our coding system, an explanation consists of a number of elements (background facts and problematic aspects of the spaceship's construction and performance) together with a hypothesis about the process that links the problematic aspects together. At first, a candidate explanation may only be very vaguely specified. It may, for example, have elements without specifying a process, or hypothesize a process without specifying elements. However, more fully fledged hypotheses are grown out of a set of these vague "kernel hypotheses" (cf. Abelson & Lalljee, 1988) through processes of elaboration (e.g., adding causal links) and further specification (being more precise about the elements concerned). These hypotheses are evaluated in terms of internal consistency and probable truth until one remains as the most probable explanation. Here, the best explanation is the one that is most likely to be true within the domain explored.

However, good explanations must be more than just true or likely to be true; they must also be felicitous (i.e., informative, relevant, and clear). Consequently, explanations may be "tuned" in various ways. For example, the "faulty seals" scenario may be felicitously explained in different ways, depending on the hearer's interests and/or knowledge state. Someone who already knew that the cold weather was in some way responsible for the accident would find a reference to the faulty seals an informative explanation, whereas someone who already knew of the role of the cold weather would find a reference to the faulty design of the seals to be an informative explanation. Both explanations are equally likely to be true, coming from the same causal scenario, but are likely to differ in how well they address the implicit focus of a causal question.

In fact, explanation tuning of the kind described may not be found in conventional newspaper reporting. This is because journalists seem to write with only one audience in mind, conceptualized as the "average" reader. Consequently, the explanation is not changed as a function of the intended audience. The exception that would seem to prove this rule is a columnist like Ann Landers, who concerns herself with responses to readers' personal problems and seems to change her explanations as a function of the source of the question (cf. Abraham, 1988).

However, in newspapers, the process of explanation tuning can be seen quite clearly in what Mackie (1974) termed "the progressive localization of cause" (p. 73). This process, whereby an explanation is made more specific, offers an interesting trade-off between the maxims of quality and quantity. A vague explanation, such as "something about the booster rocket" is quite likely to be true but too vague to be useful. In fact, the *New York Times* spent a substantial amount of time in further specifying this explanation as can be seen in Fig. 1.

Note that each time the explanation is changed by being made more precise, it is also less likely to be true, because more precise explanations have a greater chance of being falsified. That the explanations are nevertheless changed in this way clearly demonstrates that there is more to a good explanation than simply having high truth value. Thus, in this second stage of explanation tuning, the best explanations are those that are more felicitous.

The conversational model of causal explanation affords various advantages to the study of natural explanation processes. It emphasizes how explanations are grown and further specified, unlike many psychological models of hypothesis testing that simply examine how fully fledged hypotheses are tested in simple environments (e.g., Bruner, Goodnow, & Austin, 1956; Klayman & Ha, 1987). In this respect, it parallels knowledge-structure approaches to causal explanation (Abelson & Lalljee, 1988; Read, 1987), whose ideas (e.g., "kernel hypotheses") it borrows from freely. Where the conversational model can go beyond knowledge-structure approaches, however, is in explicating the intimate relationship between logic and ordinary language and thus show how the cognitive structures underlying text production and comprehension can be empirically studied. For example, the conversational model offers the important advantage of being able to interpret

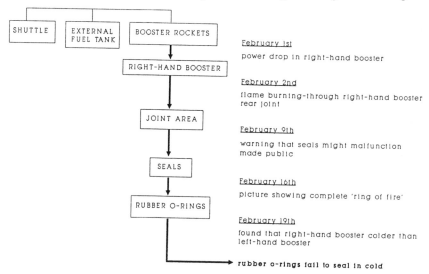

FIG. 3.1. Hypothesis generation and progressive localization of cause in response to successive inquiry findings.

the communicational function of parts of text. For example, text can be categorized in terms of whether it merely provides "background setting" for a particular audience, or whether it describes "problematic aspects" that are in focal attention as part of the story line.

We therefore believe that the conversational model can be a useful tool in the
study of natural explanation processes. However, in order to apply it systematically to the analysis of text, particular kinds of methodological requirements need
to be met. We detail some of these requirements later, and specify how text needs
to be analyzed in order to enable tests of the ideas presented earlier.

THE METHODOLOGY
OF THE PRESENT INVESTIGATION

One method that is adequate to analyze media content empirically is quantitative
content analysis. This method provides intersubjective classification and measurement of targeted text characteristics. The reliability of the measurement, which
is carried out by trained coders, is controlled both before and during the coding
process. In contrast to the process of hermeneutic interpretation, the aim of content analysis is not to give a complete reconstruction of the meaning of one or
a limited number of texts, but to enable the classification of targeted characteristics of a great number of texts. Quantitative content analysis is particularly suited
for the analysis of mass media content because large amounts of text need to be
analyzed, especially when an extended period of media coverage is involved or
the coverage of several different media is compared. Thus both methodological
and pragmatic reasons contributed to the decision to use quantitative content
analysis.

Quantitative content analysis has made great progress in analyzing questions
of a high level of complexity in recent years, moving from simply structured to
more and more complex category systems. Three kinds of complexity in particular need to be considered.

First, the category system is *differentiated,* which means that the category system does not simply contain categories on a general level, but also different levels of specific categories within a hierarchical structure. For example, the shuttle
as a whole represents a category on the general level; whereas the orbiter, booster
rockets, and external fuel tank represent categories at the first level of specificity; the booster segments, joints, fuel/propellant, nose, nozzle, sensors, and other
parts of the booster rocket represent the second level of specificity; the segment
edges, seals, O-rings, grooves, and other parts represent the third level of specificity, and so on. This allows for a very detailed description and analysis of text
content, which enables us to study, for example, how causes are progressively
localized.

Second, the category system is *multidimensional,* which means that text content is analyzed on several dimensions. For example, we classify every given explanation in terms of its level of specificity and its extent of elaboration. To give another example, we coded the problematic aspects of explanations according to their truth value as well as according to the definition of abnormality with various specifications. This multidimensional approach allows for a highly elaborated relational analysis, as will be shown below.

Third, the category system is *relational,* which means that single elements are not coded in isolation but that the interrelations between these elements and groups of elements are coded. Thus both the individual characteristics of causal explanations and their relations to each other are coded. For example, we can code the interrelationships between particular causal explanations and responsibility attributions. This relational approach avoids an "atomistic" analysis, which has been one of the major criticisms of quantitative content analysis (cf. Kracauer, 1952), and enables analysis of the coherence and complexity of the given explanation. For example, Bock (1990) presented an analysis of West German newspaper theories about AIDS. His system does not, however, enable representation of how particular theories grew and evolved in complexity.

These complex category systems constitute what we call the module system (Kepplinger & Mathes, 1988) and network technique of content analysis (Mathes, 1988, 1989). *Modules* consist of a set of related categories measuring different aspects of one topic unit. Since our category system should be able to distinguish between the three main types of causal inference, we distinguished between three main modules: *assessment of consequences, generation of causal explanations,* and *attribution of responsibility.* Each module was further divided into submodules and categories. Thus the module *attribution of responsibility* consisted of the three submodules *responsibility, blame* and *punishment.* The submodule of responsibility, for example, consisted of the categories *grounds for the attribution or denial of responsibility* and *mitigating circumstances.* The individual modules are connected to each other as a network, with the connections reflecting the relations among different types of causal inferences. Attribution of responsibility may thus be determined by a specific causal explanation or by the assessment of a specific consequence, or may even be attributed directly without a specified causal explanation. Figure 2 gives an overview of the modules and their connections.

AN EXAMPLE: THE GENERATION
OF EXPLANATIONS MODULE

In order to give a fuller picture of the logic of our category system, we will describe the internal structure of the generation of explanations module. According to our definitions, causal explanations consist of a potentially unlimited number of elements and specified or unspecified hypotheses about the causal process whereby

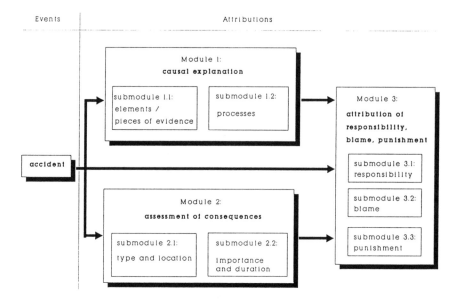

FIG. 3.2.   Basic structure of the category system (from Hilton, 1991. Copyright
© Wiley. Reproduced with permission of John Wiley & Sons, Ltd.).

these elements are connected to each other. The elements, which are coded in
submodule 1, are defined as all features of the event that may be relevant to its
explanation. We further distinguish these elements in terms of whether they are
background facts or problematic aspects. Problematic aspects are all those elements that have been identified as problematic and worthy of further attention.
They could be either potential weak points of the shuttle construction or empirical observations of events pertaining to the liftoff. For each problematic aspect,
we code its asserted or implied truth-value on a 7-point scale ranging from *im-
possible/can be excluded* to *possible/true*. We code the truth value as it is presented
by the media, not its actual truth.

    In all cases we code the way the abnormality of a problematic aspect is defined
in more detail. First we code the extent to which the problematic aspect is considered to be normal/abnormal, second whether there is an implicit or explicit reference to abnormality, and third, which contrast case (comparable or ideal) is used.
This enables us to test the applicability of the abnormal conditions focus model
(Hilton & Slugoski, 1986) to explanations provided by the mass media (see Fig.
3). One particular trend that can be tested is whether contrast cases change from
comparable to ideal cases as the inquiry moves from causal to responsibility questions (cf. Hilton, 1988, 1990). So, for example, we can test if the relevant contrast case in initial stages is likely to be other liftoffs of the space shuttle
(comparable cases) as opposed to the ideal performance of the space shuttle and
its parts if it/they performed according to the design specifications (ideal cases).

The hypotheses about the causal processes whereby the background facts and the problematic aspects are linked together are coded in submodule 2. We code the kernel hypothesis underlying the causal explanation or leave it unspecified if an element is suggested as being causal without any particular process being implied. When the process is specified, we code the kernel elements and the kernel processes in more detail. In addition we classify the character of a given explanation using distinctions drawn from medical diagnosis (Pople, 1981). Nosological explanations mainly deal with the question of which particular system the problem is located in. Mechanical explanations mainly describe the causal processes that work together to produce the accident. Aetiological explanations mainly deal with the historical circumstances leading to the malfunctioning process. By coding these distinctions, we may observe a change in the character of explanations over time, as we move from nosological through mechanical to aetiological.

Finally, we code the level of specificity and the extent of elaboration (number and type of causal links) of a given explanation at each stage of its generation. By these means we are able to study the processes of progressive localization of cause and of causal scenario generation (see Fig. 4). Coding these features enables us to differentiate cases where the explanation given is changed because it is a more specific or elaborated version of the explanation already given from genuine changes of hypothesis. For example, if the explanation of the disaster is made more specific (e.g., from "because of a fault in the booster rocket" to "because of a fault in the booster joint"), we can recognize that this does not imply a genuine change of hypothesis (e.g., from "because of a fault in the booster rocket" to "because of a fault in the external fuel tank"). Although the "surface structure" of these changes in explanation is the same, we need to use world knowledge (e.g., of the parts of the booster rocket) to recognize that their "deep structure" is quite different. By doing so we can avoid important ambiguities in terminology that have proved problematic in earlier studies of causal explanation (cf. Hilton & Erb, 1990).

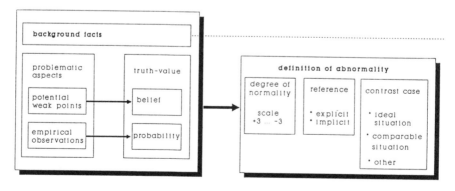

FIG. 3.3. Causal explanation module
Submodule 1: Elements.

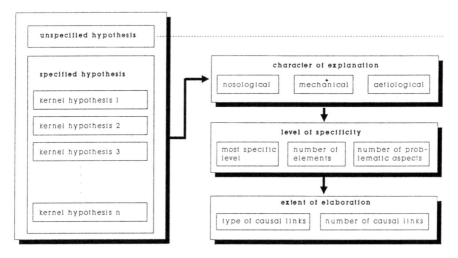

FIG. 3.4. Causal explanation module
Submodule 2: Processes

PRELIMINARY RESULTS

The content analysis scheme presented above has, at the time of writing, not been applied to the analysis of a full range of newspaper articles. However, we have obtained results using a preliminary version of the scheme. The first author coded the first 30 days of *New York Times* reports of the Challenger disaster, and two undergraduate research assistants coded the first and last 15 days, respectively. A conservative procedure was adopted of only including items coded by both coders. Figure 5 shows the number of consequences, causal hypotheses, and responsibility hypotheses reported on each day. Several patterns appear clear.

First, there is extensive reporting of the consequences of the disaster in the first 5 days after the accident, which then tails off. In the case of the Challenger accident, the consequences were relatively easy to assess.

Throughout the whole time period, there is extensive hypothesis generation, with a gradual decrease over the month. However, it is important to note the cyclic nature of hypothesis generation, with peaks of high activity following valleys of relative inactivity. When Chart 1 is compared to Figure 1 it becomes possible to see that new observations appear to prompt new cycles of hypothesis generation.

The processes of responsibility attribution are relatively inactive during this time period, though showing a slight tendency to increase, as opposed to causal hypotheses, which showed a marked tendency to decrease. Responsibility attributions were mentioned a total of 3 times in the first 15 days of coverage and

12 times in the second 15 days. Causal hypotheses were mentioned 88 times in the first 15 days of newspaper coverage and 46 times in the second 15 days. A chi-square analysis comparing responsibility attributions and causal hypotheses in the first and second 15 days was calculated, and this confirmed that the relative increase in responsibility attributions and decrease in causal hypotheses was significant ($\chi^2 = 8.20$, df $= 1$, p $< .005$). Informal observation of news reports over the subsequent 5 months suggests that this trend continued, in that the causal inquiry later began to focus very much more on responsibility questions after the causal questions had been settled, as is predicted by Fincham and Jaspars' (1980) entailment model of responsibility attribution. In addition, after the causes of the accident had been established after approximately 6 weeks, consequences were once again mentioned. By locating the source of the accident, causal explanations enabled more specific consequences for the space program to be assessed regarding the future of manned space flights.

CONCLUSIONS

Analyses of causal explanation drawn from ordinary language philosophy can be applied to in-depth analysis of mass media coverage of a major disaster. We have shown how sophisticated content analytic techniques can enable us to test a variety of hypotheses, using natural rather than experimentally generated data. In addition, we are able to empirically study processes of causal inference that

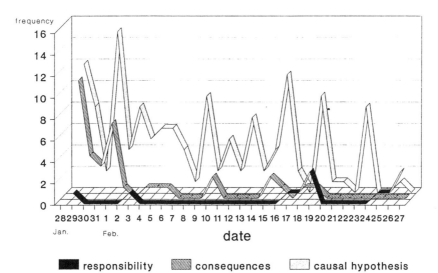

FIG. 3.5. Frequency of references to causal explanations, responsibility attributions and consequences in the first 30 days of New York Times' reports on the Challenger disaster.

have not yet been studied experimentally. Thus we are able to track how hypotheses "grow" (cf. Abelson & Lalljee, 1988), and how causes are progressively localized (Mackie, 1974). We are also able to distinguish whether changes in explanation are due to changes in hypothesis or due to fine tuning of explanations, a distinction that has only recently been studied experimentally (cf. Hilton & Erb, 1990).

The preliminary analyses of our data encourage our belief that these methods yield clear results. Future studies will test the present data set in more detail and can be applied to other reports of the disaster as well. For example, it might be that *Pravda* would report the Challenger disaster from a different perspective, using different "norms" that might in turn lead to different abnormal conditions and causes being identified. In addition, the method needs to be applied to reports of other disasters, such as the Chernobyl fire, to test its generalizability.

More generally, the method developed here enables new questions about causal reasoning to be asked and rigorously tested on naturalistic data sets. Whereas we have focused on the role of the conversational model of causal explanation in highlighting important aspects of the explanation process, the method can in principle be used to evaluate a variety of models. Propositions from knowledge-structure theory about the role of "kernel hypotheses" (e.g., Abelson & Lalljee, 1988) can be tested using such techniques, as can proposals concerning the relationship between causal and responsibility attribution (e.g., Fincham & Jaspars, 1980; Lloyd-Bostock, 1983). Nor need the techniques be limited to media analysis. Many of the techniques presented here could be applied to the analysis of "think-aloud" protocols of the kind used to study real-world decision-making processes, such as clinical diagnosis (e.g., Elstein, Shulman, & Sprafka, 1978). Consequently, the development of such methods holds considerable promise for deepening our understanding of natural processes of causal explanation.

ACKNOWLEDGMENT

Denis Hilton was supported during the period of this research by fellowships from the Alexander von Humboldt Foundation and the Cognitive Science Committee of the University of Illinois at Urbana-Champaign. We thank Jim Ball, Laurie Newman and Kurt Openlander for their help in the coding and analysis of the data, and Anke Bathelt and Anabel Schaus for their constructive comments on the coding scheme presented here.

REFERENCES

Abelson, R. P., & Lalljee, M. G. (1988). Knowledge structures and causal explanation. In D. J. Hilton (Ed.), *Contemporary science and natural explanation: Commonsense conceptions of causality* (pp. 175–203). Brighton, England: Harvester.

Abraham, S. C. S. (1988). Seeing the connections in lay causal comprehension. In D. J. Hilton (Ed.), *Contemporary science and natural explanation: Commonsense conceptions of causality* (pp. 175–203). Brighton, England: Harvester Press.

Bock, H. (1990). AIDS in der Presse: Voruberlegungen und Planungen fuer eine vergleichende sprach-psychologische Untersuchung zur Berichterstattung uber die Krankheit AIDS in Print Medien. *Forschungsberichte zur Psychologie der Kommunikation und Informationsverarbeitung*, (Tech. Rep. No. 16).

Bohner, G., Bless, H., Schwarz, N., & Strack, F. (1988). What triggers causal attributions? The impact of valence and subjective probability. *European Journal of Social Psychology, 18,* 335–345.

Bruner, J. S., Goodnow, J. J., & Austin, G. A. (1956). *A study of thinking.* New York: Wiley.

Cheng, P. W., & Novick, L. R. (1990). A probabilistic contrast model of causal induction. *Journal of Personality and Social Psychology, 58,* 545–567.

Elstein, A. S., Shulman, L. S., & Sprafka, S. A. (1978). *Medical problem solving: An analysis of clinical reasoning.* Cambridge, MA: Harvard University Press.

Fincham, F. D., & Jaspars, J. M. F. (1980). Attribution of responsibility: From man-the-scientist to man as lawyer. In L. Berkowitz (Ed.), *Advances in experimental social psychology* (Vol. 13, pp. 81–138). New York: Academic.

Försterling, F. (1989). Models of covariation and attribution: How do they relate to the analogy of analysis of variance. *Journal of Personality and Social Psychology, 57,* 615–626.

Garland, H., Hardy, A., & Stephenson, L. (1975). Information search as affected by attribution type and response category. *Personality and Social Psychology Bulletin, 4,* 612–615.

Graesser, A. C., Robertson, S. P., & Anderson, P. A. (1981). Incorporating inferences in cognitive representations: A study of how and why. *Cognitive Psychology, 13,* 1–26.

Graesser, A. C., Robertson, S. P., Lovelace, E. R., & Swinehart, D. M. (1980). Answers to why-questions expose the organization of story-plot and predict recall behaviors. *Journal of Verbal Learning and Verbal Behavior, 19,* 110–119.

Grice, H. P. (1975). Logic and conversation. In P. Cole & J. L. Morgan (Eds.), *Syntax and semantics 3: Speech acts* (pp. 41–58). New York: Academic.

Hart, H. L. A., & Honoré, T. (1985). *Causation in the law* (2nd ed.). Oxford: Clarendon Press.

Harvey, J. H., & Weary, G. (1984). Current issues in attribution theory and research. *Annual Review of Psychology, 35,* 427–460.

Hastie, R. (1984). Causes and effects of causal attribution. *Journal of Personality and Social Psychology, 46,* 44–56.

Heider, F. (1958). *The psychology of interpersonal relations.* New York: Wiley.

Hesslow, G. (1983). Explaining differences and weighting causes. *Theoria, 49,* 87–111.

Hesslow, G. (1988). The problem of causal selection. In D. J. Hilton (Ed.), *Contemporary science and natural explanation: Commonsense conceptions of causality* (pp. 11–32). Brighton, England: Harvester Press.

Hilton, D. J. (1985). Causal beliefs: From attribution theory to cognitive science. In J. Allwood & E. Hjelmquist (Eds.), *Foregrounding background* (pp. 75–86). Lund: Boksforlaget.

Hilton, D. J. (1988). Logic and causal attribution. In D. J. Hilton (Ed.), *Contemporary science and natural explanation: Commonsense conceptions of causality* (pp. 33–65). Brighton, England: Harvester Press.

Hilton, D. J. (1990). Conversational processes and causal explanation. *Psychological Bulletin, 107,* 65–81.

Hilton, D. J. (1991). A conversational model of causal explanation. In W. Stroebe & M. Hewstone (Eds.), *European Review of Social Psychology* (Vol. 2, pp. 51–81). Chichester, England: Wiley.

Hilton, D. J., & Erb, H-P. (1990). *Mental models and causal explanation: Judgments of probable cause and explanatory relevance.* Unpublished manuscript.

Hilton, D. J., & Knibbs, C. S. (1988). The knowledge-structure and inductivist strategies in causal attribution: A direct comparison. *European Journal of Social Psychology, 18,* 79–92.

Hilton, D. J., & Slugoski, B. R. (1986). Knowledge-based causal attribution: The abnormal conditions focus model. *Psychological Review, 93,* 75–88.

Jones, E. E., & Davis, K. E. (1965). From acts to dispositions: The attribution process in person perception. In L. Berkowitz (Ed.), *Advances in experimental social psychology* (Vol. 2, pp. 219–266). New York: Academic.

Kelley, H. H. (1967). Attribution theory in social psychology. In D. Levine (Ed.), *Nebraska Symposium on Motivation* (Vol. 15, pp. 192–241). Lincoln, Nebraska: University of Nebraska Press.

Kelley, H. H. & Michela, J. L. (1980). Attribution theory and research. *Annual Review of Psychology, 31,* 457–501.

Kepplinger, H. M., & Mathes, R. H. (1988). Kuenstliche Horizonte. In J. Scharioth & H. Uhl (Eds.), *Medien und Technikalakzeptanz* (pp. 111–152). Munich: Oldenbourg.

Klayman, J. & Ha, Y-W (1987). Confirmation, disconfirmation and information in hypothesis testing. *Psychological Review, 94,* 211–228.

Kracauer, S. (1952). The challenge of qualitative content analysis. *Public Opinion Quarterly, 16,* 631–642.

Lalljee, M. G., & Abelson, R. P. (1983). The organization of explanations. In M. Hewstone (Ed.), *Attribution theory: Social and functional extensions.* Oxford, England: Basil Blackwell.

Lalljee, M. G., Lamb, R., Furnham, A., & Jaspars, J. M. F. (1984). Explanations and information search: Inductive and hypothesis-testing approaches to arriving at an explanation. *British Journal of Social Psychology, 23,* 201–212.

Lloyd-Bostock, S. (1983). Attributions of cause and responsibility as social phenomena. In J. M. F. Jaspars, F. D. Fincham, & M. R. C. Hewstone (Eds.), *Attribution theory and research: Conceptual, developmental and social dimensions.* London: Academic Press.

Mackie, J. L. (1974). *The cement of the universe.* London: Oxford University Press.

Marx, R., Stubbart, C., Traub, V., & Cavanaugh, M. (1987). The NASA space shuttle disaster: A case study. *Journal of Management Case Studies, 3,* 300–318.

Mathes, R. H. (1988). "Quantitative" Analyse "qualitativ" erhobener Daten? Die hermeneutisch-klassifikatorische Inhaltsanalyse von Leitfadengespraechen. *ZUMA-Nachrichten, 22,* 60–78.

Mathes, R. H. (1989). Modulsystem und Netzwerktechnik. ZUMA-Arbeitsbericht, ZUMA, Mannheim.

Mill, J. S. (1973). System of logic (8th ed.). In J. M. Robson (Ed.), *Collected works of John Stuart Mill* (Vols. 7 and 8). Toronto, Canada: University of Toronto Press. (Original work published 1872)

Newcombe, R. D., & Rutter, D. R. (1982). Ten reasons why ANOVA theory and research fail to explain attribution processes: 1. Conceptual problems. *Current Psychological Reviews, 2,* 95–108.

Pople, H. E. (1981). Heuristic methods for imposing structure on ill-structured problems: The structuring of medical diagnostics. In P. Szolovits (Ed.), *Artificial intelligence in medicine.* Boulder: Westview Press.

Propp, V. (1968). *The morphology of the folktale.* Austin: University of Texas Press.

Read, S. J. (1987). Constructing causal scenarios: A knowledge structure approach to causal reasoning. *Journal of Personality and Social Psychology, 52,* 288–302.

Ross, M., & Fletcher, G. J. O. (1985). Attribution and social perception. In G. Lindzey & E. Aronson (Eds.), *Handbook of social psychology. Vol. 2. Special fields and applications* (pp. 73–122). New York: Random House.

Schank, R. C., & Abelson, R. P. (1977). *Scripts, plans, goals and understanding: An inquiry into human knowledge structures.* Hillsdale, NJ: Lawrence Erlbaum Associates.

Trabasso, T., & van den Broek, P. (1985). Causal thinking and story comprehension. *Journal of Memory and Language, 24,* 612–630.

Trabasso, T., and Sperry, L. L. (1985). The causal basis for deciding importance of story events. *Journal of Memory and Language, 24,* 595–611.

Turnbull, W. M. (1986). Everyday explanation: The pragmatics of puzzle resolution. *Journal for the Theory of Social Behavior, 16,* 141–160.

Turnbull, W. M., & Slugoski, B. R. (1988). Conversational and linguistic processes in causal attribution. In D. J. Hilton (Ed.), *Contemporary science and natural explanation: Commonsense conceptions of causality* (pp. 66–93). New York: New York University Press.

Weiner, B. (1985). "Spontaneous" causal thinking. *Psychological Bulletin, 97,* 74–84.

Wilensky, R. (1978). Why John married Mary: Understanding stories involving recurring goals. *Cognitive Science, 2,* 235–266.

Wilensky, R. (1983). *Planning and understanding: A computational approach to human reasoning.* Reading, Massachusetts: Addison-Wesley.

4

▼▼▼▼▼▼▼

An Economy of Explanations

John McClure
Victoria University of Wellington, New Zealand

How many causes or conditions constitute a satisfactory explanation of an action? What are the factors that affect people's perception that an explanation is sufficient? Do people perceive explanations of actions as less plausible if several alternative explanations are available?

In attribution theory these issues are approached through the classic discounting principle, which proposes that the role of any cause in producing a given effect is discounted if other plausible causes are present (Kelley, 1973). In line with the general idea that attributions simulate scientific inference, the discounting notion reflects the view that scientific explanations are simple and elegant. The discounting notion acquired wide acceptance within and beyond attribution theory, and it is widely assumed that the concept has been confirmed and established by research (e.g., Kelley & Michela, 1980).

Recent investigations concerning explanations point in rather different directions. Investigators have developed concepts of causal relations and causal structures that challenge the notion that causes are always inversely related. Several developments suggest the importance of differences between causal categories in shaping the structure of explanations. These developments imply an interaction between content and process, or at least, they imply that inference processes reflect the content of the logical relations between causes. Increasing attention is paid to knowledge structures that are in some respects similar to the schema framework used in orthodox discounting models but that in other respects imply a very different process of causal selection. A further emerging issue is that the cause that is communicated in a public explanation may not be the only or primary perceived determinant of the event. Other authors suggest that lay explanations may sometimes serve the goals of concealment or distraction rather than of matching the eliminative strategies of scientific inference, as implied by the discounting principle. These various conjectures are linked to new theoretical perspectives such as knowledge structures, conversational models, and discourse analysis. These perspectives have very different implications from some of the classic analogs applied to causal selection and causal reasoning.

This chapter first presents a brief survey of research relating to causal selection, discounting, and conjunctions, and then turns to various conceptual issues that surround this research and to new theoretical perspectives that account for some of the findings and are reframing the issues. Particular attention is paid to knowledge-structure theories and the conversational approach.

RESEARCH ON DISCOUNTING AND CONJUNCTION EFFECTS

Research that has examined discounting and related issues has been framed in the form of two slightly different questions. First, how are causes perceived concurrently? This question subdivides into such issues as whether causes for an effect are inversely related and whether conjunctions are perceived as more plausible than single causes. A second question concerns the effect of introducing a second cause on ratings of a first cause. Does the presence of an alternative explanation lead to discounting of a previous explanation? Research addressing both questions is summarized here; a fuller review is contained in McClure (1989).

Are Person and Situation Causes Inversely Related?

Initial claims about discounting suggested that ratings of person and situation causes are inversely related and that higher ratings of one lead to lower ratings of the other. It was claimed, for example, that Thibaut and Riecken's (1955) classic experiment showed that people discount pressure as a cause of giving to charity in high status persons and discount charitability as a cause of giving in low status target persons (e.g., Kelley, 1973). One problem with this interpretation is that this study used an attribution measure inappropriate for measuring discounting: a forced-choice measure that required subjects to attribute only one cause to each target person and a different cause in either case (McClure, 1989). So the study did not establish whether the participants actually perceived both causes as contributing significantly to the outcome.

Thibaut and Riecken's experiment is not the only one to use measures that are problematic for interpretations concerning discounting. Other studies examining ratings of persons and situations have used measures that impose constraints on responses. These studies were not always designed to test the discounting principle, but their findings are relevant for that principle in that they show whether high ratings of one cause are accompanied by lower ratings (or discounting) of a second cause. In his review of studies examining ratings of persons and situations, Solomon (1978) pointed out that the inverse relation between the two ratings in many studies was accentuated by the researchers' use of bipolar scales, where *person* and *situation* are at opposite ends of a single scale. Solomon noted that while these studies using bipolar measures obtained negative relations between ratings of the person and the situation, studies using separate scales for persons and situations found that variations on one scale were not accompanied by variations on the other scale (see also Billig, 1982; Taylor & Koivumaki, 1976). Subsequent studies have reinforced the finding that attributions to persons and situations are often not inversely related (Lalljee, Watson, & White, 1982; Wimer & Kelley, 1982). These studies show that an increase in the rating of one cause often does not effect the rating of a second cause, a conclusion that challenges the discounting principle. The research suggests that people may perceive situational and personal factors as jointly contributing to an outcome, and that the presence of one of these causes may have no automatic implications for the presence of the others.

Are Two Reasons Better than One?

A second paradigm that has been applied to discounting compares ratings of the probability of individual and conjunctive statements. From the discounting principle one might expect a preference for individual causal statements for common events and a preference for conjunctive statements for extreme events, where multiple causation is necessary to produce the affect (Kelley, 1973; Locksley & Stangor, 1984). The paradigm employed to rate causes adapts the procedure that was first applied to perceptions of personal characteristics (Tversky & Kahneman, 1983). Here people receive information about a given target person that identifies that person as a certain type; they then rate the probability of various statements about the person. Some statements are representative of that category of person, and some statements are unrepresentative of that category of person. In the example of Linda, who is portrayed as a "radical" person, people rate the probability that Linda is a bank teller (unrepresentative of radical persons) and that Linda is active in the feminist movement (representative of radical persons). Conjunctions typically combine a representative and an unrepresentative statement. Tversky and Kahneman found that people rated conjunctions as more probable than the constituents, a judgment that contravenes logical probability as well as suggesting implications contrary to the discounting principle. Wells (1985) replicated this finding and showed that the preference for conjunctions did not extend to combinations of two representative statements. Markus and Zajonc (1985) surmised that the higher ratings of conjunctions might reflect some artifact, in that the simultaneous presentation of conjunctions and component statements might create an improper sample space. For example, an item format where the conjunction is "Bob has a high paying job and is handsome" and the constituent is "Bob has a high paying job" could imply that in the constituent item Bob is not handsome. However, studies have shown that the item format has little effect, and the same outcome is obtained, for example, when the constituent is rewritten as "Bob has a high-paying job whether or not he is handsome" (e.g., Morier & Borgida, 1984).

Leddo, Abelson, and Gross (1984) adapted this paradigm to explanations of actions. Participants read action descriptions (e.g., Mike went into the restaurant) and rated the probability of explanations for the actions, presented either as conjunctions or single causes. Leddo and Abelson (1986) found the same tendency to give higher ratings for the conjunctions than for the constituent causes, a tendency they designated *conjunction effects*. This effect was found across a broad range of events and explanations, including important events, such as a career choice, and mundane events, such as stopping at a restaurant, and with conjunctions containing two goals and conjunctions containing goals and preconditions. Read (1988) showed that the effect also occurs when respondents are explaining a choice between two options, even when the explanation of the choice includes causes common to the option that is not chosen, that is, causes that are not unique to the option that the target person chose. This suggests that the preference for conjunctions overrides considerations about how informative a cause is in explaining an action. Clearly, if a cause is common to both the chosen and the nonchosen alternative, it doesn't explain the particular choice that is made; it is not informative (cf. Hilton, 1990).

Despite this strong tendency to favor conjunctions, theoretically interesting boundary conditions do exist. In Leddo et al.'s second study, no conjunction effects occurred with explanations of incomplete or failed actions, a finding that Leddo et al. attributed to knowledge structures that contain a single slot for failed events. Subsequent studies show that conjunction effects actually do occur with failed actions when the causes being rated are competing or alternate goals. Conversely, conjunction effects do not occur with completed actions when the causes refer to the absence of competing goals and preconditions (McClure, Lalljee, Jaspars, & Abelson, 1989; Zuckerman, Eghrari, & Lambrecht, 1986). These results suggest that conjunction effects occur with causes that are present, such as the presence of causes and preconditions, but not with causes that are absent, such as the absence of goals and preconditions. For example, a conjunction of obstacles that are present is rated probable as a cause of failure. So ratings of conjunctions are affected by the status of the causes, as well as the valence of the outcome being explained. In addition, Read (1988) showed that conjunction effects are reduced in explanations of a sudden change of mind where people have a choice between two actions that have some common effects and some distinct effects. This particular condition sensitizes people to the factor that is distinct to the option being chosen, and other causes lose their explanatory value. Finally, Abelson, Leddo, & Gross (1987) reported that conjunction effects do not extend to predictions of future behavior.

These exceptions do not challenge the finding of a general tendency toward conjunction effects with both goals (or intentions) and preconditions. On the other hand, Hilton's "abnormal-conditions focus" analysis suggests that whereas conjunctions of goals and preconditions may indeed be necessary for actions, the presence of a goal (or intention) is sufficient to explain the action's occurrence. Hilton (1990) drew a distinction between intentions and preconditions, and suggested that intentions are typically abnormal conditions that make the difference to the action occurring. In regard to Leddo et al.'s (1984) and McClure et al.'s (1989) finding that people preferred conjunctions over single causes in many conditions, Hilton claimed that people often perceive an intention as a sufficient explanation. Hilton and Knott (1988) adapted Leddo et al.'s and McClure et al.'s items to a conditional-reasoning format that distinguishes necessary and sufficient causes. They found that whereas preconditions were perceived only as necessary for the action (if they were absent, the action did not occur), intentions were perceived as both necessary and sufficient (if they were present, the action would occur). Hilton reiterated Heider's (1958) view that intentions are sufficient causes for actions.

In a sense, the abnormal-conditions component of Hilton's argument can be adapted to reach the same conclusions about preconditions that Hilton applies to intentions. Any cause, and not only an intention, can serve as the abnormal condition that makes the difference to the occurrence of the action. A precondition is likely to be a sufficient explanation in situations where a goal is highly probable and may be largely taken for granted. Take an example where a precondition is the availability of an affordable medicine that cures AIDS, and we are wanting to explain why Peter, who has AIDS, acquires the medicine. The presence of the precondition is likely to be a more sufficient explanation than the goal of Peter wanting to get well, which is likely to be considered uninformative. A precondition is also likely to be a more sufficient explanation in a situation where a goal is probable but cannot be easily realized. The presence of a precondition that enables that goal to be realized is likely to be a sufficient explanation of the action. In this type of case the presence of a precondition is likely to be the "abnormal" feature, more than the intention or goal. The argument here is that any cause or category of cause may be the abnormal condition, depending on the context in which the explanation is offered. While for some actions the nature of the causes that may be presupposed does not vary much across specific instances, for many actions the specific causal context does vary, and this condition is perceived as an abnormal condition (Hart & Honoré, 1985).

It remains to be shown whether the probability ratings obtained by Leddo et al. and McClure et al. or the conditional reasoning format used by Hilton correspond more closely to explanations in unstructured response settings. But it can be noted at this point that conjunction effects have implications that are contrary to the discounting principle. Whereas the discounting principle implies that when two causes for an effect are available the attributor discounts one cause, the conjunction effect implies that explanations with two causes are rated as more probable than explanations with one. The discounting principle implies that people choose an explanation that is simple, at the expense of completeness, whereas the conjunction effect implies that people choose an explanation that is complete, at the expense of simplicity. This tendency suggests that people perceive that any effect may involve several causes. The studies in the previous section show that people do not see the two broad categories of person and the situation causes as having necessary implications for each other's presence. The studies in this section show that people also see more specific causes as compatible, and not implying each other's absence. However, these studies also reveal boundaries to the preference for conjunctions that indicate that for certain explanations, single causes are preferable or sufficient.

Contextual Effects on Dispositional Inferences

The research described up to this point concerns the issue of how causes are perceived concurrently. A second way of approaching discounting concerns the effect of introducing a second cause on ratings of a first cause. This paradigm is applied in studies examining Jones and Davis' (1965) theory of correspondent inference; these studies examine the conditions in which people take situational factors into account when attributing attitudes to others (e.g., Jones & Harris, 1967). Attributions are elicited after target persons have performed a pertinent action, such as reading a statement expressing a particular attitude. The studies vary the absence or presence of instructions (the situational cause) and the extremity of the expressed attitude. The finding relevant to discounting has occurred where the person is instructed to perform the action and where the expressed attitude is extreme or unexpected. In this condition, respondents have attributed the relevant attitude to the person significantly less than when instructions were absent (i.e., they discounted to some extent), but they still attributed a stronger attitude to the person than in conditions where a moderate attitude was expressed. In other words, attributors did not fully discount the attitude, even though the instructions were a sufficient explanation of the action. This partial discounting has been described by both Kelley (Kelley & Michela, 1980) and Jones (1979) as "insufficient" discounting, because there is a cause present (the instructions) that is sufficient to explain the outcome. There is not complete agreement on the reasons for this lack of discounting, although most explanations emphasize the role of some perceptual or inferential failure (e.g., Quattrone, 1982). What is clear is that people fail to discount dispositional factors in these conditions unless the sufficiency of the external cause is made exceptionally salient (Ajzen, Dalto, & Blyth, 1979). As with studies described in previous sections, these studies suggest that the presence of situational causes has no necessary implications for the efficacy of dispositional causes.

The Effects of Added Causes on Ratings

A paradigm designed specifically to examine discounting compares ratings of the likelihood that an isolated cause determined an outcome, and ratings of the same cause when other causes are present (Einhorn & Hogarth, 1983, Experiment 1; Hansen & Hall, 1985; Kruglanski, Schwartz, Maides, & Hamel, 1978; Rosenfield & Stephan, 1977). Using this procedure, Kruglanski et al. focused on particular motives for actions rather than the general categories of person and situation. For example, an item stated "Frank gave a donation to charity. Frank wants to take the donation as a tax deduction. His boss is on the charity's board of directors." Covariation information indicated whether the causes accompanied the action on previous occasions. In the absence of this information, subjects rated a single motive lower in the presence of the alternative motive, indicating some discounting. But covariation information reinforcing the alternative motive did not strengthen this effect, whereas information reinforcing the initial motive increased the rating of that motive. Kruglanski et al. observed that this finding disconfirms the discounting principle: "The idea that a strong well-documented alternative (buttressed by covariation evidence) may not detract from one's confidence in the focal hypothesis any more than would a considerably weaker alternative . . . seems inconsistent with the discounting rule itself" (p. 182).

Kruglanski et al. questioned this implication of their data on the grounds that the discounting rule "was well established in this and other research" (p. 182). But similar inconsistencies with the discounting principle have been found by other authors using similar procedures. Rosenfield and Stephan (1977), for example, presented subjects with information about the probability of internal and external causes prior to observing an actor's (aggressive) behavior. When subjects received information implicating both causes, the information concerning one cause had no affect on ratings of the other cause. The authors found the result "surprising in light of the many studies cited in the introduction that have found discounting effects" (p. 100). It was only when subjects received no information about one cause that the cause was discounted.

A precise measurement of this type of effect is provided in Einhorn and Hogarth's (1983) studies. Here subjects were first presented with an effect and a single cause, which they rated, providing a "gross" rating of the cause. They were then presented with an alternative explanation, for which a gross rating had been obtained from other subjects, and made a new "net" rating of the initial cause. Ratings of the first cause were lower after the introduction of the alternative causes, but the decrease failed to reflect the ratings of the gross strength of the causes in isolation. This "underadjustment" led Einhorn and Hogarth to conclude that "a single explanation is not greatly discounted by alternatives" (p. 32). Hansen and Hall (1985) found a similar underadjustment in explanations of physical effects. An interesting feature of these experiments concerns the effect of background information implicating the causes. When this information accompanies both causes, participants exhibit some underadjustment, or no discounting at all. Where evidence implicates several causes in an affect, people apparently perceive that effect in terms of multiple causes, rather than discounting. Causes described as alternatives by the researchers are not treated as complete alternatives by the subjects. The results recall the findings of Leddo et al. (1984) that two reasons are often better than one, as far as the lay person is concerned.

The experiments also demonstrated that discounting was limited largely to causes other than the first cause encountered. Subjects appear to anchor on the first cause and take little account of the strength of alternative causes. As a consequence, they make insufficient downward adjustments in the strength of the prior "focal" cause. Independent support for this view appears in Shaklee and Fischhoff's (1982) finding that subjects' strategies of information search followed a "truncated search pattern" (p. 521). People tend to anchor on the first explanation they possess, rather than following the discounting principle.

These studies are more consistent with other findings than the authors recognize. Kruglanski, Baldwin, and Towson (1978), Rosenfield and Stephan (1977), and Einhorn and Hogarth (1983) treat their findings of limited discounting as exceptions to a firmly established pattern. But other experiments on discounting, counter to what is often claimed, demonstrate similar constraints on discounting to those that these authors found. The results of these studies suggest that people systematically deviate from the discounting rule and frequently make attributions consistent with multiple causation.

The Effect of Extremity

One issue that has generated interest is the relation of the extremity of events to discounting. Kelley (1973) proposed that with extreme events people see several causes as necessary, a perception that he linked to a "multiple-necessary" cognitive schema. In this case they are less likely to discount than with moderate effects. It is claimed that research has supported this proposition (e.g., Kelley & Michela, 1980), but in fact the results are much less straightforward. Kun and Weiner (1973), for example, who examined attributions for extreme and moderate success and failure in exams, found that while the participants perceived two causes to be present more for extreme success than moderate success, a single cause was perceived sufficient to account for both moderate and extreme failure. They attributed this asymmetry to the negative connotations of failure, but it may alternatively reflect the fact that they included only internal causes in their measures, as these causes are typically associated more with success than failure. McClure et al. (1989) showed that the asymmetry that Kun and Weiner obtained is reversed for external causes, with conjunctions being rated more probable for failure than success, relative to single causes. This reversal suggests that the likelihood of a conjunctive explanation reflects the category of cause being considered rather than the positivity or negativity of the outcome. The extent to which people discount for success and failure is contingent on the causes being considered.

The issue of whether more causes are invoked for extreme than moderate effects was also examined by Cunningham and Kelley (1975), who required participants to rate explanations for events portrayed in mild and extreme form. Participants rated the two causes as being *more true* for extreme than moderate effects, as Kelley predicted. But the measure for these ratings did not permit people to rate the strength of the two relevant causes independently, so it is unclear whether the increase was due to a perception of one cause or both. Other measures in the study, however, suggested that some effects were linked to one of the causes, rather than both. The idea that some extreme effects are attributed to a single extreme cause rather than a conjunction was explored in a series of studies by McClure, Lalljee, and Jaspars (1991), who obtained explanations on two measures: a free response measure and a choice format requiring a choice between a conjunction and a single cause matching the effect. Responses with both formats indicated that while some extreme achievements and actions were attributed to conjunctions, others were attributed to single "extreme" causes. Participants invoked causes like brilliance in the case of great achievements and insanity in the case of bizarre criminal actions. This use of single causes differs from Kelley's prediction that extreme events are explained by a conjunction of causes. However, both forms of explanation are consistent with the idea that explanations correspond to the extremity of the effects being explained. In the case of a single extreme cause, this correspondence is achieved by increasing the magnitude of one cause, and in case of conjunctions, it is achieved by increasing the number of causes that are involved.

What happened with moderate outcomes? In some cases, participants used the disjunctive (A or B) explanations predicted by Kelley or the fairly equivalent single-cause (A only) explanations. In other cases, however, participants invoked two opposing causes linked by an adversative conjunction, such as "but" or "however" (A but B). For example, they might explain a moderate result by suggesting that Josephine was intelligent but that she didn't work very hard. Clearly people perceive that outcomes may reflect opposing causal influences as well as congruent causal influences (cf. Wilensky, 1983). This possibility is recognized in concepts such as augmentation, which occurs where a cause contributing to an effect is countered by an opposing cause. But the role of opposing causes has not been incorporated into models and predictions dealing with discounting and causal schemata. The strategy of explaining moderate events by two opposing causes is consistent with the strategy of explaining extreme events in terms of single causes (McClure, 1991). Attributing extreme success to a single cause (she is intelligent) is consistent with attributing moderate success to the same cause countered by an opposing cause (she is intelligent but didn't work hard).

These suggestions are not challenged by a further study examining the effects of extremity that was performed by Locksley and Stangor (1984). The study used the conjunction-effects procedure described earlier in this chapter and produced stronger conjunction effects with extreme than with moderate items. There are difficulties in interpreting the study, relating to the fact that the authors used completely different items for extreme and moderate effects. This method renders the results ambiguous, as the result could be due to the particular content of the item rather than extremity per se. So this study contains no more unambiguous support than other studies for Kelley's proposition that extreme effects elicit conjunctive explanations.

This survey suggests that extreme effects may be attributed either to a single extreme cause or to conjunctions of causes, whereas moderate events are attributed either to alternative congruent causes linked by a disjunction or to opposing causes linked by an adversative disjunction. The structure of the explanation is subject to the content of the effect being explained and the causes that are invoked.

THEORETICAL PERSPECTIVES

Cognitive Bias and Reflection of Reality

Many of the recent studies examining discounting suggest that people discount less than attribution theories proposed. This finding seems to derive from two factors. In the first case, some nondiscounting results from cognitive biases and inferential "failures." An example is where people anchor on a cause and fail to discount that cause even when evidence suggests that another cause was responsible for the effect (Shaklee & Fischhoff, 1982). This tendency appears where people are presented causes sequentially rather than concurrently. People anchor on the first perceived cause and give insufficient weight to evidence implicating other causes (Einhorn & Hogarth, 1983; Kruglanski et al., 1978; Rosenfield & Stephan, 1977; Schustack & Sternberg, 1981; Shaklee & Fischhoff, 1982).

A second reason why people don't discount is that two or more causes are often perceived as impinging on a situation. Here people do not discount because they perceive that the causes jointly determine the effect. This occurs both with person and situation ratings (e.g., Taylor & Koivumaki, 1976; Wimer & Kelley, 1982) and goals and preconditions (Leddo et al., 1984; McClure et al., 1989; Read, 1988; Zuckerman et al., 1986). As Kelley (1983) proposed, people's explanations reflect causal structures that include several categories of causes applying to any given action (cf. Leddo et al., 1984). Where people perceive the contribution of several causes, the presence of one category of cause does not necessarily imply the absence of another category of cause (McClure, 1991). When a person is violent, for example, the fact that the individual is drunk does not entail that provocation was absent. Similarly, when someone performs an action, the fact that the person has a goal does not suggest that he or she lacks the preconditions required to carry out the action. Nor does the presence of one goal indicate that other goals are absent (Leddo et al., 1984; Wilensky, 1983). If several causes are effective in many actions, then one would not expect the presence of one of these causes to produce discounting of others (McClure, 1985). Multiple causal influences are involved in moderate effects as well as extreme effects. The distinct quality of extreme actions is that one can expect an unusual *magnitude* of one or more causes, not a greater *number* of causes per se. The research suggests that if the available information suggests that two (or more) causes contribute to an effect, people do not discount either cause (e.g., Einhorn & Hogarth, 1983). In short, some cases of nondiscounting are reflections of multiple causation in the actual events being explained, rather than cognitive bias.

Logical Relations Among Causes

This argument does not imply that discounting never occurs, but rather that discounting reflects logical relations between causes. Discounting is likely to be greatest where the relevant causes are mutually exclusive or incompatible (Kruglanski, 1980). A more moderate level of discounting is likely where the causes are clear alternatives, such as alternative goals, although it should be remembered that alternative goals are not necessarily mutually exclusive. In fact people see an alternative explanation as having only weak implications for a given explanation (e.g., Einhorn & Hogarth, 1983; Kruglanski et al., 1978; Leddo et al., 1984). Less discounting may be expected where causes are not potential alternatives, as in the case of a goal and the relevant preconditions (Leddo et al., 1984). If future research takes more account of the distinction between causes that are alternatives and those that are not, it is likely to generate more accurate predictions of discounting and causal selection. An obvious example that has been overlooked in some of the research is that where two causes are both necessary for an effect to occur, such as a goal and a precondition, the presence of one of the causes is not likely to produce much discounting of the other cause. If research takes account of the logical relation between different causes and effects, it will clarify when discounting (or nondiscounting) is due to this logical kind of factor rather than cognitive biases.

Knowledge Structures. Are the logical relations among causes in the real world reflected in cognitive structures? Expressed in different terms, do cognitive schemas and structures assume particular causal relations (cf. Kelley, 1973)? Leddo et al. (1984) linked ratings of conjunctions and single causes to knowledge structures and, in particular, to cognitive frames that reflect people's notions about a complete explanation of an event. For completed actions, the frame has multiple slots for the goals and preconditions that typically produce the action, whereas for failed actions, the frame contains a single slot for a cause that can disenable the event. The higher rating of conjunctions for completed actions reflects the concordant match between the cognitive frame and the explanation (cf. Leddo & Abelson, 1986; Read, 1987). This model is supported by Read's (1988) study of ratings of conjunctions where people chose between two alternatives that have some common effects. Even when conjunctions included causes common to the chosen and nonchosen alternative, the participants rated conjunctions that included those causes as highly probable. This suggests that the preference for conjunctions can override considerations about how informative a cause is in explaining an action. Clearly, if a cause is common to both the chosen and the nonchosen alternatives, it doesn't "explain" the particular choice that is made (cf. Hilton, 1990).

The knowledge-structure model has been qualified by findings that ratings of causes are affected by the type of cause being examined. The pattern of ratings obtained with causes that contribute to success is reversed with causes that contribute to failure (McClure et al., 1989). To account for these findings, the cognitive-slot notion would need to be inverted with causes that contribute to failure, in that these causes would require more slots for action failure than action completion. The model should also take account of Hilton and Knott's (1988) demonstration that single causes can be treated as sufficient explanations for completed actions, rather than a conjunction of causes. Hilton claimed this feature particularly in regard to intentions, but, as was noted above, preconditions are more likely to be sufficient explanations in many circumstances. An example is where the intention is highly probable and can be assumed, but where the preconditions necessary for completion of an action are not readily available.

Knowledge-structure models have been relatively sensitive to content and real-world material, in contrast to more abstract approaches. Yet the knowledge-structure model of conjunctions needs to become more sensitive in this regard to reflect the finding that causal judgments are subject to the type or content of the cause, and the relation of each cause to the outcome. There may be several causal knowledge structures, much as Kelley (1973) suggested several causal schemata that guide causal inferences. In an important respect, Leddo et al. (1984) recognized the range of possible logical relations between causes when they deliberately selected combinations of causes that are neither competing nor cooperative—the causes are neutral to each other. In real-world situations, of course, other combinations occur frequently, and this is likely to affect the rating of conjunctions. For example, a conjunction of two mutually exclusive causes is not likely to be seen as plausible. In this instance, as elsewhere, the rating of causes is subject to the content of the individual causes and their relation to each other. The knowledge-structure approach needs to be adapted to address this variability in causal relations. At the same time, there needs to be firmer evidence that causal inference does involve a process of matching explanations to a knowledge structure.

Read (1987) suggested that the causal schemata that Kelley (1973) proposed can be incorporated into a knowledge-structure framework. In a sense, the multiple-slot structure of Leddo et al.'s knowledge structures for completed actions resembles Kelley's multiple-necessary schema, whereas the single-slot structure of knowledge structures for incompleted actions resembles Kelley's multiple-sufficient schema. However, the concept of necessity in Kelley's multiple-necessary schema does differ somewhat from the meaning of necessary causes in other models (Hilton, 1990; Leddo & Abelson, 1986). Any synthesis of the two models should be sensitive to the research findings concerning the different status of various causes and the logical relation between those causes.

Conversation and Discourse. How is discounting and causal reasoning affected by the particular goals of a communication and by the norms applying to normal conversation? A recent development construes explanation as a process that conforms to the rules of conversation (Hilton, Mathes, & Trabasso, chapter 10, this volume). The link between this model and earlier approaches such as Kelley's (1967) covariation model is Mill's (1973/1872) method of difference, which proposes that explanations explain events by selecting the factor that makes the difference between the particular instance and the situations where the effect does not occur. Hilton and Slugoski's (1986) "abnormal-conditions focus" model retains the idea that explanations explain abnormal events, but it emphasizes that norms vary depending on the context in which the explanation occurs. In normal human discourse the context is conversation, and, according to the conversational analysis, explanations reflect the rules of conversation, such as those defined by Grice (1975).

As Hilton (1990) observed, this model provides a considerable advance over previous models of the inference process. Yet it remains unclear to what extent explanations adhere to this model. Some explanations occur in the context of a monologue, such as a newspaper report or a political announcement, which may differ in important respects from a conversation. A different issue is that even where explanations do occur in a conversational context, it is questionable whether they always adhere to the sorts of communicative rules described by Grice, in the way that some authors imply. The conversational model emphasizes the ways explanations are affected by the context, where parameters are defined by the questioner or listener, and pays less regard to other goals of the speaker in the communication. The conversational model implies that one requirement of the explainer is to inform and be cooperative, that the explainer operates rather like the citizens' advice bureau. The quantity maxim in Grice's framework of communicative cooperativeness implies that a primary requirement of cooperative communication is that it inform the receiver. Most attribution theories assume similarly that a primary purpose of causal inference is to obtain answers to causal questions: an enlightenment function.

But, as Grice recognized, speakers may deliberately violate these rules. This is particularly likely where the explainer's goal is to impress, intimidate, or mislead the listener, rather than to inform. At odds with the enlightenment view of explanations are theories that suggest that communication functions as much to misinform as to inform, and as much to obscure as to clarify (e.g., Billig, 1982; Snyder & Wicklund, 1981). An illustration of this tendency is seen in governments and bureaucracies that follow principles of uncooperativeness in their presentation of mis-information and non-information. The maxim operating here is to tell people (the public) nothing that they do not know already, to release information that tells people what they already know, or to provide information that is uninformative with regard to the question being asked.

Snyder and Wicklund (1981) observed that the function of some explanations is the opposite to the reductive and eliminative process of discounting. They challenged whether people are usually "pulled toward ruling out certain causes in favor of other causes" (p. 197) and proposed in contrast that "the attributor . . . often is motivated to move *away* from the direction of attributional specificity. Rather than narrowing the range of causes to arrive at a single dominant explanation, we should at times expect efforts to break open the range of causality—to locate multiple causes and to render the end result of the 'search' for causality ambiguous" (p. 198). Snyder and Wicklund invoked occasions when a sufficient cause or motive for an action is present, but because individuals wish to obscure that cause, they increase the ambiguity of their actions. People often confuse or muddy the nature of a threatening attribution by "inventing additional causes . . . in order to prevent specificity" (p. 198). Snyder and Wicklund restricted these claims to actors' explanations of their own actions, by contrast with observers' explanations. But they provide no clear rationale for this qualification; there is certainly no a priori reason for thinking that a threatening explanation of other people's behavior is less worrying than a threatening explanation of one's own behavior.

The idea that certain circumstances lead people to add causal explanations rather than to discount was also noted in explanations of social conditions such as unemployment. Billig (1982) suggested that when people dislike an available explanation of a social outcome, they muddy the picture by adding or emphasizing other factors. This principle applies to causal chains as much as individual causes. One account of the ways that people obscure sufficient explanations with inaccurate causal chains is supplied in Kelley's (1980) description of the manipulations used by magicians to control audiences' attributions. Kelley suggested that magic tricks involve two causal sequences: a real causal sequence that the magician knows, and an apparent causal sequence constructed by the magician that is meant to be followed by the audience. Kelley noted that knowledge about causal manipulation obtained from magic tricks "suggest ways in persons other than magicians—political leaders, salesmen, and others—can create false scenarios of the causes of events" (1980, p. 34). Wilensky (1983) has offered a similar operationalization of techniques of disguise and camouflage in explanations. In these cases, the techniques involve causal disguise and invention rather than causal clarification and reduction (discounting).

The goal of obscuring the most accurate or plausible causes for actions applies in any impression management that serves to justify, excuse, and condemn actions. People may add redundant causes when a sufficient cause is present or discount causes that are already available. In the case of negative actions by an ingroup member, for example, personal causes may be discounted and mitigating situational factors may be augmented. Conversely, with positive actions in ingroup members, personal factors may be augmented and situational factors discounted. The pattern is inverted with outgroups (e.g., Hewstone, Jaspars, & Lalljee, 1982). In this instance discounting and augmentation function to express or reinforce the prejudices of the group.

These models of causal management allow that people discount causes in some conditions, but in this case discounting is guided not by the motive to be economical (the scientist analogy) or the requirement to inform (the cooperator model), but by the motive to justify a particular action or to obscure a particular cause. When people's motive is to simplify or to inform, they are likely to discount, but when their motive is to obscure an explanation, even when that explanation comprises a sufficient cause for the effect, they are likely to add further causes, rather than discount.

The conversational/Gricean model implies that speaker and hearer both recognize certain underlying rules of conversation. Austin (1962) described ways in which these conversational rules are breached by accidental infelicities, but breaches are not only accidental (Grice, 1975). Habermas (1979) noted that the norms of conversation reflect the particular social relationships in which speakers and hearers are embedded and that communications may deliberately challenge that relationship rather than reinforce it. A speech act may be rejected on the grounds that the social relationship that the speech articulates is unacceptable to the listener (Bowers, 1988). Habermas suggested that "the attempt a speaker makes with a [sic] illocutionary act may founder for contingent reasons on the refusal of the addressee to enter into the proffered relationship" (p. 59). Applied to notions like discounting, these observations suggest that the degree to which people will select and reduce causes will reflect their acceptance of the relationship in which the communication is embedded.

The muddying nature of explanations described by Snyder, Wicklund, and others relates to the variability in discourse described by Potter and Wetherell (1987). For example, they reported that their own research on New Zealanders' discourse about Maoris revealed numerous contradictions rather than a clear, consistent stereotype. Their interviewees referred to Maoris as "lazy" and "such hardworking people," almost in the same breath (p. 124). Potter and Wetherell inferred from this variability that discourse reflects a particular situation or function rather than internal attitudes. It is disputable whether this variability in people's discourse constitutes evidence that people lack internal dispositions or coherent cognitions (McClure, 1991). Variability in people's discourse may reflect stable but inconsistent cognitions in the form of contradictions in attitudes

(Billig, 1982). Contradictions in discourse may also reflect contradictions in people's circumstances rather than be tactics of double-think (Bowers, 1988).

Certainly these contradictions involve different causal structures from those described in classic discounting scenarios. Billig has described one way in which people link oppositional views together. For example, in regard to unemployment, a person may assert that the economy plays a part, but clearly it is up to the person to get a job. In these cases the opposing emphases are linked grammatically by adversative conjunctions (such as but or however), which are the connectives that link opposing propositions, rather than by the additive conjunctions (A and B) or disjunctions (A or B) described by Kelley (1973). Billig linked these combinations of opposing propositions to moderate political stances, in contrast to extremist views that discount one of the opposing propositions. This "balancing of oppositions" structure in explanations that express moderate views parallels the structure of explanations for moderate outcomes described earlier, where combinations of opposing causes were invoked (McClure et al., 1991). In both cases, one of the opposing elements that is invoked in a moderate event or stance is discounted with an extreme event or stance.

Explanations in a Communicative Context.   Research relating to discounting has tended to treat people's response to attributional questions as a direct indication of the person's perceptions of the causes of events. This practice ignores an important distinction between perceived causes and communicated causes, or explanations. There is a difference between the question of whether a cause is perceived as contributing to an effect and the question of whether a cause is included in an explanation. Where explanations refer only a single cause, it is possible that the person perceives several causes to determine the outcome. Where people select a single cause and apparently discount others, they may do so for reasons other than thinking that the omitted causes are weak or uncertain. An explanation may include only the most proximate cause that preceded an action and omit important distal causes (Hart & Honoré, 1985; Kelley, 1983). Causes may be omitted because reference to them is seen as uninformative (Grice, 1975), and people think that these causes can be taken for granted, even though they contributed to the effect. Ivan Lendl attributed his many victories in tennis tournaments in 1985 to a change of diet; other causes that are likely to have contributed, such as skill and effort, were omitted from the explanation. Presumably this is not because these causes were perceived to be absent, but because they are uninformative in this context. A recent study with a bearing on this point examined people's explanations of extreme success in different contexts, exam success and scientific achievement (McClure, Lalljee, & Jaspars, 1991). Kelley's (1973) prediction that people present conjunctions for extreme effects was supported in the explanations of exam results in terms of conjunctions such as ability and effort, but the scientific success was explained more often purely in terms of a single cause: the ability of the scientist. This difference suggests that effort may not be taken for granted with school children, but it is taken for granted with the scientist and, hence, omitted from the explanation, not because it is perceived to be absent, but because it is taken for granted.

It would be useful to clarify the status of causes that people omit from their explanations to establish whether these causes are perceived as not contributing to the effect or whether they are taken for granted, despite being perceived as important factors. This question could be examined counterfactually by tapping people's perception of what effect would have occurred if a causal aspect of the situation had been different (Wells & Gavanski, 1989). Going beyond ratings of particular causes, questions could inquire whether people who made an attribution thought that an effect would have occurred if a particular cause that was not included in their attribution had been absent. This inquiry would clarify whether some causes that are omitted from explanations are perceived as important or necessary for the action being explained.

As Hilton (1990) pointed out, this issue is also relevant to people's choice of higher level action descriptions, such as a goal, or lower-level action descriptions, which refer to the behaviors used to achieve the goal. Vallacher and Wegner (1987) noted that lower-level capacities are usually not focused on unless actions fail; as Hilton observed, lower-level capacities are typically presupposed and are hence uninformative. It can be suggested that this pattern would be reversed where the purpose of a communication is to mislead or conceal, as described in the previous section. If a person wishes to conceal the higher-level goal of their action, they may describe their action in lower-level terms. If someone interrupts burglars in a garden and asks what they are doing, the burglars may reply that they are simply crossing the garden, rather than divulge their goal in crossing the garden. So while not all the relevant causes are included in the explanation, the selection of causes reflects the particular motives of the speaker in that situation, rather than a single universal pattern.

Analogs with Scientific and Legal Inference

What implications does this survey suggest for the idea that discounting parallels scientific inference (e.g., Kelley, 1973)? The low levels of discounting obtained in many studies reviewed earlier appear to challenge this analog, but there are grounds for querying whether even scientists' causal decisions correspond to a discounting principle. Scientific theories are certainly meant to be parsimonious, in the sense that one should choose the simplest of the alternative models (e.g., Nagel, 1961). But this principle applies primarily to models and theories rather than to specific causes (Walker, 1977), and even a simple theory may invoke several causal influences to explain an event. Scientific theories may actually include more causes than lay accounts because causal conditions must be specified for prediction and measurement and cannot be taken for granted as they might be in common sense (cf. Grice, 1975). A scientific explanation of a riot, for example, may include background factors that are absent in lay explanations. So analogs with scientific inference are not invalidated by evidence that lay persons "fail" to discount multiple causes.

An aspect of the discounting analog that does need reevaluation concerns the proposition that discounting applies when attributors lack information about contending causes (Kelley, 1973). In scientific inquiry, when there are two competing explanations of an event, scientists are supposed to reserve judgment and construct tests to determine which explanation is most correct rather than discount one explanation in the absence of relevant information. Furthermore, when they find that one explanation is plausible and the other is not, then the latter explanation is no longer plausible. Discarding a potential explanation because it is implausible is different from discounting one of two plausible causes for the sake of economy. It is more like the discounting of situational effects reported by Reeder, Messick, and van Avermaet (1977), where only ability was considered a plausible cause of success (see also Thibaut & Riecken, 1955).

This point applies equally to legal inference, which has been advocated as an alternative analog for lay explanation (e.g., Fincham & Jaspars, 1980). When determining whether a homicide constitutes murder or manslaughter, for example, the legal process goes to some lengths to establish whether intent, premeditation, and provocation contributed to the offense (Hart & Honoré, 1985). Again, discounting reflects evidence concerning causes, rather than occur where that evidence is lacking, which is where attribution theories predict discounting. In fact, research on discounting that has examined the role of information about causes indicates that discounting can be affected where information points to the role of one of the causes (e.g., Einhorn & Hogarth, 1983). So lay inference may be similar in this regard to scientific and legal inference.

Despite these possible similarities, lay explanation sometimes differs markedly from scientific explanation. As was noted earlier, explanations sometimes function to obscure causes or motives for actions rather than to clarify the causes for actions. In these cases, causes that obscure an available explanation for an action may be added even though the available explanation is apparently sufficient—a pattern that represents the opposite tendency to discounting. Analogs with scientific inference may be heuristic where the goals of the lay attributor and the scientists are similar, but not where they diverge (cf. Fischhoff, 1976).

The conversational and discourse models discussed in the previous sections reach contrary conclusions about the value of analogs with scientific enterprise. In his formulation of the conversational model, Hilton (e.g., 1990) claimed that the classic analog with scientific explanations should be discarded because scientific explanation does not occur in a conversational context and is a solitary activity; the model implies causal explanations are "essentially intrapsychic in nature" (p. 65). On the other hand, models of discourse analysis treat scientific relationships and discourse as a prime target of investigation (e.g., Potter & Mulkay, 1982). The different treatment of scientific discourse derives from different perceptions of scientific activity: the classical attribution model treats the scientist as a logical analytical individual, whereas discourse analysis treats science as a social enterprise subject to social and psychological analysis (cf. Kruglanski, Baldwin, & Towson, 1983). Clearly, in general terms, this latter principle is compatible with the conversational model of explanation. The conversational model, however, provides a specific model of the structure and pattern of that discourse, whereas the discourse approach draws on broader theoretical perspectives dealing with the structure of discourse.

CONCLUSION

Clearly explanations often deviate from the straightforward discounting path suggested by classic attribution theories. In some cases this is an effect of cognitive biases and cognitive structures, but in other cases it reflects the fact that actions and outcomes are embedded in a range of causal influences, and people see little reason to discount one of those influences simply because another one is present. The newer models of causal selection, such as knowledge structures and conversational analysis, encompass some of these findings. However, as the previous discussion suggests, there are several issues that should be taken account of. First, explanations reflect aspects of particular situations and particular categories of cause, rather than a universal cognitive structure. This view does not require a naive realism, but it does require a connection between cognitions and actual events and a recognition of the logical relations between causes and effects. Tied in with this point is the issue that communicated explanations may omit some perceived determinants of events. Discounting the strength of a cause has to be differentiated from omitting a cause in a communication. A further point is that explanations serve a range of purposes and do not always function to assist or inform an inquirer or to provide the simplest explanation. Explanations may serve a path of enlightenment or a perpetuation of false consciousness. People's goals in their communications and explanations shape their causal selections.

REFERENCES

Abelson, R. P., Leddo, J., & Gross, P. (1987). The strength of conjunctive explanations. *Personality and Social Psychology Bulletin, 13*, 141-155.

Ajzen, I., Dalto, C. A., & Blyth, D. P. (1979). Consistency and bias in attribution of attitudes. *Journal of Personality and Social Psychology, 37*, 1871-1876.

Austin, J. L. (1962). *How to do things with words.* London: Oxford University Press.

Billig, M. (1982). *Ideology and social psychology.* Oxford: Basil Blackwell.

Bowers, J. (1988). Review essay. Discourse and social psychology: Beyond attitudes and behaviour. *British Journal of Social Psychology, 27*, 185-192.

Cunningham, J. D., & Kelley, H. H. (1975). Causal attributions for interpersonal events of varying magnitude. *Journal of Personality, 43*, 74-93.

Einhorn, H., & Hogarth, R. (1983). A theory of diagnostic inference: Judging causality. Unpublished manuscript, Center for Decision Research, University of Chicago.

Fincham, F. D., & Jaspars, J. M. F. (1980). Attribution of responsibility: From man the scientist to man as lawyer. In L. Berkowitz (Ed.), *Advances in experimental social psychology* (Vol. 13, pp. 81–138). New York: Academic Press.

Fischhoff, B. (1976). Attribution theory and judgment under uncertainty. In J. H. Harvey, W. J. Ickes, & R. F. Kidd (Eds.), *New directions in attribution research* (Vol. 1, pp. 421–452). Hillsdale, NJ: Lawrence Erlbaum Associates.

Grice, H. P. (1975). Logic and conversation. In P. Cole & J. Morgan (Eds.), *Syntax and semantics 3: Speech acts* (pp. 41–58). New York: Academic Press.

Habermas, J. (1979). *Communication and the evolution of society.* Boston: Beacon Press.

Hansen, R. D., & Hall, C. A. (1985). Discounting and augmenting facilitatory and inhibitory forces: The winner takes almost all. *Journal of Personality and Social Psychology, 49,* 1482–1493.

Hart, H. L. A., & Honoré, T. (1985). *Causation in the law* (2nd ed.). Oxford: Clarendon Press.

Heider, F. (1958). *The psychology of interpersonal relations.* New York: Wiley.

Hewstone, M., Jaspars, J., & Lalljee, M. (1982). Social representations, social attribution and social identity: The intergroup images of 'public' and 'comprehensive' schoolboys. *European Journal of Social Psychology, 12,* 241–269.

Hilton, D. J. (1990). Conversational processes and causal explanation. *Psychological Review, 107,* 65–81.

Hilton, D. J., & Knott, I. C. (1988). *Explanatory relevance: Pragmatic constraints on the selection of causes from conditions.* Unpublished manuscript.

Hilton, D. J., & Slugoski, B. R. (1986). Knowledge-based causal attribution: The abnormal conditions focus model. *Psychological Review, 93,* 75–88.

Jones, E. E. (1979). The rocky road from acts to attributions. *American Psychologist, 34,* 107–117.

Jones, E. E., & Davis, K. E. (1965). A theory of correspondent inferences: From acts to dispositions. In L. Berkowitz (Ed.), *Advances in experimental social psychology* (Vol. 2, pp. 219–266). New York: Academic Press.

Jones, E. E., & Harris, V. A. (1967). The attribution of attitudes. *Journal of Experimental Social Psychology, 3,* 1–24.

Kelley, H. H. (1967). Attribution theory in social psychology. In *Nebraska symposium on motivation* (Vol. 15, pp. 192–238). Lincoln: University of Nebraska Press.

Kelley, H. H. (1973). The processes of causal attribution. *American Psychologist, 28,* 107–128.

Kelley, H. H. (1980). Magic tricks: The management of causal attribution. In D. Gorlitz (Ed.), *Perspectives on attribution research and theory: The Bielefeld Symposium* (pp. 19–35). Cambridge, MA: Ballinger.

Kelley, H. H. (1983). Perceived causal structures. In J. Jaspars, F. D. Fincham, & M. Hewstone (Eds.), *Attribution theory and research: Conceptual, developmental and social dimensions* (pp. 343–369). London: Academic Press.

Kelley, H. H., & Michela, J. L. (1980). Attribution theory and research. *Annual Review of Psychology, 31,* 457–501.

Kruglanski, A. W. (1980). Lay epistemo-logic—Process and contents: Another look at attribution theory. *Psychological Review, 87,* 70–87.

Kruglanski, A. W., Baldwin, M. W., & Towson, S. M. J. (1983). The lay epistemic process in attribution making. In M. Hewstone (Ed.), *Attribution theory: Social and functional extensions* (pp. 81–95). Oxford: Blackwell.

Kruglanski, A. W., Schwartz, J. M., Maides, S., & Hamel, I. Z. (1978). Covariation, discounting, and augmentation: Towards a clarification of attributional principles. *Journal of Personality, 64,* 176–189.

Kun, A., & Weiner, B. (1973). Necessary versus sufficient causal schemata for success and failure. *Journal of Research in Personality, 7,* 197–207.

Lalljee, M., Watson, M., & White, P. (1982). Explanations, attributions and the social context of unexpected behaviour. *European Journal of Social Psychology, 12,* 17-29.

Leddo, J., & Abelson, R. P. (1986). The nature of explanations. In J. Galambos, R. P. Abelson, & J. B. Black (Eds.), *Knowledge structures* (pp. 103-122). Hillsdale, NJ: Lawrence Erlbaum Associates.

Leddo, J., Abelson, R. P., & Gross, P. H. (1984). Conjunctive explanations: When two reasons are better than one. *Journal of Personality and Social Psychology, 47,* 933-943.

Locksley, A., & Stangor, C. (1984). Why versus how often: Causal reasoning and the incidence of judgmental bias. *Journal of Experimental Social Psychology, 20,* 470-483.

Markus, H., & Zajonc, R. (1985). Social cognition. In G. Lindzey & E. Aronson (Eds.), *Handbook of social psychology* (pp. 137-230). Reading, MA: Addison-Wesley.

McClure, J. L. (1985). The social parameter of "learned" helplessness: Its recognition and implications. *Journal of Personality and Social Psychology, 48,* 1534-1539.

McClure, J. L. (1989). *Discounting causes of behavior: Two decades of research.* Unpublished manuscript.

McClure, J. L. (1991). *Explanations, accounts and illusions: A critical analysis.* Cambridge: Cambridge University Press.

McClure, J. L., Lalljee, M., & Jaspars, J. (1991). Explanations of moderate and extreme events. *Journal of Research in Personality, 25,* 146-166.

McClure, J. L., Lalljee, M., Jaspars, J., & Abelson, R. P. (1989). Conjunctive explanations of success and failure: The effect of different types of causes. *Journal of Personality and Social Psychology, 56,* 19-26.

Mill, J. S. (1973). System of logic. In J. M. Robson (Ed.), *Collected works of John Stuart Mill* (8th ed., Vols. 7 and 8). Toronto: University of Toronto Press. (Original work published 1872)

Mischel, W. (1968). *Personality and assessment.* New York: Wiley.

Morier, D. M., & Borgida, E. (1984). The conjunction fallacy: A task specific phenomenon? *Personality and Social Psychology Bulletin, 10,* 243-252.

Nagel, E. (1961). *The structure of science: Problems in the logic of scientific explanation.* New York: Harcourt Brace Jovanovich.

Potter, J., & Mulkay, M. (1982). Making theory useful: Utility accounting in social psychologists' discourse. *Fundamenta Scientiae, 34,* 258-278.

Potter, J., & Wetherell, M. (1987). *Discourse and social psychology: Beyond attitudes and behaviour.* London: Sage.

Quattrone, G. A. (1982). Overattribution and unit formation: When behavior engulfs the person. *Journal of Personality and Social Psychology, 42,* 593-607.

Read, S. J. (1987). Constructing causal scenarios: A knowledge structure approach to causal reasoning. *Journal of Personality and Social Psychology, 52,* 288-302.

Read, S. J. (1988). Conjunctive explanations: The effect of a comparison between a chosen and a nonchosen alternative. *Journal of Experimental Social Psychology, 24,* 146-162.

Reeder, G. D., Messick, D. M., & van Avermaet, E. (1977). Dimensional asymmetry in attributional inference. *Journal of Experimental Social Psychology, 13,* 46-57.

Rosenfield, D., & Stephan, W. G. (1977). When discounting fails: An unexpected finding. *Memory and Cognition, 5,* 97-102.

Schustack, M. W., & Sternberg, R. J. (1981). Evaluation of evidence in causal inference. *Journal of Experimental Psychology: General, 110,* 101-120.

Shaklee, H., & Fischhoff, B. (1982). Strategies of information search in causal analysis. *Memory and Cognition, 10,* 520-530.

Snyder, M. L., & Wicklund, R. A. (1981). Attribute ambiguity. In J. H. Harvey, W. Ickes, & R. F. Kidd (Eds.), *New directions in attribution research* (Vol. 3, pp. 197-221). Hillsdale, NJ: Lawrence Erlbaum Associates.

Solomon, J. (1978). Measuring dispositional and situational attributions. *Personality and Social Psychology Bulletin, 4,* 589-594.

Taylor, S. E., & Koivumaki, J. H. (1976). The perception of self and others: Acquaintanceship, affect, and actor-observer differences. *Journal of Personality and Social Psychology, 33*, 403-408.

Thibaut, J. W., & Riecken, H. W. (1955). Some determinants and consequences of the perception of social causality. *Journal of Personality, 24*, 113-133.

Tversky, A., & Kahneman, D. (1983). Extensional versus intuitive reasoning: The conjunction fallacy in probability judgement. *Psychological Review, 90*, 293-315.

Vallacher, R. R., & Wegner, D. M. (1987). What do people think they're doing? Action identification and human behavior. *Psychological Review, 94*, 303-315.

Walker, N. (1977). *Behaviour and misbehaviour: Explanations and non-explanations.* Oxford: Basil Blackwell.

Wells, G. L. (1985). The conjunction error and the representativeness heuristic. *Social Cognition, 3*, 266-279.

Wells, G. L., & Gavanski, I. (1989). Mental simulation of causality. *Journal of Personality and Social Psychology, 56*, 161-169.

Wilensky, R. W. (1983). *Planning and understanding: A computational approach to human reasoning.* Reading, MA: Addison-Wesley.

Wimer, S., & Kelley, H. H. (1982). An investigation of the dimensions of causal attribution. *Journal of Personality and Social Psychology, 43*, 1142-1162.

Zuckerman, M., Eghrari, H., & Lambrecht, M. R. (1986). Attributions as inferences and explanations: Conjunction effects. *Journal of Personality and Social Psychology, 51*, 1144-1153.

5

▼▼▼▼▼▼▼

Lay Explanations

Adrian Furnham
University of London

A great deal of everyday, commonplace social conversation concerns explanations: explanations to others about one's own beliefs and behaviors; explanations to oneself and others about people; explanations about social, scientific, political, economic, and even theological phenomena. Popular newspapers, magazines and television programs seek to offer explanations to their consumers, using metaphors, analogies, models, and language they can understand. This chapter concerns lay explanations as opposed to scientific explanations. It concentrates on the content rather than on the process of lay explanations and the understanding of social rather than strictly personal phenomena. Furthermore, because the context in which the explanation is offered shapes both its form and content, this chapter concentrates on certain contextual effects.

Ever since the pioneering work of Heider (1958), psychologists have been interested in lay, implicit, commonsense explanations for psychological phenomena such as how, when, and why people explain themselves to others. Heider argued that common sense lay explanations were worth studying for two reasons: first, a person's commonsense psychology (belief, assumptions, axioms) guides behavior and hence must be taken into consideration in any causal analysis of the behavior; and second, commonsense psychology contains various truths not found in scientific writing! In many ways Heider's work was the precursor of attribution theory—concerned with the process whereby ordinary people understand the causes of their own and others' behavior—which has dominated social psychology over the past 2 decades (Kelly & Michela, 1980).

There seem to be five rather different psychological approaches to the study of lay explanation that result partly from what researchers understand by *lay explanation* or its many synonyms (Furnham, 1990). Three of these approaches are *process* oriented, one *content* oriented and one *context* oriented (Furnham, 1983, 1988). *Attribution theory* may be seen as a process-oriented approach to common sense, as it seeks to explain, or at least describe, how ordinary people make sense of their world specifically by focusing on their understanding of social causation (Heider, 1958; Jones & Davis, 1965; Kelley, 1973; Pettigrew, 1979; Ross, 1977; Zuckerman, 1979). Attribution theor*ies*, for there are more than one, seek to understand how people seek out, select, interpret, integrate, and communicate information about themselves, others, and their social world. Whereas the theories focus on how the processes occur, the research seems specifically concerned with how errors occur. Psychologists have been particularly interested in the inferential errors that people make in the processing of social information and the attributional egotism involved in the process. Hence one finds a great deal of research being done on errors, biases, and inaccurate self-centered processing strategies such as the fundamental attribution error—the tendency to overattribute to internal causes and underattribute to external causes (Zuckerman, 1979); the ultimate attribution error—the tendency to "explain away" positive behavior by a member of a disliked group (Pettigrew, 1979), and so forth. Attribution research, then, tends to focus on logical and inferential errors that are made by lay people, thus stressing the fallibility of lay explanation, particularly of one's own behavior (Furnham, 1982).

A second process-oriented approach to common sense can be seen in the work of Smedslund (1978, 1979, 1984) who, rather than stress the negative features of lay explanation, tended to stress the opposite, namely that common sense (and lay theories) is made up of intuitively obvious truths and inherent logic. Whereas attribution researchers seek to contrast erroneous, naive, commonsense theories with correct, sophisticated, "scientific" theories, Smedslund contrasted logically necessary and true commonsense understanding with pseudoempirical scientific research, which rather than explain the unknown tends either to explicate or occasionally obfuscate the well known. For Smedslund there is a "deep structure" of logic called common sense—a Platonic world of perfect forms. There is, therefore, an ideal and elegant Euclidean geometry of the mind; from a relatively simple number of logical axioms a range of necessarily correct theories can be derived and tested. These are not empirical tests but logical tests. Smedslund's geometry of the mind has received both favorable and unfavorable attention and criticism (Sjoberg, 1982; Valsinger, 1985). Many who take issue with him support the necessity for empirical work on commonsense understanding and lay explanation, the kind he believes is unnecessary.

A third content approach may be called the knowledge-structure approach, which focuses on preexisting theories. Hilton (1988) and others like Abelson and Lalljee (1988) have been concerned with how lay explanations of all sorts are dependent on prior knowledge structures called schema or prototypes. A knowledge-based approach emphasizes that coherence derives from both the internal causal structure of a conceptual domain and the position of the concept in the complete knowledge base. Concepts are viewed as embedded in theories and are coherent to the extent that they fit people's background knowledge or theories about their world. Hilton argued that commonsense description of cause depends on the operation of two elements—the counter factual and contrastive criterion. These two criteria allow distinctions like necessary and sufficient to be made, which he argues is of fundamental logical and psychological importance. Essentially this approach is critical of, but not dissimilar to, the first approach, which looks at the logical structure of explanations as a function of the knowledge structure of the individual.

The fourth approach to common sense is the content-oriented approach. Essentially this approach is descriptive and taxonomic, as it seeks to ascertain what lay people believe: that is, what the factual content is of their commonsense beliefs and understandings about their own and others' behavior. Furnham (1988) reviewed the content of lay theories from issues as varied as alcoholism and anorexia to smoking and schizophrenia. Nearly all of these lay theories are about the causes of various phenomena, though recent research has looked at lay theories of cures (as they relate to the cause) (Furnham 1989, 1990; Furnham & Henley, 1989). What is particularly interesting about the content-oriented studies of lay theories is the topics that have, and have not, attracted research attention (Furnham, 1988). To a large extent this is determined by the *Zeitgeist* of research in various disciplines, but it means that whereas some areas of research are almost excessively researched (such as lay theories of depression or unemployment), others are, mysteriously, totally neglected (such as sexual dysfunction, debt, or genetics). In this sense content-oriented researchers are interested in the geography rather than the geometry of the mind. In setting about this task, various features of the commonsense terrain are considered. Explorers in this landscape may wish to map various features of it.

The fifth type of approach is primarily contextual and is nicely illustrated by many of the chapters in this volume. The emphasis of this approach is how the social context (specific situation) and the presence of hearers (evaluators) shape explanations for events. It is argued that lay people adapt, accommodate, and adjust the explanations that they give to others based on the rules, requirements, and etiquette governing the situation in which they find themselves. This approach draws on many theoretical traditions, including work on impression management (Snyder, 1979) and the extensive literature on situational determinants of social behavior (Argyle, Furnham, & Graham, 1981). Argyle et al. argued that lay explanations are adjusted to the intellectual, cultural, and linguistic capacity of the receivers; also they are usually presented to elicit a positive response.

The process, content, and context approaches are by no means mutually exclusive; they simply focus on different features of the attribution and explanatory behavior. It is probably true that the most work has gone into the process approach, followed by the content and then the context approach. This chapter tends to focus on the content approach but will consider how, why, and when contextual features may influence the way explanations are publicly presented.

RESEARCH IN LAY EXPLANATIONS

What are the central issues in the content approach to lay explanation? What research program could (and should) be undertaken to investigate the nature and process of lay explanation? The following 10 topics certainly merit empirical research.

The Etiology or Development of Lay Explanations

It is impossible to understand fully the nature of lay theories or commonsense assumptions without understanding their origin. Whereas developmental psychologists have always been interested in how, when, and why children learn the use of various systems of physical concepts of mass, time, and space, and to a lesser extent how they come to understand aspects of society (economics, politics), comparatively little work has been done on children's understanding of individual needs, motives, and emotions. However, there is now more and more work on children's and adolescents' understanding of psychological (Harris, 1989) and sociological concepts (Furnham & Stacey, 1991; Stacey, 1982). Some have speculated on the origin of these beliefs. Sarbin, Taft, and Bailey (1960) have listed four main sources: induction or experience; construction or inference; and deduction from observational analogy or extrapolation from specific encounters; and authority or acceptance of ideas from others, the media, and so on. Vygotsky (1962) has shown how deeply the learning of a language is implicated in the acquisition of this conceptual system. Thus it may be that subtle differences occur in the content and presentation of lay theories as a function of the native language of the holder of the theory. Although there has been some work on children's moral and cognitive development that has attempted to identify stages of development, there is no parsimonious theory that might account for why people hold different, contradictory, or similar beliefs or common sense theories. We need to establish which socialization experience and/or maturational process contributes to the establishment of specific, stable integrated beliefs (lay theories) about human behavior. It is also important to know how these beliefs develop and change once they have been established.

The Relationship Between Different Aspects of Lay Explanations

Just as reviewers have attempted to classify formal academic theories of, say, personality into psychodynamic, learning theory, and phenomenological (Furnham, 1988) or alcoholism into biological/pharmacological, psychological/trait, and sociological/sociostructural (Furnham & Lowick, 1984) *and* specify the relationship between them, so it is possible to examine the relationship between various commonsense belief systems. Furnham and Lewis (1986) have noted that there are three equally important but distinct areas of research on the relationship between commonsense beliefs: the relationship between specific beliefs (lay theories) within an individual or group; the relationship between various beliefs about different aspects of social life whose implications or assumptions are mutually contradictory; and the relationship between commonsense beliefs and actual social behavior.

There exist many excellent attempts to discriminate between and taxonomize various commonsense beliefs in specific areas and then see how they interrelate, as well as how they relate to other issues. Good examples are Forsyth's (1980) work on ethical ideologies and moral judgment; Paulus' (1983) work on spheres of perceived control; and Eysenck's (1978) work on social attitudes. Despite the variety of topics about which lay people have "theories," it might be possible to have a single, sensitive, taxonomic system to describe and structure them.

The Function of Lay Explanations

Much of cognitive social psychology is concerned with how people make sense of the social world by selecting, integrating, and retrieving social information. That is, various belief systems (locus of control, just world beliefs, Protestant work ethic) are said to serve to make, for the adherer, the world a stable, orderly, and predictable place. The function of these beliefs is probably to establish a cause and effect relationship between phenomena, which in turn enables one to apportion blame, praise, or responsibility. For instance, Lerner (1980) argued that just world beliefs are functional and essential in that they are ways of adapting to a world in which one feels relatively helpless by attributing absolute virtue to the sociopolitical and legal system, and of sustaining a commitment to the individualistic ideologies of postmedieval societies.

Functionist theories, though somewhat unfashionable, provide useful insights into why people maintain and change various commonsense beliefs. It has long been suggested that functional theories are teleological and thus incur the logical error of placing the cause of an event after it in time. However, this takes place in any self-regulating system with a negative feedback loop. For example, in a thermostat the behavior of the system leads to the goal of a certain temperature being attained, though the goal was actually set before this temperature was reached. It has also been objected that functionalism encourages or reflects a conservative bias by emphasizing the positive functions of every aspect of the *status quo*. Advocates of social change can try to bring about alternative institutions to meet the same needs, or to meet them better, and to avoid areas of dysfunction in society. Functionalism does, however, contain a warning for reformers—that existing institutions may be serving hidden functions and it is important to understand these hidden functions before attempting change (Argyle, Furnham, & Graham, 1981; Cohen, 1968).

Thus if lay explanations serve unspecified or not well-understood functions they may be very difficult to change. Hewstone (1983) has specified three functions of social attribution (1) control, (2) self-esteem, and (3) self-presentation (which, he argued, is a useful first taxonomy). It has been observed that scientists hold on to theories or at least explanatory metaphors long after they have proved erroneous or redundant presumably because they continue to serve useful personal and psychological functions.

The Stability and Consistency of Lay Explanations

The question of how and when individual commonsense beliefs change is of considerable interest to educators, advertisers, and politicians. The stability of beliefs refers to their similarity over time (in expression, perceived truthfulness, applicability, etc.), whereas consistency of beliefs refers to whether they are held across similar or different situations. The stability and consistency of lay beliefs of social behavior have important implications for measurement; if commonsense beliefs are fairly inconsistent and influenced greatly by the context in which they are gathered (e.g., market interview), it is important to make reference to the context when evaluating the evidence. Similarly, if they are relatively stable over time, results from surveys and interviews may be safely generalized to predict future beliefs, provided the appropriate nexus of conceptual relations has already been acquired.

If cultural factors influence commonsense beliefs (as they surely do), changes in the culture (if it is becoming more or less permissive) may well affect many lay-belief systems. People's commonsense beliefs, and hence lay theories, not only change over time but may be expressed differently in different situations. A person may describe his or her understanding of a particular feature or process (e.g., influenza, inflation) quite differently to an adult and to a child. Also, depending on the nature of the person, he or she might express beliefs and attitudes that seem most congruent with, or attractive to, the hearers in the situation rather than express what he or she actually believes (Lalljee, Brown, & Ginsburg, 1984; Snyder, 1979). Just as people use high and low forms of language in different situations so equally they may express their theories in different forms, depending on the context in which they are expressed. This is a basic theme throughout this volume.

The Consequences of Lay Explanations

Commonsense beliefs—like attitudes and explanations—do have consequences for the development of other beliefs and for behavior. Central to a great deal of the early psychological work on attitudes is the concept of balance (Heider, 1958).

Balance, congruity, and dissonance theory each assumes that people are motivated to be and to appear consistent, that an awareness of imbalance or inconsistency is tension producing and not easily tolerated, and that attitude change is a principal tool for resolving inconsistencies. Thus, if one major core belief changes, for whatever reason, others related to it are likely to change. For instance, Furnham and Bland (1983) found, as predicted, that Protestant work ethic beliefs are closely related to more general conservative social attitudes. They also argued that if, as has been suggested, work ethic beliefs are on the decline one might expect conservative social attitudes to change; likewise, as there is no evidence of the latter, one should not necessarily infer the occurrence of the former. Certainly people are soon charged with lying and hypocrisy if they are inconsistent in the explanations they offer.

Should lay beliefs also have behavioral consequences? As Furnham and Lewis (1986) noted, lay economic beliefs can actually affect economic behavior. Consumer sentiment has consequences for consumer demand in that if people believe high inflation is likely to continue they may spend rather than save and have high wage demands, which partly account for the continuance of high inflation. Similarly, Katona (1971) found that public pessimism about the economy showed a sharp decline about 6-9 months *before* a major recession. Of course, it is impossible to tease out cause and correlation when examining lay beliefs and behavior, and it is probable that some form of reciprocal determinism operates.

The Changing of Lay Explanations

Central to theories of attitude change are the best and most effective methods of changing them (Furnham, 1988). There are a number of different approaches, including learning and reinforcement theories based on behaviorist ideas of stimulus-response learning, social judgment and consistency theories, which stem from the Gestalt tradition, and functional theories, which place most emphasis on human needs. These theories devote varying degrees of attention to the causes and methods of change and are, in large part, mutually exclusive. Applied research in many areas has revealed the difficulty of attitude change, which is due to the complexity of the process and the number of internal and external factors involved (Furnham, 1990). There are many examples of how religious experiences change people's entire lay-belief systems. Commonsense beliefs about racial differences and sex roles appear to have changed over time, though it is not entirely clear why that is the case (Furnham, Johnson, & Rawles, 1985). The style and the content of lay explanations change over time such that an acceptable way of explaining one's self to others in terms of motives, needs, and beliefs is no longer applicable, and alternative metaphors and explanations have to be found.

The Manipulation of Lay Explanations

There is a whole range of groups of people interested in changing lay beliefs about politics, the economy, their own health, or minority groups. Politicians, advertisers, health educators, pressure groups, managers, and trade unions all attempt to change beliefs and behaviors to suit their own ends. Often their aims are to change specific beliefs or encourage a change in one particular behavior (e.g., voting, buying). Marxists, psychoanalysts, and some fundamentalist Christian groups propagate "grand," all-encompassing theories that they expect their converts to "use" to explain practically everything in their daily lives. The manipulation of commonsense beliefs may also be observed in extreme situations of brainwashing or torture. Clearly a highly relevant applied question refers to how to most effectively change commonsense beliefs and the behaviors that result from them (Furnham & Lewis, 1986).

The Structure of Lay Explanations

Many social scientists have attempted to taxonomize belief systems into discrete categories along various dimensions. For instance, Furnham & Lewis suggested that lay economic beliefs may fall nicely into four quadrangles described by two dimensions: individualistic–collectivistic; tough minded–tender minded. The first dimension would reflect right-wing, conservative capitalism, free-enterprise beliefs versus left-wing radical, socialist, state control beliefs. The second dimension would reflect economic policy implications, with tough-minded beliefs emphasizing state, legal, or political action, whereas tender-minded beliefs would emphasize passive, consensual, or conventional rather than interventionist policies. Given that explanations differ as a function of the situation in which they are given, it might be just as important to look at a taxonomy of situations that affect lay explanations (Argyle, Furnham, & Graham, 1981). Thus it may be possible, in due course, to develop a diagnostic grid with a taxonomic structure of social situations and explanation types that explains how and when explanations are tailored to specific situations.

The Language of Lay Explanations

Smedslund (1984) argued that there is a logic of ordinary language such that given one set of propositions, others either follow or are necessarily excluded. Hence "a proposition in a given context belongs to common sense if and only if all competent users of the language involved agree that the proposition in the given context is true and that its negation is contradictory or senseless" (p. 243). Therefore, it isn't an empirical fact that a child is not an adult; it is a grammatical fact.

However, empirical studies are worth doing on the use and choice of language.

For instance, some people describe illness and the body using the "plumbing" model, with which it is conceived as a series of chambers connected by pipes and tubes, whereas others use the machine model in which the body is thought of as an internal combustion engine. Helman (1978) illustrated this point nicely in describing differences between colds and fevers. The former are seen to result from penetrations of the natural environment across the boundary of the skin and, because they are brought about by one's own behavior, they provoke little sympathy, whereas the latter are caused by invisible, amoral germs and bugs that penetrate the body by its orifices, and hence the victim is blameless and worthy of help and care.

It is, then, the choice of metaphor, idiom, concepts, or simple words to describe phenomena that merits attention. Within any set of similes and metaphors there may well be an organized, logical system that does not merit research because it simply demonstrates what is necessarily true. What does merit further investigation, however, is the difference between individuals in their choice of linguistic terms and devices to describe and explain their own behavior in specific situations. Thus some metaphors may be context specific, that is, only appropriate or acceptable in certain situations, whereas others are seen to "travel" and be less contextually constrained.

Lay Explanations About Social Science
Versus Social Scientists' Beliefs about Lay Explanations

Whether they make it explicit or not, many academic social scientists hold specific beliefs about the behavior (and beliefs) of lay people. Economists devise sophisticated models of the economy based on axiomatic beliefs about an individual's purchasing, saving, and spending strategies. Similarly, health educators devise instructive posters and other material based on what they think lay people believe about their health, and politicians hope to present themselves in accordance with the belief system of prospective voters. Certainly the content and style of lay explanations about behavior (self or others) is significantly different from the scientifically acceptable and required types of explanations.

There has been very little work done on social scientists' views of human nature and human behavior, though these are often implicit in the schools of thought within various disciplines (Furnham et al., 1985). Much more work appears to have been done on ordinary people's beliefs about science than scientists' beliefs about ordinary people. Indeed, the extent to which scientists could be said to have common sense is debatable!

One way to examine these two groups' theories about science and common sense is to examine some of the more celebrated quotes of (more-or-less) famous people.

Table 5.1 shows the range of beliefs that lay people and scientists have about common sense (lay explanations) and science (including "social science"). Not

TABLE 5.1
A Battery of Quotes For and Against Science and Common Sense

Pro-Science.

- A scientist is a man who would rather count than guess. *M. Gluckman.*
- Science is organized common sense where many a beautiful theory is filled by an ugly fact. *T. H. Huxley.*
- Science may be described as the art of systematic oversimplification. *K. Popper.*
- The man of science does not discover in order to know: He wants to know in order to discover. *A. N. Whitehead.*
- Science increases our power in proportion as it lowers our pride. *C. Bernard.*
- Science is what you know, philosophy is what you don't know. *B. Russell.*
- You know very well that unless you are a scientist, it's much more important for a theory to be shapely, than for it to be true. *C. Hampton.*

Anti-Science.

- Science is always wrong: it never solves a problem without creating ten more. *G. B. Shaw.*
- I am tired of all this thing called science. . . . We have spent millions on that sort of thing for the last few years, and it is time it should be stopped. *S. Cameron.*
- One of the most pernicious falsehoods ever to be universally accepted is that scientific method is the only reliable way to truth. *R. Bube.*
- Traditional scientific method has always been, at the very least, 20-20 hindsight. It's good for seeing where you've been. *R. Pirsig.*
- Though many have tried, no one has ever yet explained away the decisive fact that science, which can do so much, cannot decide what it ought to do. *J. W. Krutch.*
- Look at those cows and remember that the greatest scientists in the world have not discovered how to make grass into milk. *M. Pulin.*

Pro-Common Sense.

- It is a thousand times better to have common sense without education than to have education without common sense. *R. Ingersol.*
- Common sense in an uncommon degree is what the world calls wisdom. *S. T. Coleridge.*
- The philosophy of one century is the common sense of the next. *H. W. Beecher.*
- The best prophet is common sense. *Euripides.*
- If a man has common sense he has all the sense there is. *S. Rayburn.*
- Common sense is instinct and enough of it is genius. *H. W. Shaw.*
- Common sense is the wick of the candle. *R. W. Emerson.*
- Fine sense and exalted sense are not half so useful as common sense. *B. Gracian.*
- The crown of all faculties is common sense. It is not enough to do the right thing: it must be done at the right time, and place. *W. Matthews.*

Anti-Common Sense.

- Common sense is the collection of prejudices by the age of 18. *A. Einstein.*
- Logic is one thing and common sense another. *E. Hubbard.*
- Common sense is in spite of, not the result of, education. *V. Hugo.*
- Common sense is, of all kinds, the most uncommon. *T. Edwards.*
- Common sense, however logical and sound, is after all only one human attitude among many others, and like everything human, it may have its limitations—or negative side. *W. Barrett.*
- Common sense is the most fairly distributed thing in the world, for each thinks he is so well endowed with it that even those who are hardest to satisfy in all other matters are not in the habit of desiring more of it than they already have. *R. Descartes.*
- If common sense were as unerring as calculus, as some suggest, I don't understand why so many mistakes are made so often by so many people. *C. Winkel.*

TABLE 5.2
Possible Dimension Along Which Prototypically Scientific
Vs Common Sense Lay Explanations Differ

	"Scientific" Explanations	"Lay" Explanations
1. Explicit & Formal	Frequently explicit	Rarely explicit
2. Coherent & Consistent	Frequently consistent	Rarely consistent
3. Verification vs Falsification	Falsification	Verification
	Deductivism	Inductivism
4. Cause & Consequence	Rarely confuses cause of effect	Often confuses cause of effect
5. Content vs. Process	Often process oriented	Often content oriented
6. Internal vs. External	Cognizant of both factors	Underestimates external factors
7. General vs. Specific	Mostly specific	Mostly general
	Some general	Some specific
8. Strong vs. Weak	Strong	Weak

only are some of these quotes memorable and amusing but they are succinct and critical statements of varying theoretical positions. Although attacks on science are more common from artists and writers, and attacks on common sense mostly from "hard" scientists, there is sufficient crossover between these two rather simple stereotypes. Certainly, enough people support the idea that the lay person is not an ignorant, biased simpleton compared to the clear thinking, disinterested (perhaps indifferent) "scientist."

Furnham (1988) has, in fact, suggested that lay explanations theories differ from scientific theories on a number of specifiable dimensions.

Clearly there are many exceptions to this rather simplified picture. However, it may serve to highlight some of the major differences between the two approaches that can frequently occur. Of course the scientist is frequently a layperson outside either his/her laboratory and more particularly the domain or discipline that makes him or her an expert. Some scientists are required to offer different explanations for the same phenomena given the situation (TV, studio, peer seminar). Indeed, a scientist's ability to be able to offer equally clear explanations of the same phenomena in different contexts could be seen as a major skill.

THEORIES AND EXPLANATIONS

What is the difference between an account, a belief, an explanation, and a theory? It is possible in terms of dictionary definitions and philosophy of science tracts to distinguish conceptually between a hypothesis, law, model, paradigm, principle, and theory. But how could one do that in terms of lay theories? It does seem that there are various features to a lay theory that would distinguish it from a mere collection of attitudes and beliefs.

First, these ideas of components in a lay theory are structured, albeit relatively simply, into a logical, quasi-logical or indeed psycho-logical structure. In this sense, beliefs in a theory or schema are interconnected in a structural *and* functional way more so than in a simple collection of unrelated beliefs. Thus a theory dictates what constitutes a legitimate explanation—as well as a correct one—and what does not. Indeed the structure of lay theories has been a topic of psychometric research for many years. Clearly there is some basic level of structure and organization that allows a collection of attitudes to be seen as a theory. Although the holder of the theory may not be able to articulate it very clearly, it can be shown that such a theory exists. Indeed, it is in the process of attempting to articulate a theory that a lay person may be said to "hold" a theory (Furnham, 1988).

Second, the theory has some explanatory power in that it accounts for a variety of observable phenomena more than a simple unconnected, isolated event. The bigger, more powerful a theory, the more phenomena it can explain. Thus Marxism is a powerful theory, as is psychoanalysis. Some lay people hold theories about the nature of man that can (supposedly) account for almost all types of behavior; their own and that of all the people (Furnham, 1988).

Third, lay theories are relatively stable and difficult to change compared to many isolated attitude statements. Because they are functional and interconnected, they are not susceptible to change as easily.

Fletcher and Haig (1989) argued that the factors or values that psychologists look for in good theories, such as explanatory depth, unifying power, fertility, simplicity, application, internal and external coherence, and predictive accuracy, are also found in lay theories. They admit that "baser concerns relating to the maintenance of self-esteem" (p. 21) may also play a part in lay theories but that it is possible to (and lay people do) evaluate their own and other people's theories with respect to these criteria. Thus it is possible to classify explanations of oneself to others along a number of discrete, orthogonal dimensions.

LAY EXPLANATIONS OF CHILD DEVELOPMENT

It is perhaps fruitful to consider, albeit briefly, some of the research in lay theories in one quite distinct area: parents' beliefs about child development and rearing. This area has not been chosen at random. Parents frequently seek and give explanations for their child-rearing patterns. They seek explanation from doctors, teachers, parents, and popular books and give explanations not only to those who ask, but also when they think an explanation is required.

There have been a number of studies on parents' beliefs about child rearing, parenting, and education, as well as studies on their knowledge of behavioral principles (McLoughlin, 1985; Stevens, 1988). Some have been concerned mainly with preschool children, where, for instance, Lawton, Schules, Fowell, and Madser (1984) found that parents appear to be more certain of their actual parenting and its relation to their children's social development, followed by intellectual development, and least certain of its relation to their physical development. Others have been interested in how parental beliefs (particularly about sex-typing) influence behavior towards the child or toward particular types of education.

"Naive" or lay theories of child development are, however, culture specific. Keller, Miranda, and Ganda (1984) found numerous differences between German and Costa Rican mothers' beliefs about child development and optimal parenting. For instance, German women expect infants to see, think, understand words, and identify pictures or objects earlier than do Costa Ricans. Parental ideas of development (and education) would thus appear to be culture specific and also class specific. No doubt the explanations are not only affected by demographic differences of nationality and class but also situational or contextual features.

There are a number of reasons why the study of parental beliefs has been considered important. Goodnow (1981, 1984) argued that parents' beliefs illuminate effects of culture and class but, more importantly, parental beliefs relate to child-rearing practices, which in turn have developmental outcomes for the child. Holden (1988) found, as one might predict, that sex and care-giving experiences influence how individuals solve child-rearing problems.

There is also evidence for a systematic bias differentiating parents' and childrens' explanations. For instance, Compass, Adelman, Freunde, and Taylor (1982) showed that when asked to explain behavior, parents made more attributions than their children to the characteristics of the child, rather than the environmental factors. More interesting, however, was the finding that parents and children differed in their locus of attributions when interviewed individually, but that these differences were not present when families were interviewed with both parents and children present. This suggests that attributions, attitudes, beliefs, and theories are expressed and formulated quite differently depending on the context in which they are required (Furnham, 1988).

Less work has been done on the educational theories of people with and without children, before and after they have children, or on parents from different socioeconomic groups. There is sufficient evidence from studies on social mobility to suggest that parents' beliefs and responses are the major determinants of the education outcomes of their children. Clearly this is an important applied and relatively neglected area of lay theory research. Change agents interested in improving parenting would do well to understand parents' explanations of their behavior to each other, teachers, doctors, and educationalists. Such explanations reflect the theories of child development and growth that parents hold that may be seriously handicapping their children.

CONTEXTUAL DETERMINANTS
OF LAY EXPLANATION

From a diverse number of studies in very different disciplines ranging from anthropology to sociology, it has been observed that contextual factors can have an important influence on a wide number of aspects of language and, therefore, the way in which lay explanations are expressed. These include the following:

1. Language Choices, Codes and High/Low Forms

Multilingualism. Many people who are able to speak two or more languages are often influenced by contextual cues in their choice of the language spoken. These include: when the language is used in a setting that is public rather than private; when the language spoken may be interpreted as providing cues to group identification or conformity to group norms (e.g., when the relative prestige of the optional language is high, when there is a public derogation of one language, or where language tolerance is low); and where the speaker wishes to identify or be identified with a particular group, such as when the speaker is a marginal person or has strong loyalty. The choice of language may also be used to define situations—as informal, political, educated, and so on (Argyle et al., 1981). Formality of the situation—a dimension identified by many studies—appears to be the main determinant of language choice especially for festive or rites-of-passage settings. The grammar and idioms available in a language equally determine the type of explanation that may be given in that language and context.

High and Low Forms. Many languages have both high official formal and low informal forms. Brown and Fraser (1979) have noted that across various languages high forms tend to reflect phonological precision and rhythmicity as well as an elaboration of syntax and lexicon, whereas low forms have properties characterized by ellipsis, repetition, and increased speech. High forms of speech tend to be used in formal, task-oriented contexts that require the accurate, efficient transmission of complex material. High forms of speech may also be used in ritualistic settings (religious ceremonies, courtrooms, doctors' surgeries) that emphasize the difference in power or status between people. Low forms of speech, on the other hand, are used in informal, socioemotional settings that are more concerned with general social goals (such as expression of friendship, group cohesion) than the exchange of information. High forms may allow quite different explanation than low forms.

Elaborated and Restricted Codes. This is similar, but not identical to the above distinction made famous by Bernstein (1959). Restricted as opposed to elaborated codes are grammatically simpler, have a smaller vocabulary, and are more full of categorical assertions and reasoned conclusions. Although the existence of these code differences has been found in different countries, research has been mainly concerned with examining and explaining class differences. Offering an explanation in an elaborate code is quite different from that of a restricted code.

2. Grammar and Vocabulary

Not only does the form, code, or actual language and explanations chosen differ as a function of certain specific contextual factors, but the lexicon and grammar may also vary as a function of specific situational constraints.

Grammar. Grammar and sentence construction, and therefore explanations, vary as a function of whether a high or low or restricted or elaborated code is spoken. For instance, Brown and Fraser (1979) have noted that high forms of language have more nouns, adjectives, and prepositions than low codes, which have more verbs, adverbs, and pronouns. The social goal of the context, however, may also influence the grammar. A job interview seeks to obtain (primarily) and convey (secondarily) information and hence will consist mainly of questions and answers in asymmetrical contingency, in which one person has a plan while others react to what the former person does. A talk show interview seeks to entertain and arouse interest and may consist of some questions and answers but in a sort of pseudocontingency where interactors are not really reacting to each other in timing but are playing out a prepared script. Similarly, the way in which an item is described for the purpose of selling may be quite different from the description used to instruct a person on how to use it.

Finally, the topic of conversation (often dictated by the situation) affects the grammar. Cazden (1970) found that children produce longer and more complex sentences when talking about things that personally involve them, presumably because they are trying to explain phenomena. Any form of explanation usually involves a more complex sentence. The grammar may also mirror that which is being explained: hence the careful use of order ("first"; "and then"; "third"; "finally") when giving directions; or "if—then," "when you do this," that occurs when explaining physical phenomena (e.g., engineering, chemistry).

Vocabulary. It is an obvious but important point to note that certain terms are context specific. Staples and Robinson (1964) showed how form of address between working colleagues differed considerably as a function of the context in which they found themselves. In order to communicate in a particular situation, people need to know the words for describing features of that situation—mostly nouns but also verbs and adverbs. Again in formal, work, education, and professional settings a wider, often situation-specific vocabulary is needed that improves the speed and effectiveness of communication. Furthermore, task-related, context-specific vocabulary often becomes abbreviated, shortened to capital letters, or nicknamed, which serves the function of both. It is not only the task-related nature of the context that may determine vocabulary changes but also the role and status relationships signified by the situation. Many languages have a range of personal pronouns (e.g., tu/vous) that are used to signify differences of status. Highly formal, ritualized context often demands correct, polite, standard vocabulary; hence "class" becomes "socioeconomic status"; "heart attack" becomes "coronary infarction"; "piss" becomes "urine," and so on. Indeed, to avoid ambiguity and/or reduce prejudice, certain situations (e.g., courtrooms) demand that only certain words and explanations be used.

These factors are summarized in Table 5.3.

TABLE 5.3
Possible Speech Variations According To Situation Type

Explanation	Context	Informal socio-emotional
Multilingualism	International Language	Immigrant dialect
Form	High	Low
Code	Elaborated	Restricted
Grammar	More nouns, adjectives	More verbs, adverbs, pronouns
Vocabulary	Correct	Loose
Accent	Received	Local
Speed	Slow	Fast
Paralanguage	Few disfluencies	Many disfluencies

OTHERS EXPLAINING ONESELF TO ONESELF!

The focus of this volume, as the title suggests, is on the nature (content, function, bias) of people's explanation for their own behavior: the reasons (attributions) they give in particular social contexts. But people consult "professionals" to have their own behavior and makeup "explained" to them. When and why do they believe or disbelieve these explanations? The importance of this research literature for the present concern is that quite possibly the same factors that determine whether people believe feedback about themselves from others determine how they themselves explain their behavior to others!

It was the famous circus owner Phineas T. Barnum who lent his name to the *Barnum effect* with phrases such as "There is a sucker born every minute" and "a little something for everybody." The phenomenon, which has been extensively researched and reviewed (Furnham & Schofield, 1987), refers to the fact that lay people believe/accept personality feedback about themselves as true because it has been derived from "proper tests."

In 1949 Forer wrote a critical paper questioning the validity of personality interpretations and measuring instruments, posing the problem of the gullibility or suggestibility of participants when evaluating these feedback statements. He argued that there was a "fallacy of personal validation" (p. 119) in that because people frequently accept as correct generalized, vague, bogus descriptions of themselves that have high base-rate occurrence in the general population and that their acceptance of the accuracy of personality interpretations in general cannot be used to support the validity of an instrument. Meehl (1956), who borrowed the concept from his colleague D. G. Patterson, later labeled this the "Barnum effect," a phenomenon whereby subjects accept personality feedback as true, whether it is universally valid or trivial, because it is supposedly derived from personality-assessment procedures. Since then researchers have explored various aspects of the phenomenon and have generally confirmed early findings that, it is argued, partly explain why people believe horoscopes and other quasi-scientific personality assessment procedures (graphology, tarot cards) to be true (Tyson, 1982).

Although research has also looked at personal and interpersonal determinants of the Barnum effect, most of the research has concentrated on three crucially important "situational" factors, or experimental variables, that strongly influence the validation of bogus feedback.

Generality of Feedback

That subjects believe that Barnum statements are accurate descriptions of their personality has been explained by the very vague, ambiguous, and general nature of the statements themselves (Snyder, Shenkel, & Lowery, 1977). However, a rather different, but related question has also been asked: Can subjects distinguish between genuine and false personality descriptions of themselves? That is, if given accurate, honest feedback from properly constructed and validated personality questionnaires, could subjects distinguish between their actual profile and an inaccurate description from another (possibly very different) individual and/or simply bogus, but very flattering, profile? Sundberg (1955), in an early study using Minnesota Multiphasic Personality Inventory (MMPI) found that they could not pick out their own genuine personality descriptions better than might be expected by chance. Similarly, Dies (1972) reported that even when an "objective, nonpathologically oriented, and comprehensive framework" (p. 49) was provided, students were still unable to pick out their genuine feedback from the false (bogus) feedback. In fact, Merrens and Richards (1970) reported a preference for generalized feedback over actual feedback in terms of their perceived accuracy and specificity. However, a study by Harris and Greene (1984) showed subjects could discern relevant aspects of feedback, perceiving trivial (bogus) feedback as less unique, but more accurate than actual test-derived (CPI) or inaccurate (opposite, inverses) feedback, which was thought of as more useful. Thus, if asked, subjects *can* distinguish between general and specific, unique and common, and accurate and inaccurate; but the real question remains—do they?

Favorability of Feedback

People tend to believe that positive, favorable, flattering feedback is more accurate than negative feedback. To some extent favorability of feedback is linked to its base-rate accuracy. Layne (1978, 1979) argued that Barnum feedback is more accurate and socially desirable than real feedback. Furthermore, Snyder and Shenkel (1976) suggested that the differential acceptance that has been attributed to levels of favorability may reflect the fact that positive feedback has a higher base-rate accuracy. When they analyzed their results of higher acceptance of favorable interpretation by controlling base-rate accuracy related to favorability, no significant acceptance effects were obtained, suggesting that subjects may have been responding to the more true of the two personality descriptions (which happened to be more positive). Snyder et al., (1977) argued that this raises serious questions about previous Barnum research that has analyzed favorable feedback without considering the possibly confounding effect of base-rate accuracy.

The interaction of relevance of feedback and favorability has been considered. Snyder and Schenkel (1976) found that subjects tend to see favorable feedback as less true of people in general than of themselves and unfavourable feedback as being no less true of others than themselves.

Therefore, it seems that favorable feedback leads to higher acceptance than unfavorable feedback, but this may be due to higher base-rate accuracy of positive feedback, actor versus observer, attribution errors, or the fact that in some cases the positive feedback was actually more true for the subjects.

Test Situation and Procedure

A study by Richards and Merrens (1971) used three different personality assessment techniques (Bernreurer, life history questionnaire, and abbreviated Rorschach) that were supposedly to derive the Barnum statements, which were subsequently rated by participants in terms of accuracy, depth, and efficiency. They found that the Rorschach test tends to be seen as producing feedback of greater depth than the other test and argued that this could be due to the more ambiguous and less straightforward nature of this test (adding some "symbolic" or "deep underlying" meaning to its feedback). They also noted that this test has been popularized by the media and hence the respondents may be responding to the test's reputation. This obviously has important implications for the Barnum effect because it implies that the test's format, fame, and feedback clarity are as important as its validity and reliability in terms of providing feedback acceptable to a respondent or client.

A critical review of the literature in this field therefore indicates that the effect of the nature of the feedback statements and the test situation are the most important factors in predicting the acceptance of personality feedback. Indeed, favorability of feedback seems to be very influential on the acceptance phenomenon. Recent research on the universality of statements, the perceived uniqueness of these statements for the individual, and the base-rate accuracy of these statements has cast doubt on the previous research that led Snyder et al. (1977) to conclude that feedback that was of a general and favorable nature with a high base-rate accuracy that was presented as being unique to the individual would elicit the acceptance phenomenon (albeit that it was bogus). However, the actual test situation does seem to be significant in eliciting the Barnum effect. Together with the aforementioned research that suggests participants can discriminate the nature of Barnum feedback (correct, incorrect, bogus) if asked the right questions, it may be that the testing situations' contexts or conditions are the most significant factor on the explanation of the Barnum effect.

Early research on the Barnum effect seemed to suggest that people also made serious errors in accepting bogus information about themselves as accurate. However, later studies using genuine feedback, more sensitive questioning, and more powerful statistics have suggested that people are not as naive as heretofore presumed. This is not to suggest that the warning for therapists and researchers in the Barnum Effect literature should be ignored. Nor is it to suggest that personal or acceptance validation should be used exclusively or primarily as material with which to validate a theory or measurement tool (Bayne, 1990). However, to reject all feedback validation from genuine instruments would seem rash, if not foolish.

Although much of the concern about the Barnum effect has been expressed by clinical psychologists (most of the early work was published in clinical journals) because of the pressures on psychotherapists to maintain good relationships with their clients, most of the research has been with students doing pencil-and-paper tests. Snyder and Shenkel (1975) have written that "a comfortable collaborative illusion emerges, formed between the buyer and the seller of the test results, psychological advice, astrological reading, or handwriting analysis" (p. 54). This certainly may be true of the latter three categories, but not of the former. Few, if any, psychometrically devised and assessed psychological tests are validated by feedback or personal acceptance.

People go to astrologers, graphologists, psychologists, as well as friends, religious preachers, and others to get insight into themselves. Often these "others" provide interesting, useful, and surprising information about oneself, but sometimes it is trite. The work in this area gives one insight into the criteria lay people use in evaluating the veridical nature of lay explanations. Indeed the main factors, listed earlier, that influence the generality of feedback may well determine the explanations people supply about their own behavior, in the sense that they may learn a content, style, or category of explanation from others that they then use themselves.

CONCLUSION

This chapter has been concerned with lay theories and explanations. It was argued that research into lay theories/common sense and explanations merited serious consideration regarding a number of facets: etiology, relationship, function, stability, consequences, change, manipulation, structure, language, and comparison. Lay theories differ from scientific theories in sophistication rather than kind, yet there are supporters and detractors of both types of theory. The chapter set out to document studies on lay explanations of child development to illustrate the literature in this area. The chapter not only examined the content of lay explanation but how contextual features influence language and speech and therefore—in various subtle ways—the nature of explanations themselves. Finally the extensive and highly relevant and salient literature of the Barnum effect was reviewed. This research demonstrates the gullibility of people to accept as true to themselves bogus, but positive high base-rate information. Further, more careful research has shown that lay people are not as naive and unsophisticated as originally suspected, though there remain many logical traps and biases for people to fall into in explaining themselves to others in a variety of social contexts.

REFERENCES

Abelson, R., & Lalljee, M. (1988). Knowledge structure in causal explanation. In D. Hilton (Ed)., *Contemporary science and natural explanation* (pp. 175–203). Brighton England: Harvester.

Argyle, M., Furnham, A., & Graham, J. (1981). *Social situations*. Cambridge, England: Cambridge University Press.

Bayne, R. (1991). Interpretations and uses of research on "Barnum" personality statements. *British Journal of Guidance and Counselling, 8*, 223–236.

Bernstein, B. (1959). A public language: Some sociological implications of a linguistic form. *British Journal of Sociology, 10*, 311–326.

Brown, P., & Fraser, C. (1979). Speech as a marker of situation. In C. Scherer & H. Giles (Eds.), *Social markers in speech*. Cambridge, England: Cambridge University Press.

Cazden, C. (1970). The situation: A neglected source of social class differences in language use. *Journal of Social Issues, 26*, 35–60.

Cohen, P. (1968). *Modern social theory*. London: Heineman.

Compass, B., Adelman, H., Freundle, P., & Taylor, L. (1982). Parent and children causal attributions during clinical interviews. *Journal of Abnormal Psychology, 10*, 77–84.

Dies, R. R. (1972). Personal gullibility of pseudo-diagnosis: A further test of the "Fallacy of Personality Validation." *Journal of Clinical Psychology, 28*, 47–50.

Eysenck, H. (1978). *Psychology is about people*. Harmondsworth, England: Penguin.

Fletcher, G., & Haig, B. (1989). *The lay person as "naive scientist": An appropriate model for sociology psychology?* Unpublished manuscript.

Forer, B. (1949). The fallacy of personality validation. *Journal of Abnormal and Social Psychology, 44*, 118–123.

Forsyth, D. (1980). A taxonomy of ethical ideology. *Personality and Social Psychology Bulletin, 7*, 218–223.

Furnham, A. (1982). The medium, the context and the message. *Language and Communication, 2*, 23–47.

Furnham, A. (1983). Social psychology of common sense. *Bulletin of the British Psychological Society, 36*, 105–110.

Furnham, A. (1988). *Lay theories: Everyday understanding of problems in the social sciences*. Oxford: Pergamon.

Furnham, A. (1989). Overcoming "psychosomatic illness." *Social Science and Medicine, 29*, 61–67.

Furnham, A. (1990). The psychology of common sense. In J. Siegfried (Ed.), *The status of common sense in psychology*. New York: Ablex.

Furnham, A., & Bland, K. (1983). The Protestant work ethic and conservatism. *Personality and Individual Differences, 4*, 205–206.

Furnham, A., & Henley, S. (1989). Lay beliefs about overcoming psychological problems. *Journal of Social and Clinical Psychology, 26*, 423–438.

Furnham, A., Johnson, C., & Rawles, R. (1985). The determinants of belief on human nature. *Personality and Individual Differences, 6*, 675–686.

Furnham, A., & Lewis, A. (1986) *The Economic Mind*. Brighton, England: Harvester.

Furnham, A., & Lowick, V. (1984). Lay theories of the cause of alcoholism. *British Journal of Medical Psychology, 57*, 319-332.

Furnham, A., & Schofield, S. (1989). Accepting personality test feedback. *Current Psychological Research and Reviews, 6*, 162-178.

Furnham, A., & Stacey, B. (1991). *Young people's understanding of society.* London: Routledge.

Goodnow, J. (1981). Everyday ideas about cognitive development. In J. Forgas (Ed.), *Social cognition: Perspectives on everyday understanding.* London: Academic Press.

Goodnow, J. (1984). Parents' ideas about parenting and development: A review of issues and recent work. In M. Lamb, A. Brown, & B. Rogoff (Eds.), *Advances in development psychology*, Vol 3. Hillsdale, NJ: Lawrence Erlbaum Associates.

Harris, M. E., & Greene, R. L. (1984). Students' perception of actual, trivial and inaccurate personality feedback. *Journal of Personality Assessment, 48*, 179-184.

Harris, P. (1989). *Children and emotion: The development of psychological understanding.* Oxford: Blackwell.

Heider, F. (1958). *The psychology of interpersonal relations.* New York: Wiley.

Helman, C. (1978). "Feed a cold, starve a fever": Folk models of infection in an English suburban community, and their relation to medical treatment. *Culture, Medicine and Psychiatry, 2*, 107-137.

Hewstone, M. (Ed.). (1983). *Attribution theory: Social and functional extensions.* Oxford; Blackwell.

Hilton, D. (Ed.). (1988). *Contemporary science and natural explanation.* Brighton, England: Harvester.

Holden, E. (1988). Adult's thinking about a child-rearing problem: Effect of experience, parental status, and gender. *Child Development, 59*, 1623-1632.

Jones, E., & Davis, K. (1965). From acts to dispositions: the attribution process in social perception. In L. Berkowitz (Ed.), *Advances in experimental social psychology.* New York: Academic Press.

Katona, G. (1971). Consumer durable spending: Explanation and prediction. *Brooking Papers on Economic Activity, 4*, 234-239.

Keller, J., Miranda, D., & Ganda, G. (1984). The naive theory of the infant and some maternal attitudes: A two country study. *Journal of Cross Cultural Psychology, 15*, 165-179.

Kelley, H. (1973). The processes of causal attribution. *American Psychologist, 28*, 107-128.

Kelley, H., & Michela, J. (1980). Attribution theory and research. *Annual Review of Psychology, 31*, 457-503.

Lalljee, M., Brown, L., & Ginsburg, G. (1984). Attitudes: Disposition, behavior or evaluation. *British Journal of Social Psychology, 23*, 233-244.

Lawton, J., Schules, S., Fowell, N., & Madser, M. (1984). Parents' perception of actual and ideal child-rearing practices. *Journal of Genetic Psychology, 145*, 77-87.

Layne, C. (1978). Relationship between the Barnum Effect and personality inventory responses. *Journal of Clinical Psychology, 34*, 94-97.

Layne, C. (1979). The Barnum Effect: Rationality versus gullibility. *Journal of Consulting and Clinical Psychology, 47*, 219-221.

Lerner, M. (1980). *The belief in a just world: A fundamental delusion.* New York: Plenum Press.

McLoughlin, C. (1985). Utility and efficiency of knowledge of behavioral principles as applied to children. *Psychological Reports, 56*, 463-467.

Meehl, P. (1956). Wanted—a good cookbook. *American Psychologist, 11*, 262-272.

Merrens, M. R., & Richards, W. S. (1970). Acceptance of generalized versus bona-fide personality interpretations. *Psychological Reports, 27*, 691-694.

Paulus, P. (1983). Sphere-specific measures of perceived control. *Journal of Personality and Social Psychology, 44*, 1253-1265.

Pettigrew, T. (1979). The ultimate attribution error: Extending Allport's cognitive analysis of prejudice. *Personality and Social Psychology Bulletin, 5*, 461–476.

Richards, W. S., & Merrens, M. R. (1971). Student evaluation of generalized personality assessment as a function of method of assessment. *Journal of Clinical Psychology, 27*, 457-459.

Ross, L. (1977). The intuitive psychologist and his shortcomings. In L. Berkowitz (Ed.), *Advances in experimental social psychology* (pp. 174–216). New York: Academic Press.

Sarbin, T., Taft, R., & Bailey, D. (1960). *Clinical inference and cognitive theory.* New York: Holt, Rinehart and Winston.

Sjoberg, L. (1982). Logical versus psychological necessity: A discussion of the role of common sense in psychological theory. *Scandinavian Journal of Psychology, 23,* 65–78.

Smedslund, J. (1978). Some psychological theories are not empirical: Reply to Bandura. *Scandinavian Journal of Psychology, 19,* 101–102.

Smedslund, J. (1979). Between the analytic and the arbitrary: A case study of psychological research. *Scandinavian Journal of Psychology, 20,* 129–140.

Smedslund, J. (1984). What is necessarily true in psychology? In J. Royce & C. Mos (Eds.), *Annals of theoretical psychology* (pp. 91–109). New York: Plenum.

Snyder, C. R., & Shenkel, R. J. (1975, March). Astrologers, handwriting analysts, and sometimes psychologists use the P T Barnum Effect. *Psychology Today,* pp. 52–54.

Snyder, C. R., & Shenkel, R. J. (1976). Effects of favourability modality and relevance upon acceptance of general personality interpretations prior to and after receiving diagnostic feedback. *Journal of Consulting and Clinical Psychology, 44,* 34–41.

Snyder, C. R., Shenkel, R. J., & Lowery, C. R. (1977). Acceptance of personality interpretations: The "Barnum Effect" and beyond. *Journal of Consulting and Clinical Psychology, 45,* 104–114.

Snyder, M. (1979). Self-monitoring processes. In L. Berkowitz (Ed.), *Advances in experimental social psychology* (pp. 86–126). New York: Academic Press.

Stacey, B. (1982). Economic socialization in the pre-adult years. *British Journal of Social Psychology, 21,* 159–173.

Staples, L., & Robinson, W. (1974). Address forms used by members of a departmental store. *British Journal of Social and Clinical Psychology, 13,* 131–142.

Stevens, J. (1988). Shared knowledge about infants among fathers and mothers. *Journal of Genetic Psychology, 149,* 515–525.

Sundberg, N. (1955). The acceptability of "fake" versus "bona fide" personality test interpretations. *Journal of Abnormal and Social Psychology, 50,* 145–147.

Tyson, G. (1982). People who consult astrologers: A profile. *Personality and Individual Differences, 3,* 119–126.

Valsinger, J. (1985). Common sense and psychological theories: The historical nature of logical necessity. *Scandinavian Journal of Psychology, 26,* 97–109.

Vygotsky, L. (1962). *Thought and language.* Cambridge, MA: MIT Press.

Zuckerman, M. (1979). Attribution of success and failure revisited or: The motivation bias is alive and well in attribution theory. *Journal of Personality, 47,* 245–287.

6

▼▼▼▼▼▼▼

A Conversation Approach to Explanation, with Emphasis on Politeness and Accounting

William Turnbull
Simon Fraser University, British Columbia, Canada

INTRODUCTION

Everyday explanation is and should be a topic of considerable interest to social psychology. Explanation seeking and giving are activities people engage in strategically to attain personal and interpersonal goals. For example, an individual might ask for an explanation in an attempt to gain greater intimacy with someone or in order to understand. An explanation might be offered to make the self look better in the eyes of others or to fill a gap in someone's knowledge. In addition to its strategic nature, everyday explanation is an eminently social phenomenon in two important senses: Everyday explanation both structures and is structured by the social world.

The ways in which explanations structure social life have been explored extensively and predominantly from an attributional perspective, the central tenet of which is that the explanation given for a behavior influences the important processes of social perception and social interaction. By contrast, the ways in which conceptions of the social world structure everyday explanation have received comparatively little attention from psychologists. Yet, when an explanation is required, why it is required, and what would constitute an acceptable explanation crucially depend on the social relationship, social situation, and culture of the individuals involved. Consider in this regard how different the explanation of an event would be if one's goal were to clarify the event rather than excuse it, or if the explanation were given to a child rather than an adult. The importance of the social world for everyday explanation derives not only from its determining role on the form and content of explanation but also from the fact that, once given, explanations affect the very social structures from which they arise.

In this chapter, the strategic nature of explanation and the impact of social structure on explanation are explored from the perspective of a conversation model of everyday explanation (Turnbull, 1986). The basic postulates of the conversation model—that explanations involve contrasts, and acceptable explanations have explanatory relevance—are briefly reviewed. The bulk of the chapter examines the interpersonal, rather than strictly informational determinants and consequences of explanation. The emphasis is on the impact on explanation of conversationalists' concerns about own and others' image or face. In particular, I explore how accounts, explanations of face-threatening behavior, are influenced by the politeness strategies conversationalists employ in order to protect face. The influence of politeness on accounting is illustrated with data from an experiment assessing the impact of status on the structure of refusals. The chapter concludes with a consideration of certain important yet unresolved issues pertinent to a social psychology of politeness and everyday explanation.

CONVERSATION, CONTRASTS, AND EXPLANATORY RELEVANCE

The vast majority of everyday explanations are given in conversations or their written equivalents. Accordingly, the central claim of a conversation model of explanation is that conversational principles and processes strongly influence the content and structure of everyday explanation (Turnbull, 1986; Turnbull & Slugoski, 1988). Explanations are best conceived of as conversational units or moves; specifically, explanations are answers to explicit or implicit *why* questions. Questions about why a behavior occurred arise when an actor's behavior is perceived to contrast with what is taken for granted or presupposed about that actor and that behavior under those circumstances. Thus, it is misleading to say that Event A needs to be explained and that E is an explanation of Event A. What needs explaining and what an explanation explains is the contrast of why Event A occurred rather than some other event perceived to be more normal, expected, or ideal (Hesslow, 1983, 1984, 1988; Kahneman & Miller, 1986; Turnbull, 1986).

But a serious problem arises given this conception of explanation: For any event there are a host of norms with which it potentially contrasts, and different explanations are appropriate for different contrasts. How do interactants pick out the relevant contrast and explanation? The solution lies in conversationalists' mutual assumption that explanations will follow the maxims of Grice's (1975) Cooperative Principle and be true (Quality); as informative as required but no more (Quantity); relevant (Relevance); and clear, unambiguous, brief, and orderly (Manner). Belief that the maxims are being followed allows conversationalists to identify the particular contrast at issue and give explanations with explanatory relevance (Hilton, 1990), explanations with a content and form consistent with observance of the Cooperative Principle.

A recent study by McGill (1989) provides a vivid example of the importance of explanatory relevance. A classic attributional bias is the actor/observer difference, the tendency for actors to explain their own behavior mainly in terms of situational factors, and the behavior of others mainly in terms of personal factors (Jones & Nisbett, 1972; Nisbett, Caputo, Legant, & Maracek, 1973). McGill (1989) proposed that the actor–observer difference in attribution is not due to a difference in explanation offered for the same event but rather arises from a difference in the contrasts being explained. According to McGill, when actors explain their own behavior the contrast is "why in this situation rather than in other situations?"; but when explaining the behavior of others, the contrast is "why that particular person rather than other people?" Situational factors have explanatory relevance for a stimulus contrast (actor), whereas personal factors have explanatory relevance for a person contrast (observer). When McGill explicitly manipulated the contrast to have either a person or a stimulus focus, the explanations of actors and observers were equivalent when the same contrast was involved.

CONVERSATION AND POLITENESS

Explanations that have explanatory relevance efficiently fulfill the transactional function of conversation, the transmission of factual or propositional information. However, explanations with explanatory relevance can be expressed in a wide variety of ways to different effect. Consider, for example, a student who does much better than anyone else on a very difficult examination. When asked by a class member, "How come you did so well?" the student could answer, "It's simple. I'm a lot smarter than the rest of you," or "I dunno. Somehow I was just able to figure out what the questions were likely to be, and so I was well prepared." The first explanation is likely to lead to the perception that the speaker is smug and insensitive; whereas, in contrast, by playing down the superior performance, the second explanation both attests to the speaker's modesty and protects the other student's sense of competence. Clearly the only student in a class who is able to infer the questions that are on an examination is a superior student. But the two ways of expressing the same information have very different interpersonal effects.

This example illustrates that conversation conveys not only factual information but also information about the personal and interpersonal world; that is, conversation has a phatic or interpersonal function. Because conversationalists are implicitly aware of the interpersonal implications of their talk, they tailor what they say to establish, maintain, or redefine desired images of themselves, others, and their social relationships. In spite of the fact that desired images of self differ from person to person, there is regularity in the interpersonal claims that people make in conversation. Specifically, people try to avoid threatening and try to protect their own image and others' images of self (Goffman, 1967, 1972). The above example illustrates just how strong one's expectation is that people generally do try to protect their own and others' image: there is a tendency to interpret the first, image-threatening explanation as facetious and, therefore, reflective of a modest speaker who does care about the other's image.

It can be expected that the pursuit of identity and relationship goals, given their importance, will exert a strong influence on conversation and explanation. Specification of the precise nature of this influence is a difficult task. There are, after all, a vast number of techniques of self/other impression management (Baumeister, 1982, 1986; Cody & McLaughlin, 1989; Schlenker, 1980, 1985). Perhaps all the theorist can do is catalogue this array of rhetorical devices and identify some general principles such as "Be Modest" or "Be Tactful" (cf. Leech, 1983, for an intriguing discussion of such principles). Unfortunately, taking this approach leaves the theorist with the difficult issues of specifying the circumstances in which each principle applies and the details of its application (e.g., How modest should one be in these circumstances? Exactly what does one say to project modesty?).

A solution to these difficulties, in the form of an ostensibly pan-universal model of the influence on conversation of the goal of protecting the image of self and other, has been proposed by Penelope Brown and Stephen Levinson (1987). These authors observed that, on the surface, the vast majority of everyday talk is non-Gricean. Yet, Brown and Levinson assumed that conversation *is* cooperative in intent, and proposed that the surface deviations from Grice's maxims arise mainly from conversationalists' attempts to balance the competing goals of message clarity and the protection of one's own and the other's face. The concept of *face* (Goffman, 1967) refers to the desire to have others accept the positive image one claims for oneself, to have others value one's values—positive face; and the desire to be free to pursue one's goals—negative face.

Because people depend on others for the attainment of many of their goals, social interaction is rife with the potential to threaten face. For example, in order to pursue my own goals, I might need to request something of you. You might, of course, disagree with what I am trying to attain, and our disagreement would be a threat to the positive face of each of us. Even if you were willing to cooperate, thereby protecting my positive face, my request would threaten your negative face, your freedom to do what you wished rather than what others wished of you.

How could I enlist your cooperation without threatening your face? According to Brown and Levinson, people solve this dilemma by employing politeness strategies. Consider an example. Suppose that my intention was to borrow money from an acquaintance, and I said, "I just don't know what I'm going to do. I left my wallet at home and I need a dollar to get the bus home." My request is very indirect: I never did *ask* anyone to give or loan me money.

Indirectness has important phatic functions. Although it would be clear to both interactants that a request had been made and that requests are face-threatening, the speaker conveys respect for the addressee's negative face by producing a surface assertion rather than a request. And it is the mutual recognition of the speaker's concern about face that protects the addressee's face. More generally, one's face is protected through the recognition of the displayed concern of others for one's face.

The justification provided by the speaker for his request serves to protect the positive face of both speaker and addressee. Because the speaker's need is one any of us might have, on some other occasion the addressee too may want the same thing. Thus, the justification communicates a shared need, a sense that the wants of the speaker are the wants of the addressee. In sum, indirectness and justification are strategic moves to protect face.

Let's change the example slightly so that now I want to borrow bus fare from a friend rather than an acquaintance: "Chuck, could you loan me a dollar?" Granted, I use a conventionally indirect request, but the request is quite direct, contains no justifications, and generally reflects less attention to face than the request made of a mere acquaintance. The example illustrates two important points. First, the use of politeness strategies incurs certain costs: namely, the speaker's (transactional) message is transmitted less efficiently. In general, the greater the use of politeness strategies, the less Gricean talk becomes; and the greater the concern with transactional efficiency, the less polite talk becomes. Secondly, the use of politeness strategies varies depending on certain as yet unspecified variables (given our example, social distance, or solidarity, would appear to be one such variable).

The politeness model addresses both issues. Brown and Levinson proposed that the extent to which an act is perceived to threaten face—its weightiness (W_x)—is determined by the equation:

$$W_x = P(H,S) + D(S,H) + R_x$$

$P(H,S)$ refers to the relative power of the addressee (hearer) over the speaker. $D(S,H)$ refers to the degree of social distance between the speaker and addressee. And R_x refers to the degree of imposition of the act, the extent to which it interferes with an individual's face-wants (e.g., asking to borrow a dime versus $100; asking someone to give their name versus a description of their sexual fantasies). According to the equation, W_x increases with increases in any of $P(H,S)$, $D(S,H)$, or R_x.

Interactants' perceptions of the weightiness of a face-threatening act influence the relative concern they demonstrate with message clarity and face saving. Specifically, as W_x increases interactants become more and more concerned with protecting face and less concerned with transactional clarity. Face-saving is accomplished through the use of a specific politeness strategy drawn from a set of more general superstrategies. When W_x is very low or when transactional clarity is more important than face, speakers go *Bald on record*. An utterance is *on record* when it is clear to addressees exactly what meaning the speaker intended to convey by producing that utterance. An on record utterance that pays no attention to face is *Bald on record*; for example, if the addressee were in danger of being hit by a falling tree, the speaker might yell, "Run!" or "Watch out!" Moderate levels of W_x lead to on record strategies with some component oriented to redressing potential face threat. Speakers can go *on record with positive politeness*, the underlying strategy of which is to indicate that S wants what A wants, that speaker and addressee are similar sorts of people with similar values and interests. Refusing an invitation to a party by saying, "That sounds really fun and I'd love to come but . . ." provides a good illustration of positive politeness. Speakers may go *on record with negative politeness*, a superstrategy with which the speaker indicates respect for the addressee's right to be free and suggests that there is no real imposition on the addressee or that it is negligible. Apologizing for the imposition, being indirect, being pessimistic, hedging one's message, and minimizing the imposition are typical strategies of negative politeness, as in, "I'm sorry, I hate to bother you but I was wondering if I mightn't borrow a smidgen of black pepper?" As W_x becomes increasingly more serious, speakers may choose to go off record. Use of an *off record* strategy results in utterances that have a number of interpretations, are therefore ambiguous with regards to the speaker's actual intention, and as a consequence leave the speaker a way out if challenged on his or her intention. For example, a child might go off record in asking for a particular birthday gift by telling mother that a friend has "the most fantastic video game I've ever seen." Finally, if W_x is perceived to be too high, a speaker might decide to *fail to perform* the face-threatening act.

The experimental evidence tends to support the politeness model. Confirmation comes from studies testing the importance of the relative Power of speaker and addressee (Baxter, 1984; Cansler & Stiles, 1981; Falbo & Peplau, 1980; Gonzales, Pederson, Manning, & Wetter, 1990; Holtgraves, 1986), and of the degree of imposition on or cost to the addressee (Baxter, 1984; Cody, McLaughlin, & Schneider, 1981; Gonzales, Pederson, Manning, & Wetter, 1990; Lustig & King, 1980). The Distance dimension has fared less well (Baxter, 1984; Slugoski & Turnbull, 1988; R. Brown & Gilman, 1989), but Slugoski and Turnbull (1988) provided evidence that revising the model to distinguish between the dimensions of interpersonal Distance and Affect is sufficient to handle the apparently nonsupportive data (see also R. Brown & Gilman, 1989).

The experimental data supporting the politeness model must be interpreted with caution. Most experiments employ a role-play methodology, typically some type of discourse completion task in which a situation is described to the subject who is then asked to respond appropriately. The difficulties of interpreting evidence of how one thinks one would respond as evidence about how one does respond are well known (Nisbett & Wilson, 1977). A technique that avoids this problem involves the collection of spontaneous conversational data that are then coded in terms relevant to the politeness model. This methodology has yielded evidence inconsistent with the politeness model (e.g., Holmes, 1990; Wolfson, 1981, 1988). However, being correlational, this method is subject also to problems of interpretation. An intriguing experimental methodology that elicits spontaneous speech was described by Gonzales et al. (1990). These researchers created a situation in which subjects were lead to believe they had damaged a high or low status person's (Power) important versus nonimportant possessions (R_x). Subjects' responses to this face-threatening act were surreptitiously videotaped and subsequently coded for politeness. Results only partially supported the politeness model; in particular, status influenced politeness only for the low severity of damage condition. In view of these somewhat inconsistent findings and associated problems of interpretation, the empirical basis for the politeness model is uncertain. What is needed are further tests of the model based on experimental paradigms in which subjects are unaware both that their speech is being recorded and that it is the object of study.

EXPLANATIONS AND POLITENESS

Concerns about politeness influence both requests for explanation and explanations themselves. As demonstrated by studies of pluralistic ignorance (cf. Miller & McFarland, 1987), people may fail to ask for explanations that they need (i.e., they fail to perform a face-threatening act) because of the fear of embarrassment that would follow from the implication that they are unintelligent or uninformed. Being aware that this is a common fear of students, teachers who want to encourage questions from their students do not ask, "Is there anyone who doesn't understand?" but instead ask, "Is there anything that needs further discussion?" The latter question is an off record way of asking whether the students understand, and it invites the implication that any failure to understand is due to factors such as the inherent difficulty of the material rather than to the ignorance/stupidity of the student or the inadequacy of the teacher's instructional technique. Because of the politeness devices incorporated into this question, students can ask for explanation without a loss of own face and without threatening the face of the teacher. Speakers' desire to avoid threatening both the positive and negative face of their addressees by putting them on the spot is reflected also in the infrequency of direct, overt "why" questions of the form, "Why did you do that?"

Because addressees are aware that explanation seekers are concerned with the impression they convey, explanations are likely to be phrased in ways that avoid leaving the inference that the questioner is ignorant about something that should be known or that he/she is incapable of deep understanding. The tension between satisfying explanatory relevance and protecting face is well illustrated by the not uncommon situation academics encounter in which they must decide at what level of detail to explain their research to a curious non academic. An extensive explanation may threaten the negative face of the audience (i.e., by implicating that the audience is willing to expend the time and effort needed to understand at a deep level). An overly cursory explanation may threaten the audience's positive face (i.e., by implicating that the audience is too uneducated or too unintelligent to understand or that the audience is not worth the time it would take to give a fuller explanation). Such situations are difficult interpersonally precisely because they call for a most delicate balancing of explanatory relevance and politeness. The impact of politeness is so pervasive that it seems even to influence scientific writing, an enterprise one might have thought would be immune to such considerations. Using a corpus of journal articles in molecular biology, Myers (1989) argued convincingly that the use of such devices as the passive voice, hedging, and the citation of related research do not reflect the norms of science but rather the operation of politeness strategies.

ACCOUNTS, PREFERENCE, ORGANIZATION, AND POLITENESS

The scientific sense of *explanation* is not its only sense. Being asked to explain oneself often carries a connotation of blame: One is being brought to task for an act of moral violation. The underlying contrast is, "Why did you do X when you ought not to have done it/when you ought to have done Y?" The appropriate "explanation" in such circumstances is an *account*, "a statement made by a social actor to explain unanticipated or untoward behavior" (Scott & Lyman, 1968, p. 46). Classically, accounts consist of *justifications*, claims that the actor is responsible for the act but that no offense was committed, and *excuses*, claims that the actor committed the offense but was not responsible for its occurrence (Austin, 1961). (More extensive taxonomies of accounts, some including the additional account types of *concessions, refusals, apologies, requests*, and *disclaimers*, have been variously proposed (Hewitt & Stokes, 1975; Schonbach, 1980; Semin & Manstead, 1983; Tedeschi & Riess, 1981).

The social-psychological approach to accounting is to examine how individuals construct particular types of excuses, justifications, and apologies to preserve a public and private self-image (Arkin & Baumgardner, 1985; Cupach, Metts, & Hazelton, 1986; Kernis & Granneman, 1990; Leary & Shepperd, 1986; Ohbuchi, Kameda, & Agarie, 1989; Schlenker & Darby, 1981; Snyder & Higgins, 1988; Snyder, Higgins, & Stucky, 1983; Weiner, Folkes, Amirkhan, & Verette, 1987). In this literature, accounts are conceptualized as impression-management techniques that actors use in an attempt to manipulate observers' attributions for the actor's behavior. From this perspective a transgressor's goal in making excuses, for example, is to maintain a positive image of self by lessening the responsibility for negative acts attributed by observers to the transgressor. The relevant evidence is consistent with this view; for example, Snyder and his colleagues (Snyder & Higgins, 1988; Snyder, Higgins, & Stucky, 1983) have found that a common and effective way to excuse behavior is to attribute it to external, variable, and specific factors (the so-called EVS pattern), a pattern consistent with an attribution of low personal causation.

Both the impression-management and conversation approaches emphasize the strategic nature of accounting. They differ in that the impression-management perspective focuses on the actor's goal of effectively presenting a positive image of self to both the self and the audience, whereas the conversation perspective focuses in addition on the actor's goal of conveying a positive image of the audience. This difference derives mainly from the essentially individualistic orientation of the impression-management perspective as compared to the interactional stance of the conversation approach. Given that accounting is a coordinated activity of two or more people performed in the course of interaction, an interactional model seems more appropriate. Interestingly, interactional issues are implicit in the impression-management literature. For example, the tendency for actors to be modest rather than boast about their accomplishments is viewed as a tactic that presents the actor as competent but also as likable (Gollwitzer & Wicklund, 1985; Schlenker & Leary, 1982; Stires & Jones, 1969; Tetlock, 1980). But why does boasting lead to less liking than does being modest? One answer is that boasting shows no concern for the face of the audience: Boasting threatens both the audience's positive face ("You are not as accomplished as me") and negative face ("I am better at this than you and therefore I should do it rather than you"). Modesty is preferred to boasting because modesty is a politeness tactic that displays a concern for the face of the audience. Displaying concern for the audience is likely to lead to the actor, in turn, being accorded concern by the audience.

In sum, it would appear that the appropriate conception of accounting is interactional, with concerns about politeness being a central component. Such a perspective is broader in scope than the existing views of impression management. Further, it allows for specific predictions to be made from politeness theory about the microstructure of accounting as a function of the social structure of the situations in which accounts occur.

In order to illustrate the interactional approach to accounting, I examine the specific case of the impact of differences in status on the accounts that occur when requests are refused. Although requests have been studied in detail, there is very little empirical work on refusals. The present analysis leads to a number of hypotheses about the structure of refusals. Because refusing a request is an instance of a ubiquitous class of behaviors known as a dispreferred second, it can be expected that the structure of refusals should display some very general aspects of accounting.

PREFERENCE ORGANIZATION
AND POLITENESS: REFUSING REQUESTS

According to the research of Cody and McLaughlin (1988, 1985), accounting episodes for acts external to a conversation (e.g., dropping a plate of food) often consist of a reproach ("What happened?"), an account ("The plate was too hot to hold"), and an evaluation ("That's okay. Don't worry about it"). However, when accounting for an act internal to a conversation (e.g., accounting for refusing a request), typically there is no overt reproach. There is, however, an implicit reproach.

Consider an example. According to a best-seller on assertiveness training (Smith, 1975), when asked to do something they do not want to do, assertive people clearly and directly say, "No." Furthermore, they do not account for their refusal in any way for to do so would violate an important principle of assertiveness; namely, "You have the right to offer no reasons or excuses to justify your behavior" (p. 47). Contrary to Smith's admonitions, if politeness principles constrain social life, assertive behavior will be highly disruptive of social interaction and, therefore, extremely infrequent. Instead, "nonassertive" behaviors such as weakening one's refusal or providing an account are to be expected. Further, such behaviors should occur regardless of the presence of an overt reproach.

Indirect support for this claim is provided by the study of preference organization in conversation (Schegloff, Jefferson, & Sacks, 1977) and its relation to adjacency pair structure. The request–compliance/refusal structure is one example of a ubiquitous conversational structure called *adjacency pair structure* (Schegloff, 1968; Schegloff & Sacks, 1973). Other examples include greeting-greeting, question–answer, offer–acceptance, and blame–denial. Production of the first part of such a structure sets up the expectation that the addressee will produce an appropriate second part that is oriented to the first part in some way. Although specific first parts call up specific second parts (e.g., questions call up answers but not greetings), for any particular type of first part there is a range of allowable types of second parts. Thus, for example, the allowable second parts to questions include, among others, answers, questions of clarification, protestations of ignorance, claims that the question is illegitimate, and refusals to answer. For any particular type of first part, the type of second part that is the most frequent response in everyday conversation is described as the *preferred second*. Any response to the first member of an adjacency pair other than the preferred second is described as a *dispreferred second*.

The terms *preferred* and *dispreferred* are somewhat misleading as they suggest something about the speaker's desire to produce or to avoid some response. No such connotation is intended (Atkinson & Drew, 1979, p. 59). Clearly, speakers may wish to refuse a request rather than grant it, or avoid answering a question rather than answer it; that is, speakers may want to produce the dispreferred second. What the terms are meant to suggest is a difference in the simplicity and directness of the language used in preferred and dispreferred seconds. Preferred seconds are more frequent; tend to occur without delay after the first part; are clear, brief, and to the point; that is, they are Gricean. In addition to being less frequent, dispreferred seconds occur after a delay; are longer, vague, and rambling; contain words like "well" and "oh," in addition to a lot of "ums" and "ahs"; involve indirect meanings; and often contain excuses or justifications; in other words, they are non-Gricean (see Atkinson & Heritage, 1984, Part II, and Levinson, 1983, p. 334 for summaries).

One explanation for the differences in structure of preferred and dispreferred seconds is that they reflect differences in politeness strategies; specifically, dispreferred seconds are conversational moves that threaten face and their non-Gricean structure arises from attempts to protect face (Heritage, 1984). The typical characteristics of dispreferred seconds are consistent with this view. Indirectness, excuses, and apologies are all standard politeness strategies. Additionally, a delay in responding, the presence of a marker indicating the dispreferred status of the response, and other delaying tactics such as the presence of an insertion sequence may comprise "other-initiated self-corrections" (Schegloff, Jefferson, & Sacks, 1977), attempts to get the original speaker to change the first part so that a dispreferred second will not occur. An off record attempt to get someone to self-correct is less face-threatening than a direct, bald on record correction.

Because a refusal is a dispreferred second, refusals should exhibit the characteristic structure of dispreferred seconds, including the presence of accounts. Supportive evidence comes from a study by Wootton (1981), who examined parents' grantings and nongrantings (refusals) of their children's requests as they occurred in spontaneous conversations. As would be expected, refusals exhibited the typical characteristics of dispreferred seconds. Two characteristics in particular stood out. First, parents avoided the use of the direct refusal token "no" and instead used weakened or mitigated forms, such as "not yet," "not now," and "no, darling." The refusal was weakened also by use of an initial "Oh" or "Well," as in, "Oh, no" or, "Well . . . <pause>." Second, parents accounted for their refusals; in particular, they nearly always justified their behavior and sometimes excused it.

The literature on preference organization and the specific data of Wootton are consistent with the view that the structure of refusals reflects the use of politeness strategies. The evidence, however, is weak because it is only correlational. A stronger test of this claim would involve the manipulation of the extent to which a refusal threatened face. Conversation analysts, from whom the concept of preference organization is borrowed, explicitly argue against the use of experimental data for testing hypotheses about conversation (cf. Heritage, 1988; Potter & Wetherell, 1987). However, as I argued previously, experimental analyses are required to test adequately hypotheses about the causal impact of particular variables on the degree and expression of politeness. Accordingly, a methodology is required in which the determinants of degree of face threat can be manipulated under conditions that appear relatively natural to the respondent and in which the respondent is unaware that his or her refusal is the object of study.

EXPERIMENTAL PARADIGM
FOR THE STUDY OF ACCOUNTS: REFUSALS

A common and frequent part of social psychological research involves telephoning people in an attempt to recruit them as subjects. By varying how much time and effort is required of potential subjects (i.e., by manipulating R_x), the rate of acceptance and rejection of the request can be manipulated. Variations in how the caller identifies him or herself (e.g., Susie versus Dr. Robinson; a student from one's own university versus a student from a rival university) or in the degree of politeness encoded in the request can be used to manipulate degree of face threat of the request. Such conversations can be tape-recorded, subsequently transcribed, and then coded in terms of relevant categories, these being in the present context the characteristics of dispreferred seconds.

Consider a specific instance of the above methodology employed to test the hypothesis that the higher the status of a person making a request relative to that of the person who refuses the request, the greater the degree of politeness of the refusal. Seventy-eight subjects were chosen at random from a subject pool at Simon Fraser University. None had been called previously to participate in a study. Because of the nature of the study, it is important to convey some information about these subjects. At the beginning of each semester, research assistants obtain permission from instructors of high enrollment courses throughout the university to solicit names of students who may be willing to participate in a psychology experiment. Interested students give their names and telephone numbers, and they expect to be contacted during the semester for one or more experiments. They are informed that if contacted, they are quite free to refuse any request if they so wish. No course or other university credit is given for participation. In sum, the potential subjects are volunteers who come from all disciplines within the University, they anticipate being asked to participate in one or more psychology experiments, and they are fully aware that they are quite free to refuse any request made of them.

The research assistant telephoned students picked at random from this subject pool and asked for the student by name. Once she had reached the student, she identified herself in one of three ways. The requester's ostensible identity constituted the manipulation of relative status:

High Status Requester: Hi. My name's Dr. Robinson. I'm head of the Social Psychology Research Lab at Simon Fraser University.

Equal Status Requester: Hi. My name's Susie. I'm a first-year student at Simon Fraser University and I'm helping out at the Social Psychology Research Lab.

Low Status Requester: Hi. My name's Susie. I'm a high-school student and I'm helping out at the Social Psychology Research Lab at Simon Fraser University.

The condition to which a subject was assigned was determined randomly. Following this introduction, the experimenter then requested the subject's participation in an experiment as follows:

I'm phoning to see if you'd like to participate in a psychology experiment. The experiment will take place up at the university this coming Saturday morning from 7:00 o'clock until about 10:30.

The wording of this request was similar to the normal requests the research assistant made of subjects in her daily activity of telephoning potential subjects to recruit them for specific experiments. After the assistant had made the request, she did not speak again until the subject made a response. If the subject asked about the nature of the study, the assistant told him or her that it involved an investigation of the effects of electric shock. The assistant was instructed not to lead the subject in any way and to answer all queries as if the study really were going to be carried out as indicated. Once the subject had replied, the responses of the experimenter were dependent in part on the subject's responses, and thus the experimenter's remarks though similar were not completely constant across conversations. In order to ensure that the assistant carried out this procedure in the required manner, twenty practice telephone calls were made and the conversations recorded. Times at which the assistant lead the conversation or otherwise prompted the subject were identified so that the assistant could improve her performance.

Once the conversation had proceeded to the point at which the subject tried to terminate it by saying, "Goodbye" or its equivalent, the caller interrupted the subject and revealed the true reason for the call. Subjects were informed that the study was being performed for Dr. Turnbull of the Psychology Department, who was interested in how people respond to an extremely demanding request. They were told that the call had been recorded and why this was necessary. They were assured of anonymity and asked permission to use the conversation. All subjects willingly gave permission to use their conversation for the study.

A copy of each conversation was made beginning at the point in the conversation at which the caller said ". . . until about 10:30" and ending just before the debriefing began. The copy was transcribed by another research assistant who remained blind to both the experimental hypotheses and the experimental condition of the subject. The conversations were transcribed in standard orthography using the notation common to conversation analysis (cf. Atkinson & Heritage, 1984, pp. ix–xiv). The initial transcripts were checked by a second research assistant who subsequently met with the original transcriber to resolve any discrepancies. The transcribed conversations were coded for the typical characteristics of dispreferred seconds.

Certain conversations were excluded from further analysis after they had been transcribed. These included conversations in which the subject complied with rather than refused the request (High status N = 5; Equal status N = 2; Low status N = 4); the subject voiced suspicion about the experiment (High status N = 1; Equal status N = 2; Low status N = 1); plus one Equal status subject who was the intended subject's father, and one Low and one High status subject who had difficulty with English as a second language. The reported analyses are based therefore on 19, 21, and 20 subjects for each of the High, Equal, and Low status requester conditions, respectively.

In order to assess the effectiveness of the experimental manipulations, an additional 45 subjects listened to a recording of the research assistant's request (15 subjects for each of the experimental conditions). They rated the requester on three 7-point scales designed to assess perceptions of the requester's status and solidarity/social distance relative to the subject, and the pleasantness of the requester; namely, the scales weak (1)−powerful (7), not at all similar to me (1)−very similar to me (7), and seems very unpleasant (1)−seems very pleasant (7). Analysis revealed, as predicted, a significant effect for the Status manipulation (means of 6.5, 4.8, and 3.4 for the High, Equal, and Low status requester, respectively; all t's significant at $p < .05$). There was also a significant effect of the manipulations on ratings of similarity. Paired comparisons indicated no significant difference in the rated similarity to the subject of the Equal and Low status requester (means of 4.2 and 3.3, respectively; $t < 1$, ns), but both were rated as more similar to the subject than the High status requester (mean of 1.6; both comparisons significant at $p < .05$). There were no significant differences in ratings of how pleasant the requester seemed to be (means of 5.6, 5.8, and 5.3 for the High, Equal, and Low status requester, respectively, all t's < 1, ns).

Predictions

Consistent with Wootton (1981), it can be expected that subjects will avoid the use of direct refusals and instead delay, weaken, and mitigate them. (It is unlikely that this will be accomplished by terms of endearment such as 'darling.') Further, subjects should account for their refusal by making excuses. Justifications should not occur, because respondents know the caller had reason to believe both that the subject was an appropriate person of whom to make the request and that the subject had previously indicated a willingness to participate in an experiment. Because of this, it would be inappropriate to attempt to justify the refusal, for example by saying, "I wouldn't be a good subject; you'd be better off with someone else." or "I'm doing nothing wrong by refusing because you have no right to call and make such a request." Finally, it can be expected that subjects might apologize for their refusal and also possibly provide restitution (McLaughlin, Cody, & O'Hair, 1983). Two forms of restitution seem likely: subjects might offer to be a participant on some other occasion, or they might indicate how interested in and how much they would have enjoyed the study. Of course, the offer might not be sincere in that the subjects may count on it being rejected, and their display of interest in the study may not be sincere either. Nevertheless, each is a positive politeness strategy addressed to restoring the loss of face of the requester.

These predictions should hold regardless of the status of the requester. In addition, there should be effects of the status manipulation. Specifically, since the degree of face-threat of a refusal increases as the subjects' status relative to the requester decreases, the degree of politeness encoded into a refusal should increase likewise. It should be noted that the unexpected effect of the manipulations on ratings of perceived similarity does not compromise the predictions. The politeness model prescribes greater politeness with increases in interpersonal distance. Thus, the significant differences in the manipulation of status and of similarity both lead to a prediction of greater face threat, and therefore greater politeness, in refusals given to High than to Low status requesters.

Results

Transcripts were coded for the presence of those characteristics typical of the structure of dispreferred seconds generally and of refusals in particular; namely, a delay between the request and the first sound or word that the subject made in response; markers indicating the dispreferred status of the response, including words such as "well," "oh," "um" and "ah"; delaying tactics, such as an insertion sequence prior to refusal; mitigated refusals; statements indicating appreciation that the request was made, or interest in the study; accounts; apologies; and offers. The relevant data are presented in Table 6.1.

As can be seen in Table 6.1, across experimental conditions the structure of refusals corresponds to predictions. This finding provides support for the viability of an experimental analysis of preference organization and accounting.[1] Certain details of these findings need to be stressed (data relevant to accounts, apologies, and offers are discussed in detail in later sections). The average delay in responding of greater than 1 second is noteworthy because preferred seconds are often produced before or simultaneously with the completion of the first speaker's turn, a finding replicated by Wootton (1981). By delaying their response, subjects

---

[1]An additional 67 subjects were telephoned and asked to participate in a study described as taking place at 2:30 p.m. on a week day and lasting about 20 minutes. The status of the caller was manipulated as in the refusals study. The acceptances (20 in each of the three status conditions) were coded for the presence of a direct acceptance token plus all categories relevant to preferred and dispreferred seconds. Results indicated that the structure of these experimentally induced acceptances closely paralleled the structure of preferred seconds observed in spontaneous conversation. In particular, acceptances followed the request immediately (and often overlapped with the requester's last word or two); less than 5% included insertion sequences; 92 percent of the acceptances contained a direct agreement token ("yes," "okay," or "sure" being most common); and they contained far fewer words and hesitations than the refusals. These data offer additional support for the validity of the experimental paradigm.

TABLE 6.1
Number and Percentage of the Attributes of Refusals
as a Function of the Relative Status of the Requester

	Requester Status					
Attribute	High		Equal		Low	
Pause	Mean = 1.1 seconds		Mean = 1.3 seconds		Mean = 1.2 seconds	
Initial Marker	13	(68%)	15	(71%)	17	(85%)
Delaying Tactic	6	(32%)	11	(52%)	7	(35%)
Mitigated Refusal	12	(63%)	17	(81%)	15	(75%)
Appreciation	4	(21%)	3	(14%)	5	(25%)
Excuse	13	(68%)	21	(100%)	19	(95%)
Apology	12	(63%)	15	(71%)	13	(65%)
Offer	0	(0%)	12	(57%)	2	(10%)

Note: The data are based on N = 19, 21, and 20 subjects for the *High*, *Equal*, and *Low* requester status conditions, respectively.

may have communicated their reluctance to refuse the request, while at the same time allowing the requester to modify or retract the request. The other major delaying tactic identified in the literature is the placement of insertion sequences between the first and second parts of adjacency pairs. In the present data, insertion sequences were questions either about the time the study would take place or what it would involve. Thirteen subjects checked on the time the study was to take place (2, 10, and 1 subjects in the High, Equal, and Low status conditions, respectively). The relatively large number of queries about time in the Equal status condition is interesting because these subjects used the query as a way of introducing the claim that if the study had been taking place at any other time they would have been eager to participate. There were 11 sequences involving what the study was about (4, 1, and 6 queries for the High, Equal and Low status conditions, respectively). It might be objected that telling subjects that the study involved electric shock might have influenced the results in some odd way. Contrary to this view, the pattern of results for these subjects mirrors that of subjects who did not ask what the studies involved. Of particular interest is the fact that all 4 subjects in the High status requester condition who asked what the study involved refused to participate with a direct "no," whereas only one of six in the Low status condition did so.

The category of "mitigated refusal" included all refusals that did not use the direct refusal token "no." As illustrated below, refusals coded as mitigated varied widely in terms of how indirect and mitigated they were. Note that in all examples, E is the experimenter and S the subject. Unless otherwise indicated, the examples begin with the first response the subject made after the experimenter's request. Numbers in parentheses indict delays timed to one-tenth of a second. Some refusals were off record, as in (1):

(1) S: (0.6) Oh, I've got an exam.

The most common form of mitigation was the use of hedges, particularly the hedge, "I don't think so":

(2) S: (1.2) Umm, I don't think so. Yeah, I'm a little busy right now. Is there any other time?

As can be seen in Table 6.1, expressing interest in, appreciation of, and desire to comply with the request prior to refusal was another tactic of mitigation commonly employed:

(3) S: (0.7) Oh, I'd love to but I have to work.

The most direct form of refusal not involving the word "no" was the phrase "I can't," but in every case it occurred with an apology and usually also an initial mitigating "oh":

(4) S: (0.7) This coming Saturday?
    E: Yes.
    S: Oh, I'm sorry, Saturday I can't make it.

Perhaps the most vivid illustration of the tendency to protect face by mitigating a refusal is to be found in the data for those subjects who used the word "no." Only 27% (16 out of 60) of the conversations included a refusal employing the word "no" (7, 4, and 5 for the High, Equal, and Low status requester conditions, respectively). In every case but one, these refusals were mitigated by being delayed, softened by an initial "oh" or "um," and accompanied by at least one of account, an apology, or an offer:

(5) S: (0.7) Oh, no, I'm sorry, can't, I'm going home.

The pressure to avoid saying "no" directly is illustrated also by a subject who preceded the direct "no" with an agreement token:

(6) S: (1.9) Oh. Yeah. Uh, huh, huh <giggle>. Um, no, I don't think so. Okay?

Overall, these data offer strong support for the claim that various tactics of mitigation are employed when requests are refused. It was predicted that the frequency or type of mitigation would be related to the degree of face-threat. The apparent lack of any differences in mitigation as a function of the experimental conditions appears therefore to be problematic for politeness theory.

Accounts

As predicted, all accounts in the data are excuses. Both direct and indirect accounts are included in Table 6.1. Of these, 80% (48 out of 60) are *direct* excuses, explicit explanations for why the subject could not comply with the request:

(7) S: (0.9) Umm, I'd love to <short laugh> but I can't make it Saturday, I have to work.

In addition, there were 6 instances of *indirect* excuses (5 in the High and 1 in the Low status conditions), in which the subjects implied that the reason for refusing the request was that the experiment conflicted with some other unspecified activity:

(8) S: (0.6) When was it?
    E: 7 o'clock this Saturday morning.
    S: Until?
    E: Until about 10:30.
    S: Uh huh.
    E: It takes about three and a half hours.
    S: Oh, so it's going to take the whole time.
    E: Right.
    S: Oh, I can't.

On the basis of the excuses used in the practice conversations, it was expected that the content of excuses would involve the categories of conflict with work, conflict with school assignments, being out of town when the experiment was scheduled, and unspecified time conflicts. This expectation was borne out. The content of 49 excuses out of a total of 54 fell into the above categories, with the remaining 5 excuses involving the refuser claiming sickness (N = 3), fear of shock (N = 1), and need to attend a wedding ceremony (N = 1). Conflict with work was the most frequent content (N = 17), followed by unspecified conflict due to time (N = 15), leaving town (N = 9), and conflict with school assignments (N = 8). There were no significant condition differences. Examples of excuses, in the order of frequency of content, include:

(9) S: (0.7) Ooooh, that's bad for me. I gotta work.

(10) S: (0.8) Oh, ah, sorry <laugh>. That's a bad time for me, I'm afraid.

(11) S: (0.9) Actually, we're going away on Friday night so I won't be <short laugh> able to make it.

(12) S: (1.6) Uuuumm (1.2) hum (1.5) until 10:30, I have an exam that day (2.7) soo (0.6) I don't think I should.

(13) S: (0.4) I'm sorry, I can't. I'm really sick right now.

The content of the excuses is what would be expected from a strategic view in which excuses are a means of reducing the negative implications of face-threatening behavior. In our society, having a job, needing time for schoolwork, and leaving to visit one's hometown take precedence over being in an experiment. The "unspecified time conflict" excuse is more ambiguous as to its acceptability; but, of course, prior commitments typically do take precedence. In sum, every excuse was based on the claim that some other activity took precedence over the requested activity. Owen (1983) found this type of excuse to be the most common in her corpus of remedial interchanges, and it may be that it is generally the most common type of excuse. It should be noted also that such excuses are likely to be sanctioned in our society and that they fit the EVS pattern of excuse-making (Snyder & Higgins, 1988).

Apologies and Offers

Owen (1983) identified three classes of apology on the basis of the keywords "apology/apologize," "sorry," and "afraid." In the present corpus 95% (38 out of 40) of the apologies incorporated the word "sorry," and the remaining two used "I'm afraid" in an apology mode. These data replicate those of Owen, who found apologies with "sorry" to be by far the most frequent in her corpus of remedial interchanges.

It was predicted that subjects might provide restitution for their refusal in the form of statements of appreciation and offers to participate in the study at some other time. Some subjects did employ these tactics of face saving (see above for discussion of appreciations):

(14) S: (0.9) Um, I'd love to <laugh> but I can't make it Saturday. I
         have to work (0.8) Um (0.8) if we could make it another time,
         I mean, well it's really up to you but <laugh>.

On the basis of McLaughlin et al. (1983) it was expected that as face threat increased subjects would be more likely to apologize and give restitution, strategies that are the most face saving. As can be seen in Table 6.1, the data offer no support for this prediction. Indeed, no offers were given in the most face-threatening condition (High status requester) and, contrary to predictions, 86% (12 out of 14) of the offers occurred in the Equal status condition.

In this case, comparison of the results for the High and Low status conditions provides the cleanest test of the Brown and Levinson model. As indicated, an attribute-by-attribute comparison of these conditions yields results contradictory to those predicted from the model. However, many of these differences are small and it could be objected that they reflect sampling error rather than true disconfirmations. The overall pattern of results is not consistent with this objection. On every one of the eight attributes in Table 6.1, the difference between the High and Low status conditions is directly opposite to predictions. The overall pattern of results provides strong disconfirmation of the politeness model.

Refusal-Excuse Structure

As has been documented, the structure of refusals is orderly, consisting of those characteristics typical of the structure of dispreferred seconds. The issue of whether there is structure internal to this overall pattern of characteristics can be addressed through an examination of the order of occurrence of the functional components of refusals (see Owen, 1983, for a similar analysis of apologies). Four functional units or moves are sufficient to describe over 90% of all the refusals; namely, the components of excuse, refusal, appreciation, and apology. The most frequent structure is [appreciation] but [excuse]:

(15) S: (1.0) Oh, I wish I could but I'm working at that time.

A minor variation is [appreciation] but [excuse] [apology]:

(16) S: (0.9) Ooh, I'd really like to but I have an exam on ah Monday and I really need the time < sigh > I'm really sorry.

In order of frequency, other common structures include [excuse] so [refusal], [refusal][excuse], [excuse], and [apology][refusal][excuse]:

(17) S: (1.2) Mmmm, I'm busy during Saturday. I have to work, so I wouldn't be able to take p-part in it.

(18) S: (3.1) I don't think so, huh, I have an exam that afternoon huh, ooh.

(19) S: (0.6) Oh, I've got an exam.

(20) S: (0.4) I'm sorry, I can't. I'm really sick.

To capture the structure in all remaining conversations, offers have to be added to the allowable moves. There is no apparent regularity to the placement of offers, other than they never occur in initial position.

POLITENESS AND EVERYDAY EXPLANATION: PROBLEMS AND PROSPECTS

The failure to find the predicted differences in refusals as a function of status raises a number of issues that, although specific to the study, are important generally to an analysis of politeness and its relation to explaining and accounting. One major unresolved issue concerns the appropriate measure of politeness. Since testing hypotheses about politeness requires the computation of a quantitative measure of degree of politeness, the refusals data may reflect use of an incorrect measure of politeness rather than conceptual difficulties with the politeness model. This possibility would be easy to assess if there existed clear and agreed on criteria for measuring politeness. Unfortunately this is not the case. A variety of measurement schemes have been proposed (cf. Blum-Kulka, 1987; Blum-Kulka & Olshtain, 1984; P. Brown & Levinson, 1987; R. Brown & Gilman, 1989; House & Kasper, 1981; Penman, in press; Schonbach, 1980; Wood, Farquharson, Arrowood, & Kroger, 1989). Even though many are grounded theoretically on the Brown and Levinson model, significant differences exist among them. But the mode of P. Brown and Levinson is not the only theoretical approach to politeness (see Fraser, 1990, for a recent review), and measurement schemes with different theoretical bases can be very divergent (cf. Penman, in press; Wood et al., 1989). Until agreement is reached on the measurement issue, it will be difficult to interpret any test of the politeness model.

A second major issue exemplified by the refusals study is that the concept of *Power* in the Brown and Levinson model is underanalyzed (a similar criticism can be made of the concepts of *Distance* and degree of imposition, R_x). In the refusals study, Power was manipulated by differences in status and it might be asked how status confers interpersonal power. According to French and Raven (1959), the bases of social power are the ability to reward or punish the other, the legitimacy of one's position, liking or identification with the other, expertise, and information. Given that subjects were no doubt aware that there was nothing concrete the requester could do to coerce compliance (e.g., she could neither lower nor raise the subject's grade nor take away or give course credit), the requester's status was unrelated to the control she could exercise over the subject. Relative status also was unrelated to legitimacy since in all three conditions subjects had granted the requester prior permission to make such a request. It would appear, then, that the only bases for differences in the requester's perceived power were her expertise and knowledge, attributes that were more or less equivalent in the context of the study. (If identification can be equated with similarity independent of liking, it is possible that this factor differentiated between the Low and Equal versus High status conditions). Thus, the hypothesis actually tested in the study is that differences in perceived expertise of a requester influence the structure of refusals. And it may be that the Brown and Levinson model only applies to situations in which power is based on factors other than expertise/knowledge. Clearly, there is a need for closer conceptual analysis of the relation between different types of power and politeness.

A related conceptual issue concerns the expressions of power rather than its determinants. Individuals can be sensitive to face without behaving in the ways prescribed by the model. For example, high-power persons sometimes act with kindness or compassion towards an inferior; that is, they act graciously (the concept of *noblesse oblige*). In the refusals study, subjects may have felt sorry for the high school student who was trying to recruit subjects, and accordingly responded with kind consideration. When refusing the High power requester, they may have felt much less need to protect feelings. To assess this possibility, it is necessary to determine whether graciousness can be equated with greater politeness, as defined by the politeness model, or whether a different type of politeness is involved (e.g., perhaps graciousness is entirely an other-oriented politeness strategy). Additionally, it is necessary to specify the particular conditions that elicit graciousness rather than "less polite" behaviors. Although highly speculative, I suggest that graciousness occurs when there are large differences in power (e.g., as observed when the President talks to an army private) or when the face-threatening act is necessitated by the speaker's role. Based on the second condition, it can be predicted that a request for participation in one's own thesis research will be treated with little politeness by a high power requestee, whereas when the request occurs as part of one's job, graciousness will occur.

The above speculations can be used to explain away data that appear inconsistent with the politeness model. However, such explanations are *post hoc* and thus have some serious deficiencies. A study by Cherry (1988) exemplifies the difficulties involved with post hoc explanations. Cherry examined letters written to a university president protesting the denial of promotion and tenure to a faculty member in that university. The letters were coded for politeness, and the politeness level was correlated with the academic rank of the letter writer. Contrary to predictions, the letters written by assistant professors and graduate students were less polite than those written by associate professors. Cherry interpreted this result as the reflection of a deliberate rhetorical strategy in which politeness principles were flouted in order to create a stronger impression of outrage (akin to a Gricean implicature). On this interpretation, data that appeared to be inconsistent with the politeness model were actually consistent with it. Reasoning of this sort renders the politeness model unfalsifiable. Avoiding this serious problem calls for the specification of the particular antecedent conditions that give rise to certain expressions of "politeness" rather than others. As this discussion has demonstrated, such specification will require deeper social psychological analyses of the determinants and expressions of politeness than are presently available.

Despite these problems, politeness theory offers the social psychologist an innovative approach to the study of attribution. Certainly social cognition, the dominant theoretical orientation in social psychology, has proven to be a most fertile ground from which to analyze everyday explanation. Social cognition, however, has been criticized for overemphasizing the cognitive component while ignoring those social factors necessary for a truly *social* cognition (Forgas, 1981; Higgins, McCann, & Fondacaro, 1982; Markus & Zajonc, 1985). Politeness theory is a social model par excellence: social motivation and strategic social interaction are central to it. But while politeness theory informs social psychology, the converse is also true. Using the methodology of social psychology and incorporating social psychological analyses of the determinants, forms, expressions, and consequences of interpersonal power and of solidarity/intimacy (cf. Brehm, 1985; Kelley et al., 1983) into politeness theory can lead to fine-grained conceptualizations of the impact of the motive to protect face on social life.

ACKNOWLEDGMENTS

I wish to thank Rolf Kroger, Dale Miller, Linda Wood, and the editors for their insightful comments on an earlier version of this chapter. Correspondence should be addressed to William Turnbull, Department of Psychology, Simon Fraser University, Burnaby, British Columbia, Canada, V5A 1S6.

REFERENCES

Arkin, R. M., & Baumgardner, A. H. (1985). Self-handicapping. In J. H. Harvey & G. Weary (Eds.), *Basic issues in attribution theory and research*, (pp. 169-202). New York: Academic Press.

Atkinson, J. M., & Heritage, J. (Eds.). (1984). *Structure of social action: Studies in conversation analysis*. Cambridge: Cambridge University Press.

Atkinson, J. M., & Drew, P. (1979). *Order in court: The organization of verbal interaction in judicial settings*. London: MacMillan Press

Austin, J. L. (1961). A plea for excuses. In J. O. Urmson & G. J. Warnock (Eds.), *Philosophical papers of J. L. Austin*, (pp. 123-152). Oxford: Oxford University Press.

Baumeister, R. F. (1982). A self-presentational view of social phenomena. *Psychological Bulletin, 91*, 3-26.

Baumeister, R. F. (Ed.). (1986). *Public and private self*. New York: Springer-Verlag.

Baxter, L. A. (1984). An investigation of compliance gaining as politeness. *Human Communication Research, 10*, 427-456.

Blum-Kulka, S. (1987). Indirectness and politeness in requests: Same or different? *Journal of Pragmatics, 11*, 131-146.

Blum-Kulka, S., & Olshtain, E. (1984). Requests and apologies: A cross-cultural study of speech act realization patterns (CCSARP). *Applied Linguistics, 5*, 196-213.

Brehm, S. S. (1985). *Intimate relationships*. New York: Random House.

Brown, P., & Levinson, S. (1987). *Politeness: Some universals in language usage*. Cambridge: Cambridge University Press.

Brown, R., & Gilman, A. (1989). Politeness theory and Shakespeare's four major tragedies. *Language in Society, 18*, 159-212.

Cansler, D., & Stiles, W. (1981). Relative status and interpersonal presumptuousness. *Journal of Personality and Social Psychology, 17*, 459-471.

Cherry, R. D. (1988). Politeness in written persuasion. *Journal of Pragmatics, 12*, 63-81.

Cody, M. J., & McLaughlin, M. L. (1985). Models for the sequential construction of accounting episodes: Situational and interactional constraints on message selection and evaluation. In R. L. Street & J. N. Capella (Eds.), *Sequence and pattern in communicative behavior*, (pp. 50-69). London: Edward Arnold.

Cody, M. J., & McLaughlin, M. L. (1988). Accounts on trial: Oral arguments in traffic court. In C. Antaki (Ed.), *Analyzing everyday explanation: A casebook of methods*, (pp. 113-126). London: Sage Publications.

Cody, M. J., & McLaughlin, M. L. (1989). *The psychology of tactical communication*. London: Multilingual Matters.

Cody, M. J., McLaughlin, M. L., & Schneider, M. (1981). The impact of relational consequences and intimacy on the selection of interpersonal persuasion tactics: A reanalysis. *Communication Quarterly, 29*, 91-106.

Cupach, W. R., Metts, S., & Hazelton, V., Jr. (1986). Coping with embarrassing predicaments: Remedial strategies and their perceived utility. *Journal of Language and Social Psychology, 5*, 181-200.

Falbo, T., & Peplau, L. A. (1980). Power strategies in intimate relationships. *Journal of Personality and Social Psychology, 38*, 618-628.

Forgas, J. P. (1981). *Social cognition: Perspectives on everyday understanding*. London: Academic Press.

Fraser, B. (1990). Perspectives on politeness. *Journal of Pragmatics, 14*, 219-236.

French, J. R. P., Jr., & Raven, B. H. (1959). The bases of social power. In D. Cartwright (Ed.), *Studies in social power*, (pp. 150-167). Ann Arbor: University of Michigan Press.

Goffman, E. (1967). *Interaction ritual: Essays on face to face behavior*. Garden City: Doubleday and Company.

Goffman, E. (1972). *Relations in public: Microstudies of the public order.* New York: Basic Books.

Gollwitzer, P. M., & Wicklund, R. A. (1985). Self-symbolizing and the neglect of others' perspectives. *Journal of Personality and Social Psychology, 48,* 702-715.

Gonzales, M. H., Pederson, J. H., Manning, D. J., & Wetter, D. W. (1990). Pardon my gaffe: Effects of sex, status, and consequence severity on accounts. *Journal of Personality and Social Psychology, 58,* 610-621.

Grice, H. P. (1975). Logic and conversation. In P. Cole & J. L. Morgan (Eds.), *Syntax and semantics, Vol. 3, Speech Acts,* (pp. 41-58). New York: Academic Press.

Heritage, J. (1984). *Garfinkel and ethnomethodology.* Cambridge: Cambridge University Press.

Heritage, J. (1988). Explanations or accounts: A conversation analytic perspective. In C. Antaki (Ed.), *Analyzing everyday explanation: A casebook of methods* (pp. 127-144). London: Sage.

Hesslow, G. (1988). The problem of causal selection. In D. J. Hilton (Ed.), *Contemporary science and natural explanation: Commonsense conceptions of causality* (pp. 11-32). Brighton: Harvester Press.

Hesslow, G. (1984). What is a genetic disease? On the relative importance of causes. In L. Nordenfelt & B. I. B. Lindahl (Eds.), *Health, disease and causal explanations* (pp. 16-28). Dordrecht: Reidel.

Hesslow, G. (1983). Explaining differences and weighting causes. *Theoria, 49,* 87-111.

Hewitt, J. P., & Stokes, R. (1975). Disclaimers. *American Sociological Review, 40,* 1-11.

Higgins, E. T., McCann, C. D., & Fondacaro, R. (1982). The "communication game": Goal-directed encoding and cognitive consequences. *Social Cognition, 1,* 21-37.

Hilton, D. J. (1990). Conversational processes and causal explanation. *Psychological Bulletin, 107,* 65-81.

Holmes, J. (1990). Apologies in New Zealand English. *Language in Society, 19,* 155-199.

Holtgraves, T. (1986). Language structure in social interaction: Perceptions of direct and indirect speech acts and interactants who use them. *Journal of Personality and Social Psychology, 51,* 305-314.

House, J., & Kasper, G. (1981). Politeness markers in English and German. In F. Coulmas (Ed.), *Conversational routine* (pp. 157-185). The Hague: Mouton.

Jones, E. E., & Nisbett, R. E. (1972). The actor and observer: Divergent perspectives of the causes of behavior. In E. E. Jones, D. E. Kanouse, H. H. Kelley, R. E. Nisbett, S. Valins, & B. Weiner (Eds.), *Attribution: Perceiving the causes of behavior* (pp. 79-94). Morristown, NJ: General Learning Press.

Kahneman, D. A., & Miller, D. T. (1986). Norm theory: Comparing reality to its alternatives. *Psychological Review, 93,* 136-153.

Kelley, H. H., Berscheid, E., Christensen, A., Harvey, J. H., Huston, T. L., Levinger, G., McClintock, E., Peplau, L. A., & Peterson, D. R. *Close relationships.* New York: Freeman.

Kernis, M. H., & Granneman, B. D. (1990). Excuses in the making: A text and extension of Darley and Goethal's attributional model. *Journal of Experimental and Social Psychology, 26,* 337-349.

Leary, M. R., & Shepperd, J. A. (1986). Behavioral self-handicaps versus self-reported handicaps: A conceptual note. *Journal of Personality and Social Psychology, 51,* 1265-1268.

Leech, G. N. (1983). *Principles of pragmatics.* London: Longman.

Levinson, S. C. (1983). *Pragmatics.* Cambridge: Cambridge University Press.

Lustig, M. W., & King, S. (1980). The effect of communication apprehension and situation of communication on strategy choice. *Human Communication Research, 7,* 74-82.

Markus, H., & Zajonc, R. B. (1985). The cognitive perspective in social psychology. In G. Lindzey & E. Aronson (Eds.), *The handbook of social psychology, 3rd edition, vol. 1* (pp. 137-230). Reading, MA: Addison-Wesley.

McGill, A. L. (1989). Context effects in judgments of causation. *Journal of Personal and Social Psychology, 57,* 267-279.

McLaughlin, M. L., Cody, M. J., & O'Hair, H. D. (1983). The management of failed events: Some contextual determinants of accounting behavior. *Human Communication Research, 9*, 208-224.

Miller, D. T., & McFarland, C. (1987). Pluralistic ignorance: When similarity is interpreted as dissimilarity. *Journal of Personality and Social Psychology, 53*, 298-305.

Myers, G. (1989). The pragmatics of politeness in scientific articles. *Applied Linguistics, 10*, 1-35.

Nisbett, R. E., Caputo, C., Legant, P., & Maracek, J. (1973). Behavior as seen by the actor and as seen by the observer. *Journal of Personality and Social Psychology, 27*, 154-164.

Nisbett, R. E., & Wilson, T. D. (1977). Telling more than we can know: Verbal reports on mental processes. *Psychological Review, 84*, 231-259.

Ohbuchi, K., Kameda, M., & Agarie, N. (1989). Apology as aggression control: Its role in mediating appraisal of and response to harm. *Journal of Personality and Social Psychology, 56*, 219-227.

Owen, M. (1983). *Apologies and remedial interchanges: A study of language use in social interaction.* New York: Mouton.

Penman, R. (in press). Facework and politeness: Multiple goals in courtroom discourse. *Journal of Language and Social Psychology.*

Potter, J., & Wetherell, M. (1987). *Discourse and social psychology: Beyond attitudes and behavior.* London: Sage.

Sacks, H. (1973). Unpublished lecture notes. Summer Institute of Linguistics, Ann Arbor, Michigan.

Schegloff, E. A. (1968). Sequencing in conversational openings. *American Anthropologist, 70*, 1075-1095.

Schegloff, E. A., Jefferson, G., & Sacks, H. (1977). The preference for self-correction in the organization of repair in conversation. *Language, 53*, 361-382.

Schegloff, E. A., & Sacks, H. (1973). Opening up closings. *Semiotica, 7*, 289-327.

Schlenker, B. R. (1980). *Impression management: The self-concept, social identity, and interpersonal relations.* Monterey, CA: Brooks/Cole.

Schlenker, B. R. (Ed.). (1985). *The self and social life.* New York: McGraw-Hill.

Schlenker, B. R., & Darby, B. W. (1981). The use of apologies in social predicaments. *Social Psychology Quarterly, 44*, 271-278.

Schlenker, B. R., & Leary, M. R. (1982). Audiences' reactions to self-enhancing, self-denigrating, and accurate self-presentation. *Journal of Experimental and Social Psychology, 18*, 89-104.

Schonbach, P. (1980). A category system for account phases. *European Journal of Social Psychology, 10*, 195-200.

Scott, M. B., & Lyman, S. M. (1968). Accounts. *American Sociological Review, 33*, 46-62.

Semin, G. R., & Manstead, A. S. R. (1983). *The accountability of conduct: A social psychological analysis.* London: Academic Press.

Slugoski, B. R., & Turnbull, W. (1988). Cruel to be kind and kind to be cruel: Sarcasm, banter and social relations. *Journal of Language and Social Psychology, 7*, 101-121.

Smith, M. J. (1975). *When I say no, I feel guilty.* New York: Bantam Books.

Snyder, C. R., & Higgins, R. L. (1988). Excuses: Their effective role in the negotiation of reality. *Psychological Bulletin, 104*, 23-35.

Snyder, C. R., Higgins, R. L., & Stucky, R. J. (1983). *Excuses: Masquerades in search of grace.* New York: Wiley

Stires, L. K., & Jones, E. E. (1969). Modesty versus self-enhancement as alternative forms of ingratiation. *Journal of Experimental Social Psychology, 5*, 172-188.

Tedeschi, J., & Reiss, M. (1981). Verbal strategies in impression management. In C. Antaki (Ed.), *The psychology of ordinary explanations of social behavior,* (pp. 231-309). New York: Academic Press.

Tetlock, P. E. (1980). Explaining teacher explanations of pupil performance: An examination of the self-presentation position. *Social Psychology Quarterly, 43*, 283-290.

Turnbull, W. (1986). Everyday explanation: The pragmatics of puzzle resolution. *Journal for the Theory of Social Behavior, 16*, 141-160.

Turnbull, W., & Slugoski, B. R. (1988). Conversational and linguistic processes in causal attribution. In D. Hilton (Ed.), *Contemporary science and natural explanation: Commonsense conceptions of causality* (pp. 66-93). New York: New York University Press.

Weiner, B., Folkes, V. S., Amirkhan, J., & Verette, J. A. (1987). An attributional analysis of excuse-
giving: Studies of a naive theory of emotion. *Journal of Personality and Social Psychology, 52,*
316-324.

Wolfson, N. (1981). Invitations, compliments, and the competence of the native speaker. *International Journal of Psycholinguistics, 24,* 7-22.

Wolfson, N. (1988). The bulge: A theory of speech behavior and social distance. In J. Fine (Ed.),
Second language discourse: A textbook of current research (pp. 21-38). Norwood, NJ: Ablex.

Wood, L. A., Farquharson, M., Arrowood, A. J., & Kroger, R. (1989). *A manual for coding and
scoring for the politeness of discourse,* (Version Two). Unpublished manuscript, University of
Guelph.

Wootton, A. J. (1981). The management of grantings and rejections by parents in request sequences.
Semiotica, 37, 59-89.

7
▼▼▼▼▼▼▼

Excuses in Everyday Interaction

Bernard Weiner
University of California, Los Angeles

To develop and maintain bonding with others, we must effectively use social conventions, social skills, and social strategies. If successful, then others will think and feel positively about themselves and us. If unsuccessful, however, then their interpersonal thoughts and feelings will be negative, thereby endangering relationships. The strategies that might be used to promote positive relationships include communication of acceptance, admiration, appreciation, compliments, and on and on; these may be somewhat unconscious, automatic reactions, or conscious and thoughtful ploys; and they may be truthful and reflect our beliefs and feelings, not directed by intended goals, or they may be fabrications guided by desired outcomes.

In this chapter, I examine one communication strategy that manipulates the thoughts and feelings of others: namely, the giving of excuses. I will consider the following questions and issues:

1. How are excuses defined?
2. How prevalent are they?
3. What are the intentions or goals of excuse-givers?
4. What are the antecedents and social contexts for excuses?
5. What are the contents of excuses, that is, how can they be described?
6. How should the contents of excuses be taxonomized, or classified along theoretically meaningful properties?
7. What is the excuse-giving process?

8. Can excuses be detected as lies?
9. What are the consequences of excuses, that is, do they "work"?
10. What are some typical excuse-giving scenarios, considering context, antecedents, and consequences?
11. Is there an association between excuse-giving and general psychological functioning?

Some of the above questions can be answered, whereas others as yet cannot; some unknown answers appear to be readily ascertainable, whereas others do not; and some answers can be guided by extant empirical and theoretical knowledge, whereas others cannot. I believe, however, the reader will find that this area of study is more tractable than might have been intuited: Progress has been made and additional advances are foreseeable. Excuse-giving therefore provides a rich context that is ripe for more exploration.

DEFINITION

Unlike many other fields of psychological study where the definition of the phenomenon under investigation is not essential, a formal meaning of *excuse* is needed because this determines the phenomena to be studied. Disparate definitions have been proposed, and they incorporate different observations. Each definition has a legitimate claim of being "correct"; time will have to determine which is most fruitful and best imposes boundary conditions for the phenomena under investigation.

All definitions are guided by the notion that an excuse (ex = from; cuse = cause) shifts the cause of an event. According to Snyder and Higgins (1988), excuses are characterized as: "the motivated process of shifting causal attributions for negative personal outcomes from sources that are relatively more central to the person's self to sources that are relatively less central" (p. 23). For example, a baseball player may come to believe: "I missed the ball because the sun was in my eyes," rather than the true and initially accepted cause, which is that he or she is a poor baseball player. In this example, the cause of a negative event is shifted from internal to the person to external circumstances.

Given this definition, the excuse-giver may or may not publicly communicate the external cause, but he or she must consciously believe it and must not consciously be aware of the causal substitution, for this would undermine its effectiveness. Hence, an excuse is analogous to a defense mechanism that protects the self-esteem and self-worth of the person. To study excuses, the investigator may examine a variety of esteem-related defenses and processes including rationalization, hedonic biasing, self-handicapping strategies, and so on (see Snyder & Higgins, 1988). With this definition and approach, the study of excuses is best considered within the rubric of clinical psychology.

On the other hand, my colleagues and I (Weiner, Amirkhan, Folkes, & Verette, 1987; Weiner, Figueroa-Muñoz, & Kakihara, 1991; Weiner & Handel, 1985; Yirmiya & Weiner, 1986) have suggested a more restrictive and social definition of *excuse*: a consciously used device, communicated to someone else, primarily to foster a positive relationship. This can be accomplished by creating a positive image of the other or of the self, preventing another from becoming angry at oneself, inducing positive expectancies about one's future interpersonal actions, and so on. Excuses thus manipulate the thoughts and feelings of the listener (rather than of the self) to the ultimate interpersonal benefit of the communicating excuse-giver.

In contrast to the definition offered by Snyder and Higgins, excuses need not shift causality away from the self, for some excuses internal to the actor are quite functional (e.g., "I could not come to the party because I was ill" may be a more adaptive internal causal communication than the true cause, which is that the person did not want to go). In addition, excuses may protect the self-esteem of the listener rather than of the self (e.g., "I cannot go on a date with you because I already have plans" is often perceived as more adaptive than conveying the true cause, which is that the requester is considered boring). Further, excuses might occasionally involve positive outcomes. For example, a teacher might believe that the students did well on an exam because of good teaching but creates a favorable self-impression of modesty by telling parents that their children were successful because of good parenting practices. It is evident, therefore, that given our meaning, excuses must be publicly communicated, they must not be believed by the communicator, and the excuse-giver must be consciously aware of the causal substitution. Thus, an excuse is a type of lie, although not all lies are excuses, inasmuch as many lies do not involve a causal substitution (e.g., "I was home at 10:00" is a lie if the adolescent came home after midnight; it is not, however, an excuse). Given this perspective, the study of excuses is more central to social rather than to clinical psychology, and social transgressions rather than personal failure are primarily the acts to which an excuse is attached.

Excuses are not the only type of account offered publicly, yet they are distinguishable from other accounts, including denial, justification, and confession (see Schonbach, 1980). Given a denial, the untoward act is not admitted, whereas given an excuse, the act is accepted. When there is an excuse, however, the actor denies personal responsibility for the action (if this is implicated), whereas when a justification or confession is communicated, responsibility is accepted. Given a justification, the legitimacy or permissibility of the act is asserted (e.g., "I came late on purpose so I would not hurt Joan's feelings"), whereas if there is a confession, then blame as well as personal responsibility is accepted (see Weiner, Graham, Peter, & Zmuidinas, 1991). In sum, an excuse is a unique and untruthful impression management ploy or tactic in which an act, but not responsibility for the act, is assumed.

PREVALENCE

It certainly is reasonable to inquire about the prevalence of excuses: Do they rarely occur, or are they quite widespread and common components of everyday social interaction? An answer to this question would require interaction sampling, or perhaps a sampling of written material. These, however, have not been and are not likely to be undertaken (but see Cody & McLaughlin, 1988). One has to then infer prevalence from other indicators. For example, when our experimental subjects have been asked to recount a time they gave an excuse (i.e., to recall a false reason that was communicated), they do so apparently with little difficulty (Weiner et al., 1987; Weiner, Figueroa-Muñoz, & Kakihara, 1991). Not one of over 300 subjects we have asked to freely recall a personal occasion of giving an excuse has failed to find one in memory. In addition, known phrases such as "that is no excuse" or "that is a poor excuse" attest to the typicality of unacceptable reasons for a negative act, as do aphorisms such as "he who excuses himself accuses himself." In sum, although there are little (or no) data regarding the actual number of excuses communicated in everyday life, there are many reasons to contend that they are indeed frequent.

INTENTIONS OR GOALS OF EXCUSE-GIVERS

It has already been suggested that excuses are given for the benefit of the excuse-giver: He or she wants to establish or maintain a social bonding and increase social rewards as well as decrease social punishments. After all, in most societies rewards and punishments require the cooperation of others. But this basic function subsumes a variety of specific and immediate goals.

In one investigation (Weiner, Figueroa-Muñoz, & Kakihara, 1991), 69 college students were asked to recall a time when they gave an excuse. They also indicated the goal or hoped-for result of this false communication. For some of the research participants, more than one goal was recounted. Table 7.1 shows that five general categories of objectives were reported. Most frequent was the

TABLE 7.1
Goals of the Excuse-Giver

Goals	% Frequency
Not engage in the behavior	29
Maintain esteem of other	22
Change expectancy	18
Reduce anger	16
Maintain self-esteem	7
Miscellaneous	8

Note: data from Weiner, Figueroa-Muñoz, & Kakihara, 1991

desire not to engage in a particular action. For example, in response to his father's query, "Why has the garbage not been taken out yet?" one of our respondents reported that his reply was: "I have to study," when the real reason was that he just did not want to do the task. The other categories of excuse-giving goals shown in Table 7.1 were to maintain the self-esteem of the other, change the expectancy of the listener, reduce the listener's anger, and maintain one's own self-esteem. Only this latter objective is consistent with the position of Snyder and Higgins (1988).

ANTECEDENTS AND CONTEXT

A number of the antecedents that promote the conveying of an excuse have been suggested earlier in the chapter, in part by the imposed definition of this tactical communication. First, an excuse usually (but not always) follows a social transgression such as coming late for a party, not handing in a school assignment, and so on. The exception to this rule may be when there is a rejection of another. Further, when there is a social transgression, then the excuse-giver is responsible but seeks to deny that responsibility. In addition, the situation must elicit the belief that a causal attribution is called for, that is, either the listener must ask a question like, "Why were you so late?" or the excuse-giver anticipates that this question is expected to be answered. And finally, an assumption is made that the excuse will be effective in reaching some goal, such as reducing listener anger. Note, therefore, that the initiation of excuse-giving requires an active, lay psychologist as communicator—one having expectations and presumptions about the thoughts and feelings of others and holding naive rules about cognitive and emotional change.

In addition to a variety of intrapsychic antecedents, excuses also are likely to be manifested in particular social contexts. Inasmuch as most social influence attempts are directed towards parents, siblings, roommates, and friends (see review in Cody & McLaughlin, 1990, p. 11), this is expected to be the dominant setting for excuse-giving. Our research (Weiner, Figueroa-Muñoz, & Kakihara, 1991) has revealed that nearly 75% of excuses are given in affiliative, as opposed to achievement settings. Excuses thus involve friendships, personal bonding, rejection, and the maintenance of the social fabric.

CONTENTS

Let us review briefly the discussion thus far. It has been proposed that excuses are untrue, tactical communications, given primarily to deny responsibility for a social transgression. They are frequent and conveyed primarily in affiliative contexts, most likely to relatives and friends, to get out of an action, reduce listener

TABLE 7.2
Content of True (Withheld) and False Causes (Excuses) in Three Investigations

Content Categories	Weiner et al., 1991 (Exp. 1)		Weiner et al., 1991 (Exp. 2)		Weiner et al., 1987	
	True	Excuse	True	Excuse	True	Excuse
Parents	1%	7	0	0	0	14
Friends	4	7	0	0	0	6
Illness	0	21	4	16	0	5
Other Commitment	2	24	4	3	1	19
Transportation	0	2	2	16	0	11
Work/Study	2	15	4	27	0	12
Forget/Negligence	12	2	28	6	34	8
Intent	70	2	53	1	60	1
Misc.	9	24	5	0	5	24

Note: data from Weiner et al., 1987; Weiner, Figueroa-Muñoz, & Kakihara, 1991

anger, increase positive interpersonal expectancies, or enhance listener self-esteem. These specific goals serve the more basic function of maintaining favorable relationships.

But how specifically does the excuse-giver go about this task? What true causes are withheld and what actually is communicated? In prior research, we have examined these questions with a variety of methodologies. In two research investigations we asked the research participants (college students) to recall a time when they gave an excuse and to report this incident as well as the real (withheld) cause and the falsely communicated cause (the excuse) (Weiner et al., 1987; Weiner, Figueroa-Muñoz, & Kakihara, 1991). In another investigation, we had respondents recall excuses associated with the distinct goals of either to raise the self-esteem of the listener, reduce the listener's anger, or increase the listener's expectancies regarding the excuse-giver (Weiner, Figueroa-Muñoz, & Kakihara, 1991). And using a very different laboratory experimental procedure, in one investigation some subjects were "intercepted" and compelled to come 15 minutes late for an experiment where another subject was waiting. These delayed subjects also were asked to give an excuse for arriving late (Weiner et al., 1987).

In each of these studies, we grouped the withheld reasons and/or the excuses. Eight categories were sufficient to describe virtually all of the causes (See Table 7.2). Considering first the withheld or true causes, Table 7.2 reveals that across three studies, nearly 85% of the reasons that are withheld are forgetting/negligence or intention ("I did not want to . . ."). Thus, excuse-givers indeed perceive themselves as responsible when giving an excuse. Furthermore, intention was more than twice as likely to be the true cause of the social transgression than was forgetting/negligence. That is, the excuse-giver purposively planned the social misdeed. Thus, the offense calling forth an excuse falls within the category of murder (a misdeed with conscious intent) rather than manslaughter (a misdeed without intent). Little wonder, then, that the excuse-giver wants to escape punishment and deny responsibility!

Table 7.2 also reveals the causes that are communicated by the excuse-giver. They fall within six general categories: parents ("My parents would not let me go"), friends ("I had to help Mary"), illness ("I had the flu"), other commitments ("I had to take my mother to the airport"), transportation ("The bus came late"), and work/study ("My boss made me work overtime"). Among these, other commitments and work/study requirements are most frequent. The excuses given are rather mundane and prosaic, most likely out of fear that any unusual explanation will not be believed.

A THEORETICALLY DERIVED
TAXONOMY OF EXCUSES

The classification shown in Table 7.2 is merely a grouping of phenotypically similar situations; it goes little beyond description, it is not theoretically generated, nor does it address genotypic similarity. In a genotypic grouping, classification is based on the principle of underlying shared properties that are not immediately evident.

To derive a theoretically driven taxonomy of excuses, it is first necessary to examine the basic dimensions or properties of phenomenal causality. A number of research investigations, guided by attribution theory, have been undertaken to determine the dimensions of causal ascriptions (see review in Weiner, 1986). On the basis of factor analytic, concept formation, and multidimensional scaling research, it frequently has been suggested that three properties of perceived causality are locus, controllability, and stability. That is, causes can be perceived as internal or external to the actor, controllable or not controllable by the actor or others, and varying or unvarying over time. In the affiliative domain, for example, physical attractiveness as a cause of rejection generally is construed as internal to the rejected person, not subject to volitional change, and constant over time. On the other hand, refusal of a social engagement because the rejector is ill typically is perceived as external to the rejected person (internal to the rejectee), not subject to volitional control, and unstable.

Inasmuch as excuses are particular types of causes, they also are classifiable according to the basic dimensions or properties of phenomenal causality, that is, they can be internal or external to the communicator, controllable or not controllable by that person, and stable or unstable over time. Table 7.3 summarizes data from three investigations conducted by my colleagues and me (Weiner et al., 1987; Weiner, Figueroa-Muñoz, & Kakihara, 1991) regarding the causal properties of real reasons and excuses. It reveals that the causes that are withheld are internal to the transgressor, controllable by that person, and somewhat unstable. For example, if a person did not go to a party because that individual merely

TABLE 7.3
Dimensional Classification of True (Withheld) and
False Causes (Excuses) in Three Investigations

	Withheld (Real)	Revealed (Excuse)
Locus		
Weiner, Figueroa-Muñoz, & Kakihara, 1991	94%[1]	23
Weiner, Figueroa-Muñoz, & Kakihara, 1991	97	19
Weiner et al., 1987	92	32
Controllability		
Weiner, Figueroa-Muñoz, & Kakihara, 1991	94	6
Weiner, Figueroa-Muñoz, & Kakihara, 1991	98	15
Weiner et al., 1987	90	10
Stability		
Weiner, Figueroa-Muñoz, & Kakihara, 1991	48	10
Weiner, Figueroa-Muñoz, & Kakihara, 1991	47	15
Weiner et al., 1987	8	2

Note: data from Weiner et al., 1987; Weiner, Figueroa-Muñoz, & Kakihara, 1991
[1]Percentage figures refer to internal, controllable, and stable causes.

decided not to go to any parties, then that cause would be classified as internal to the transgressor, under that person's control, and stable. This indicates that there was an intent not to attend the party. Forgetting to go to the party also is an internal and controllable cause, but it is unstable. Forgetting is considered controllable because others hold the individual responsible and blame him or her, and the forgetting person is likely to experience guilt. On the other hand, communicated causes are external to the offender, not controllable by that person, and unstable. For example, missing a party because one's car is said to have a flat tire or because one's mother had to be driven to the airport are external to the offender, not subject to volitional alteration, and not enduring over time.

In sum, both the withheld causes as well as the excuses tend to have very discernible causal properties. The greatest difference or shift between the true cause and the excuse is on the dimension of controllability. As indicated in the definition of an excuse, the excuse-giver perceives that he or she is indeed responsible for a misdeed, but conveys that he or she is not. This often is accomplished (but need not be) by a shift in causality from internal to the person to external (e.g., from negligence to a flat tire). But, as previously indicated, an excuse such as "I was ill" can be appropriate and is used inasmuch as illness is not perceived as controllable by the person, although it typically is construed as internal to that individual. Nonetheless, it also is the case that the majority of excuses are external to the excuse-giver.

WHAT IS THE EXCUSE-GIVING PROCESS?

Inasmuch as an excuse requires the substitution of one communication (the lie) for a true cause, one wonders about the cognitive processes that are involved to execute this sequence. When a social contract is broken, a transgressor may consider the real explanation (e.g., "I did not want to go"), analyze this explanation for causal properties (internal, controllable, and stable), anticipate the negative consequences of communicating that cause, and then make an action decision (withhold revealing that cause). This captures a thought (causal analysis)–anticipated affect–action sequence.

When considering what excuse to substitute, however, the process may or may not be the same. It may be that the communicator has a scheme or a model for a good excuse (external, uncontrollable, and unstable), selects an excuse meeting those properties ("My car broke down"), and then communicates this explanation. But time constraints in a conversation or the sudden confrontation of a "Why didn't you show up?" question may not permit this degree of cognitive work. Hence, it is quite possible that we already have a list of "good" and "bad" excuses from which to draw and we do that without going through a more complete causal analysis. This sequence, however, also may not capture the full complexity of the decisionmaking process, for some excuses that reduce responsibility are not likely to be communicated in certain contexts (e.g., students may not want to tell their parents that they failed to come home during Christmas because of illness—an uncontrollable and, therefore, a good excuse). However, the fact that virtually all excuses exhibit the same causal properties suggests that individuals are "cognitive misers" as well as "cognitive functionalists." That is, strategies that "work" and do not require a great deal of cognitive stress are adopted to respond to the immediate demands of the environment.

Obviously, one can hypothesize other possible processes, from the most simple habits or scripts to extremely complex chains of reasoning. This topic remains a totally uncharted area of study.

DETECTION

Inasmuch as the communication delivered by the excuse-giver is a lie, there is a risk of detection, that is, the excuse-giver may be "uncovered." It is known, however, that in general individuals are very poor at discriminating false from true communications (Ekman, 1984). It should not be very surprising, then, to find that this is also the case regarding excuses. Folkes (1982) reported that when being rejected for a date, nearly 75% of the reasons that are given are accepted as real or true. In contrast, rejectors report that only about 50% of the reasons they report are valid. In addition, Weiner et al. (1987) found that about 12% of the communications regarding the reasons for a broken social contract are perceived by the communicator to be disbelieved by the listener. Of these, about one-half were in fact true, and the other one-half were false. Thus, persons are not able to identify excuses as lies; the saying that "he who excuses himself accuses himself" is not correct inasmuch as excuses are not detected as false.

There is one detection clue that relates to the content of the excuse itself rather than to conceivable nonverbal cues such as sweating, stuttering, and so forth. Table 7.4 shows the types of reasons communicated for a social transgression as a function of their truth or falsity (from Weiner et al., 1987). Table 7.4 reveals that when transportation problems are the conveyed reason for a social transgression (e.g., "The bus was late"; "My car broke down"), then it is more likely to be the truth than a lie. This also is the case when the uttered reason is negligence or a desire to do or not to do something. Indeed, when someone who did not appear at a party says, "I did not want to go," then it is almost certainly the truth rather than a fabrication. On the other hand, if the explanation given is work/school demands or other commitment, then that statement is more likely to be false than true. Hence, if a student handing in a late paper tells the teacher, "I had to work overtime," then it is about twice as likely to be a lie than the truth. Although content provides far from definitive evidence of falsity or truthfulness, it is one source of detection information (although this content-based clue is unlikely to be realized by the listener).

DO THEY "WORK"?

Let us again take stock. Excuses are frequently given, perhaps "unthinkingly," and are generally undetected lies, having the structural characteristics of external, uncontrollable, and unstable causes. But do they accomplish their goals? Are they dependable tactics? Do they work?

TABLE 7.4
Categories of Explanation and Percentage Frequency as a
Function of Type of Reason and Truth or Falsity

Category of Explanation	% True	% False (Excuse)
Transportation	24[1]	15
Work/school	14	25
Other commitment	13	22
Illness	12	16
Negligence	17	6
Preference	9	1
Misc.	10	15

Note: from Weiner et al., 1987, p. 317
[1]Indicates percentage of true causes

To understand if excuse-related goals are reached, we again have to turn to attribution theorists and the more general understanding of phenomenal causality. It has been documented that the three underlying properties of causality previously discussed have unique psychological affects. Turning first to the locus dimension of causality, it has been found that causal locus influences self-esteem. For example, an "A" in a class because of internal factors such as high ability and effort enhances self-esteem and pride in accomplishment. Conversely, an "A" attributed to external causes including the objective ease of the task or good luck neither increases personal esteem nor generates feelings of pride. Similarly, in affiliative contexts a rejection because of internal causes such as perceived low attractiveness lowers self-esteem, whereas a rejection because the other person is ill has no such consequences (see review in Weiner, 1986).

The controllability dimension of causality relates to a variety of affects, including anger and pity. Anger primarily is experienced when an individual has engaged in a controllable or volitional action that harms others (see Averill, 1983). Pity and sympathy, on the other hand, are aroused by uncontrollable plights such as those associated with the handicapped, the retarded, the aged, and so on (see Weiner, Graham, & Chandler, 1982).

The third dimension of causality, causal stability, is linked with expectancy of success (see review in Weiner, 1986). An outcome such as exam failure ascribed to a stable cause (e.g., low aptitude) is expected to be repeated, inasmuch as low aptitude is perceived as enduring over time. On the other hand, ascription of failure to temporary illness or bad luck will not produce decrements in the future expectancy of success. This merely is restating the logic of cause–effect laws: if the cause remains the same, then the effect is anticipated to remain the same, whereas if the cause changes, then the effect also is subject to change.

In sum, the three dimensions of phenomenal causality are related to affects including self-esteem (for locus) and anger and pity (for controllability), as well as to thoughts (expectancy of success for stability). Inasmuch as excuses are causal substitutions, they also should alter self-esteem, anger and pity, and expectancy of success in the manner indicated for all causal beliefs. Furthermore, virtually all excuses have the properties of externality, uncontrollability, and instability, whereas withheld causes primarily are described as having the properties of internality, controllability, and partial stability. Hence, an excuse should enhance the self-esteem of the listener or of the excuse-giver, reduce anger and increase sympathy toward the excuse-giver, and alter expectancies in a positive manner.

The published research confirms that excuses do have the consequences suggested by attribution theorists. For example, in one study reported by Weiner et al. (1987), following the recounting of an excuse for a social transgression, participants were queried with regard to the consequences of the communicated explanation for their relationship with the listener, their personal image, their perceived responsibility for the transgression, and anger reactions. They also answered these questions while imagining that the true (the withheld) reason was actually communicated.

The results of this investigation are shown in Table 7.5. The ratings reveal that excuses enhance the personal relationship, maintain the self-image of the excuse-giver, lessen that person's responsibility, and reduce the anger of the listener toward the excuse-giver, when compared with the estimates of the effects of the withheld cause.

In another study reported in Weiner et al. (1987), a confederate intentionally coming late for an experiment that involved other subjects communicated either a "good" excuse ("The professor in my class gave an exam that ran way over time") or a "bad" excuse ("I was talking to some friends I ran into in the hall, and that's why I'm late"). Note that the former explanation has the characteristics of an excuse in that it is external, uncontrollable, and unstable, whereas the latter explanation is internal to the excuse-giver and controllable (as well as unstable). Ratings were subsequently made by the waiting subjects of their emotional reactions toward the confederate, his or her perceived personality characteristics, and prosocial behaviors they would display toward that person. As predicted, the good excuses produced more positive emotional reactions, perceptions of the excuse-giver as having more positive traits, and greater tendencies to exhibit positive behaviors toward the excuse-giver than did the bad explanations. These findings also were replicated using a procedure in which the late arriver was actually a naive subject asked to make up his or her own "good" or "bad" reason to communicate.

In sum, excuses do accomplish their aims. There is a very pleasing parsimony in the understanding of the relations between the goals of excuses, their structure, and their consequences. Attribution theorists have established a taxonomy of causal dimensions with the properties of locus, controllability, and stability. Among the stated goals of excuse-givers are to preserve self-esteem of the self or the other, minimize anger, and maintain positive expectancies, all in service of interpersonal bonding. These excuse-related goals can be respectively reached by shifting perceived causality along the three identified dimensions of causality. Specifically, to minimize loss of self-esteem, locus of causality for rejection or failure of another can be altered from internal to the rejected or failed person

TABLE 7.5
Perceived Consequences of Explanations (True Causes Versus Excuses)

Dependent Variable	Withheld	Excuse
Relationship suffer	3.72	1.87
Personal image suffer	4.27	1.23
Responsibility	4.72	2.33
Anger	4.39	2.26

Note: adopted from Weiner et al., 1987, p. 318

to external; to reduce anger, perceived controllability for a broken social contract can be manipulated from controllable to uncontrollable by the transgressor; and to induce positive expectancies, causal stability for a negative consequence can be changed so that the cause is perceived as unstable rather than stable. The excuse-communicator does this, shifting internal and controllable causes so they are external, uncontrollable, and unstable. The excuse-giver seems to adopt a very simple strategy that is able to reach all the attributionally linked goals simultaneously. That is, over-determined excuses are communicated that can satisfy multiple objectives, saving the excuse-giver from cognitive work.

COMPLETE SCENARIOS

Our research has pointed out three prototypical excuse patterns that reflect the content as well as the theoretical characteristics of both the withheld (true) and the false (excuse) explanations (see Weiner, Figueroa-Muñoz, & Kakihara, 1991). One grouping includes affiliative contexts, esteem-related excuses, intention as the true cause, and a variety of communicated causes such as other commitment. For example, a person is asked to a party but does not want to spend time with the person issuing the invitation. The rejector then says that he or she has already accepted another invitation. The listener accepts the excuse, thus maintaining his or her self-esteem. The absence of hurt feelings then contributes to a positive relationship.

A second, less prevalent pattern includes affiliative contexts, anger reduction excuses, forgetting as well as intention as the causes, and a variety of causal communications. For example, a person arrives late for a date. The reason was that he or she did not really hurry when getting ready. The individual then states that the traffic was unusually heavy. The listener believes this excuse and anger is reduced. Lack of anger enhances their interpersonal bonding.

Finally, a third grouping consists of achievement contexts, expectancy altering excuses, forgetting and intention among the true causes, and disparate excuses. For example, a student does not complete an assignment on time. He or she actually went to a party instead of doing the assigned paper. The student then reveals that he or she had to work overtime because the boss demanded it on that special occasion. The teacher accepts the excuse, has positive anticipations about the outcome of the next assignment, and continues to have a good relationship with the student.

RELATION TO GENERAL PSYCHOLOGICAL FUNCTIONING: USE BY AT-RISK CHILDREN

When considering the relation between excuse-giving and general psychological functioning, what perhaps first comes to mind is whether there are individuals who are pathological excuse-givers, always denying responsibility for their misdeeds. This tendency then actually is the cause of, contributes to, or may be a correlate of poor general adjustment. Whereas this seems to be a reasonable sup-position, I know of no data that addresses this topic, which appears more ap-propriate for a clinical than for a social psychologist.

There is a somewhat different way to approach the relation between excuse-giving and psychopathology, which is to ask if particular groups follow different rules in excuse communication or perceive cause–consequence associations in a manner that disagrees with normal functioning groups of individuals. This could then produce, or again be a correlate of, interpersonal psychological difficulty.

My colleagues and I (Caprara, Pastorelli, & Weiner, 1990) conducted research guided by the latter paradigm, using Italian school children as subjects. First, two groups of 10- to 12-year-old children were identified: a normal functioning group, and one that was considered at-risk and was currently displaying aggres-sive behaviors. We tested these children in an investigation concerned with ex-cuses. Scenarios were presented that depicted a broken social contract (from Wein-er & Handel, 1985). For example, in one vignette a boy did not show up at a friend's house when he had promised to do so. Controllable and uncontrollable reasons were then provided for the transgression (e.g., "He watched TV instead" versus "His mother would not let him go"). The normal and the at-risk children then rated the extent to which the victim of this social transgression would be angry if these causes were known to him or her. The children were also asked if they would or would not reveal these causes.

Following the logic of the prior discussion, controllable causes were expected to elicit anger and therefore would not be revealed, whereas uncontrollable causes were not expected to evoke anger and therefore should be communicated. However, we wondered if this pattern would be less in evidence for the at-risk children, who might display weaker associations between controllable causes-anticipated anger-response withholding, and uncontrollable causes-anger absence-response revealing, than would the normal functioning children. These deficien-cies could contribute to aggression inasmuch as the at-risk children would be, for example, more likely to expect others to respond inappropriately with anger and more likely to communicate controllable causes that do arouse anger. Such beliefs and behaviors could then initiate a sequence of aggression.

Table 7.6 shows the mean anticipated anger and revealing judgments as a func-tion of the subject population and the controllability of the cause of the broken social contract in this investigation. Examining first the judgments of anticipated anger, the data replicate the established finding that controllable causes are per-ceived to elicit more anger than uncontrollable causes of a broken social agree-ment. In addition, there is an effect of subject population, with at-risk children anticipating more anger from others than do normal children. Hence, not only are these children more aggressive, but they also expect others to be aggressive. Of most importance, there was a Cause X Group interaction. This interaction is traced to the finding that, given controllable causes, the difference in anticipat-ed anger between the two subject populations is relatively equal (3.82 vs. 3.39).

TABLE 7.6
Rated Anticipated Anger and Intention to Withhold or Reveal the Cause
of a Social Transgression as a Function of the Controllability of the
Cause and the Subject Population (At-Risk versus Normal Children)

	At-Risk Children		Normal Children	
	Controllable Cause	Uncontrollable Cause	Controllable Cause	Uncontrollable Cause
Anticipated Anger	3.82	2.38	3.39	1.29
Intention to Reveal	3.95	5.13	3.57	5.36

Note: data from Caprara, Pastorelli, & Weiner, 1990

On the other hand, given uncontrollable causes of the social transgression, there was much greater anger anticipated by the at-risk (2.38) than by the normal children (1.29). Hence, at-risk children have relatively incorrect expectations regarding the actions of others when the excuse is "good" in that it decreases personal blame.

Turning next to the data regarding excuse-revealing, also shown in Table 7.6, there again is a highly significant effect due to the transgression attribution—controllable causes were more likely to be judged as being withheld than uncontrollable causes (or, stated in the converse manner, uncontrollable causes were more likely to be revealed than controllable causes). But at-risk children were marginally more likely to reveal the controllable reasons than were the normal children (3.95 vs. 3.53), whereas the normal children were more likely to reveal uncontrollable causes of the transgression than were the at-risk children (5.36 vs. 5.13). This interaction is consistent with the more adaptive picture than has been painted of the normal than the at-risk children.

In sum, it was documented by Caprara et al. (1990) that at-risk children anticipate more anger from others, particularly when the cause of the transgression was uncontrollable and therefore not the "fault" of the transgressor. In addition, there was a tendency for at-risk children to reveal more controllable or "bad" reasons and fewer uncontrollable or "good" reasons than the normal functioning children. Thus, children at-risk appear less functional in their use and understanding of excuses (although they certainly still adhere to the general attribution-emotion-behavior patterns). Caprara et al. (1990) therefore proposed that dysfunctional cognitive interpretations of the social world and consequent emotional reactions could provide clues to the understanding of aggressive behavior. One avenue to search for shortcomings in the cognitive-emotional-behavioral sequence is in the study of excuse-giving.

GENERAL CONCLUSION

Often studies of impression management have focused on the distinctions between the various strategies that are used to influence others, such as denial, confession, and so on. In this chapter, I tried to progress from taxonomic considerations and description to a detailed analysis of one particular communication strategy—conveying an excuse.

Excuse-giving is a powerful interpersonal tool, effective in its goals of maintaining bonding. Attribution theory enabled us to understand that the roots of this effectiveness can be traced to the structural properties of excuses and the association between these causal properties and their linkages to affect and to expectancy. Excuses thus can be incorporated within a larger theoretical network involving the rules of phenomenal causality, and this tie with general social psychological theory has fostered our comprehension of both everyday, normal functioning and maladaptive patterns of responding.

REFERENCES

Averill, J. A. (1983). Studies on anger and aggression. *American Psychologist, 38,* 1145-1160.

Caprara, G. V., Pastorelli, T., & Weiner, B. (1990). *A social-cognitive approach to the understanding of at-risk children.* Unpublished manuscript, University of Rome, Italy.

Cody, M. J., & McLaughlin, M. L. (1988). Accounts on trial: Oral arguments in traffic court. In C. Antaki (Ed.), *Analyzing everyday explanation: A casebook of methods* (pp. 113-126). London: Sage.

Cody, M. J., & McLaughlin, M. L. (1990). Introduction. In M. J. Cody & M. L. McLaughlin (Eds.), *The psychology of tactical communication* (pp. 1-28). Clevedon, England: Multilingual Matters Ltd.

Ekman, P. (1984). *Telling lies.* New York: Norton.

Folkes, V. S. (1982). Communicating the causes of social rejection. *Journal of Experimental Social Psychology, 18,* 235-252.

Schonbach, P. (1980). A category system for account phases. *European Journal of Social Psychology, 10,* 195-200.

Snyder, C. R., & Higgins, R. L. (1988). Excuses: Their effective role in the negotiation of reality. *Psychological Bulletin, 104,* 23-35.

Weiner, B. (1986). *An attributional theory of motivation and emotion.* New York: Springer-Verlag.

Weiner, B., Amirkhan, J., Folkes, V. S., & Verette, J. A. (1987). An attributional analysis of excuse giving: Studies of a naive theory of emotion. *Journal of Personality and Social Psychology, 52,* 316-324.

Weiner, B., Figueroa-Muñoz, A., & Kakihara, C. (1991). The goals of excuses and communication strategies related to causal perceptions. *Personality and Social Psychology Bulletin, 17,* 4-13.

Weiner, B., Graham, S., & Chandler, C. C. (1982). Causal antecedents of pity, anger, and guilt. *Personality and Social Psychology Bulletin, 8,* 226-232.

Weiner, B., Graham, S., Peter, O., & Zmuidinas, M. (1991). Public confession and forgiveness. *Journal of Personality, 59,* 281-312.

Weiner, B., & Handel, S. (1985). Anticipated emotional consequences of causal communications and reported communication strategy. *Developmental Psychology, 21,* 102-107.

Yirmiya, N., & Weiner, B. (1986). Perceptions of controllability and anticipated anger. *Cognitive Development, 1,* 273-280.

II

Explanations and Social Contexts

8

▼▼▼▼▼▼▼

Legal Fictions: Telling Stories and Doing Justice

W. Lance Bennett
University of Washington

The role of stories in social explanation has been analyzed in fields as diverse as psychology (Hastie, Penrod, & Pennington, 1983; Rumelhart, 1975; Wilensky, 1983), sociolinguistics (Sacks, 1972), political science (Bennett & Edelman, 1985), history (White, 1984), anthropology (American Ethnological Society, 1988; Clifford & Marcus, 1986), law (White, 1985), communications (Fisher, 1985, 1987) and economics (McClosky, 1985). The explanatory power of narrative has also been recognized in popular intellectual circles, heralded by the Public Broadcasting System's "Joseph Campbell and the Power of Myth" (Moyers, 1987) and the subsequent appearance of Campbell's works on national best-seller lists. In more recent days, a prominent national magazine published a debate by a group of leading Democrats who agreed on little else but the fact that the party needed a "new story" to explain itself to the people (Hitt, 1990).

It is particularly gratifying to see the passage from academy to society occurring with my own work, co-authored with Martha Feldman, on storytelling in criminal trials (Bennett, 1978, 1979; Bennett & Feldman, 1981). The idea that jurors' legal judgments are derived from narrated constructions of evidence and testimony has been greeted with academic responses (Jackson, 1988; King, 1986; Twining, 1987), attention in lawyers' professional magazines (e.g., Call, 1986), and coverage in law school textbooks on trial advocacy (Berger, Mitchell, & Clark, 1988; Berger, Mitchell, & Clark, 1989). This chapter carries on both the theoretical and the applied branches of this dialogue by exploring what makes lawyers' courtroom explanations either more or less "hearable" (knowledgeably decidable) by jurors.

Many of the issues here are similar to problems raised in the knowledge-structure approach to social reasoning (see, for example, Schank & Abelson, 1977, and Read, 1987). While formal models of scripts, scenarios, and schemas are useful for refining specific conceptual issues (particularly through artificial intelligence and experimental applications), there remains a unique virtue to using narratives or, more simply, stories as a theoretical framework for analysis. To put it simply, stories are intelligible to both academic and lay audiences. On the one hand, stories can be highly formalized for theoretical purposes, as shown by the work of Propp (1968), for example. At the same time, stories are presentable to every day actors as commonsense accounts of what they are doing in particular situations.

This is not to say that more abstract knowledge-structure approaches represent mutually exclusive alternatives to narrative formulations. On the contrary; many "causal scenarios" (Read, 1987) when elaborated in social contexts quickly become recognizable as stories. Indeed, one can define *story* or *narrative* as a causally (or at least temporally) organizable sequence of events, moved by human actions toward a point of interpretive ambiguity, followed by a more or less satisfactory resolution of that interpretive issue. Consider, in a similar fashion, our (Bennett & Feldman, 1981) proposition that jurors reach legal verdicts by "mapping" categories of legal instructions provided by judges onto the narrative categories that emerge from courtroom testimony and argument. This idea has been developed usefully through the more formalized approach of Pennington & Hastie (1986). Likewise, our structural explanation of what makes stories coherent and believable (Bennett and Feldman, 1981) can be linked fruitfully to Thagard's (1989) principles of "explanatory coherence."

In addition to productive connections between narrative theory and knowledge structure models, there also are important ties to be established between our broad propositions about narrative "logic" and the more finely detailed approaches of discourse analysis in both simulated and real legal settings (e.g., Conley & O'Barr, 1990). For example the work of Aronsson and colleagues (Adelsward, Aronsson, & Linell, 1988; Aronsson & Nilholm, 1990; Aronsson & Nilholm, this volume) demonstrates how narratives are constructed, negotiated, and defended in group legal decision contexts. A logical next step is to link up the broad narrative strategies used by lawyers with the discourse patterns and dilemmas encountered by juries and other legal decision makers.

All of this said, this chapter continues developing earlier ideas about how narratives cohere and where they break down as explanations of legally disputed social actions. In particular, the present discussion looks at lawyers' practical explanatory problems in constructing legal cases as hearable stories for lay jurors. These practical problems further illustrate the above-mentioned merits of using narrative as an analytical framework: namely, the capacity to develop theory based on critical inputs both from formalized academic approaches and from the results of lawyers' practical applications of storytelling in legal training and trial advocacy. First, a brief review of the main points from our earlier research is in order.

A BRIEF OVERVIEW
OF THE STORYTELLING APPROACH

The central point of our earlier work (Bennett, 1978, 1979; Bennett & Feldman, 1981) can be summarized as follows: Jurors "hear" a case by assembling a narrative about what happened. Competing stories emerge from the chaotic proceedings of the trial. Thus, lawyers who understand the explanatory power of stories tend to fashion their opening and closing remarks as narratives and try to fit evidence and testimony during the trial into those narrative frameworks. The goal is to explain what happened in a dispute in a way that helps jurors draw conclusions favorable to the case. Through comparison and synthesis of the main plot lines and multiple subplots that emerge from testimony, lay persons (e.g., jurors) are able to judge what happened and then decide its legal significance. Some of the main points to emerge from our analyses of cases and simulations of storytelling with actual audiences are the following:

1. Stories enable people (in this case, jurors) to manipulate complex and often disjointed bodies of information into decidable explanations.

2. The "structure of coherence" in these "everyday narrative theories" (about what happened in a disputed legal case) revolves around the central plot action. Everyday familiarity with narrative structure makes it possible for hearers to decide what the central (interpretive) plot ambiguity is (i.e., the disputed criminal activity) and interpret that action in relation to logical and empirical connections with other plot elements. As mentioned earlier, Thagard's (1989) work is a complementary addition to these problems of coherence and belief.

3. Both narrative coherence and assignments of belief or "truth" are problematical because complex stories often require rich background understandings that jurors and lawyers may not have. Judgments about truth and coherence also may be problematical because basic forms of narration itself may vary from one language community or subculture to another, leading to communication breakdowns between lawyers, witnesses, defendants and jurors. *One implication of this to be explored in the present discussion is how lawyers (who are aware of the requisite background assumptions and narrative conventions) can "educate" juries to better hear otherwise puzzling accounts.*

4. Because of the above difficulties in disentangling coherence, plausibility, and "truth," there is little or no correlation between the actual truth-status ("facticity") of a story and its ultimate believability for a second-hand audience. Truth lies (so to speak) in coherence first, and supporting evidence second.

5. Final verdicts result from mapping the legal categories of judge's instruc-

tions onto the narrative framework itself. (See the useful elaboration of this in Pennington & Hastie, 1986).

As these generalizations suggest, a narrative theory of justice frees our understandings about law and legal judgment from positivistic notions of "truth" and "objectivity," revealing, instead, a rich process of persuasion and symbolic construction in which courtroom dramaturgy has considerable influence. Storytelling also helps explain how an "objective," or truth-seeking process can operate in the frequent absence of agreement among the accounts of witnesses, the accused, and victims.

JUST STORIES

What jurors hear in court are at once "just stories," and at the same time, stories that carry the added weight of having to "do justice" as part of the process of interpreting them. Narrative thus becomes a useful bridge between common sense and formal judgment, as well as a bridge between ordinary explanation processes and those special explanations that carry the added burden of justice with them.

Viewing justice processes as narrated social constructions, or "legal fictions," thus addresses both the inner workings and the problematic nature of social explanation in legal judgment. Introducing a realistic element of uncertainty into the legal explanation process sharpens our understanding of what is perhaps the major concern about law in society: the nature of injustice. The legal requirement that juries distill a single narrative reality from the multiple, often conflicting accounts presented in a trial explains why injustice is part and parcel of the justice process. In other social contexts that rely on narrative accounts, discrepant realities are more likely to be tolerated and, in some cases, even celebrated. For example, spouses may learn to live with differing versions of shared experiences, at times bridging the reality gap with playful humor, sometimes indulging in ritualized bickering, and occasionally advancing contradictory accounts as evidence of mutual independence and strength of character. By contrast, courtroom pressures to reach a verdict can result in the denial or distortion of personal experiences, leaving participants with little sense of vindication. In extreme cases, even those who "win" their days in court may walk away unsatisfied that their stories have been told—or heard—adequately (e.g., Conley & O'Barr, 1988). Beyond what it may tell us about legal explanation, then, the analysis of storytelling in trials offers insights about justice and injustice as people actually experience them.

The forms of injustice that may be linked to narrative explanations in the courtroom can be much more subtle than the overt prejudices that jurors and judges may hold against minorities, women, or the poor. This is not to say that racism, sexism, or class prejudices do not enter the justice process directly as corrupting influences. They do. However, the ability of lawyers to screen prospective jurors, combined with growing social awareness of overt expressions of prejudice, make it hard to reconcile large numbers of well-meaning, conscientious jurors with the equally high numbers of poor and minority defendants who experience injustice in the legal process. Operating beneath the surface of prejudice in society are great and incomprehensible gaps in social reality. These multiple realities make it difficult for people to communicate and understand how disputed activities might have occurred. Injustices often flow from procedurally correct legal explanations not only because people experience the same situation differently, but also because they may have trouble communicating about their disparate realities. Narratives that make perfect sense to one audience may seem ludicrous or implausible to another. This is why "a jury of one's peers" is at once an indispensable precept of justice and, at the same time, often impossible to realize in a heterogeneous, impersonal modern society.

As noted earlier, the primary goal of this essay is to understand the broad outlines of how lawyers develop and defend the stories they offer as explanations to juries. Given the ambiguities of narration and interpretation in a polarized setting like the courtroom, it is difficult to separate theoretical questions about how justice is done from questions about where injustice enters the process. Put most bluntly, I will argue that the nature of legal explanation in American society contains the seeds of injustice itself.

Since this is a delicate point, let me make one thing perfectly clear. The implication of this argument is not that we should dispense with narratives or otherwise change the current procedures for "doing justice." Rather, there are two other normative implications of this analysis. First, it is useful to draw attention to the disparities between idealized assumptions about justice and the practical realities encountered by many people who seek justice. Second, by recognizing these disparities, lawyers can try to adjust the way they present stories to juries in an effort to compensate for potential injustices in specific cases. These normative points merit brief elaboration because they tie the model of explanation developed here to practical, real world applications: namely, the crafting of legal explanations aimed at reducing the incidence of "routine" (i.e., communication-related) injustice in trials.

As suggested, a key normative problem that our empirical theory can address is the founding assumption of the justice process itself: that defendants will be judged by juries of their peers. This romantic notion, with origins in earlier times and simpler places, assumes a uniformity of social experience, language, and communication skills that is hard to find in noncommunitarian, heterogeneous societies. However, dispensing with stories would not solve the problem; far from it. Narratives are the only conceivable means for ordinary people to use in organizing, recalling, comparing, and testing the vast amounts of information that go into American-style legal judgments. Moreover, they are the only obvious means of bridging the gap between the commonsense, experiential understandings of jurors and the abstract legal categories in which judgments must be announced. This is where the empirical and normative aspects of our theory come together. Stories are an inseparable part of legal explaining, yet it is in perfectly good story explanations that injustice can be done. Because stories are not "optional" (i.e., juries will reconstruct cases in narrative terms even when lawyers are unaware that storytelling is going on at all), it becomes important for lawyers to understand the uses and effects of the kind of explanations they are building. Thus, a second normative contribution of this essay is to show that when lawyers develop a conscious understanding of their roles as chief storytellers in trials, they are in a much better position to recognize and prevent the injustices that may result when the right story is heard by the wrong jury. We will return to this point later.

STORIES IN THEORY AND PRACTICE

Whereas our earlier work dealt primarily with the ways in which stories are heard and misheard by juries, this essay puts the emphasis on the role of lawyers as storytellers. This shift from how juries hear stories to how lawyers both tell them and orchestrate their telling through witnesses is a step toward a more complete empirical and normative theory of what goes on in the trial justice process.

This analysis of legal explanation giving addresses three very different kinds of explanatory problems that must be handled within a single narrative framework:

1. The problem of developing a narrative to fit a lawyer's "case theory," which defines the defendant's actions in terms of law, evidence, anticipated strategies of the opposition, and probable instructions of the judge to the jury.

2. The problem of anticipating and responding to the complexity of courtroom proceedings in which a narrative may be damaged as it runs into ambiguous evidence; poor performances by key witnesses; and "noise" introduced by conflicting or confusing testimony, sheer volume of information, multiple plots and subplots, and obfuscating maneuvers by the opposition.

3. The problem of having to "educate" a jury of "non-peers" about the world of the defendant.

These areas represent the major kinds of "work" that defense lawyers must do in order to construct successful explanations. First, they must transform legal cases into commonsense, narrative terms. Then, the chosen narrative must be guided safely through the often confusing maze of opponent attacks and witness testimony during the trial. In the process, lawyers must anticipate (and correct) problems the jury may have understanding and believing the story or drawing the proper conclusions from it. These troublesome aspects of courtroom storytelling have been raised in a series of very helpful responses to our earlier work, most notably from legal scholars William Twining (1987) and Bernard Jackson (1988), and in stimulating conversations with Alan Kirtley and John Mitchell, two lawyers who have used narrative theory to train lawyers in courtroom advocacy techniques.[1] To simplify the analysis of these three "problem areas" in legal explanations, the following discussion takes the point of view of an ideal-type (i.e., unusually self-conscious) defense lawyer. The implications for complementary prosecution cases should be easy to derive from the analysis.

Turning Case Theories into Stories

Consider, first, the problem of how stories about everyday life fit into the rarefied context of law and evidence normally associated with lawyers' case theories. Twining pointed out that it is not obvious from our earlier work how lawyers develop a narrative from the starting point of a legal theory of a case. Classical accounts of case construction, Twining goes on to argue, tend to regard narrative strategies as incidental or inferior elements in the grand scheme of inductive logic that draws evidence into the legal reasoning process. For example, the "scientific" case construction approach of John Henry Wigmore (1937) introduced a "chart method" to replace the crude "narrative method" of laying out the logic of a case for presentation to the jury. Wigmore relegated the narrative method of case construction to the standing of an inferior alternative. However, Twining pointed out that it is virtually impossible to use Wigmore's method of case construction without resorting at least implicitly to narrative formulations of strategic "logical" choices, thus suggesting a complementarity between narrative and legal reasoning in case construction. At the same time, he concluded that our earlier emphasis on narrative went too far in the other direction, obscuring the important question of how a lawyer trained in legal reasoning translates technical matters of fact and law into a story for the jury. Fair enough.

The answer, I think, can be found in the practical model of trial advocacy advanced by Berger, Mitchell, & Clark (1988). Expanding on our earlier work, they argued that a case theory consists of two parts: a legal theory and a factual theory. The legal theory is an interpretation of legal rulings that seem relevant to the dispute. The factual theory defines the facts in the case in a way that supports the most desirable legal theory. The lawyer plays law and facts off against each other until a legal theory and a factual theory fit snugly together in a hypothetico-deductive relationship of the form, "If the facts exist as alleged, the client is legally entitled to the relief sought" (p. 17).

---

[1]I would like to acknowledge many valuable conversations with Kirtley and Mitchell. Their "lawyers' reactions" combined with their sensitive understandings of the narrative perspective provided just the kind of cross-disciplinary dialogue that is required to build good theory. John B. Mitchell has served as Director of Legal Training at the Seattle law firm of Perkins Coie and teaches at the University of Puget Sound School of Law. Alan Kirtley is Senior Lecturer at the University of Washington School of Law and Supervising Attorney at the University of Washington Civil Law Clinic.

Where do stories come into the picture? The answer is that the lawyer's factual theory *is* a story. Since facts can only be defined and evaluated in relation to one another, there must be an interpretive framework that both structures the facts and gives them a common meaning that can be judged according to the legal theory of the case. The authors tell law students reading their book that this framework is "more than an accumulation of relevant information. To be sure, it is constructed from the mass of information you have and which you might subsequently obtain to support your legal theory. It is, nonetheless, a 'story' and you must always think of it that way" (p. 22).

In response to Twining, then, a story evolves as a full complement to a legal theory, constituting the factual component of a theory of the case. As various legal theories are considered, different stories are fashioned from the facts to test the fit between alternative legal interpretations and the evidence. Consider, for example, the hypothetical case of a defendant charged with robbery. He has been identified by three witnesses as the driver of the getaway car following the hold-up of a convenience store. The legal theory in this case is fairly straightforward: the defendant was aiding and abetting the robbery, and therefore he is subject to prosecution on armed robbery charges.

There are two theoretical questions for the defense attorney at this point: Does the evidence in the case support a factual theory that disconnects the defendant from knowing involvement in the crime? Alternately, are there weaknesses in the available evidence and testimony that warrant the defense strategy of not putting the defendant on the stand at all, while playing up "reasonable doubts" about the prosecution theory of the case? Working between available evidence and possible narrative constructions, we see that two of the "classic defenses" clearly do not apply in this particular case. One factual theory quickly dismissed is "mistaken identity." That is, the defendant is not the same person who drove the car. In this case there are three convincing witnesses, all of whom are sure they saw the defendant drive out of a well-lit parking lot. Nor can the defendant provide a convincing alibi about what he was doing on the night in question, if not driving the car. A second "classical" theory is that the defendant was forced at gunpoint to drive the car and had reason to fear for his life if he refused. The trouble with this story is that a witness from the defendant's neighborhood will testify that the defendant and his two passengers were laughing and joking in a neighbor's front yard before they got into the car and drove off. Scratch story number two. (Note: The implication here is not that lawyers run through a list of stories in hopes of finding one that fits the facts. This would, at the very least, be unethical. Moreover, representing the narrative construction process in this way would play into unflattering popular stereotypes about how lawyers operate. All of this said, there is, it seems to me, an obvious interplay that must go on between the available evidence and familiar narrative framings for that evidence. Out of this "narrative testing" of evidence comes a lawyer's sense of the strength of a case, the pitfalls of a chosen defense, and the best rhetorical – that is, storytelling – strategy for constructing "the facts" in the case.)

A third narrative framing both fits with and emerges from the evidence well enough to provide a defensible factual theory. The defendant swears that he never saw the two robbers before the evening of the crime. He met them at the neighbor's house, and they seemed friendly when he joked with them. When he was ready to leave for a drive around town, they asked if they could come, too. He said yes. After driving around for a half an hour or so on a hot summer night, one of them suggested pulling into the convenience store to get something to drink. The defendant parked on the side of the store, thus making it impossible to see what the two men were doing inside. He sat in the car listening to the radio until they came back with a bag of sodas. They got in and he drove off. They went back to the neighborhood where the two men thanked him for the ride and walked off down the street. He didn't see where they went. An hour later, the police arrived (after tracing his license plate) and arrested him.

Once he or she decides that this story provides a good fit between the evidence and the legal theory of the crime, the lawyer is ready to confront the next explanatory problem: how to guide the story safely through all the complexities of the trial. Opposition challenges, weak or implausible testimony, secondary stories introduced by witnesses, and many other distractions in the courtroom can make it difficult for the jury to hear the primary story clearly. The problem for the lawyer becomes how to steer the story safely through this maze of distracting information.

Protecting the Story During the Trial

In his helpful criticisms of our earlier work, Bernard Jackson (1988, Ch. 3) raised two important questions. First, how do we explain the emergence of a dominant narrative from the confusion of information and competing stories introduced by witnesses during a trial? Second, what effect does all this distracting and often conflicting information have on the dominant story?

The overriding answer to these questions is that listeners assemble stories by finding the most general plots that subsume the lesser subplots. Competing plots can then be compared to see how well they contain the same information and how they hold together under various sorts of informational strain and conflict. Lawyers play the key role in managing the information load on a plot. In this process, the juror's prior familiarity with a "deep grammar" of stock legal plots surely comes into play to help recognize the narrative possibilities within the trial discourse. However, I do not think that evoking these familiar plots is as tricky as Jackson seems to imply. Rather, I propose that the key explanatory challenge is to sustain and defend a preferred narrative line once it has been evoked (in opening remarks, for example).

As each bit of information is introduced in subsequent testimony, the lawyer must guide it into context, exerting considerable influence on the way potentially flawed or overly complex stories are heard. Needless to say, some lawyers are only minimally aware of the relationship between evidence, testimony, and narrative, thus leaving jurors to draw their own inferences from weak testimony and structurally confusing story lines. However, lawyers who see the importance of narrative can contextualize uneasy bits of information in two ways: first, by *preparing* juries (both during *voir dire* and in opening remarks) to hear dissonant information before witnesses deliver it, and, second, by *repairing* any damage done during the trial.

Anticipated "problems" with story structure or content can be addressed by "preparing" the jury. Damaging juror biases and useful commonsense insights can be flagged while jurors are screened and selected during *voir dire*. During opening remarks, lawyers can tell the complete story to the jury, offering it as an information-processing framework to use in keeping track of the mass of information about to follow. To the extent that damaging witnesses and strong counterstories can be anticipated, juries can be prepared for hearing them. For example, the lawyer in our hypothetical case might warn the jury that they are about to hear three sincere and truthful witnesses identify the defendant as the driver of the car. The jury must remember, however, that in order to find the defendant guilty he had to know what he was doing. Thus, being the driver of the car in no way establishes an intent to rob the store. The lawyer might further prepare the jury to hear the accusation that the defendant parked on the side of the building because he didn't want to be seen driving the car. This is absurd, the defense lawyer might contend, because the store is so busy that people are always milling about in the parking lot. There were, after all, three witnesses who saw the defendant driving away. No, the defendant parked on the side of the store simply because all the spaces in front were full. And for that reason, he didn't know about the robbery until he was arrested later that night.

No matter how well a lawyer prepares a jury to hear a story in a particular way, there will almost always be weak or damaging testimony that requires on-the-spot "repair" work. Suppose, for example, the neighbor is called to the stand to testify that the defendant met the two men at her house for the first time on the night of the robbery. Unfortunately, the neighbor adds an ambiguous element not contained in her pretrial statement. Although she cannot specifically remember them meeting before, it seems that the two men and the defendant were having a "very friendly" conversation about sports. Suddenly a bit of ambiguous testimony invites speculation that their meeting might not have been spontaneous, after all. One way to repair this problem would be to ask the witnesses if that particular conversation contained any specific references that might distinguish it from the kind of conversation that any men (including strangers) might have about a subject as general as sports. Perhaps the judge would permit calling a very close friend of the defendant's to testify about past contact between the defendant and the robbers (although this strategy probably would be ruled inadmissible). A final bit of repair work might involve reinforcing the preferred interpretation of the ambiguous testimony during closing remarks. In this way, a strong narrative line can be preserved amidst the complex web of testimony, opposition maneuvers, subplots, and uneven witness credibility.

Another word is in order here on Jackson's (1988) concern about how the relationship is developed between the narrative "whole" and the multitude of informational "parts" in a trial. Talking about rhetorical "preparing" and "repairing" may not satisfy his interest in how lawyers engage or call on the "deep grammar" structures that select and organize information during a story's telling. I agree that structural theories of the sort proposed by Propp (1968), by Jackson (1985) in his adaptation of Greimas, by Mandler and Johnson (1977), and Wilensky (1983) explain how people can "recognize" a familiar story plot amidst the chaos of a trial. It is clear that lawyers routinely make use of a "folklore" of familiar crime plots to serve as "deep" structural models or grammars to constrain the idiosyncratic evidence of a given case. Indeed, a bit of research that should be done is to parallel Propp's work on Russian folktales with a similar generative plot analysis of a given culture's "crime and justice tales." One suspects that under the blooming, buzzing confusion of specific legal incidents there is a greatly reduced set of generic plots that lawyers and jurors intuitively search and use in building explanations of a given case. Among the plots that come immediately to mind are mistaken identity, accidental commission of a harmful act, ignorance, victim of circumstances, and wrongful behavior forced against the defendant's will. But the general point for this discussion is that the explanatory challenge is not in bringing these plots to mind. It is easy to evoke any of these deep plot outlines either through extensive "plotting" during opening or closing remarks, or with even the most minimal cues and references imbedded within questions put to witnesses. Surely the ensuing confusions and sheer information load in a trial may weaken an evoked plot line. However, I suspect that the problems created by fragmentary testimony or noncredible witnesses seldom affect the "recognition" of a story, but bear, instead, on its believability. In other words, when a witness appears to be confused or lying, what is normally damaged is not the "deep structural" form of the offered explanation (i.e., the story plot) but its credibility.

In most trials, the jury will "recognize" the plot outlines of the competing stories as soon as the opening remarks are delivered. These salient models are not likely to be driven easily out of mind, but they are subject to minute-to-minute refutation and skepticism. For this reason, an analysis of deep grammar structures may tell us less about the effects of particular events during a trial than will an analysis of the techniques lawyers use to prepare and repair damage to the credibility of the narrative.

Educating the Jury

There are cases in which repairing specific plot elements does little to enhance the overall plausibility of the story. Some stories simply raise questions about "whether things like this ever happen in the real world." That is, jurors may understand perfectly well what the defense is claiming, but have trouble imagining such goings-on. The internal structure or consistency of these accounts may be less important than juror assessment of the odds that the described events happen in the world they know and live in. The problem of explanation here requires the lawyer to educate jurors familiar only with their own social reality about the patterns of life and the probabilities of events in the defendant's world.

Consider the possible problems presented in our hypothetical case. Suppose that the issue of prior contact between the defendant and the gunmen has been handled well by the lawyer (e.g., several witnesses testify that the men were never seen in the same circles before the night of the robbery). Suddenly, a new problem is created – particularly if the jury comes from a white, middle class suburban world, and the defendant, say, belongs to an urban ethnic subculture – not with the deep grammar structure of the story, but with the particular variant offered in the defense case. That is, the jury can perfectly well understand and believe the *possibility* of someone getting caught up in wrongdoing without being aware of what was happening. The trouble is, they might not buy the particular circumstances in this case because they are not easily imaginable in the white suburban world. In that world, people do not meet total strangers on the street and invite them for a drive around town. Thus, the lawyer faces a dilemma: the more successfully he or she removes doubts about whether the men knew each other before the incident, the more the entire story enters the realm of the unimaginable and improbable. In other words, a jury might buy the idea that innocent bystanders can get caught up in crimes, but not buy the idea that it can happen like this.

The lawyer is faced with the challenge of "educating" the jury to accept the idea that chance encounters among strangers in some social worlds may result in subsequent activities that probably would not develop in the jurors' worlds. Moreover, this education must convey the idea that these differences are just that: differences. Not signs of guilt or some other suspect motivation, but simply naturally occurring differences in lifestyles. The problem with developing this background knowledge in a trial is that the assumption of a jury of peers implies that commonsense realities are shared by jurors and defendant alike and, therefore, lifestyle differences should not become issues in court. Whereas lawyers may call expert witnesses to educate juries about uncommon background knowledge in technical areas like medicine or engineering, it is generally more difficult to qualify a sociologist or anthropologist as an expert witness to explain variations in social norms and customs across subcultures in the same society.

Yet the successful outcome of our hypothetical case may well depend on a jury's accepting the idea that in some neighborhoods people may meet on the street and spend the rest of the evening socializing together. And some of those people may well be carrying guns. And they may not know where the others live. They may not even bother to ask or remember names.

In some cases, a lawyer may be able to convince a judge early on that educating the jury about social norms in the defendant's world is crucial for accepting the idea that an otherwise well-documented story could have happened at all. Perhaps an open-minded judge would allow a sociologist, a social worker, a minister, or an anthropologist to be called as an expert witness. More likely, however, the lawyer will not think of it, or the judge will not hear of it, and the lawyer is forced to educate the jury during opening and closing remarks.

Various educational strategies suggest themselves in this case. To begin with, it is easy to point out that this sort of behavior occurs all the time, that it is a perfectly accepted mode of social contact, and that it rarely ends up in armed robberies. In other words, the defendant was doing nothing unusual and surely had no reason to suspect the gunmen of being anything but friendly strangers interested in a ride around town. Perhaps the normative implication here can be brought even closer to home. Parents on the jury may be reminded that this sort of social encounter may be similar to what their own children do at the shopping mall or while cruising. The point not being to elicit approval, but to spark some recognition that this kind of thing "happens." Sometimes it happens without leading necessarily to any criminal outcomes, and at other times innocent children get caught up unwittingly in crimes committed by their cohorts. Let us draw the normative parallels even closer to home. Isn't it possible that members of the jury have met total strangers, say at a cocktail party, and spent a pleasant evening with them without ever knowing their names or worrying about their backgrounds? We are talking about the same kind of social encounter here, but one that just happens to occur differently in different subcultures.

If successful, these educational efforts can provide the normative understanding necessary for jurors to see a particular defense story as an acceptable variant of some commonly understood plot within the cultural story grammar. Such education is often crucial to the success of narrative explanation. Even a well-structured, well-defended story can fall on deaf ears if audiences lack the background information to interpret it or to regard it as "possible" in the same "real world" they know and live in.

JUST STORIES (REVISITED)

All of this brings us back to the question of justice. In many cases, explanations may not be accepted by juries simply because they are unfamiliar with background knowledge or the narrative style required to find a particular narrative coherent and consistent with a body of evidence. Lawyers face an unusual set of dilemmas in educating juries. The most basic obstacle, of course, is that lawyers may be unaware or only dimly aware that their courtroom arguments must satisfy the above requirements of narrative presentation. Beyond this, even "aware" lawyers may not know much about the social world or the language community to which their clients belong. In the best of cases, this means that lawyers must learn about these things before devising an educational strategy for jurors. In the worst of cases (e.g., overloaded public defenders), this self-education may be too much to ask.

Yet the fact remains that the basic link between ordinary stories and the narratives that must "do justice" is making sure the audience can hear the story adequately. It is ironic that this turns out to be more difficult in the courtroom than in many, and perhaps most, everyday life settings. Indeed, people in a variety of social settings do this sort of education all the time when it is not clear that audiences will draw the right inferences from otherwise well-crafted stories. For example, a television comedian began a story about the Donald and Ivana Trump marriage battle by educating the audience about the fact that Ivana was Czechoslovakian. It then became possible to deliver the joke: "I bet this is the first time anybody as rich as Donald Trump ever bounced a check (Czech)!" As this example from television indicates, the "social realities" against which people judge narratives need not be their own immediate experience. People may receive their social models through a variety of media like television dramas and the news, all of which can make the grounds for social prejudice and misunderstanding more subtle and pervasive (e.g., "realistic" stereotypes of criminals and victims portrayed in various popular culture forms). At the same time, however, the receptiveness of jurors to mediated social experiences provides room for lawyers who are versed in strategies of narration to use storytelling techniques to educate jurors in the ways of hearing those stories. (I am indebted to Bernard Jackson for bringing these points to my attention in a personal correspondence.)

As the example of the television comedian suggests, without the addition of a missing piece of background information, a communicated message (in this case, a joke) can be virtually uninterpretable. Similarly, without important bits of background information about defendants' worlds, otherwise well crafted stories would be hard for jurors to make sense of. The explanatory dilemma, of course, is that there may be little difference in a juror's mind between a story that falls apart due to weak evidence or noncredible witnesses and one that suffers due to a lack of social understandings. Both may result in unfavorable verdicts.

CONCLUSION

What, then, is the role of narrative theory in understanding stories as legal explanations? Theories of narrative, particularly grammar structure theories, are important first of all for understanding how lawyers select a single narrative out of all the possible "factual theories" that might apply to a particular collection of evidence and legal charges. Then, after the trial begins, the deep structure of a story may be helpful in deciding how damaging a particular bit of weak testimony really is—a judgment that will help determine how much time and energy to put into the rhetorical repair process. In our earlier work (Bennett & Feldman, 1981) we showed that the impact of weak or noncredible elements of stories becomes greater the more closely those elements are connected to the central action of the plot. The central action corresponds to the alleged criminal activity disputed in the trial. While reference to the underlying story structure (of "deep" cultural justice tale) may help lawyers estimate the degree of potential interpretive damage caused by any particular event in a trial, controlling that damage is less likely to involve work on the story structure than on the weak element itself. Juries are not likely to forget the story or to have problems distinguishing a central story from lesser ones. Rather, they are likely to have trouble believing particular elements of the main story. These elements require rhetorical attention if the explanation is to work.

If, after any necessary preparation and repair work is done, the whole story is the thing that seems out of focus or hard to understand, then the explanatory problem is not one of simple witness credibility or weak evidence. The trouble is more likely to involve basic background understandings that are not shared by juror and defendant. In this case, the lawyer must educate jurors about norms or other background understandings they need to know in order to recognize the defendant's case as a plausible variant of some familiar cultural plot structure.

This distinction between repairing weak elements in an otherwise familiar story and making a "strange" story plausible has subtle but crucial implications for justice and injustice. Whether or not weak or contested story elements can be repaired is fundamentally a question about truth, which is the proper concern of legal explanations. On the other hand, when a story simply cannot be heard by a jury as a reasonable variant of some familiar cultural plot, we have entered a dark area of injustice. Juries are not supposed to experience judgment dilemmas of the latter sort because panels are supposed to be composed of "peers" from social backgrounds similar to the defendant's. Yet it is precisely the difficulty of matching up peers in a heterogeneous society that confounds the former type of explanatory problem with the latter.

In the process of building an adequate courtroom explanation, then, lawyers must be prepared to employ three very different types of storytelling operations: choosing a story that provides a good structural fit between the facts and the legal issues in the case; preparing and repairing weak elements in that story; and educating jurors who may lack the relevant background knowledge to believe or even to understand the story at all. Only when a narrative is adequate on all three levels does its use as a courtroom explanation satisfy the ideals of justice in (American) society.

ACKNOWLEDGMENT

I would like to thank the editors, particularly Steven Read, for their very helpful criticisms and suggestions. Alan Kirtley and John Mitchell have also provided valuable insights by using the framework presented here in training lawyers in narrative methods of trial advocacy.

REFERENCES

Adelsward, V., Aronsson, K., & Linell, P. (1988). Discourse of blame: Courtroom construction of social identity from the perspective of the defendant. *Semiotica, 71*, 261–284.

American Ethnological Society (1988, March). *Narrative resources for the creation and mediation of conflict.* Annual meeting, St. Louis, MO.

Aronsson, K., & Nilholm, C. (1990). On memory and the collaborative construction and deconstruction of custody case arguments. *Human Communication Research, 12*, 289–314.

Bennett, W. L. (1978). Storytelling in criminal trials: A model of social judgment. *Quarterly Journal of Speech, 64*, 1–22.

Bennett, W. L. (1979). Rhetorical transformation of evidence in criminal trials: Creating grounds for legal judgment. *Quarterly Journal of Speech, 65*, 311–323.

Bennett, W. L., & Edelman, M. (1985). Toward a new political narrative. *Journal of Communication, 35*, 156–171.

Bennett, W. L., & Feldman, M. S. (1981). *Reconstructing reality in the courtroom: Justice and judgment in American culture.* New Brunswick, NJ: Rutgers University Press.

Berger, M., Mitchell, J., & Clark, R. (1988). *Pre-trial advocacy: Planning, analysis and strategy.* Boston: Little, Brown.

Berger, M., Mitchell, J., & Clark, R. (1989). *Trial advocacy: Planning, analysis and strategy.* Boston: Little, Brown.

Call, J. A. (1986, November). The trial as story. *Trial, 84*, 6–9.

Clifford, J., & Marcus, G. E. (Eds.). (1986). *Writing culture: The poetics and politics of ethnography.* Berkeley: University of California Press.

Conley, J. M., & O'Barr, W. M. (1988, March). *Lay ideologies of law: The construction of meaning by informal court litigants.* Paper presented at the Annual Meeting of the American Ethnological Society, St. Louis, MO.

Conley, J. M., & O'Barr, W. M. (1990). Rules versus relationships in small claims disputes. *Conflict talk.* Cambridge: Cambridge University Press.

Fisher, W. R. (Ed.). (1985). "Homo narrans." [Special issue]. *Journal of Communication, 35.*

Fisher, W. R. (1987). *Human communication as narration: Toward a philosophy of reason, value and action.* Columbia: University of South Carolina Press.

Hastie, R., Penrod, S., & Pennington, N. (1983). *Inside the jury.* Cambridge, MA: Harvard University Press.

Hitt, J. (1990, January). What's wrong with the Democrats? *Harper's, 280*, 45–55.

Jackson, B. S. (1985). *Semiotics and legal theory.* London: Routledge and Kegan Paul.

Jackson, B. S. (1988). *Law, fact and narrative coherence.* Unpublished manuscript.

King, M. (1986). *Psychology in and out of court.* Oxford: Pergamon Press.

Mandler, J., & Johnson, N. S. (1977). Remembrance of things parsed: Story structure and recall. *Cognitive Psychology, 9*, 111–151.

McClosky, D. (1985). *The rhetoric of economics.* Madison: University of Wisconsin Press.

Moyers, B. (1987). *Joseph Campbell and the power of myth.* Public Broadcasting Corporation, six part series.

Pennington, N., & Hastie, R. (1986). Evidence in complex decision making. *Journal of Personality and Social Psychology, 51,* 242-258.

Propp, V. (1968). *Morphology of the folktale.* Austin: University of Texas Press.

Read, S. J. (1987). Constructing causal scenarios: A knowledge structure approach to causal reasoning. *Journal of Personality and Social Psychology, 52,* 288-302.

Rumelhart, D. E. (1975). Notes on a schema for stories. In D. G. Bobrow & A. Collins (Eds.), *Representation and understanding: Studies in cognitive science* (pp. 211-236). New York: Academic Press.

Sacks, H. (1972). On the analyzability of stories by children. In J. J. Gumperz & D. Hymes (Eds.), *Directions in sociolinguistics: The ethnography of communication* (pp. 329-345). New York: Holt, Rinehart and Winston.

Schank, R., & Abelson, R. P. (1977). *Scripts, plans, goals and understanding.* Hillsdale, NJ: Lawrence Erlbaum Associates.

Thagard, P. (1989). Explanatory coherence. *Behavioral and Brain Sciences, 12,* 435-502.

Twining, W. (1987). *Lawyers' stories.* Unpublished manuscript.

White, H. (1984). The question of narrative in contemporary historical theory. *History and Theory, 25,* 1-33.

White, J. B. (1985). *Heracles' bow: Essays on the rhetoric and poetics of the law.* Madison: University of Wisconsin Press.

Wigmore, J. H. (1937). *The science of judicial proof* (3rd ed). Boston: Little, Brown.

Wilensky, R. (1983). Story grammar versus story points. *The Behavioral and Brain Sciences, 6,* 579-623.

9

▼▼▼▼▼▼▼

The Account Episode
in Close Relationships

Frank D. Fincham
University of Illinois at Champaign-Urbana

Psychologists have expended considerable energy studying marital communication, and much has been learned about the behaviors of distressed and satisfied spouses in problem-solving discussions (for a review see Weiss & Heyman, 1990). Surprisingly, however, marital researchers have paid little attention to talk *qua* talk, an omission that also is evidenced in the psychological literature on close relationships (Duck & Pond, 1989). In view of psychologists' rejection of the sociological tradition of marital research, it is ironic that sociologists have long noted the importance of talk in social interaction, particularly in close relationships.[1] Berger and Kellner (1970), for example, observed that "the reality of the world is sustained through conversation with significant others" (p. 53) and that "in the marital conversation a world is not only built, but it is also kept in a state of repair and ongoingly refurbished" (p. 61).

A particularly important element of marital conversations is the effort to maintain and restore meaningful interaction when it is threatened or disrupted by a spouse's behavior. Such "aligning actions" (Stokes & Hewitt, 1976) include several concepts discussed by sociologists including motive talk (Mills, 1940), remedial interchanges (Goffman, 1971), quasi-theorizing (Hall & Hewitt, 1970), and the offering of accounts (Scott & Lyman, 1968). Only the last of these, accounts, has received much attention in the psychological literature (cf.

---

[1]Unfortunately, the theoretical importance accorded talk by sociologists has not been matched by the emergence of data on this topic. Although the body of data collected by marital researchers in psychology might address some aspects of talk, the codes used in observational research fail to capture many relevant aspects of linguistic inquiry.

Schonbach, 1990) and in the study of close relationships (cf. Burnett, McGhee, & Clark, 1987).

Because systematic data on accounts are still relatively rare (not only in psychology but also sociology and communication studies) and pertain to contexts (e.g., courtrooms, Cody & McLaughlin, 1988; the social science experiment, Blumstein et al. 1974) that are quite different from interaction between intimates, the present chapter offers a conceptual analysis of accounts in close relationships that might facilitate research on this topic. The chapter is organized into four sections. In the first, distinctions among the related concepts of account, attribution, and explanation are noted. This serves as a springboard for the second section, which offers specific hypotheses regarding the elements of an account episode. The third section analyzes the account episode in terms of a dynamic model of marriage. The chapter concludes with a summary of the main arguments.

ACCOUNTS, ATTRIBUTIONS, AND EXPLANATIONS

Perhaps the most important feature of the terms *account, attribution,* and *explanation* is that each has several denotations. It is not surprising, therefore, that the literature associated with each includes the study of multiple phenomena. For example, accounts have been studied as "a statement made by a social actor to explain unanticipated or untoward behavior" (Scott & Lyman, 1968, p. 46) and as "story-like explanations of past actions and events which include the characterizations of self and significant others" (Harvey, Agostinelli, & Weber, 1989, p. 40). Despite some apparent similarity (e.g., the central role of explanation), there are important differences between these two lines of inquiry: the former focuses specifically on interpersonal communication in which actions are subject to "valuative inquiry," whereas the latter is not limited to interpersonal contexts and focuses more generally on "packages of attributions" for any life experience or event (for an extended discussion of different conceptions of accounts see Antaki, 1987 and Harvey, Orbuch, & Weber, in press-a, in press-b).

It follows that the degree of overlap among research on accounts, attributions, and explanations depends on the referents adopted for each. Although this is not the context in which to offer an extensive analysis of these constructs, it is important to note that in all three cases a distinction can be drawn between private events involving purely intrapersonal processes and public events or social acts that necessarily entail overt behavior. These two classes of events are related and most likely influence each other, but it would be a mistake to view them as representing the same phenomenon; despite possible overlap, each is likely to have different correlates, to be influenced by different factors, to serve different functions, and so on (cf. Bradbury & Fincham, 1988). Within each domain, attributions, accounts, and explanations are not isomorphic. For example, in the public domain, explanations may refer to various statements that often have little or nothing to do with causal attributions or accounts (Draper, 1988), whereas accounts may take many forms other than causal explanations. In view of their various referents, it behooves researchers who study accounts, attributions, and explanations to specify precisely the subject of their inquiry.

The present chapter examines accounts as communications that occur when a person feels or is made to feel answerable for his/her behavior or beliefs. The nature of such communications may vary, ranging from a single attribution to a complex narrative. Although this definition follows closely Scott and Lyman's (1968) view of accounts, it does not imply that other approaches to accounts or that work on attributions and on explanations are irrelevant to the present chapter. On the contrary, with a clear conception of the subject of inquiry, it is easier to use treatments of related concepts to inform the current analysis without proliferating confusion. Two such bodies of scholarship are particularly germane in the present context. First, the literature on responsibility attribution is relevant because the central meaning of the word "responsible" appears to be "answerable, accountable to another for something; liable to be called to account" (Oxford English Dictionary). Second, the analysis of explanations in terms of conversational processes (e.g., Hilton, 1990) has much to offer an understanding of the account as a "linguistic device employed [to] prevent conflicts from arising by verbally bridging the gap between action and expectation" (Scott & Lyman, p. 46). However, a conversational analysis of accounts is beyond the scope of this chapter and is, in any event, available elsewhere (Heritage, 1988).

BUILDING BLOCKS
FOR UNDERSTANDING ACCOUNTS
IN CLOSE RELATIONSHIPS

Building on prior research, this section analyzes four elements of account episodes: namely, the conditions that instigate an account, the reproach that usually follows and gives rise to the account, the account itself, and account evaluation. The discussion of each element concludes with specific postulates that might inform future research. This analysis of the account episode is then related to a dynamic model of marital interaction in the next section.

Instigating Conditions

To account is a three-place predicate: *someone* accounts for *something* to *someone*. That is, for an account to occur a spouse must recognize and accept the need to offer an account. This recognition may be self-initiated (e.g., "I really should tell him why I didn't renew our subscription to *Newsweek*") and result in a spontaneous account (e.g., "I think we need to tighten our budget and so I didn't renew our *Newsweek* subscription"). Spontaneous accounts convey implicitly the importance attached to the smooth functioning of the relationship, and the spouse's offering a spontaneous account is likely to be seen as sensitive, especially when the account addresses a concern that the partner planned to share with him or her. Alternatively, the account may be instigated by a partner's reproach (e.g., "Weren't you going to renew our subscription to *Newsweek*?"). These two cases illustrate an important feature of accounts in close relationships: The need for an account may be recognized by only one spouse or by both spouses. As a consequence, reproaching the partner may not necessarily result in an account and could, in some cases, lead to the spouse's being called to account for offering the reproach.

In light of the above observations, the *something* for which a partner is accountable is likely to vary from simply being a matter of individual judgment to carrying the force of a moral imperative about which there is little dispute. In analyses of accounts (e.g., Scott & Lyman, 1968) and responsibility attribution (e.g., Fincham & Jaspars, 1980), the violation of expectations is the *something* for which one is held accountable/responsible. However, expectations can vary on a number of dimensions that have important implications for the instigation of accounts. First, expectations can be implicit or explicit. Implicit explanations may reflect tacit knowledge that partners bring to the relationship or may develop in the course of the relationship. Wittgenstein's (1953) concept of language games is useful here in that expectations, like the rules of language, are learned and made manifest by experiencing the relationship (playing the language game). Second, expectations may or may not have been affirmed (tacitly via behaviors or overtly via explicit agreements).

The nature of the expectation that is violated may also influence the *someone* to whom the spouse is accountable. Expectations vary in the extent to which they reflect group norms and therefore gain importance from forces (e.g., moral, legal, religious) that transcend the individual or the relationship. Violation of an expectation therefore may also challenge a group norm and create even greater indignation in the offended spouse.

> Postulate 1. A self-initiated account for an expectancy violation is more likely to be favorably evaluated than an account that is instigated by a partner's reproach.
>
> Postulate 2. Violation of expectations that have been affirmed by previous behavior, result from explicit agreements, or that reflect group norms are most likely to threaten the smooth functioning of the relationship and therefore result in reproaches.
>
> Postulate 3. Reproaches by a spouse are most likely to be challenged when they arise from violation of implicit expectations that do not reflect group norms, are seen by the partner to arise *de novo*, or that result from explicit agreements involving miscommunication.

Reproach

Accounts follow a reproach for behavior that violates an expectancy. As noted, a spouse may offer an account spontaneously, in which case the spouse reproaches him or herself; in such cases the reproach most often takes the form of an intrapersonal cognitive event. More frequently, the reproach constitutes an interpersonal event in which the partner will reproach the spouse in some way (for a taxonomy of reproaches see Schonbach, 1990; Cody & Braaten, this volume). For example, the partner may make the need for an account apparent from his or her nonverbal behavior (e.g., raises eyebrows in a questioning manner) or verbally call the spouse to account. Verbal reproaches may simply ask for an account (e.g., "Why did you do that?") or involve further material, including a projected account for the violation (e.g., "You must have been pressured into it"), a comment on the violation (e.g., "You've done it twice this week!"), a comment on the spouse's intent/motivation (e.g., "I know you tried your best to fit into my schedule"), a comment on the spouse's personality (e.g., "You are such an inconsiderate oaf"), or a comment on the relationship (e.g., "I guess we can tolerate these irritations between us").

Because verbal reproaches constitute speech acts (Austin, 1962), their nature is best understood not only by what is said (the locutionary act) but also the act performed by the utterance (e.g., request, threat—its illocutionary force) *and* the effect of the act on the beliefs, attitudes, or behavior of the addressee (e.g., making the partner feel guilty, consoling the partner—its perlocutionary effect).

Whether nonverbal or verbal, reproaches differ in perceived severity or negativity. This dimension is viewed as more fundamental for understanding the impact of the reproach than previously investigated factors such as the content of what is said or the verbal versus nonverbal nature of the reproach (e.g., McLaughlin, Cody, & O'Hair, 1983). The illocutionary and perlocutionary force of the reproach are most likely to determine its perceived severity/negativity. Research on accounts (cf. Cody & McLaughlin, 1988) and on marital interaction (cf. Weiss & Heyman, 1990) suggests that severe reproaches are particularly important because they are likely to evoke similarly negative responses.

Postulate 4. The expectancy violations characterized in Postulate 2 are likely to produce the most severe/negative reproaches.

Postulate 5. Reproaches that are seen as disproportionately severe/negative relative to the expectancy violation are most likely to result in defensive responses (e.g., be challenged).

Postulate 6. Severe reproaches are likely to lead to negative responses to the reproach (e.g., defensiveness).

Account

Most early research on accounts was descriptive and focused on developing tax-onomies of accounts (e.g., Semin & Manstead, 1983; Tedeschi & Reiss, 1981). Consequently, initial reliance on Austin's (1961) distinction between excuses (where one admits that the violation was wrong but denies responsibility for it; e.g., "I couldn't make the salad because I was kept at a meeting with the visiting divisional manager") and justifications (where one denies that the violation was wrong but admits responsibility for it; e.g., "The most important thing is the main course. I can run out and pick up a salad") has been replaced by comprehensive taxonomies of accounts. Several additional account categories have been proposed, the most influential being concessions (i.e., admission of the violation being wrong and of responsibility for the violation; this may be simply a confession or be ac-companied by an apology, offer of restitution, etc.) and refusals (i.e., denial of the violation, personal involvement in it, etc., either directly or indirectly through such tactics as silence or irrelevant talk, or refusal to acknowledge the other per-son's right to reproach; see Schonbach, 1980).

Although the above-mentioned taxonomies are valuable, it is instructive to note the advance in attribution research that occurred when attention turned from the content of attributions (e.g., effort, ability) to their underlying dimensions (e.g., stable, unstable). This change reduced significantly the problem of sampling from the vast domain of possible attributional content because attributions reflected a relatively small number of underlying dimensions. Investigation of these dimen-sions resulted in a more integrated literature that facilitated comparisons across studies. A similar advance is represented by McLaughlin, Cody, and O'Hair's (1983) use of the aggravation-mitigation continuum as a dimension underlying accounts: refusals are viewed as most aggravating, justifications somewhat less aggravating, excuses are somewhat mitigating, and concessions most mitigating. In a similar vein, Schonbach (1990) investigated the defensiveness of accounts. These are important concepts but they may not capture fully the interpersonal aspect of understanding accounts, which is fundamental in close relationships.

It is proposed therefore that a critical feature of accounts in close relation-ships is their *responsivity,* that is, the extent to which they address the communica-tive *and* metacommunicative aspects of the partner's reproach. Consider, for ex-ample, a wife who, upon discovering that her husband made a major household purchase without consulting her, asks, "Why did you do that?" By supplying in-formation relevant to the question, the husband would address the manifest content of the communication. Although important, content is less critical than the meta-communicative aspects of the reproach. That is, the manner in which the wife asked the question conveys more than simply a request for information; the tone of her voice and her nonverbal behavior show a concern that her husband no longer values her opinion. This concern is important because of its possible implications for the relationship. The husband may address this concern explicitly in the content of his account (e.g., "I really care about your opinion but this was on a one hour floor sale and I couldn't get hold of you") or by the manner in which it is communicated (e.g., taking the wife's question seriously and offering an earnest and sincere account).

The concept of responsivity is consistent with analyses of conversation offered by ethnomethodologists and linguists. Specifically, a central assumption in conversational analysis is that a speaking turn address the matters raised by the turn preceding it (e.g., adjacency pairs, Schegloff & Sacks, 1973; cf. Werth, 1981). Similarly, in pragmatics Grice (1975) offers four conversational maxims, one of which states that a partner's contribution to a conversation is "appropriate to immediate needs at each stage of the transaction" (p. 47). In fact, attempts have been made to reduce Grice's four maxims to a single maxim of relevance (e.g., Sperber & Wilson, 1986). Although responsivity is not accorded the normative status given to relevance, it is nonetheless likely to be critical in close relationships. This may reflect the fact that being responsive in itself shows respect for the partner, a concern that is central in marriage (Gottman, 1979).

Postulate 7. The more responsive the account to the reproacher's concerns, the more likely it will repair or mitigate the fracture produced by the expectancy violation.

Postulate 8. Accounts are likely to be most responsive to the concerns expressed via the reproach when they address both its communicative and metacommunicative aspects. When conflict exists between these two dimensions, accounts that address the metacommunication are likely to be seen as more responsive.

Postulate 9. The responsivity of an account is likely to influence the evaluation of the expectancy violation for which it is offered. Failure to be responsive will confirm any negative inferences raised by the violation and result in its being judged more harshly. Conversely, a responsive account is likely to result in a more benign evaluation of the violation.

Account Evaluation

The evaluation of an account is a complex process, and several observations have already been made about the success or honoring of accounts. It remains to specify further conditions that are likely to determine the perceived responsivity of accounts and to identify additional factors that might influence their evaluation.

Perhaps the most important consideration here is the knowledge that the spouse brings to the evaluation of his or her partner's account or what Scott and Lyman (1968) call "background expectations." The account must be consistent with the evaluator's knowledge (e.g., of relationships, physical causality) to be judged as reasonable and appropriate (e.g., an account that appeals to divine intervention would not be acceptable to an atheist). In addition, the knowledge that the evaluator develops about the current relationship is likely to influence his or her evaluations (e.g., an account based on a relationship rule that is not seen to exist by the evaluator is likely to fail).

In addition to evaluating the content of the account, the spouse evaluates other aspects of the partner's communication, including his or her responsiveness to the metacommunication associated with the reproach. This evaluation will often take place at a tacit level without awareness. However, the product of this evaluation is potentially available to the spouse (e.g., "I felt good about his answer," "She really tried to help me understand what happened"). Factors likely to influence this evaluation include the spouse's ability to interpret accurately the partner's nonverbal behavior, sensitivity to such behavior, understanding of the situation in which the communication takes place, and so on. In sum, the prototype of a successful account is one that is considered reasonable and is experienced as responsive by the reproaching spouse.

Although it is possible to distinguish the responsivity and reasonableness of an account and to imagine extreme situations in which they might conflict, it is likely that in most contexts they may be indistinguishable. That is, a spouse who feels that his or her partner has been responsive, rather than unresponsive, is likely to view the account offered as more reasonable. Finally, the spouse's evaluation of an account may remain private or it may be communicated to the partner and lead to further elaboration of the account, a new account, conflict that generalizes beyond the expectancy violation at hand, and so on.

> Postulate 10. All else being equal, the more an account is consistent with the reproacher's knowledge or background expectations, the more likely it is to be honored.

Coda

The present analysis of elements in an account episode emphasizes the total communicative context in which each occurs. Of particular relevance to this analysis are the perlocutionary effects of speech acts. Because speech acts can constitute any of the elements in an account episode (i.e., the expectancy violation, reproach, account, or communication of the account evaluation), their perlocutionary effects are particularly important for understanding the account episode. In this regard it is imperative to distinguish the intended from the actual perlocutionary effect of the spouse's speech act. It is the intended perlocutionary effect *as perceived by the partner* that is critical in our analysis and gives rise to a postulate that is independent of account element.[2]

---

[2]Most research on accounts appears to be based primarily on the content of what is said (cf. extensive use of stimulus vignettes). Such research necessarily yields an incomplete picture of the account episode because it does not incorporate the complete communicative context (including paralinguistic cues). Because talk in account episodes (and perhaps in the relationship) represents an attempt to influence the partner, we need to study the complete context of the communication that influences the partner's response in order to understand it.

Postulate 11. The spouse's perception of the intended perlocutionary effect of the speech act occurring in the account episode is likely to influence the partner's response to it (e.g., reproaches seen to have negative intent will be reciprocated and lead to minimally responsive accounts).

THE ACCOUNT EPISODE IN CLOSE RELATIONSHIPS

Drawing from a recent model of marital interaction, this section offers an analysis of the account episode as it unfolds in close relationships. It is guided by the premise that what happens during such episodes necessarily requires consideration of what each spouse brings to the interaction. This premise is supported strongly by Schonbach's (1990) finding that individual differences in need for control and self esteem have a profound influence on account episodes. Although particular attention will be paid to the most frequently studied construct in marriage, relationship satisfaction, additional factors critical to an understanding of accounts are identified.

The Context of the Accounting Episode

According to the contextual model of marriage (Bradbury & Fincham, 1989, 1991), the psychological characteristics that spouses bring to an interaction influence processing of their partner's behavior (i.e., the behaviors attended to, initial affective responses to the behaviors, and their interpretation), which, in turn, affects overt responses to the behavior. These characteristics fall into two classes: (a) momentary thoughts and feelings, or *proximal context,* and (b) relatively stable, intransient characteristics (e.g., chronic mood states, personality traits, relationship beliefs) or *distal context.* Proximal and distal context variables are related bidirectionally, indicating that momentary thoughts and feelings during an interaction reflect stable aspects of the spouse, which, in turn, can change as a function of these thoughts and feelings. Finally, thoughts and feeling that occur before and after interactions, *appraisals,* influence and are influenced by proximal and distal contexts and can thus affect indirectly the processing of behavior during an interaction. These appraisals can also change a spouse's understanding of an action, interaction episode, aspects of the self, the partner, or the relationship (for a more complete description of the contextual model see Bradbury & Fincham, 1989, 1991; Fincham & Bradbury, in press).

How can consideration of contextual variables enrich our understanding of accounts? To address this question, two examples of an accounting episode are contrasted. This comparison is then analyzed in terms of relevant contextual variables. It will be argued that what each spouse brings to an interaction can affect whether an expectancy violation is perceived and, if so, the manner in which the account episode unfolds, and that the outcome of the accounting sequence may depend on subsequent appraisals in addition to what happens during the account episode.

Illustrating the Importance of Context

Two Contrasting Account Episodes.   Consider the situation in which a husband is late in meeting his wife. His wife, who has high self-esteem, feels secure, tends to be optimistic, is feeling quite relaxed in anticipation of the upcoming meeting, and may even be enjoying some pleasant fantasies about it. Although the purpose of the meeting is an instrumental one, to look for a new house, the wife's fantasies focus on the shared experience with her husband and how it represents yet another step in their relationship. She fondly recalls earlier developments in their relationship and she looks forward to enjoying the experience. Under these circumstances, it is possible that she may not even notice that her husband is 5 minutes late, and thus the need for an account may not arise. When her husband spontaneously offers an account for his lateness she may express surprise and may attend more to supporting her husband who is frustrated at being caught in traffic than to evaluating his account.

Alternatively, she may notice the lateness. However, the impact of the observation is likely to be mitigated by her current positive mood. At this point three courses of action are possible. First, she may downplay the expectancy violation (e.g., saying to herself, "It gave me a little more time to enjoy the fresh air") and fail to offer a reproach. Second, she may spontaneously evaluate several reasons for the lateness. Those that occur to her are relatively benign and serve to minimize her husband's responsibility for being late (e.g., he was caught in the traffic). Upon her husband's arrival she simultaneously notes the expectancy violation (e.g., she pointedly glances at her watch) and seeks validation of her understanding ("You look pooped. Been struggling in the traffic?"). Her communication, however, conveys supports and allows the disruption caused by the lateness to be minimized. The husband can accept the account ("Yeah, it was pretty bad") or offer an alternative account. Feeling supported, he is able to accept responsibility for the violation and at the same time acknowledge the possible negative impact of his action by offering an apology (e.g., "No, I got caught up at the office. I am really sorry"). Third, the wife may notice the lateness without evaluating possible reasons for it. When her husband arrives she may simply ask him why he is late or, touching his hand affectionately, express a specific complaint (e.g., "I don't like being kept waiting"). In her current state she is predisposed to evaluate favorably even a minimally responsive statement ("It's a long story. I don't want to talk about it").

Contrast this scenario with one in which the wife is an insecure person with low self-esteem who tends to be pessimistic. She is also anticipating the meeting with her husband, but it makes her feel tense as she recalls prior conflicts about major decisions in the marriage. Not surprisingly, she fantasizes about possible disagreements with her husband. Anxious to get the matter settled, she is hyper-vigilant in monitoring the time. Under these circumstances, she may reproach her husband even if he is only seconds late.

The extra 5 minutes that she spends waiting for him increases her tension. They may be accompanied by thoughts about why he is late (e.g., "He really doesn't care enough about our future," "He thinks my time is less valuable than his") and about possible accounts he might offer (e.g., "Let him just try and tell me that he got lost! It better be a pretty good story"). In any event, she is likely to reproach her husband immediately upon his arrival (thereby making it difficult for him to offer an account spontaneously). Moreover, the approach is likely to be severe and attacking, reflecting her strong negative feelings (e.g., "You're a lost cause – can't even keep an appointment," "I suppose you are going to tell me your watch broke. You really think I am stupid"). Responding to the metacom-munication ("There is nothing you can say to redeem yourself"), the husband feels defensive and counterattacks in a way that challenges the reproach (e.g., "You said sometime between 4:30 and 4:45, not 4:30 on the dot! Why are you being so difficult?" – miscommunication in this relationship is frequent). Alternatively, he may accept the reproach but still respond by attacking the wife (e.g., "It was bad enough being caught in the traffic . . . I'm in no mood to deal with your nagging"). His account is hardly noticed by the wife as she responds (e.g., "If you shaped up, I wouldn't have to nag").

To the extent that the wife engages in an evaluation of the account, she is like-ly to process it in terms of the negative concepts that she has accessed prior to and during the interaction (e.g., "If this was important enough to you, you would have left before the rush hour"). Wanting to end the negative interaction, the hus-band elaborates on his account (e.g., "I wanted to leave early because this *is* im-portant to me but Mr. Brown called an emergency meeting as I was about to leave. Please let's leave this for now . . . we are already late") and his tone of voice and earnest demeanor convey a strong positive metacommunication (e.g., "I care about us and you have every right to be mad at me"). Although not satis-fied the wife agrees, thinking that she will raise the issue later.

While bathing that evening the wife recalls the account episode. Her memory is colored by the fact that they saw a house that both spouses liked. In her ap-praisal of the episode she finds herself thinking that she was unreasonable about her husband's lateness. She reevaluates her husband's last statement during the episode as reassuring and wonders how he sometimes puts up with her.

Relationship Satisfaction, Individual Differences, and Partner Goals. From these scenarios we can begin to identify some important contextual varia-bles that have the potential to advance our understanding of the account episode in close relationships. Perhaps the most obvious is the wife's general sentiment towards the relationship, her relationship satisfaction. In fact, this distal context variable is thought to be a stronger determinant of a spouse's action than the partner's behavior to which it is a response (the sentiment override hypothesis, Weiss, 1980). It therefore may not be surprising that marital satisfaction is related to a variety of interactional behaviors: In the first example the wife is responsive to her husband, accepting of his statements, offers a specific behavioral complaint, and couples her complaint with a positive affective cue, all of which are behaviors associated with marital happiness. In contrast, the wife in the second example complains about her husband's personal characteristics, couples the complaint with negative affect, and shows more negative behaviors. These observations, together with the fact that this couple showed a sequence of reciprocated negative behaviors, suggests that they are a maritally distressed couple (cf. Weiss & Heyman, 1990).

There are few data that evaluate directly the operation of sentiment override. However, even if this hypothesis proves to be incorrect, marital satisfaction is likely to influence a spouse's behavior via its impact on the spouse's processing. That is, the wife's relationship satisfaction most likely affected her thoughts and feelings (appraisal) about the upcoming interaction (e.g., by affecting access to memories, priming positive vs. negative constructs that are used to process the behavior) and may have played a role in bringing about her current mood, which, in turn, affected her processing of the husband's behavior (for a summary of mood effects on judgments in close relationships see Forgas, 1991). Moreover, her happiness with the marriage is likely to have affected the attributions she generated spontaneously for the lateness and her acceptance of the attributions in her husband's account (for a review of the association between attributions and marital satisfaction, see Bradbury & Fincham, 1990). Perhaps most importantly, relationship satisfaction is likely to influence the perceived perlocutionary effect of partner statements (for a review of research on the intent and perceived impact of partner communications see Bradbury & Fincham, 1987).

In sum, relationship satisfaction is relevant to many of the postulates outlined earlier. Specifically, compared to happily married spouses, dissatisfied spouses are likely to offer fewer spontaneous accounts (Postulate 1), view expectancy violations as abrogations of explicit agreements (Postulate 2), offer reproaches that are seen to be disproportionately severe/negative (Postulate 5), exhibit negative behavior in response to negative reproaches (Postulate 6), offer accounts that are low in responsivity (Postulates 7, 8, and 9), and make more negative inferences about the perlocutionary force of partner statements (Postulate 11).

Notwithstanding the importance accorded satisfaction in marital research and in the above analysis, the scenarios emphasize additional factors that are likely to be particularly important in understanding accounts, including current mood, concepts in working memory, individual difference variables, and spouse goals. The last two are discussed briefly in view of the relative paucity of research devoted to them.

Individual differences or personality factors are particularly relevant because they predispose partners to process information in a particular manner. For example, negative affectivity or the tendency "to focus differentially on the negative aspects of themselves, other people, and the world in general" (Watson & Clark, 1984, pp. 481–482) is a dimension that captures a difference between the two wives in the above scenarios and is likely to influence the aspects of behavior they attend to and how they interpret them. Because close relationships are likely to be an important source of self-esteem, especially for individuals with low self-esteem, self-esteem may similarly influence processing of partner behavior. In the scenarios, the wives differ in self-esteem, a factor that might reduce the threshold for partner behavior to be seen as self-relevant and threatening and lead to the assumption of one's own responsibility for a partner's expectancy violations in appraisals following the account episode.

In sum, negative affectivity and self-esteem are examples of two personality factors that may exert a pervasive influence on pre-interaction appraisals, the proximal context, the processing of partner behavior, behavior itself, and postinteraction appraisals (cf. Postulate 11). Such variables are likely to limit the spouse's ability to respond maximally to normative principles of social interaction (e.g., Grice's conversational maxims) and, in terms of the present analysis, to be seen as responsive (cf. Postulates 7, 8, & 9). The importance of such individual difference variables is further emphasized by the relative paucity of recent research on personality factors in marital interaction and the need to include them in any comprehensive account of such interaction (Kelly & Conley, 1987). Nonetheless, it is important to note that the impact of individual differences is likely to vary as a function of numerous other circumstances that may be operative in a particular situation.

Finally, spouses' *goals* are likely to be critical in understanding account episodes. In any particular interaction, a spouse's momentary goals may reflect only one or a few of the many goals represented in the distal context or may not even reflect any such goals (e.g., when an otherwise cooperative partner is deeply hurt by a spouse's comment and becomes intent simply on humiliating him or her). Moreover, goals that are elements of the proximal context may vary during the course of an interaction.

Recall that for the first wife relationship goals were more salient (to enjoy the experience with her husband), whereas the second wife was more oriented to instrumental goals (to purchase a house). However, both sets of goals were available to each spouse, and external or internal stimuli could change which was most salient. For example, reassuring behavior by the second husband might have allowed his wife to focus on the shared experience of looking for a house and, in contrast to past experiences, could have led her to think that the purchase decision might actually enhance their relationship experience. Although goals vary on a variety of dimensions, the extent to which they reflect individual versus relational concerns is likely to be critical in understanding accounts. For example, after an initially defensive account motivated by the desire to save face, a spouse may decide that the escalation of conflict is too great and shift his or her focus to a relationship-oriented goal that allows the display of behavior where there is a loss of face.

To summarize, this illustration of account episodes in close relationships attempts to provide a framework that allows for both continuity and discontinuity in the behavior of partners across and within account episodes. Thus, for example, factors such as relationship satisfaction, individual differences, and goals may produce consistent response patterns across and within situations. However, the environmental circumstances in which the account episode occurs (e.g., in public versus in private) may also influence their operation, leading to variation in response patterns.

CONCLUSION

Research on accounts that occur during interaction between intimates is likely to be a fertile area of research. An analysis was offered, therefore, that might guide such inquiry. In the analysis, elements of the account episode were viewed as communications that occur in conversations. An attempt was made to illustrate the importance of understanding each partner's psychological context for studying such communications.

The present analysis is intended to illustrate, rather than document exhaustively, an approach to understanding accounts in close relationships. Although some important variables were glossed over, the approach outlined offers a perspective that has the potential to build a bridge from research on attributions, explanations, and accounts as intrapersonal events to research on these constructs as interpersonal events. A major factor that is likely to effect this transition is recognition of the importance of talk in close relationships.

The study of talk in the context of a close relationship is not easy because past interactions (i.e., a history of language games) allow partners to draw on a vast repertoire of implicit, shared assumptions and meanings in their conversation. Moreover, access to this repertoire is often hindered by the use of telegraphic utterances that may not even cue the outsider to the elaborate story conveyed by them. Finally, adherence to conversational maxims such as informativeness (Grice, 1975) may further restrict the occurrence of easily recognized accounts, explanations, and attributions in marital conversations; they may occur only at the time of novel expectancy violations that are truly surprising to the partner (accounts for other forms of expectancy violation may comprise part of shared knowledge; may not offer any information that is considered informative) and may not occur explicitly in subsequent conversations (they would comprise part of existing knowledge, and their use may therefore violate the maxim of informativeness). In view of such considerations, it is not surprising that the identification of attributions in marital conversations has posed considerable difficulty (cf. Holtzworth-Munroe & Jacobson, 1988; Bradbury & Fincham, 1988) and that the study of accounts in close relationships has not yet resulted in systematic, quantitative research (Harvey et al., in press-a). Openness to the variety of methodologies available across disciplines to study talk may therefore be essential to the emergence of a more complete understanding of accounts in close relationships.

REFERENCES

Antaki, C. (1987). Performed and unperformable: A guide to accounts of relationships. In R. Burnett, P. McGhee, & D. Clark (Eds.), *Accounting for relationships* (pp. 97–113). New York: Methuen.

Austin, J. L. (1961). A plea for excuses. In J. D. Urmson & G. Warnock (Eds.), *Philosophical papers* (pp. 329–340). Oxford: Clarendon Press.

Austin, J. L. (1962). *How to do things with words.* Oxford: Clarendon Press.

Berger, P., & Kellner, H. (1970). Marriage and the construction of reality. In H. P. Dreitzel (Ed.), *Recent sociology: Patterns of communicative behavior.* New York: Macmillan.

Blumstein, P. W., Carssow, K. G., Hall, J., Hawkins, B., Hoffman, R., Ishem, E., Maurer, C. P., Spens, D., Taylor, J., & Zimmerman, D. L. (1974). The honoring of accounts. *American Sociological Review, 39,* 551–566.

Bradbury, T. N., & Fincham, F. D. (1987). The assessment of affect in marriage. In K. D. O'Leary (Ed.), *Assessment of marital discord* (pp. 59–108). Hillsdale, NJ: Lawrence Erlbaum Associates.

Bradbury, T. N., & Fincham, F. D. (1988). Assessing spontaneous attributions in marital interaction: Methodological and conceptual considerations. *Journal of Social and Clinical Psychology, 7,* 122–130.

Bradbury, T. N., & Fincham, F. D. (1989). Behavior and satisfaction in marriage: Prospective mediating processes. *Review of Personality and Social Psychology, 10,* 119–143.

Bradbury, T. N., & Fincham, F. D. (1990). Attributions in marriage: Review and critique. *Psychological Bulletin, 107,* 3–33.

Bradbury, T. N., & Fincham, F. D. (1991). A contextual model for advancing the study of marital interaction. In G. J. O. Fletcher & F. D. Fincham (Eds.), *Cognition in close relationships* (pp. 127–150). Hillsdale, NJ: Lawrence Erlbaum Associates.

Burnett, R., McGhee, P., & Clarke, D. (Eds.). (1987). *Accounting for relationships.* New York: Methuen.

Cody, M. J., & McLaughlin, M. L. (1988). Accounts on trial: Oral arguments in traffic court. In C. Antaki (Ed.), *Analyzing everyday explanation* (pp. 113–126). Beverly Hills, CA: Sage.

Draper, S. W. (1988). What's going on in everyday explanation? In C. Antaki (Ed.), *Analyzing everyday explanation* (pp. 15–31). Beverly Hills, CA: Sage.

Duck, S., & Pond, K. (1989). Friends, Romans, countrymen, lend me your retrospections: Rhetoric and reality in close relationships. *Review of Personality and Social Psychology, 10,* 17–38.

Fincham, F. D., & Bradbury, T. N. (in press). Marital conflict: Towards a more complete integration of research and treatment. *Advances in Family Intervention, Assessment and Theory, 5.*

Fincham, F. D., & Jaspars, J. M. (1980). Attribution of responsibility: From man the scientist to man as lawyer. In L. Berkowitz (Ed.), *Advances in experimental social psychology* (Vol. 13, pp. 81–138). New York: Academic.

Forgas, J. (1991). Affect and cognition in close relationships. In G. J. O. Fletcher & F. D. Fincham (Eds.), *Cognition in close relationships* (pp. 151–174). Hillsdale, NJ: Lawrence Erlbaum Associates.

Goffman, E. (1971). *Relations in public: Microstudies of the public order.* Harmondworth: Penguin.

Gottman, J. M. (1979). *Marital interaction.* New York: Academic.

Grice, H. P. (1975). Logic and conversation. In P. Cole & J. L. Morgan (Eds.), *Syntax and semantics 3: Speech acts* (pp. 41–58). New York: Academic.

Hall, P. M., & Hewitt, J. P. (1970). The quasi-theory of communication and the management of dissent. *Social Problems, 18,* 17-27.

Harvey, J. H., Agostinelli, G., & Weber, A. L. (1989). Account-making and the formation of expectations about close relationships. *Review of Personality and Social Psychology, 10,* 39-62.

Harvey, J. H., Orbuch, T. L., & Weber, A. L. (in press-a). Convergence of the attribution and accounts concepts in the study of close relationships. In J. H. Harvey, T. L. Orbuch, & A. L. Weber (Eds.), *Attributions, accounts, and close relationships.* New York: Springer Verlag.

Harvey, J. H., Orbuch, T. L., & Weber, A. L. (in press-b). A social psychological model of account-making in response to severe stress. *Journal of Language and Social Psychology.*

Heritage, J. (1988). Explanations as accounts: A conversation analytic perspective. In C. Antaki (Ed.), *Analyzing everyday explanation* (pp. 127-144). Beverly Hills, CA: Sage.

Hilton, D. (1990). Conversational processes and causal explanation. *Psychological Bulletin, 107,* 65-81.

Holtzworth-Munroe, A., & Jacobson, N. S. (1988). Toward a methodology for coding spontaneous causal attributions: Preliminary results with married couples. *Journal of Social and Clinical Psychology, 7,* 101-112.

Kelly, E. L., & Conley, J. J. (1987). Personality and compatibility: A prospective analysis of marital stability and marital satisfaction. *Journal of Personality and Social Psychology, 52,* 27-40.

McLaughlin, M. L., Cody, M. J., & O'Hair, H. D. (1983). The management of failure events: Some contextual determinants of accounting behavior. *Human Communication Research, 9,* 208-224.

Mills, C. W. (1940). Situated action and vocabularies of motive. *American Sociological Review, 5,* 904-913.

Schegloff, E. A., & Sacks, H. (1973). Opening up closings. *Semiotica, 7,* 289-327.

Schonbach, P. (1980). A category system for account phases. *European Journal of Social Psychology, 10,* 195-200.

Schonbach, P. (1990). *Account episodes: The management of escalation of conflict.* Cambridge: Cambridge University Press.

Scott, M. B., & Lyman, S. (1968). Accounts. *American Sociological Review, 33,* 46-62.

Semin, G. R., & Manstead, A. S. R. (1983). *The accountability of conduct.* London: Academic.

Sperber, D., & Wilson, D. (1986). *Relevance: Communication and cognition.* Oxford: Blackwell.

Stokes, R., & Hewitt, J. P. (1976). Aligning actions. *American Sociological Review, 41,* 838-849.

Tedeschi, J. T., & Reiss, M. (1981). Verbal strategies in impression management. In C. Antaki (Ed.), *The psychology of ordinary explanations* (pp. 271-309). London: Academic.

Watson, D., & Clark, L. A. (1984). Negative affectivity: The disposition to experience aversive emotional states. *Psychological Bulletin, 96,* 465-490.

Weiss, R. L. (1980). Strategic behavioral marital therapy: Toward a model for assessment and intervention. In J. P. Vincent (Ed.), *Advances in family intervention, assessment and theory* (Vol. 1, pp. 229-271). Greenwich, CT: JAI Press.

Weiss, R. L., & Heyman, R. E. (1990). Observation of marital interaction. In F. D. Fincham & T. N. Bradbury (Eds.), *The psychology of marriage: Basic issues and applications* (pp. 87-117). New York: Guilford.

Werth, P. (1981). The concept of "relevance" in conversational analysis. In P. Werth (Ed.), *Conversation and discourse* (pp. 129-154). New York: St. Martin's Press.

Wittgenstein, L. (1953). *Philosophical investigations.* Oxford: Blackwell.

10

▼▼▼▼▼▼▼

Explanation as Legitimation:
Excuse-Making in Organizations

Robert J. Bies
Georgetown University

Sim B. Sitkin
University of Texas at Austin

In organizations, people often disappoint, frustrate, or even anger others with whom they work. For example, a boss gives a lower-than-expected performance rating to a subordinate; a boss informs top management that sales figures continue to decline; top management informs the organization of layoffs and budget cuts in a restructuring of the organization; one subordinate spreads malicious rumors about another co-worker to "get ahead" in an upcoming promotion decision (Bies, 1987b). In each of these examples, and many others like them, such behavior represents a violation of social expectations or role requirements and thus creates a *failure event* (Cody & McLaughlin, 1985; Schonbach, 1980) that must be explained.

The occurrence of failure events in organizations can prove costly, as violations of expectations or role requirements can undermine, if not destroy, the trust and cooperation necessary for continued organizational functioning (Sitkin & Bies, 1990). For example, take the case of a boss–subordinate relationship. On an annual basis, a subordinate may request an increase in salary and, more routinely, the subordinate may request that current procedures be changed or that new policies be made. In many situations, however, the boss may be unable or unwilling to satisfy the request. As a result, the subordinate may question the boss' motives and intentions in making the decision (Bies, 1987b) or may question the boss' influence in fulfilling the request (Pelz, 1952). Answers to such questions will influence a subordinate's support for the boss and willingness to cooperate (March & Simon, 1958), which are critical to managerial authority (Barnard, 1938). Thus, in order to maintain authority, a boss is faced with the task of legitimating the action (Izraeli & Jick, 1983).

A failure event is less likely to become destructive if it is properly managed (Cody & McLaughlin, 1985; Sitkin, in press-b). One approach to managing a failure event involves the use of accounts. An *account* is a "statement made by a social actor to explain unanticipated or untoward behavior" (Scott & Lyman, 1968, p. 46). The use of accounts is typically part of a three-phase sequence of activities involving the offending and offended parties (Cody & McLaughlin). First, there is a request for "repair" by the offended party, which is a communication to the offending party that something is wrong and needs attention (Schonbach, 1980). Second, there is a remedy, or account, supplied by the offending party (Goffman, 1971). Finally, there is an evaluation by the offended party of the account that is provided (McLaughlin, 1984). Assuming the account is acceptable to the offended party, then equilibrium is restored in the social relationship (Goffman).

In this chapter, we examine one aspect of the sequence of account-giving activities, that is, the relationship between an account provided by the offending party and the evaluation of that account by the offended party. In terms of the type of account, we restrict focus on the effects of *excuses*, which should be distinguished from *justifications*.[1] Following Austin (1961), Scott and Lyman (1968) defined an excuse as an account in which the offending party admits the behavior was bad, but denies responsibility for the offense. A justification is an account in which the party accepts responsibility for the behavior, but denies its pejorative quality.

According to Harré (1977), the offending party has two goals in mind when providing an excuse to an offended party. The first goal is to make the action in question appear *intelligible*. That is, the excuse is an explication of the behavior in question, such that the offended party has an understanding of why the action occurred. The second goal is to make the action appear *warrantable*. That is, the excuse, although acknowledging the behavior was bad, emphasizes it was the proper and appropriate action given the circumstances of the situation. If these goals are achieved, then the excuse should be *honored* or accepted by the offended party (Blumstein, 1974). In other words, an excuse acts to legitimate the action and thus restore equilibrium to the organizational relationship (Bies, 1989).

There is a great abundance of empirical evidence that excuses are used quite effectively to manage failure events in everyday situations and across social relationships (Cody & McLaughlin, 1990; Schonbach, 1990; Snyder, Higgins, & Stucky, 1983). In contrast, excuse-making in organizational settings has only recently captured the attention of researchers (Sitkin & Bies, 1990). The purpose of this chapter is to review the growing number of empirical studies on the use and effectiveness of excuse-making in organizational settings.

This chapter is divided into four sections. The first section reviews the empir-

---

[1]A few of the studies reviewed in this chapter gathered evidence on both excuses and justifications. However, for the purposes of this chapter we will report the data on excuses only.

ical studies that demonstrate that a failure event will elicit excuse-making in organizations. In the second sections, key features of excuse-making in organizations will be identified. Third, research in the effectiveness of excuse-making will be reviewed. Finally, we identify directions for future research on excuse-making in organizations.

EXCUSE-MAKING AS A LEGITIMATION STRATEGY IN ORGANIZATIONS

A number of studies support the argument that a failure event will elicit excuse-making in organizational settings. The failure events studied have included a variety of bad news (e.g., poor employee or organization performance, budget cutbacks, employee terminations), unethical behavior, and how sensitive information is handled (secrecy and disclosure). These studies are reviewed below.

Bad News

Bies (1990) conducted a study of middle managers in ten companies in which they recounted episodes in which bad news was delivered to a subordinate or a boss. Examples of bad news delivered to subordinates included budget cuts, employee termination, and unfavorable performance reviews. Examples of bad news delivered to bosses included financial losses, cost overruns, and missed deadlines. In *each* episode of bad news—whether with boss or subordinate—the managers provided an excuse when delivering the information.

Bies found that excuse-making was not limited to the direct target of the communication, but also to other internal organizational audiences For example, managers would engage in excuse-making to key and powerful people in the organization to build a "coalition" of supporters before the bad news had to be delivered. Similarly, after the news was delivered, excuse-making was at the center of "public relations" activities with those who witnessed or heard about the bad news. Thus, excuse-making was used by managers as a legitimation strategy with a broad set of organizational audiences.

Excuse-making is also prevalent when bad news is communicated to audiences external to an organization. In a series of studies of corporate annual reports, the reporting of bad news was found to be accompanied with more excuses that detail the mitigating circumstances that caused the situation than when good news was reported (Bettman & Weitz, 1983; Salancik & Meindl, 1984; Staw, McKechnie, & Puffer, 1983). In a study of how organizations managed the stigma associated with filing for Chapter 11 bankruptcy, Sutton and Callahan (1987) found that managers provided excuses to deny responsibility for the bankruptcy, including blaming the event on the environment or focusing on the faults of previous management. Similarly, in an analysis of layoffs at the Atari Company, Sutton, Eisenhardt, and Jucker (1986) found that managers focused the blame for Atari's decline not on themselves, but on those laid off.

Unethical Conduct

In a telephone survey, Garrett, Bradford, Meyers, and Becker (1989) found that managers engage in excuse-making when their organizations are faced with ac- cusations of unethical behavior. In a scenario study, Konovsky and Jaster (1989) had businessmen and businesswomen compose a "position paper" in response to allegations of questionable behavior. The results demonstrated that business people engage in excuse-making to avoid negative interpretation of their behaviors.

Handling Sensitive Information

Choosing when to disclose and when to withhold information is a key role re- quirement for managers in different industries, such as electronics and health ser- vices (Sitkin, in press-a; Sitkin & Sutcliffe, 1991). While secrecy may fulfill cer- tain role requirements, such behavior may create a failure event when questions or requests for information are denied, thus eliciting excuse-making as a strategy for legitimating secrecy. Indeed, Sitkin and his colleagues have found excuse- making used by managers to justify secrecy in the electronics (Sitkin, in press-a) and health services (Sitkin, Sutcliffe, & Reed, 1987) industries.

THE ARCHITECTURE OF EXCUSES IN ORGANIZATIONS

A few studies have identified "architectural" (e.g., structure, content) aspects of excuses in organizations (Sitkin & Bies, 1990). These features include the con- tent of excuses, the use of multiple reasons, and the timing of excuses. The studies are reviewed below.

The Content of Excuses

Several studies have focused on the identification of different types of excuses in organizations. In a survey study of subordinates' reactions to budget cuts, Bies, Shapiro, and Cummings (1988) found six categories of excuses offered by bosses for denying budget requests. The most frequent type of excuse was the boss' claim that the refusal was due to the subordinate's own behavior (e.g., insufficient preparation, incompetence). This category was followed by budget constraints (e.g., "We don't have enough money in the budget"), upper management (e.g., "My boss won't let me"), the political environment (e.g., "It would not be a politically correct thing to do now"), formal company policy (e.g., "The rules won't allow me to do it") and company norms (e.g., "Traditionally, our company has never allowed this").

Based on a study of secrecy and disclosure in the semiconductor industry, Sitkin (1986) identified four types of excuses that were used by engineers to explain why they chose to disclose or keep secret information about technical, personnel, or safety matters. Task-oriented excuses focused on the information required to do a job, such as need-to-know criteria to justify secrecy or "coordination needs" to excuse disclosure. Rule-oriented excuses concerned adhering to procedures, traditions, or authoritative instructions (e.g., "My supervisor told me to . . ."). Ethics-oriented excuses explained behavior by reference to doing "what is right" or to fulfilling an obligation to keep a secret or to share information openly. Finally, power-oriented excuses focused on the use of information to sustain the competitive or status position of the individual, their group, or their organization. Task requirements and ethical obligations were most often relied on to explain the disclosure of information. In contrast, the withholding of information was excused through the use of rules, power, and task excuses.

In another study, Sitkin et al. (1987) examined the types of excuses used by pharmacists to explain how much (or how little) information they chose to give to clients about possible prescription-related errors. These excuses included adhering to professional norms ("professional"), pursuing management's goals and rules ("managerial"), and avoiding legal liability ("legal").

In the Bies (1990) study of middle managers who delivered a variety of bad news, four different types of excuses emerged. These excuses were: mitigating situational circumstances (e.g., "The economic recession won't allow us to hire more people"), someone else's fault (e.g., "It was the previous boss's fault") and the subordinate's own behavior (e.g., "Your performance failed to meet the target"), and the boss's own behavior (e.g., "I made an error/mistake").

The Use of Multiple Reasons.

Researchers have noted that individuals often offer more than one reason in explaining behavior or other outcomes in organizations (Bies, 1987b; Sitkin & Pablo, 1988). Evidence of the use of multiple reasons can be found in two studies. In his research on excuses for organizational secrecy, Sitkin (in press-a) found that subjects used an average of 1.83 reasons to explain each incident. Sitkin et al. (1987) reported a similar level of overall use of multiple reasons (1.75 on average per incident).

The Timing of Excuses

The timing of an excuse refers to whether the excuse is provided before or after (and how long after) a failure event. For example, prior to any decision, a boss could suggest to a subordinate that "top management is considering cutbacks, so the funds we requested may be unavailable." As such, the account would act like a *disclaimer* (Hewitt & Stokes, 1975). After the decision, the boss could provide a similar account, noting that "management did not approve your request due to budget cutbacks." All of the research reviewed thus far, and most of the rest of the research reviewed in this chapter, focuses on excuse-making *after* a failure event. However, there is some evidence that excuse-making occurs *before* a failure event. In his study of middle managers who deliver bad news, Bies (1990) found managers would sometimes "build-in" possible excuses (e.g., potential mitigating circumstances) before undertaking difficult projects.

THE EFFECTIVENESS OF EXCUSE-MAKING IN ORGANIZATIONS

A growing body of empirical studies has examined the effects of excuse-making on individual attitudes and behaviors in organizations. One stream of research has demonstrated that excuse-making can mitigate negative attitudes and behaviors. A second stream of research has focused on identifying factors that influence the effectiveness of excuse-making in organizations. That is, under what conditions are excuses more likely to be honored (Blumstein, 1974). These two streams of research and the respective studies are reviewed below.

Excuse-Making Mitigates Negative Attitudes and Behavior

Several studies have demonstrated that excuses can mitigate negative attitudes and behaviors in organizations. These studies have focused on situations involving poor employee performance, underpayment, budget request refusals, job rejection, layoffs and termination, and unethical conduct.

Poor Employee Performance. Five studies have examined the effects of excuse-making in the context of poor employee performance. In a field study, Greenberg (1988) found that providing mitigating information in excuses enhanced perceptions of fairness of poor performance ratings. In two studies conducted in the laboratory and through a field survey, Baron (1990) examined the mitigating effects of excuses when a boss had given subordinates destructive criticism of (i.e., personal attacks on) their work. Baron found that excuses not only reduced the subordinates' feelings of anger and fairness, but also increased their willingness to rely on collaboration, rather than avoidance, to resolve future conflicts.

Subordinates also have been found to use excuses effectively. When subordinates offer an explanation to their boss, detailing mitigating circumstances for poor performance, that attributional information was found to reduce the blame attributed to subordinates and lessened the severity of the boss's disciplinary actions (Wood & Mitchell, 1981). Gioia and Sims (1986) found similar results in a field study of boss-subordinate interactions concerning a performance problem. Specifically, bosses were more lenient in their evaluations of subordinates after communications with the subordinates.

Underpayment. In a laboratory study, Greenberg (in press) examined the effects of an experimenter's excuse (e.g., "It's not my fault") for underpaying subjects. He was interested in whether the excuse would lessen the subjects' willingness to "steal" from the experimenter. Greenberg found subjects who received excuses were not only more accepting of being underpaid, but they also engaged in less theft, relative to subjects who received no excuse. Further, the effectiveness of the excuse in reducing theft was greater when the experimenter delivered the news of underpayment in an interpersonally sensitive (e.g., "This is unfortunate") rather than insensitive (e.g., "I don't care) manner.

Budget Request Refusals. In a survey study, Bies and Shapiro (1988, Study 2) examined subordinates' reactions to unfavorable budget allocations. They found the presence of a boss' excuse for budget cuts enhanced perceptions of procedural fairness of the action.

Job Rejection. Bies and Shapiro (1988, Study 1) conducted a business simulation study involving a key unfavorable outcome for the MBA student subjects: failure to receive a job offer. They found that "job applicants" who received an excuse for a job rejection (e.g., "A decline in the economy led to a cutback in positions available") perceived less unfairness than job applicants who received no excuse. Similarly, in a field study of the corporate recruitment process, Bies and Moag (1986) found that when job candidates received an excuse for being rejected, they perceived less unfairness and they expressed less anger than others who did not receive such information.

Layoffs and Termination. Research in field settings has found that excuse-making enhances perceptions of fairness in layoff situations (Brockner & Greenberg, 1990). In a survey study of layoff survivors, Brockner, DeWitt, Grover, and Reed (in press) found that managerial excuse-making was positively associated with survivor ratings of organizational commitment. In two additional surveys, Brockner et al. (1990, Studies 2 and 3) found a similar positive association between excuse-making and survivors' ratings of organization commitment.

The effects of excuse-making have also been studied in the context of employee termination. In a policy-capturing study, Rousseau and Anton (1988) had third-parties judge the fairness of various employee terminations. They found the presence of reasons for employee termination enhanced the perceived fairness of that action.

Unethical Conduct. In a business simulation study, Bies and Shapiro (1987, Study 1) examined the presence or absence of a boss' excuse for taking credit for a subordinate's ideas, which ended up costing the subordinate reward and recognition. In the study, the participants were in the role of an "arbitrator" who evaluated the subordinate's complaint about the boss' action. Those subjects who were presented an excuse for the boss' action perceived less unfairness in the action and were less disapproving of the boss than those subjects who received no excuse.

In a laboratory study, Shapiro and Bies (1990) examined the effects of a disclaimer—that is, an excuse prior to an action—on reactions to people who engage in bluffing, a form of lying, in negotiation. They found that negotiators who gave a disclaimer for lying were perceived much less negatively by their negotiating partners than were negotiators who lied but provided no disclaimers.

Factors that Influence the Effectiveness of Excuse-Making

The studies on factors influencing the effectiveness of excuse-making have focused on message-communicator characteristics and situational factors. These studies are reviewed below.

Message-Communicator Characteristics

Several studies have identified message-communicator characteristics of an excuse that explain its effectiveness. These factors are the perceived adequacy of the excuse and the perceived sincerity of the excuse-giver. The studies are reviewed.

Perceived Adequacy. In a business simulation study, Bies and Shapiro (1987, Study 2) examined how a subordinate would react to the presence or absence of a boss' excuse for a budget cut or a sales order cut. They found that although a boss' excuse for the decision lessened the blame attributed to the boss, as well as reduced feelings of procedural unfairness, it was the perceived adequacy of the reasoning in the excuse, when introduced as a covariate into the statistical analysis, that explained most of the variance in the subordinates' reactions. Bies and Shapiro (Study 3) replicated these findings in a field survey of subordinates' reactions to unfavorable budget decisions by their bosses.

A similar pattern of findings concerning the importance of perceived adequacy of an excuse is found in the related research program of Folger and his colleagues. In one study by Folger, Rosenfield, and Robinson (1983), subjects competed with each other in a winner-takes-all competition. The set of rules was announced before the competition, but changes in the rules for distributing the outcomes were announced after the competition was over. All subjects were informed that they had lost in the competition. However, half of the subjects were provided with "adequate" reasons (e.g., "bias" in scoring method) and the other half were provided with "inadequate" reasons (e.g., an "arbitrary" decision) for changing the rules. Subjects who received an adequate excuse for apparently arbitrary changes in the ground rules expressed less discontent (e.g., anger, resentment) than those who received an inadequate excuse.

In a follow-up study by Folger and Martin (1986), participants were denied the opportunity for a favorable outcome as the result of an experimenter's actions, and either adequate reasons (e.g., the task equipment broke down) or inadequate reasons (an arbitrary decision by the experimenter) were provided. In addition, some participants were given the opportunity to "recommend the experimenter for a permanent job as research assistant." Folger and Martin found that participants were less resentful and more willing to recommend the experimenter when they received the adequate, rather than inadequate, reasons for the experimenter's action.

A field study by Greenberg (1990) examined employee theft rates in three manufacturing plants before, during, and after a 15% pay cut was in effect for all employees. In one plant, the pay cut was announced without any explanation, while in a second plant, some "minimal" information in an explanation for the pay cut was provided. In a third plant, a highly detailed explanation of the facts was provided in an explanation for the pay cut. Although employee theft rates were found to be highest during the time of the pay cut than either before or after the pay cut, the amount of theft was influenced greatly by the explanation given for the pay cut. The minimal explanation for the pay cut had a lower theft rate than the plant in which no explanation was given. However, the lowest theft rate occurred in the third plant where the elaborate, well-detailed explanation was given.

What constitutes the adequacy of an explanation in organizations has been the focus of a few studies. In two studies, Shapiro and Buttner (1988) examined whether the excuse is logical, or makes sense, is a key feature of excuse adequacy. In a laboratory study using a loan-decision context (Study 1), Shapiro and Buttner found that logic influenced the perceived adequacy of the excuse. Similarly, in a survey of MBA student job applicants' assessments of explanations for a job rejection (Study 2), Shapiro and Buttner found logic positively associated with perceived adequacy.

The content of the excuse can influence its perceived adequacy. In their study of subordinates' reactions to budget request refusals, Bies et al. (1988) found the type of mitigating circumstance claimed in an excuse influenced the perceived adequacy of the excuse. In a content analysis of the mitigating circumstances reported in the study, they found that whereas different types of mitigating circumstances were communicated by bosses to subordinates, not all claims of mitigating circumstances were perceived as "equal" by subordinates. That is, some types of mitigating circumstances were perceived as more adequate than others. Excuses that focused on company norms, budget constraints, or formal company policy were perceived as significantly more adequate than excuses that focused on the subordinate's own behavior, upper management, and the political environment.

Perceived Sincerity.   Several studies suggest that the perceived sincerity or honesty with which one communicates an excuse is another important factor (Bies, 1987b). In a study on dyadic negotiation, Rubin, Brockner, Eckenrode, Enright, and Johnson-George (1980) unexpectedly found that a negotiator's excuse for a bargaining position resulted in higher negative ratings and more blocking and conflict from the other negotiator. The researchers concluded that the excuse (e.g., "my hands are tied") did not have the predicted effects because the negotiator may have appeared insincere in giving such an explanation. That is, the appearance of insincerity undermined the bargaining relationship, thus becoming a contributing factor to conflict (Baron, 1988).

In a field study, Bies (1987a) examined how a boss' sincerity in giving an excuse for an unfavorable budget decision influenced employees' perceptions of unfairness about the decision-making process. As part of the survey, employees were asked to assess the presence of an excuse and the sincerity of the boss in giving the excuse. The results showed that the presence of an excuse and the boss' sincerity were each independently and negatively associated with perceptions of unfairness.

In a survey of subordinates' reactions to budget request refusals, Bies et al. (1988) examined the relative importance of three aspects of an excuse—claim of mitigating circumstances, adequacy, and sincerity—on a subordinate's feelings of anger, procedural injustice, disapproval of the boss, and complaints to higher-ups. The results suggested that, while a boss' excuse for refusing a budget request can mitigate negative responses by subordinates, the subordinates' reactions were influenced most by the adequacy of the reasoning in the excuse and the boss' sincerity in communicating the excuse. Specifically, the perceived adequacy and sincerity of a boss' excuse for refusing a budget request was negatively associated with subordinates' feelings of anger, procedural injustice, and disapproval of the boss, and sincerity alone was negatively associated with complaints to higher-ups, whereas the claim of mitigating circumstances had no independent effects in any of the responses.

Situational Factors

A few studies have identified situational factors that influence the effectiveness of excuse-making. These factors include the degree of informational uncertainty, outcome importance, outcome negativity, and audience characteristics and expectations. The studies are reviewed.

Informational Uncertainty and Outcome Importance.   In a survey study of layoff survivors, Brockner et al. (in press) examined two situational conditions under which excuse-making could increase the favorability of subordinates' reactions: the degree of informational uncertainty and outcome importance. In general, the positive association between managerial excuses and the favorability of subordinates' reactions (e.g., greater organization commitment and work effort, reduced turnover intention) existed when there were conditions of high uncertainty and high outcome importance.

Outcome Negativity.   In two studies of survivor reactions to layoffs, Brockner et al. (1990) examined the influence of the perceived negativity of the outcome and whether there were reasons given for the layoffs. In one survey study (Study 2), Brockner et al. found that layoffs reduced organizational commitment in general, but did so even more strongly when no reasons were given. These researchers found a similar pattern of results in another survey of layoff survivors (Study 3).

In a survey study of MBA students' reactions to job rejection, Shapiro and Buttner (1988, Study 2) found the perceived adequacy of an excuse to be greater under conditions of perceived low-outcome severity than perceived high-outcome severity. Giacalone and Pollard (1987) found that excuses were more acceptable when there was a small, rather than large, breach of the ethical norm of confidentiality.

Audience Characteristics.   In a series of studies of how norms influence the explanations given for secrecy and disclosure, Sitkin (1986, in press-a; Sitkin et al., 1987) has found that excuses were tailored to some extent to the specific audience receiving the excuse for the disclosure or nondisclosure of information. Giacalone (1988) found the acceptability of some excuses for unethical behavior was influenced by the gender of the communicator and the gender of the audience. That is, males and females judged an excuse differently, and some excuses were more effective with males than with females. Further, Giacalone found that the audience took into consideration the previous history of the excuse-giver when determining the acceptability of the excuses for the unethical behavior.

FUTURE RESEARCH

A review of the empirical studies on excuse-making in organizations suggests a variety of tentative conclusions. First, there is consistent evidence that excuse-making is used as a legitimation strategy. Second, there is consistent evidence that excuses mitigate a variety of negative attitudes and conflictual behaviors. Third, there is an emerging pattern of evidence that the perceived adequacy of the excuse and the sincerity of the excuse-maker, along with situational factors (e.g., outcome importance), influence the effectiveness of excuse-making in organizations. While these generalizations are consistent with research findings in other social domains (see Cody & McLaughlin, 1990), there are several aspects of excuse-making in organizations that warrant more research.

First, there needs to be more research on situational conditions that influence excuse-making in organizations. While research has focused primarily on uncertainty and outcome-related variables (e.g., importance, negativity), other situational factors (e.g., audience, norms) that have already been identified still warrant more empirical study. Other additional situational factors for future research include power relationship between the parties, timing of the excuse, history and familiarity with the excuse-maker, and level of conflict (Bies & Sitkin, 1990).

Second, there needs to be more research on the use of multiple reasons in excuse-making (Bies & Sitkin, 1990). Indeed, in organizations, there are often multiple reasons given when problems arise (Sitkin, in press-a; Sitkin et al., 1987). Yet, at the same time, we know very little about the effectiveness of single versus multiple reasons given in excuse-making (Bies, 1987b). Third, although research has identified different types of mitigating circumstances, the research also suggests that they are not all perceived to be equally effective (Bies et al., 1988). One direction for future research is to compare the relative influence of different types of mitigating circumstances in excuse-making. Another research direction is to focus on the attributional dimensions of different excuses in organizations (e.g., internal–external, stable–unstable, controllable–uncontrollable), which previous research has shown to influence the effectiveness of excuse-making (Weiner, Amirkhan, Folkes, & Verette, 1987).

Fourth, the analysis presented in this chapter focused on the use of accounts as part of a one-way communication process between two parties. For example, a boss communicates an excuse to the subordinate. While many organizational communications fit this pattern (Putnam & Poole, 1987), in some cases the communication of excuses involves a two-way process. For example, in response to the boss' excuse for an unfavorable resource allocation (e.g., upper management), a subordinate may counter with an alternative excuse (e.g., boss acted arbitrarily), to relegitimate his or her initial position, or to attempt to delegitimate the boss' position (cf. Martin, Scully, & Levitt, 1990). Following this line of reasoning, whether a boss' excuse will mitigate negative responses may depend, in part, on the nature or presence of the subordinate's excuse (Bies & Tripp, 1988) and whether the two parties can negotiate a shared understanding of the situation (Harré & Secord, 1977). Thus, as an extension of the research reviewed in this chapter, the interplay between boss and subordinate excuses represents another direction for future research.

Finally, there needs to be research on the trade-offs raised by excuse-making in organizations. On the one hand, an excuse may legitimate a boss' decision (Tompkins & Cheney, 1983), and such legitimation is a critical aspect of managerial authority that ensures social order in organizations (Barnard, 1938; Simon,

1947). On the other hand, an excuse can have negative effects for the organization in the long run if it keeps organizational members from recognizing and responding to problems (Sitkin, in press-b). For example, an excuse may be used to "cool out" a potentially offended party (Goffman, 1952) and also create a false peace (Nord, 1987). If, at a later time, the individual comes to believe he or she has been intentionally deceived, the resultant feelings of betrayal, distrust, and injustice may lead to retaliation and the escalation of conflict (Jemison & Sitkin, 1986; Shapiro & Bies, 1990). In addition, given that an excuse lessens a subordinate's feelings of anger, it may also lessen his or her motivation to search for alternative solutions to the rejected proposal (Goffman, 1952) and thereby undermine some of the constructive outcomes of a failure event (Sitkin, in press-b), such as creative problem solving (Brown, 1983; Deutsch, 1973; Thomas, 1976) and positive change (Brown, 1983; Coser, 1956; Kanter, 1983).

ACKNOWLEDGMENT

We wish to thank the editors and Susan Bies for their constructive comments and suggestions on an earlier version of this chapter.

REFERENCES

Austin, J. L. (1961). *Philosophical papers*. London: Oxford University Press.

Barnard, C. I. (1938). *The functions of the executive*. Cambridge, MA: Harvard University Press.

Baron, R. A. (1988). Attributions and organizational conflict: The mediating role of apparent sincerity. *Organizational Behavior and Human Decision Processes, 41*, 111-127.

Baron, R. A. (1990). Countering the effects of destructive criticism: The relative efficacy of four interventions. *Journal of Applied Psychology, 75*, 235-245.

Bettman, J. R., & Weitz, B. A. (1983). Attributions in the boardroom: Causal reasoning in corporate annual reports. *Administrative Science Quarterly, 28*, 165-183.

Bies, R. J. (1987a). Beyond "voice": The influence of decision-maker justification and sincerity on procedural fairness judgments. *Representative Research in Social Psychology, 17*, 3-17.

Bies, R. J. (1987b). The predicament of injustice: The management of moral outrage. In L. L. Cummings & B. M. Staw (Eds.), *Research in organizational behavior* (Vol. 9, pp. 289-319). Greenwich, CT: JAI Press.

Bies, R. J. (1989). Managing conflict before it happens: The role of accounts. In M. A. Rahim (Ed.), *Managing conflict: An interdisciplinary approach* (pp. 83-91). New York: Praeger.

Bies, R. J. (1990). *The manager as intuitive politician: Blame management in the delivery of bad news*. Unpublished manuscript.

Bies, R. J., & Moag, J. S. (1986). Interactional justice: Communication criteria of fairness. In R. Lewicki, B. H. Sheppard, & M. H. Bazerman (Ed.), *Research on negotiation in organizations* (Vol. 1, pp. 43-55). Greenwich, CT: JAI Press.

Bies, R. J., & Shapiro, D. L. (1987). Interactional fairness judgments: The influence of causal accounts. *Social Justice Research, 1*, 199-218.

Bies, R. J., & Shapiro, D. L. (1988). Voice and justification: Their influence on procedural fairness judgments. *Academy of Management Journal, 31*, 676-685.

Bies, R. J., Shapiro, D. L., & Cummings, L. L. (1988). Causal accounts and managing organizational conflict: Is it enough to say it's not my fault? *Communication Research, 15,* 381–399.

Bies, R. J., & Sitkin, S. B. (1990). *Excuse-making as conflict management.* Unpublished manuscript.

Bies, R. J., & Tripp, T. M. (1988, April). *Attributional conflict and third party judgments.* Paper presented at the meeting of TIMS/ORSA, Washington, DC.

Blumstein, P. W. (1974). The honoring of accounts. *American Sociological Review, 39,* 551–566.

Brockner, J., Dewitt, R. L., Grover, S., & Reed, T. (in press). When it is especially important to explain why: Factors affecting the relationship between managers' explanations of a layoff and survivors' reactions to the layoff. *Journal of Experimental Social Psychology.*

Brockner, J., & Greenberg, J. (1990). The impact of layoffs on survivors: An organizational justice perspective. In J. S. Carroll (Ed.), *Applied social psychology and organizational settings* (pp. 45–75). Hillsdale, NJ: Lawrence Erlbaum Associates.

Brockner, J., Konovsky, M., Cooper, R., Folger, R., Grover, S., & Reed, T. (1990). *Attributions for layoffs, procedural justice, outcome negativity, and the reactions of layoff victims and survivors.* Unpublished manuscript.

Brown, L. D. (1983). *Managing conflict at organizational interfaces.* Reading, MA: Addison-Wesley.

Cody, M. J., & McLaughlin, M. L. (1985). Models for the sequential construction of accounting episodes: Situational and interactional constraints on message selection and evaluation. In R. Street & J. Capella (Eds.), *Sequence and pattern in communicative behaviour* (pp. 50–69). London: Arnold.

Cody, M. J., & McLaughlin, M. L. (1990). Interpersonal accounting. In H. Giles & P. Robinson (Eds.), *The handbook of language and social psychology* (pp. 227–255). London: Wiley.

Coser, L. A. (1956). *The function of social conflict.* New York: The Free Press.

Deutsch, M. (1973). *The resolution of conflict: Constructive and destructive processes.* New Haven, CT: Yale University Press.

Folger, R., & Martin, C. (1986). Relative deprivation and referent cognitions: Distributive and procedural justice effects. *Journal of Experimental Social Psychology, 22,* 531–546.

Folger, R., Rosenfield, D., & Robinson, T. (1983). Relative deprivation and procedural justifications. *Journal of Personality and Social Psychology, 45,* 268–273.

Garrett, D. E., Bradford, J. L., Meyers, R. A., & Becker, J. (1989). Issues management and organizational accounts: An analysis of corporate responses to accusations of unethical business practices. *Journal of Business Ethics, 8,* 507–520.

Giacalone, R. A. (1988). The effect of administrative accounts and gender on the perception of leadership. *Group & Organization Studies, 13,* 195–207.

Giacalone, R. A., & Pollard, H. G. (1987). The efficacy of accounts for a breach of confidentiality by management. *Journal of Business Ethics, 6,* 393–397.

Gioia, D. A., & Sims, H. P., Jr. (1986). Cognition-behavior connections: Attributions and verbal behavior in leader-subordinate interactions. *Organizational Behavior and Human Decision Processes, 37,* 197–229.

Goffman, E. (1952). On cooling out the mark: Some aspects of adaptation to failure. *Psychiatry, 15,* 451–463.

Goffman, E. (1971). *Relations in public: Microstudies of the public order.* New York: Basic Books.

Greenberg, J. (1988, August). Using explanations to manage impressions of performance appraisal fairness. In J. Greenberg & R. J. Bies (Co-Chairs), *Communicating fairness in organizations.* Symposium presented at the national meeting of the Academy of Management, Anaheim, CA.

Greenberg, J. (1990). Employee theft as a reaction to underpayment inequity: The hidden cost of pay cuts. *Journal of Applied Psychology, 75,* 561–568.

Greenberg, J. (in press). Stealing in the name of justice: Informational and interpersonal moderators of theft reactions to underpayment inequity. *Organizational Behavior and Human Decision Processes.*

Harré, R. (1977). The ethnogenic approach: Theory and practice. In L. Berkowitz (Ed.), *Advances in experimental social psychology* (Vol. 10, pp. 283–314). New York: Academic Press.

Harré, R., & Secord, P. F. (1973). *The explanation of social behavior.* New York: Littlefield, Adams.

Hewitt, J. P., & Stokes, R. (1975). Disclaimers. *American Sociological Review, 40*, 1-11.

Izraeli, D., & Jick, T. D. (1983). The art of saying no: On the management of refusals in organizations. In P. J. Frost, V. F. Mitchell, & W. R. Nord (Eds.), *Organizational reality: Reports from the firing line* (3rd ed., pp. 283-296). Glenview, IL: Scott Foresman.

Jemison, D. B., & Sitkin, S. B. (1986). Corporate acquisitions: A process perspective. *Academy of Management Review, 11*, 145-163.

Kanter, R. M. (1983). *The change masters.* New York: Simon & Schuster.

Konovsky, M. A., & Jaster, F. (1989). "Blaming the victim" and other ways business men and women account for questionable behavior. *Journal of Business Ethics, 8*, 391-398.

March, J. G., & Simon, H. A. (1958). *Organizations.* New York: Wiley.

Martin, J., Scully, M., & Levitt, B. (1990). Injustice and legitimation of revolution: Damning the past, excusing the present, and neglecting the future. *Journal of Personality and Social Psychology, 59*, 281-290.

McLaughlin, M. L. (1984). *Conversation: How talk is organized.* Beverly Hills, CA: Sage.

Nord, W. R. (1987, October). *On the study of conflict and false peace.* Paper presented at the Conflict and Change Conference, Minneapolis, MN.

Pelz, D. C. (1952). Influence: A key to effective leadership in the first-line supervisor. *Personnel, 29*, 209-217.

Putnam, L. L., & Poole, M. S. (1987). Conflict and negotiation. In F. M. Jablin, L. L. Putnam, K. H. Roberts, & L. W. Porter (Eds.), *Handbook of organizational communication* (pp. 549-599). Beverly Hills, CA: Sage.

Rousseau, D. M., & Anton, R. J. (1988). Fairness and implied contract obligations in job terminations: A policy-capturing study. *Human Performance, 1*, 273-289.

Rubin, J. Z., Brockner, J., Eckenrode, J., Enright, M. A., & Johnson-George, C. (1980). Weakness as strength: Test of a "my hands are tied" ploy in bargaining. *Personality and Social Psychology Bulletin, 6*, 216-221.

Salancik, G. R., & Meindl, J. R. (1984). Corporate attributions as strategic illusions of management control. *Administrative Science Quarterly, 29*, 238-254.

Schonbach, P. (1980). A category system for account phases. *European Journal of Social Psychology, 10*, 195-200.

Schonbach, P. (1990). *Account episodes: The management or escalation of conflict.* Cambridge: Cambridge University Press.

Scott, M. B., & Lyman, S. M. (1968). Accounts. *American Sociological Review, 33*, 46-62.

Shapiro, D. L., & Bies, R. J. (1990). *Threats, bluffs, and disclaimers in negotiations.* Unpublished manuscript.

Shapiro, D. L., & Buttner, E. H. (1988, August). *Adequate explanations: What are they, and do they enhance procedural justice under severe outcome circumstances?* Paper presented at the meeting of the Academy of Management, Anaheim, CA.

Simon, H. A. (1947). *Administrative behavior.* New York: The Free Press.

Sitkin, S. B. (1986, August). *Discreet excuses and excused indiscretions: Justifying secrecy and disclosure in Silicon Valley.* Paper presented at the meeting of the Academy of Management, Chicago, IL.

Sitkin, S. B. (in press-a). Secrecy norms in organizational settings. In L. D. Browning (Ed.), *Conceptual frontiers in organizational communication.* Albany, NY: State University of New York Press.

Sitkin, S. B. (in press-b). The strategy of small losses: Learning from failure. In B. M. Staw & L. L. Cummings (Eds.), *Research in organizational behavior* (Vol. 14). Greenwich, CT: JAI Press.

Sitkin, S. B., & Pablo, A. L. (1988). *The use of multiple explanations.* Unpublished manuscript.

Sitkin, S. B., & Sutcliffe, K. M. (1991). Dispensing legitimacy: Professional, organizational, and legal influences on pharmacist behavior. In S. Bacharach, S. Barley, & P. Tolbert (Eds.), *Research in the sociology of organizations.* Greenwich, CT: JAI Press.

Sitkin, S. B., Sutcliffe, K. M., & Reed, L. (1987, August). *Legal, organizational, and professional justifications for disclosive and non-disclosive behavior: Pharmacist use of social accounts.* Paper presented at the national meeting of the Academy of Management, New Orleans, LA.

Snyder, C. R., Higgins, R. L., & Stucky, R. J. (1983). *Excuses: Masquerades in search of social grace.* New York: Wiley/Interscience.

Staw, B. M., McKechnie, P. I., & Puffer, S. M. (1983). The justification of organizational performance. *Administrative Science Quarterly, 28,* 582-600.

Sutton, R. I., & Callahan, A. L. (1987). The stigma of bankruptcy: The spoiled organizational image and its management. *Academy of Management Journal, 30,* 405-436.

Sutton, R. I., Eisenhardt, K. M., & Jucker, J. V. (1986). Managing organizational decline: Lessons from Atari. *Organizational Dynamics, 14* (Spring), 17-29.

Thomas, K. W. (1976). Conflict and conflict management. In M. Dunnette (Ed.), *Handbook of industrial and organizational psychology* (pp. 889-936). Chicago: Rand McNally.

Tompkins, P. K., & Cheney, G. (1983). Account analysis of organizations: Decision making and identification. In L. L. Putnam & M. E. Pacanowsky (Eds.), *Communication and organizations: An interpretive approach* (pp. 123-146). Beverly Hills, CA: Sage.

Weiner, B., Amirkhan, J., Folkes, V. S., & Verette, J. A. (1987). An attributional analysis of excuse-making: Studies of a naive theory of emotion. *Journal of Personality and Social Psychology, 52,* 316-324.

Wood, R. E., & Mitchell, T. R. (1981). Manager behavior in a social context: The impact of impression management on attributions and disciplinary action. *Organizational Behavior and Human Performance, 28,* 356-378.

11

▼▼▼▼▼▼▼

Alternative Knowledge Sources in Explanations of Racist Events

Philomena Essed
University of Amsterdam

In a series of interviews with Black women about everyday racism, one of them offered the following story about a high school in the United States:

> When I came into high school I started off in the very lowest tracks. . . . I think that generally, in this country, we track Black children in the lower tracks so that they do not have opportunities to go to college. However, I do not think that [my case] was a result of racism, because both the teachers and the headmaster that I had . . . [gave me] a lot of encouragement and support to reach my potential so that by the time I was a junior in high school I was back on the college preparatory track. (Essed, 1991, protocol C9)

She goes on to explain that she had problems because she had gone to school at age 5 and skipped a grade when she was 7 because she was doing very well. However, she developed an adverse reaction by the time she was 10, because she could no longer cope with the fact that she would always be 2 years younger than her other (predominantly White) classmates.

This story is an example of the application of general knowledge of racism (here: overall underestimation of Black children) in understanding personal experience (being placed in the lowest tracks). It is an interesting example, because it defies the usual claims that Blacks are inclined to use any opportunity to "accuse" Whites of racism. This chapter demonstrates that knowledge of racism is a necessary precondition for making correct evaluations of racial situations. Moreover, experts in the racism problematic are well equipped to take inconsistent information into account when making inferences from material that is a

199

balanced mix of information that is racism consistent (underestimation, lowest tracks) and racism inconsistent (support and encouragement) (for further discussion see Fiske, Kinder, & Larter, 1983).

Many studies have dealt with the issue of racism, but few have addressed epistemological questions of perception and knowledge of racism. Knowledge of racism is a dynamic concept. It represents cognitions that are activated when the understander processes, stores, and retrieves specific experiences of racism. Knowledge of racism is part of a process of constant input, testing, and interpretation of new information and remodeling of previous representations. Whereas various social cognition theorists have been interested in the contents of knowledge structures and in the processes of knowledge acquisition (Kruglanski, 1988), primary attention is paid here to the relevance and use of knowledge of racism in accounting. For that purpose I suggest a tentative interpretation method for analyzing racist events. Further I discuss a method for understanding accounts of racism. Because this method was explained elsewhere and also tested on a limited scale, I concentrate in this chapter only on its application (Essed, 1988, 1990a; Louw-Potgieter, 1989). For illustration I use stories gathered in nondirective interviews with 55 black women, ages 20–45, in the United States (California) and in the Netherlands. These cross-cultural data are part of a larger project on everyday racism (Essed, 1991). The women interviewed all have, or are training for, a college degree.

The interviews addressed different kinds of experiences of racism. For illustration of the structure and use of knowledge sources in accounts I could have taken any type of experience of racism that occurs in everyday life, such as racism in selecting job applicants (Essed, 1988), patronizing behavior of White against Black women in feminist organizations (Essed, 1989) or subtle mechanisms of exclusion of Black professionals in everyday interactions with White colleagues and supervisors (Essed, 1990c). Here, I select from the interview materials the accounts of Black women about sexual harassment by White men. This artificial isolation of one type of racism is necessary in order to show that general knowledge about that particular form of racism is a necessary (though not the only) condition for understanding concrete examples of its specific manifestations in everyday life. This holds true for the layperson trying to understand her personal experiences as well as for scholars who study these experiences.

Sexual racism against Black women has been the object of many predominantly historical studies (Davis, 1981). Little attention has been paid, however, to contemporary manifestations of this problem, least of all against educated Black women. The context of discussion concerns interactions in the academic environment. More specifically, attention will be paid to the particular problem of White male professors who abuse the power attached to their function in dealing with Black female students. Although it is often assumed that middle-class Black women have much protection against unwelcome sexual advances of White men (Staples, 1973), my own study shows that, for such women (the threat of) sexual harassment by

White men is an everyday reality, whether or not actual assaults take place. Various women testified of assaults by White men in a position of authority who threatened them, or actually retaliated when the women resisted. These situations usually have further implications: A woman's education, job or career is at stake. When White men in a position of authority abuse functional power to force themselves sexually upon Black women, they are likely to use the same power to retaliate when the woman refuses. This makes it even more relevant to keep this issue on the agenda.

INTERVIEWING SOCIAL EQUALS

Accounts are partly shaped by the interview context in which they are presented (Cicourel, 1964). For various reasons I did not control systematically all the factors that affected the presentation of the accounts in the particular interview situation. The exploratory nature of the research and the sensitivity of the problem demanded flexibility and carefulness in the selection of interviewees, as well as in the manner of interviewing. Further, in each successive interview I applied insights gained in earlier ones. For these and other reasons, the characteristics of the interview situation itself cannot be used as a basis for systematic analysis. I will discuss, however, on a more general level some factors that had an impact on the sort of information I received. The first has to do with the social relationship between the interviewees and the interviewer (myself).

Most investigations in social science tend to "study down" rather than to "study up" (Lofland & Lofland, 1984). The last two decades, doing research among equals has been encouraged strongly by feminist social scientists. In certain respects the project about everyday racism held the "ideal" conditions for a nonhierarchical relationship between the interviewer and the interviewees: common experiences with the informants, similar racial background, social equality, and natural involvement with the problem at study (Mies, 1983). Being an insider provided a rich base for tentative probing. This is an important value in exploratory research.

The nature of exploratory research allows for flexibility in the way one gathers information about still unexplored phenomena in order to conceptualize key notions and characteristics of the problem. However, the method of nondirective interviewing depends completely on the memory of the informants. This can be problematic, because everyday racism often involves small, seemingly trivial events that may easily be overlooked as incidental or unimportant. When memory failed, I probed for cues, such as detail, outstanding events, specific emotions, people, or statements to stimulate the reconstruction of experiences. However, probing did not always induce successful response. In that sense, the accounts probably still represent only the "tip of the iceberg."

In exploratory research, ingenuity and flexible use of the method that is chosen inevitably play a part in determining its productiveness. This introduces the question of the reliability of the method of nondirective interviews. Conversations are "locally" produced and therefore always unique, up to a certain point. Nondirective interviews can never be repeated in exactly the same way because the interview is partly determined by the particular associations the interviewee has in reconstructing her experiences and the specifics of the interview context. Nevertheless, the fact that the same project was conducted twice, once in the United States and once in the Netherlands, and that in both countries the method gave consistent results – namely verbal reconstructions of experiences of racism in similar situations of everyday life – indicates that the method used was reliable.

Finally, one may wonder why Black women were willing to tell some of their unpleasant experiences to a stranger. Most women told me they wanted to participate because they were convinced of the importance of the project, they liked the idea of talking about their daily experiences, or they were just happy to support another Black woman doing her research. The women were open, friendly, and supportive. Their high level of trust in me suggested that they expected me to understand their experiences simply because I am another Black woman. Finch called this possibility that a particular kind of identification develops one of the special characteristics of woman-to-woman interviews when they are conducted in the way I described above, that is, without a formal questionnaire (Finch, 1984). For many women the interview was an opportunity to talk about themselves to someone who listened carefully to their daily concerns and asked questions that would stimulate them to gain a clearer picture of their own feelings and opinions, for themselves as well as for the purpose of research. At the same time these questions reflected a genuine understanding of the experience of Black women. We will see that agreeing to be interviewed in a project about racism did not mean that the women placed their negative experiences automatically in a racial context. Rather than imposing on the women an interpretative framework, I encouraged them also to voice doubts and insecurities about the meaning of some of their experiences.

THE ROLE OF GENERAL KNOWLEDGE
IN UNDERSTANDING EVERYDAY RACISM

Who is telling the truth, or whose reality counts when it concerns racism: the offender and his or her motivations or the victim for whom one particular case adds to any number of previous ones? Today, agents of racism are less likely to openly make racist statements or to openly reject Blacks because of their skin color. This makes the study of racism more complicated, but also more of a challenge because alternative ways have to be found to analyze racial situations.

Thus, in court, statistics have often been allowed as evidence in discrimination cases. Statistics not only tell something about the number of Blacks hired in an organization, but they also represent an indication of the racial structure within that organization. This introduces the way I perceive the function of general knowledge of racism in the study of racist events: General knowledge of racism can be used as evidence when assessing (potentially) racist events. Of course, general knowledge is not the only evidence. Attribution theory provides various useful concepts and instruments such as comparisons for (in)consistency and consensus, to which I shall return later. Here, it is relevant to emphasize that general knowledge of racism reflects the (historical) macrostructure of race relations that forms the framework of any situation in a racial context.

The concept of knowledge is often artificially separated from experience. While epistemological questions are not uppermost in this chapter, it is useful to make explicit that my approach follows others in rejecting the view that experience is necessarily second class compared to knowledge (Code, 1988). Here, the view is taken that one's experience may be an important knowledge source. The focus on general knowledge and comprehension of racism must be placed against the background of social cognition theory (Fiske & Taylor, 1984; Forgas, 1982). Cognitions of racism are not only unique personal representations about the stock of racism episodes experienced within one's lifetime. Representations are continually tested, adapted, and also structured by information from the social context and may therefore be regarded as belonging to the social domain. These representations may also include elements of scientific knowledge ordinary people hear about, process, and use in their everyday lives (Moscovici & Hewstone, 1983).

Before entering into a discussion of the use of knowledge of racism, it is first relevant to qualify the notion of knowledge of racism. In social psychology the idea of general knowledge of racism has hardly ever been conceptualized. In sociology the rather vague term *race consciousness* has been used instead. Hall and Allen (1989) identified the three major components of race consciousness as (a) race identification, (b) system blame, and (c) action orientation. These components can be further operationalized in terms of general knowledge features. Hypothetically, I identify the following as abstract features of general knowledge of racism: (a) the ability to explain individual experiences in terms of group experiences, (b) the acknowledgment of the historical experience of the group, (c) the explanation of (historical and contemporary) group experiences in terms of racial and ethnic domination, and (d) personal responsibility in the process of change. Through prolonged practice in dealing with racism, Black people become experts. This means that their general knowledge of racism becomes more and more complexly organized, while their interpretative strategies become more elaborate and effective (Fiske & Kinder, 1981). This theme is worked out in the rest of the chapter by analyzing accounts of racism.

ACCOUNTS OF RACISM

Accounts of racism can be seen as reconstructions of events in which the account-er gives meaning to, explains, and judges the behavior of others (agents of rac-ism). Accounts of racism are, therefore, a specific type of account: a *critique* of specific practices within a larger context of judgment and of general knowledge of prevalent racial and ethnic domination. Since knowledge of racism has been defined as a form of political knowledge, accounts of racism constitute a *political critique*. This function of accounts, namely to voice a critique of existing power relations, has as yet received little attention.

Among feminist theorists it is generally agreed that taking women's own ac-counts of their situation has been a very important improvement in the reproduc-tion of knowledge about the situation of women (Ramazanoglu, 1989; Smith, 1987). Inviting Black women to express their own experiences of racism raises problems, however, of how the knowledge produced can be validated. The researcher cannot just present everyday accounts of Black women without mak-ing some selection and evaluation of these accounts. It remains, therefore, the task of the researcher to provide concepts that enable us to understand whether specific experiences must be interpreted in terms of racism (Ramazanoglu). Claims of knowledgeability of racial issues reflect a particular perspective shaped by race, class, gender, and personality factors. Although it is often extremely difficult to construct reliable standards of evidence and norms of truth, this does not mean that informed judgments cannot be made (Hawkesworth, 1989). Provided we have sophisticated and detailed information through the analysis of accounts of ex-periences of racism, we can dispel distortions and mystifications that abound in dominant perceptions of racism.

When is a judgment about racial situations an informed judgment? This ques-tion cannot be fully answered here, but the minimal conditions are that these judgments reflect a certain degree of general knowledge, both of rules and con-ventions in nonracial situations and of racial situations and racism, for several reasons. First, racist events always involve unacceptable behavior. In order to distinguish acceptable from unacceptable behavior, knowledge is used of what acceptable behavior is, given the circumstances of that situation. Second, when unacceptable acts can be explained in terms of racial injustice and when no other plausible explanations are available, the event can be seen, hypothetically, as a racist event. In order to distinguish racial explanations from other plausible ex-planations it is at least relevant to have general knowledge of racism.

In order to establish whether judgments derive from these knowledge sources, I tested all the interviews. The systematic testing of the availability of general knowledge of rules and conventions was too broad a task to fulfill in the format of the research project. Therefore, I focused only on the second condition, the availability of general knowledge of racism. The reader must bear in mind that the women were told before that the interviews were about racism and that they could have refused to participate if they did not have any experience in that respect or if they did not know anything about that topic. Of the 55 interviewees, four (including Denise, see below) explained during the interview that they had never given much thought to racism. I compared these interviews with all the other interviews and found a major difference: Unlike the others, these women did not see their own experiences as part of the group experience. They perceived themselves as different from other Blacks. Further, they made few, if any, generalized statements about race relations, and they avoided the very words "discrimination" and "racism." Thus, it could be expected that their accounts of unfair behavior in interactions with Whites would not include the evaluative hypothesis (or conclusion) that racism was involved. Detailed analysis of their accounts showed that this was indeed the case. In the course of this chapter I explain the methods I used (a) to test whether accounts derive from knowledge of racism, and (b) to analyze the interpretative and argumentative procedures underlying accounts of sexual racism. For illustration I selected two cases from all stories about sexual harassment in a racial context.

The first example illustrates the difference between informed and uninformed assessments. For the sake of readability I call insufficiently informed judgments "subjective assessments" and sufficiently informed judgments "objective assessments." In the first example general situation knowledge and general knowledge of racism (objective criteria) suggests that the woman involved was subjected to sexual racism. According to her own assessment (subjective criteria) she only experienced unacceptable behavior. A case like this is not unique. I (1990b, 1991) pointed out that victims of racism may try sometimes to find excuses for not interpreting their experiences as evidence of racism. Typical disclaimers are, for example, "I hate using my color as an excuse" or "A few Blacks misbehave and they are spoiling everything for the rest of us." The motivational factors underlying denial deserve more attention, but it is beyond my immediate purpose to examine excuses and justifications that have the impact of mitigating racism.

ASSESSMENT OF IMPLICIT GENERAL KNOWLEDGE IN RECONSTRUCTIONS OF RACIST EVENTS

In order to study the role of general knowledge in understanding racist events, it is assumed, hypothetically, that the comprehension of racism in everyday situations can be conceptualized as a process following a specific sequence. The test sequence is only a rough outline of the cognitive economy of the use of interpretive steps. The right-hand side of Fig. 11.1 represents objective assessments. The initial interpretative steps depend on the effective use of situational knowledge (Steps 1 and 2). Subsequently, general knowledge of racism is used in order to understand the racial context of the situation (Step 3 and so on). It is likely that the more expertise one has in judging racist events the more "automatically" the

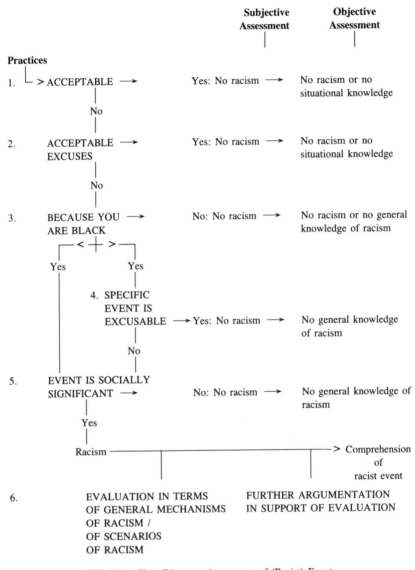

FIG. 11.1 Flow Diagram: Assessment of (Racist) Events

interpretation sequence will proceed. Hypothetically, it can be assumed that the interpretation of potentially racist events may proceed as follows:

Step 1: Acceptable or Not?

In processing new events people activate generalized episodes of that type of situation, or "scripts" (Schank & Abelson, 1977). Scripts include socially shared knowledge of rules and conventions of behavior in specific situations. Without this situational knowledge (see right-hand side of Fig. 11.1) the interpreter cannot judge whether specific practices are acceptable. Hence, subjective conclusions that these practices are acceptable and that there is no racism are, objectively speaking, either correct, or they are incorrect due to insufficient situational knowledge. Arguably, script theories are normative and they often take White (male) middle-class standards as the norm. To give an example, in a restaurant the waiter is supposed to be friendly and to respond efficiently to the demands of the clients. This is the rule, but it may well be the case that the majority of Black (and/or lower-class) clients do not normally get friendly and efficient service. It is, then, questionable whether we can use the experience of (White) middle-class clients as the standard for the definition of restaurant scripts. The examples used in this chapter are unambiguous. Whether it concerns White or Black female students, their generalized episodes of professor–student interactions may include sexual harassment as a deviation from the rule, but certainly not as the rule. Nevertheless, we must keep in mind that the concept of socially shared knowledge is problematic, first, because rules and conventions are (sub)culturally (and gender) determined and second, because these rules may be violated so often that the definition of what the rule is becomes questionable.

The first step in the sequence suggests that specific practices should be interpreted as acceptable or unacceptable, given the situational conditions. In general, behavior considered acceptable will not induce further questioning. However, insufficient knowledge of the normal rules and conventions for acceptable behavior may cause the interpreter to accept behavior that seems normal, but which is in fact not acceptable in that specific situation.

Step 2: Acceptable Excuses for Unacceptable Behavior?

Unacceptable behavior (e.g., discrimination) can only be excused when there are circumstances beyond the control of the actor. Conclusions that excuses for unacceptable behavior are acceptable are either correct (hence, no racism), or they are incorrect, objectively speaking, due to lack of sufficient situational knowledge.

Step 3: Is It Because I Am Black?

If there are no acceptable excuses, it is relevant to know if this example of discrimination (or expressed prejudice) is directed against a Black individual because of her/his racial-ethnic background. When dealing with covert racism this conclusion is hypothetical and its plausibility depends on subsequent argumentation to substantiate that conclusion. Here, I stress that preliminary conclusions about racism presuppose the ability to relate personal experiences to group experiences, and, hence, a certain degree of knowledge of race relations and of racism.

Step 4: Is the Specific Event Excusable?

This question is irrelevant for interpreters who have knowledge of racism. Moreover, making Step 4 suggests by itself failure to understand that racist discrimination cannot be excused under any circumstances. Because we want to distinguish subjective from objective assessments, Step 4 must be included in the sequence as an optional step, which can be explained as follows. If particular unacceptable behavior (Step 1) that could not be excused (Step 2), is directed against a person because she or he is Black (Step 3), the racist implications of that situation are obvious, objectively speaking. However, my earlier research showed that some interpreters tend to excuse racist behavior (Essed, 1990b). For illustration I take a commonly occurring form of racism in shopping situations. Many Black women I interviewed in two successive research projects criticized White shop attendants for checking on them conspicuously (Essed, 1990b, 1991). They felt this was not fair, because they noticed that White clients were not automatically suspected of shoplifting (Steps 1, 2, 3). Nevertheless, various women in the first project felt the shop attendants could be excused. How could one blame them, the argument went, for not knowing how to tell "honest" from "dishonest" blacks? When I interviewed these women in the early 1980s about their daily experiences with the Dutch, racism was not yet a topic of public discourse in the Netherlands. Among Blacks there was a tendency to deny that they were discriminated against. In the interviews I could not even mention the word discrimination to the women, because it was a taboo. Thus the women tended to individualize racial situations rather than connecting the personal to the group experience. This introduces the next step in the interpretation sequence.

Step 5: Is the Event Socially Significant?

Insight into racism implies that the interpreter sees specific events as the situational expression of the group experience.

Step 6:

Finally, the last step places the specific event in an evaluative framework consisting of general racism knowledge, which can be supported by other argumentation, such as comparisons with the experiences of specific other Blacks. The function and use of the evaluative framework is discussed in more detail below.

The flow diagram is discussed and applied in more detail elsewhere (Essed, 1991). Let me show, here, with one example, that lack of general knowledge of racism indeed impedes the understanding of its manifestations in one's personal experiences. For that purpose I use the account of an American Black woman, Denise A., student, 21 years old. The accounts of this particular woman were selected for the following reason. Unlike most other Black women who participated in the project, Denise A. was not prepared by her family to face United States' race relations. Her mother told her that "there's no such thing as color." She lived in an all-White neighborhood, was taught to "assimilate into White culture" and did not perceive herself as Black. In school, Blacks called her "White girl" or "oreo." In the period during which the interview with her took place, she was "searching desperately to find out about Black culture." She had hardly ever thought about the issue of racism. Her story is about her experiences with a White professor, a man in his fifties. We will see that her story includes descriptive and interpretative categories of unfair treatment, but it does not include racism (and sexism) evaluation categories:

> I was working 10 hours a day and going to school at the junior college. I failed the (calculus) class. I talked to (the professor) afterwards. . . . He said just come into my office and I'll help you. . . . I started going to his office to get help, 'cause they didn't have tutors at the junior college and he . . . would . . . say [things like], "You're attractive" and "I would like to see you" and I would go, "Well I'm sorry, I'm just here for you to help me with my calculus" and then one day . . . he was trying to kiss me and I . . . [said], "No," and he says, "Well you know that you want me to, you want this," and he says, "You're just playing around 'cause you know you started the whole thing." I was, oh, my gosh, what have I done to this man to make him think that I want him to come on to me sexually? So the only thing I could think of to do is just not to go to his office and I was scared to talk to anybody about it 'cause I thought maybe I had done something to . . . bring him on. . . . Since I didn't respond, I had a hard time in the class. So, I just flunked it again.
>
> [Eventually, Denise has to quit school. She applies at another university and she talks to the EOP adviser, a Black man.] He tried to calm me down . . . and he said, "Don't blame yourself . . . a lot of White men feel that Black women are here to be used sexually." It really was hard for me to conceive of it but it sort of clicked in the whole thing.

The flow diagram was designed with the view of testing accounts for the use of general knowledge of racism. One can easily use, however, the same diagram for inferring whether or not the accounter uses general knowledge of sexism. With the help of the flow diagram it can be illustrated, through systematic analysis, that the account does not build on implicit or explicit general knowledge of racism (or sexism):

1. Was it acceptable? No

The professor tried to take advantage of the situation and Denise is clear about the fact that she did not find that acceptable. Her solution is to give up on further tutor sessions. Later she decides to change schools.

2. Were there acceptable excuses? No (hesitantly)

Initially, Denise blamed herself for the situation. However, she feels deep down that she did not give cause. This can be inferred from her reaction to the EOP officer when he tells her that she should not torture herself with any more self-blame: "It sort of clicked."

3. Was it because you are a Black woman? Yes (hesitantly)

In the first part of the story, where Denise, in her memory, goes back to the situation, she reconstructs the story as if she did not have knowledge of an alternative conclusion (the one offered by the EOP officer). The fact that it happened to her because she is a woman was clear to Denise, but she individualizes her case ("What have I done to this man to make him think . . ."). Therefore, it can be assumed that she does not have sufficient general knowledge of sexism. In the reconstruction she does not place the event in a race relations context either. As a matter of fact, we only hear that it was a White professor when she quotes the EOP officer ("a lot of White men feel that Black women . . ."). Moreover, she distances herself to a certain extent from the explanations offered by the EOP officer. She thinks what he says must be true, because "it clicked," but at the same time she does not internalize this knowledge because she does not use it as her own explanation.

4. Was the specific event excusable? No

Although Denise is still not completely convinced that she did not give cause, she does not think the professor's behavior is excusable either.

5. Is the event socially significant?

Denise has no specific answer to this question. We have seen that she had general situational knowledge by which to distinguish acceptable from unacceptable behavior. She has new, developing notions of general knowledge of racism (which she learned from the EOP officer), but these notions are not readily available for use in the reconstructions of past events.

Unlike Denise herself, the EOP officer immediately places the event in a larger framework that includes general knowledge of sexual forms of racism against Black women. Apparently, he has general knowledge of sexism ("women are used sexually") as well as of sexual racism (White men using Black women sexually). While his knowledge structure is not made explicit by Denise, as scholars we can use other studies for outlining the main features of general knowledge the EOP officer may have used (implicitly) when he explained the situation to Denise. For that purpose, it is useful to give a brief discussion of the historical and sociological context of sex-related forms of racism in Euro-American societies and to discuss the experiences of other Black women I interviewed.

THE HISTORICAL AND SOCIAL CONTEXT OF SEXUAL RACISM

Even when many of the manifestations of sexism are similar to manifestations of sexual racism, it is relevant to make a distinction between sexism and sexual racism. Sexual racism against Black women is a hybrid form of control. On the one hand, sexual exploitation of women cannot be discussed separately from the racially specific control of women. On the other hand, racism cannot be discussed separately from the gender-specific control of Blacks emerging out of slavery. Therefore, many Black feminists agree that race, gender, and class are interlocking systems, the joint workings of which structure the experience of Black women (Collins, 1990; Hooks, 1989). This line of theorizing rejects additive approaches of oppression or the view that Black women can prioritize between sexism or racism. Some contend, however, that in relation to White society, race, rather than gender, is the primary source of oppression (Stasiulis, 1987). In other words, knowledge about the oppression of women in general is relevant, but not sufficient for understanding the issue of sexual exploitation in a racial context.

Throughout the history of White domination Black women were exploited sexually as well as economically. This combination of economic and sexual oppression refers not only to exploitation of their female biological system, that is, their reproductive function: They were also forced to have sexual intercourse with the White slave owner to satisfy his sexual passion. Black women resisted forced pregnancy and childbirth in many ways (Hine & Wittenstein, 1985), but they had but little protection against White males who exploited them sexually. This is clear from studies (Davis, 1981; Fox-Genovese, 1988; Gutman, 1976; Jones, 1985), slave narratives (e.g., Brent, 1973), and other literature (Carby, 1987). White slave owners blamed Black women themselves for their sexual exploitation. In their constructed ideology of the Black female's sexuality, she was portrayed as passionate and lascivious. Thus far, I focused on the U.S. system of exploitation of female slaves, but the same story can be told about the situation of African women who have been subjected to slavery in the former Dutch colony of Surinam (Oomens, 1987). Note, however, that, contrary to the case in the United States, sexual racism is not rooted in Dutch social relations on the European continent. This difference has bearings on the wider context of contemporary sexual racism in both countries.

In the United States, sexual racism against Black women continued to be an active component of U.S. race relations in the period of industrialization and thereafter. In the Netherlands, anti-Black racism in general and sexual racism in particular has centuries-old roots in Dutch culture (Paasman, 1987; Pieterse, 1990), but its integration into Dutch social relations goes back only to the period after World War II. Let me first explain the U.S. situation.

The end of slavery did not mean an end to the sexual exploitation of Black women (Rollins, 1985). Stereotypes of Black sexuality remained components of European and American culture and consciousness (Gilman, 1985; Hoch, 1979, Stember, 1976). Moreover, the sexual exploitation of Black women remained essential to the functioning and perpetuation of the racist system (Lerner, 1972; White, 1985). Thereby, the sexual objectification of Black women often served to maintain the double standard of sexual conduct attributing sexual purity to White women and sexual availability to Black women (Staples, 1973). Carby put it like this: "The links between Black women and illicit sexuality consolidated during the antebellum years and had powerful ideological consequences for the next hundred and fifty years" (1987, p. 39).

Black women in the United States are generally aware of these stereotypes and many of them refuse, therefore, to date White men (Staples, 1973). Little is known, however, about contemporary sexual racism in the Netherlands. The connotations of the Dutch ideological constructions of Black female sexuality are probably more closely related to notions of "savage" or "exotic" sexuality than to the image of the Black slave or domestic servant whose sexuality White males feel they can own. This can also be inferred from statements of the women, such as the following about a television commercial. Codes in the text refer to interviewees. "S" followed by a number stands for a (Surinamese) Black woman in the Netherlands, and "C" followed by a number for a (Californian) Black American interviewee: "There are very few Blacks on TV, but if you see them they are likely to be half naked. . . . It's like this one commercial about Nescafe which is full of sensual Black women . . . making and serving coffee" (S13).

These images are used to justify sexual assaults against Black women in the Netherlands. Take, for example, the case of a Dutch manager who harassed his Black secretary. This is how he defended himself: "She was asking for it. . . . These dark girls are always acting frivolously . . . shaking their butts, dressing up with nice make-up. . . . They are lively. . . . One can hardly expect me to be unsensitive to these things . . ." (S14).

Although the sociohistorical context of sexual racism is to a certain extent different in the two countries, its daily expressions are often similar. Black women
in both countries are frequently taken for prostitutes. They are abused as sexual
objects. Let me give a few examples: One Dutch woman tells about her girlfriend
whose (White, male) ex-lover dumped her with the words that "Black women
are only good enough to be fucked anyway" (S15).

A Black student in the United States refers to the same problem when she compares different dating experiences with Black and White boyfriends: "I have found
that Black men treated me a lot better. They give me respect. They show a lot
of love and gentleness whereas I have had a lot of difficulties with the White
guys that I was dating. A lot of times they felt they had the right to yell at me
and curse at me. . . . They weren't that affectionate towards me, especially publicly . . . didn't want to hold my hand in public . . ." (C28).

Another Black woman in the United States tells about her friend, a Black female student, who was raped by a White priest she had turned to when she had
psychological problems. The girl got pregnant and the priest insisted: "Oh well,
it's probably someone else's child. . . . She is a Black woman and has probably
laid down and went to bed with other people. She'll take care of it. She is just
a prostitute anyway" (C25).

One could add many more experiences of Black women to this list, such as
a Dutch social welfare inspector who blackmailed Black women in the same neighborhood with the threat that their allowances would be stopped if they did not
let him into their bedrooms. In the United States, cases were reported such as
White men who were making obscene gestures, or teachers who tried to kiss Black
female students when alone with them in the classroom. Black women in both
countries had experienced harassment personally, or vicariously, through Black
female friends or colleagues. In other words, intersubjective similarity shows that
the accounts of Black women about sexual harassment by White men are not incidental, but part of a structural problem.

A comprehensive framework of knowledge of sexual racism can be constructed on the basis of literature, research, and other studies of the problem. These
modes of knowledge (re)production are familiar to scholars. Obviously, Black
women with higher education have access to similar sources in developing and
refining their general knowledge of sexual racism. For Black women, however,
acquiring information about racism in general, and about sexual racism in particular is not an academic exercise. Knowledge acquisition and its proper application in real life is a survival strategy. For these and other reasons I do not consider the "subjective" theories underlying their descriptions and explanations of
real-life experiences less valuable than scientific theories. Moreover, the argumentative structure Black women use to validate their claim that specific events are
racist stands open to testing and exploration, just like scientific theories, which
also fulfill the search for interpretation, evaluation, and explanation (see also Groeben, 1990). Keeping this in mind, I now illustrate with the analysis of a second

account the use of different knowledge sources in reconstructing an experience of sexual racism.

THE STRUCTURE OF ACCOUNTS
OF EXPERIENCES OF RACISM

The following method for analyzing accounts of racism must be placed against the background of linguistic and social cognition theory. It borrows from narrative theory (Labov & Waletzky, 1967) some of the organizing categories of stories, that is (a) the Setting, featuring time, location, and participants; (b) the Complication, describing the things remarkable or problematic about the situation; and (c) the Resolution, indicating participants' reaction to the problem. These categories are placed in a wider context of heuristics of reality construction and systems of reference (beliefs, expectations, social knowledge, and other cognitions). Below I use several notions familiar to attribution theorists in conceptualizing heuristics of understanding, but I do not apply any specific attribution theory as such. Instead, I construct an alternative analysis. Experiential accounts form a unique source of information because they provide access to a kind of knowledge not ordinarily regarded as suitable for epistemological consideration (Code, 1989; Finch, 1984; Graham, 1984; Wilkinson, 1981). Accounts of racism can be seen as lay epistemic models based on deductive argumentation. When, in specific situations of unfair practices, the hypothesis is formed that these are covert expressions of racism, the validation of the hypothesis is accomplished deductively. Although the form of validation is deductive, this does not mean that the interpreters may not err on logical tasks. Therefore, the method of analyzing accounts must include strategies for assessing plausibility of "proof" and argumentation.

This method has been discussed and applied elsewhere (Essed, 1988, 1990a; Louw-Potgieter, 1989). Here, I only summarize its main characteristics. Accounts are usually only called for when explaining interesting behavior, or unexpected acts that cause difficulties. We have seen that in order to know whether particular acts are cases of racism these must first be tested against norms of acceptable behavior or acceptable reasons for unacceptable behavior, given the context of the situation. This implies the availability, in memory, of relevant situation scripts (Schank & Abelson, 1977). Earlier, this procedure was illustrated with the flow diagram. When actions have been interpreted as unacceptable, and there are no acceptable excuses, and if the implications of these actions are consistent with previously existing social representations of racism, the hypothesis is formed that these actions may be manifestations of racism. Then, a search for supporting information is bound to follow. Cognitive strategies and other processes of understanding on which accounts are based are very complex and cannot be analyzed in detail in this chapter. Here, it is sufficient to pay attention to two categories of heuristics: (a) inference from social cognitions of racism, including knowledge, expectations, beliefs, and opinions about racism in general and about scenarios of racism; and (b) comparison for consistency or inconsistency with other situations/actors/ingroup or outgroup members.

Let me briefly summarize the reconstruction categories I identified hypothetically as elements of accounts of racist events:

(1) Context: When, where, who was involved?
(2) Complication: What went wrong?
(3) Evaluation: Was it racism?
(4) Argumentation: Why do you think it was racism?
(5) Decision: What did you do about it?

These are organized in Table 11.1.

Not all the organizing categories and heuristics are included in all accounts. The Context, Complication and Decision represent *stable* contents of the account. They represent the facts of the situation and can be seen as the core of accounts of racism. These categories are narrative categories. But, it may be assumed that, like narrative categories, they also have a cognitive status (van Dijk & Kintsch, 1983). However, it does not mean that the storyteller memorizes always all the facts. Also the storyteller may choose to tell certain facts or not. Take Denise. She did not tell anybody that the professor was harassing her until she talked to the EOP officer, another Black. Likewise she may not have told the story to me, had I been White. In other words, the contents of the accounts are also shaped by the presence of the hearer. The structure of accounts, however, remains the same.

The Evaluation and Argumentation categories include *variable* information, because interpretations and evaluations of situations can change. We have seen a nice example of this in the account of Denise. After she had talked to the EOP officer about the situation with the White professor she started to see the case in another light.

I illustrate each account category briefly with a story selected from the interview materials. This story involves an African-American woman, Gloria S., 30 years old, who tells the following story about one professor in the college she used to visit. Unlike the story of Denise, featuring an unmistakably "bad" professor, Gloria has mixed feelings, which makes the story more complex. She finds the professor very attractive and is flattered that he likes her, but his behavior induces serious doubts about his racial morals. The reconstruction of her account has been reorganized so as to fit the order of the analytical schema (see Table 11.1). The quotes are her own words. Statements that were not relevant for the purpose of the analysis have been omitted.

TABLE 11.1

Reconstruction Categories and Heuristics of Accounts*

Type of Category	Content of Category	Form of Heuristic	Supporting References
1. CONTEXT	Description of time, place, actors, situation	–	–
2. COMPLICATION	Description and interpretation of actions	Comparison	Norms, values about acceptable/non-acceptable behavior
3. EVALUATION	Significance or value of actions	Inference	(Class/gender structured) Beliefs, expectations, social knowledge about racial issues
4. ARGUMENTATION	Statements in support of Evaluation	Inference	and about racism (gender/class domination)
		Comparison for Consistency	Experiences of other blacks Experiences with other whites Other actions of same actor
		Comparison for Consensus	Interpretations/ evaluations from others Interpretations/ evaluations from the actor
		Comparison for Inconsistency	Experiences of whites Experiences with black actors
5. DECISION	Intentions and/ or actions		Expectations about the goals of particular response

*From Essed (1988).

Context. This category gives information about the time, place, participating actors and social circumstances of the racism event:

> "There was a young *White* boy that came to teach at X University. He was a hippy kind of guy, considered himself rather liberal. . . . Many of the women thought him cute and therefore gave him some kind of special status. (And here I was), this wonderfully warm, attractive, interesting, and vibrant *Black* woman. He liked me. . . ." [italics added]

Through her use of language we can infer that the situation was about gender dynamics (cute, self-assured guy versus warm, attractive, interesting, and vibrant woman) in a racial context (White versus Black). Given the fact that the social context includes the matrix of gender and race relations, we can expect that interactions occurring within that context will either confirm or contradict the *status quo* of existing race and gender power relations. Therefore, the context is of crucial importance in determining whether specific manifestations of oppression in a particular situation (the Complications, see the following) have gender and/or racial implications.

Complication. If we may characterize society as a persisting distribution of knowledge and the practices produced by that knowledge, it means that individuals in a given society will develop systematic and detailed knowledge of what the routines are and they will be able to act in ways that take account of this (Barnes, 1989). The name of this category, Complication, literally says what it is about. It describes the acts that were interpreted as unacceptable, given the characteristics of the situation. This category is very important because the ability to interpret acts as deviant, or as discriminatory, implies that the interpreter has general knowledge about the dominant culture, specific knowledge about social rules, and expectations about "normal" behavior in the particular situation. This can be inferred also from the story of Gloria. She agrees that the attraction between this young professor and any of his female students was natural and probably rather normal. What was not acceptable, however, was the way in which this professor acted upon that: "He called me on the phone and asked me out. He asked me around some shady corner . . ."

Apart from the fact that it was not quite correct in the first place for a female student to be asked for a date by her male professor, the scene where he wanted this to take place added even more to the unacceptability of the situation. Of all other cues in the situation, suggesting that similar harassment might have happened to a White female student as well (overtures, dates, secrecy), it is perhaps the shady corner that infuriates Gloria most as a *Black* woman (see further under Evaluation). Thus, knowledge of how a man is supposed to ask a woman for a date in a nonracial situation is presupposed in the judgment of Gloria that "He could not come and face the fact that he was going to take me to a movie or whatever."

Evaluation. This category makes clear whether the event is seen as an instance of racism or not. In order to understand whether specific acts are expressions of racism one needs a larger framework of general knowledge about the nature and processes of racism. In this specific example gender oppression converges with racism. This can also be inferred from Gloria's own assessment of the situation: "There was an element of sexism and an element of racism."

Interestingly, when Denise was in a similar situation she did not place it in a racial context, nor in a context of sexism. Apparently, she did not have sufficient general knowledge of these phenomena. If Gloria had had only knowledge of sexism, or if this had happened with a Black professor, she might have interpreted the situation only in terms of sexual harassment. However, she has enough understanding of (the history of) sexual exploitation of Black women by White men to see the racist implications of the situation. She recognizes the stereotypical association of a shady corner with the Black woman who is seen as a prostitute. Even if the same professor had harassed other White students as well, the mere fact that he is White and she is Black makes the context by definition racial as well. Irrespective of the motivations of the professor, his actions are consistent with general patterns of sexual racism against Black women. This, he could have known. In fact, the Complication and the Context of the situation activate general knowledge of patterns of sexual racism, while the existence of these patterns is reconfirmed through that situation. Indeed, as I emphasized earlier, sexism in a racial context cannot be seen as just sexism, nor as just racism. In the Argumentation category, Gloria addresses both the sexist and racist implications of the situation.

Argumentation. The function of this category is to support the particular evaluation. In this sense it can also be seen as part of the Evaluation. This is the most interesting category because it deals with the question, "Why did you think what happened was racism?" In accounts of racism this question is dealt with by the rational testing of preliminary hypotheses about the situation. The Argumentation category is structured by (a) *inference* from beliefs, expectations, and knowledge about racial issues and about racism; and by (b) *comparison* for (in)consistency and consensus, among other things, with the experiences of other Blacks, with other personal experiences in similar situations, other experiences with the same actor, similarities with behavior of other Whites, and with opinions of others about the situation.

Gloria infers from general expectations and knowledge about gender issues and about racism when she substantiates why she considers the situation as sexist and racist. These highly abstract evaluative concepts may have been used as political symbols rather than as indicators of broad and abstract cognitive structures

(Sears, Huddie, & Schaffer, 1986). The data do not give sufficient information to qualify in detail the contents and structure of the cognitive structure underlying the concepts of "sexism" and "racism" as used by Gloria. However, she clearly applies these concepts at this concrete level of interaction with at least some knowledge of routine manifestations of sexism and (sexual) racism in everyday life. This can be inferred from the following arguments: "I had the same infatuation that the other female students had, but at that point I was close to being a senior and I was sophisticated enough to know that I was not going to meet anybody, least of all this White guy, around the corner someplace."

Qualifying herself as "sophisticated enough" implies that she herself finds that one needs a certain level of knowledge in order to understand the sexist and racist implications of this specific situation. Gloria does not give priority to either sexism or racism in her argumentation. She interprets it as sexism (disrespect for a woman) when her professor calls her on the spur of the moment and expects that she will readily meet him somewhere. The racial element is indicated by the fact that she was "least of all" going to be involved with a White male in that particular situation.

She further substantiates her evaluation of the situation as follows: "He was taking advantage of the fact that he was unique"; "He had some insecurities about dating a brown[1] girl."

In addition to inference from beliefs and knowledge it is relevant to make comparisons with other situations, actors, or group members in order to judge whether the specific situation is unique or systematic. These comparisons have similarities with Kelley's (1973) consensus, consistency, and distinctiveness attributions, but his covariation principle is too rigid to be considered an adequate strategy in the reconstruction of experiences. People can use information about consensus, consistency, and distinctiveness, but this does not mean that they have to in order to draw conclusions and to give explanations about events (for further discussion see Essed, 1991; Lalljee & Abelson, 1983). We will see that Gloria uses supporting argumentation, but she does not use, in her account, covariation to arrive at her conclusions. Supporting argumentation that could add to the plausibility of the fact that racism is involved in the sexual harassment of Gloria may include references to one or more of the following sources of information. I reconstructed these sources on the basis of inference from hundreds of accounts (Essed, 1984; 1991), but I do not mean to suggest that the list is complete:

1. Experiences of other Blacks in similar situations/with the same agent of racism (consistency): Had the professor tried the same with other Black female students?

---

[1] I am not sure why Gloria talks here about "brown" girls when she calls herself on all other occasions during the interview "black." Also she teaches her child that "we are black, we are African people."

2. Other personal experiences: in similar situations/with the same agent (consistency): Was it the first time that the professor hinted at getting intimate with Gloria?

3. Similarity to actions of other Whites in same or other situation (consistency): Did Gloria experience this before with other White men or did she know this was happening with other Black women?

4. Confirming statements (or confession) of the agent (Consensus): Did the professor acknowledge that it was racist and sexist to go for a cheap date with a Black woman?

5. Confirming statements about the event made by others (Consensus): Did Gloria talk about this to others and what were their conclusions?

6. Dissimilarity of perceived or expected actions in nonracial situation (Inconsistency): Would the professor also suggest to meet at some shady corner if Gloria had been White? Would he approach a White female student for a date in the first place?

7. Beliefs, expectations, knowledge, and other social cognitions about racism in general or in specific (similar) context/with the same White person: What knowledge is available about sexual abuse of Black women by White men?

Because the purpose of the interview was to get spontaneous stories rather than to search systematically for evidence, I did not pose any of these questions. However, Gloria herself came up with the following comparisons for Consistency in her account:

1. *With other situations.* Specific events only gain meaning in relation to previous experiences of racism. In other words, each new experience triggers memories of other racist events. Therefore, it is relevant to the understanding of the dating event when Gloria says, "I perceived that (dating event) as my third altercation with racism while I was at X University" (Other examples are discussed elsewhere in the interview).

2. *With behavior of the same actor in other situations.* The reader should be reminded that we are discussing Gloria's later account of the event, and not, per se, her explanation of the situation when it actually happened. Thus, she refers to the professor's behavior on later occasions to confirm the hypothesis of racism in the way the professor asked her to date him. When Gloria refuses to date the professor (see below) he retaliates: "As a result of that he begun to make an example of me in class, a bad example."

3. *With perceived or expected actions in non-racial situations.* Through comparison, dissimilarity can be found with expectations about "normal" dating situations. Apparently, the professor was not thinking about having any serious kind of relation with a Black student: "When I began to talk to him about [the fact that] any kind of relationship would become complicated for each of us, . . . the

issue of color came up immediately for me. Whether or not it was one for him, I do not know, but, he withdrew from any kind of resolution."

The function of the Argumentation category is to make plausible the hypothetical evaluation that the particular event is a racist event. Thus, even long after the event has occurred additional information can be used in order to confirm or to contradict the hypothesis. Gloria and the professor spoke to each other again on other occasions. Maybe it was because she remained "infatuated" like all the other girls, maybe it was because she was somehow "flattered" that he "liked" her, or maybe it was because she was not sure yet that he had a racial problem, but in spite of the quarrels, retaliations, and his not being "really so sure about Black women . . ." they did "continue to have a friendship." In this light must be seen the following comparison for Consistency.

4. *With behavior of the same actor in a similar situation* (when Gloria confronted him again):

> He did visit me a year later when I went to (name of place). And he went on another quest to find himself. So I think it was something unresolved that I detected in him and I think it did have to do with racial morals.

The complexity and completeness of the Argumentation category in accounts of racism is confined by the knowledge the teller has of racism in general, but also by the extent to which the interviewer succeeds in eliciting this knowledge (Evans, 1989). It would be beyond the scope of this chapter, however, to elaborate on this issue. Here, it is relevant to point out that the method for analyzing accounts can be used to assess plausibility of the story as well as to pose other relevant questions about the story. For instance, the interviewer could ask more specific questions about the teller's knowledge of sexual racism, or ask the teller to make relevant comparisons like the ones mentioned above.

The Decision category describes reactions to a racist event:

> I really did confront him with whatever his hangups were about dating a brown girl. . . . I said what do you think this is, who do you think you are? You are making an attempt to take advantage of your situation.

Although the method is based on rational inference and argumentation, it does not mean to exclude the possibility of occasional irrational evaluation of specific situations. On the contrary, if one suspects irrationality the method can be used to evaluate reconstructions of racist events on criteria of rationality. The categories of interpretation provide a rational basis to systematically examine why a specific event is perceived as racist.

CONCLUSIONS

General knowledge of racism forms the conceptual framework for interpreting specific racist events. This holds for scientific research as well as for the 'lay person's' understanding of experiences of racism in everyday life. I have tried to show that accounts of racism are not *ad hoc* stories. They have a specific structure. The discussion above focused on the use of knowledge of racism by Black women. It was pointed out that without general knowledge of racism, individuals cannot understand the meaning of racism in their lives. This does not mean to suggest that general knowledge of racism is an issue only relevant for members of the dominated group. The method for analyzing accounts offers instruments for understanding the way individual dominant group members participate in practices through which structures of racial domination are reproduced. Finally, the analytical procedures presented provide a basis for more research into this area. In particular, more sophisticated techniques must be developed for sensitizing memories that would otherwise remain incomplete or missing and for questioning accounters efficiently when seeking for hypothesis consistent or inconsistent information. This can lead to the construction of a normative model for the assessment of racial events that may also be used for other purposes such as the assessment of gender situations.

REFERENCES

Barnes, B. (1989). Ostensive learning and self-referring knowledge. In A. Gellatly, D. Rogers, & J. A. Sloboda (Eds.), *Cognition and social worlds* (pp. 190-204). Oxford: Clarendon Press.

Brent, L. (1973). *Incidents in the life of a slave girl*. New York: Harvest.

Carby, H. V. (1987). *Reconstructing womanhood*. New York: Oxford University Press.

Cicourel, A. V. (1964). *Method and measurement in sociology*. New York: Free Press of Glencoe.

Code, L. (1988). Credibility: A double standard. In L. Code, S. Mullett, & C. Overall (Eds.), *Feminist perspectives* (pp. 64-88). Toronto: University of Toronto Press.

Code, L. (1989). Experience, knowledge, and responsibility. In A. Gary & M. Pearsall (Eds.), *Women, knowledge, and reality* (pp. 152-172). Boston: Unwin Hyman.

Collins, P. H. (1990). *Black feminist thought*. Boston: Unwin Hyman.

Davis, A. Y. (1981). *Women, race and class*. New York: Random House.

Essed, P. (1988). Understanding verbal accounts of racism. *TEXT, 8*, 5-40.

Essed, P. (1989). Black women in white women's organizations. *RFR/DRF, 18*, 10-15.

Essed, P. (1990a). Against all odds: Teaching against racism at a university in South Africa. *European Journal of Intercultural Studies, 1*, 41-56.

Essed, P. (1990b). *Everyday racism*. Claremont, CA: Hunter House.

Essed, P. (1990c). The myth of over-sensitivity about racism. In I. Foeken (Ed.), *Between selfhelp and professionalism, Part III* (pp. 21-36). Amsterdam: The Moon Foundation.

Essed, P. (1991). *Understanding everyday racism*. Newbury Park, CA: Sage.

Evans, J. St. (1989). *Bias in human reasoning*. Hove: Lawrence Erlbaum Associates.

Finch, J. (1984). "It's great to have someone to talk to": The ethics and politics of interviewing women. In C. Bell, & H. Robert (Eds.), *Social researching* (pp. 70-87). London: RKP.

Fiske, S. T., & Kinder, D. R. (1981). Involvement, expertise, and schema use: Evidence from political cognition. In N. Cantor & J. F. Kihlstrom (Eds.), *Personality, cognition, and social interaction* (pp. 171–190). Hillsdale, NJ: Lawrence Erlbaum Associates.

Fiske, S. T., Kinder, D. R., & Larter, W. M. (1983). The novice and the expert: Knowledge-based strategies in political cognition. *Journal of Experimental Social Psychology, 19*, 381–400.

Fiske, S. T., & Taylor, S. E. (1984). *Social cognition*. Reading, MA: Addison-Wesley.

Forgas, J. P. (1982). Episode cognition: Internal representations of interaction routines. *Advances in Experimental and Social Psychology, 15*, 59–101.

Fox-Genovese, E. (1988). *Within the plantation household*. Chapel Hill: University of North Carolina Press.

Gilman, S. L. (1985). *Difference and pathology*. Ithaca: Cornell University Press.

Graham, H. (1984). Surveying through stories. In C. Bell & H. Roberts (Eds.), *Social researching* (pp. 104–124). London: Routledge & Kegan Paul.

Groeben, N. (1990). Subjective theories and the explanation of human action. In G. Semin & K. Gergen (Eds.), *Everyday understanding* (pp. 19–44). London: Sage.

Gutman, H. G. (1976). *The Black family in slavery and freedom*. New York: Random House.

Hall, M. L., & Allen, W. R. (1989). Race consciousness among African-American college students. In G. Berry & J. Asamen (Eds.), *Black students* (pp. 172–197). Newbury Park, CA: Sage.

Hawkesworth, M. E. (1989). Knowers, knowing, known: Feminist theory and claims of truth. In M. Malson, J. O'Barr, S. Westphal-Whil, & M. Wyer (Eds.), *Feminist theory and practice and process* (pp. 327–351). Chicago: University of Chicago Press.

Hine, D., & Wittenstein, K. (1985). Female slave resistance: The economics of sex. In F. Steady (Ed.), *The Black woman cross-culturally* (pp. 289–299). Cambridge, MA: Schenkman.

Hoch, P. (1979). *White hero, Black beast*. London: Pluto Press.

Hooks, B. (1989). *Talking back: Thinks feminist - Thinking Black*. London: Sheba Feminist Publishers.

Jones, J. (1985). *Labor of love, labor of sorrow*. New York: Basic Books.

Kelley, H. H. (1973). The processes of causal attribution. *American Psychologist, 28*, 107–128.

Kruglanski, A. W. (1988). Knowledge as a social psychological construct. In D. Bar-Tal & A. Kruglanski (Eds.), *The social psychology of knowledge* (pp. 109–141). Cambridge: Cambridge University Press.

Labov, W., & Waletzky, J. (1967). Narrative analysis: Oral versions of personal experiences. In J. Helm (Ed.), *Essays on the verbal and visual arts* (pp. 12–44). Seattle, WA: Washington University Press.

Lalljee, M., & Abelson, R. P. (1983). The organization of explanations. In M. Hewstone (Ed.), *Attribution theory* (pp. 65–80). Oxford: Blackwell.

Lerner, G. (1972). *Black women in White America. A documentary study*. New York: Vintage Books.

Lofland, J., & Lofland, L. H. (1984). *Analyzing social settings*. Belmont, CA: Wadsworth.

Louw-Potgieter, J. (1989). Covert racism: An application of Essed's analysis in a South African context. *Journal of Language and Social Psychology, 8*, 307–339.

Mies, M. (1983). Towards a methodology for feminist research. In G. Bowles & D. Klein (Eds.), *Theories of women's studies* (pp. 117–138). London: Routledge & Kegan Paul.

Moscovici, S., & Hewstone, M. (1983). Social representations and social explanations: From the "naive" to the "amateur" scientist. In M. Hewstone (Ed.), *Attribution theory* (pp. 98–125). Oxford: Blackwell.

Oomens, M. (1987). Veelwijverij en andere losbandige praktijken (Polygamy and other licentious behavior). In J. Reijs, E. Kloek, U. Yansz, A. de Wildt, S. van Norden, & M. de Baar (Eds.), *Vrouwen in de Nederlandse kolonieën* (Women in the Dutch Colonies) (pp. 152–171). Nijmegen: SUN.

Paasman, B. (1987). Mens of Dier?. De beeldvorming over negers in de tijd voor de rassentheorieën. (Images of negroes in the period before the race theories). In A. F. Stichting (Ed.), *Vreemd gespuis* (Strange scum) (pp. 92–107). Amsterdam: Anne Frank Stichting.

Pieterse, J. N. (1990). *Wit over zwart* (White on black). Amsterdam: KIT.

Ramazanoglu, C. (1989). *Feminism and the contradictions of oppression*. London: Routledge.

Rollins, J. (1985). *Between women: Domestics and their employers*. Philadelphia: Temple University Press.

Schank, R. C., & Abelson, R. (1977). *Scripts, plans, goals and understanding*. Hillsdale, NJ: Lawrence Erlbaum Associates.

Sears, D. O., Huddie, L., & Schaffer, L. G. (1986). A schematic variant of symbolic politics theory, as applied to racial and gender equality. In R. Lau & D. Sears (Eds.), *Political cognition* (pp. 159-202). Hillsdale, NJ: Lawrence Erlbaum Associates.

Smith, D. E. (1987). *The everyday world as problematic*. Toronto: Toronto University Press.

Staples, R. (1973). *The Black woman in America*. Chicago: Nelson-Hall.

Stasiulis, D. (1987). Rainbow feminism: Perspectives on minority women in Canada. *RFR/DRF, 16*, 5-9.

Stember, C. H. (1976). *Sexual racism*. New York: Harper Colophon.

van Dijk, T. A., & Kintsch, W. (1983). *Strategies of discourse comprehension*. New York: Academic Press.

White, D. G. (1985). *Ar'n't I a woman?* New York: Norton.

Wilkinson, S. (1981). Personal constructs and private explanations. In C. Antaki (Ed.), *The psychology of ordinary explanations of social behaviour* (pp. 205-219). London: Academic Press.

12

▼▼▼▼▼▼▼

The Social-Interactive Aspects
of Account-Giving

Michael J. Cody
University of Southern California, Los Angeles

David O. Braaten
University of Southern California, Los Angeles

"Afterwards, I just hung my head and said my silent prayer. I prayed that I'd win the Lottery and I'd never have to come back to this horrible place again!" (from data reported in Braaten, Cody, & Bell, 1990).

In this example, a bank employee reported on an "account episode" at work. He had arrived late, and his supervisor had been quite hostile when reproaching him about the tardiness. In fact, the supervisor had said, "Why in the hell are you so fucking late?" The worker had intended to explain that a truck carrying fruit had jack-knived on the freeway, causing him to be tardy. Such an excuse, specifying unintentional, uncontrollable, unstable, and external causes (see Weiner, this volume) should be effective in exonerating the account-giver of blame (also see review by Cody and McLaughlin, 1990). However, confronted with such hostility, the worker first attempted to defend himself by claiming that he wasn't "terribly" late. The worker then began to relate his excuse. Unfortunately, the supervisor displayed virtually no inclination to forgive the worker and barely allowed the worker to finish telling his story before ordering him to stay after work to "make up for the lost time." The worker hung his head in seething anger, dreaming of how he could leave his life at the bank behind.

Considerable attention has focused on the determinants of accounts (Cody & McLaughlin, 1990; Schonbach, 1990). There can be little doubt that the communication of an account is strongly influenced by attributions, normative expectations, beliefs concerning the probable effect accounts have on different receivers, and beliefs about receivers' emotional reactions to accounts. However, many accounts are communicated in face-to-face contexts, and a reproacher's behavior in requesting an account also serves as a determinant of accounting behavior. A severely phrased form of reproach often impacts on the account episode in three ways. First, as indicated in our story, *extremely hostile forms of reproach often cause defensive reactions on the part of account-givers.* Confronted with hostility, the bank employee defended himself against the claim that he was "terribly" late.

Second, *reproachers who employ severely phrased reproaches are predisposed to rejecting the account, no matter what type of account is communicated.* As Schonbach (1990) recently argued, a need for consistency or consonance predisposes the reproacher to terminate the episode with a relatively negative evaluation. When a reproach is harshly phrased, the reproacher claims (or strongly implies) that the account-giver is guilty, and this public commitment to the prejudged guilt places a constraint on the reproacher. A reproacher would lose credibility by first accusing a worker of wrongdoing using a severely phrased assertion of guilt, only to retreat to honoring after the account is communicated. Several projects have in fact found that reproachers who employ severely phrased rebukes usually reject the account that was communicated (Braaten, Cody, & Bell, 1990; Schonbach, 1990).

The consequences entailed in the use of employing severe or harsh forms of reproaches are also of concern. By initiating a request in a harsh manner, a reproacher dramatically increases the probability that the communication exchange will escalate to conflict (see Schonbach, 1990). The use of severe forms of reproach is associated with more frequent complaints filed by organizational members and higher ratings of stress, dissatisfaction, and anger (Braaten et al., 1990). A third hypothesis, then, is that *severe forms of reproach will result in more negative relational and emotional consequences than less severe forms of reproach.*

In this chapter we will overview the limited research conducted to date concerning forms of reproach and account episodes. Three general areas will be discussed. First, we will overview the basic research paradigm investigating the "account episode." Second, we will review the few studies that have examined different types of reproaches and the impact reproach forms have on accounts, and on the consequences of account episodes. Third, we will outline needed research.

THE ACCOUNT EPISODE

The Basic Structure of the Account Episode

There exists a basic structure or pattern to an account episode. First, a need exists to explain the occurrence of a *failure event.* The account phase is initiated with a perception or a realization that the actor (the account-giver) is held (rightly or falsely) to be at least partly responsible by the reproacher for an action that is either a violation of normative expectation (i.e., "You wore *that* dress to a job interview?") or an omission of an obligation (i.e., "Why didn't you pay the phone bill on time?"). However, no single typology of failure events exists. In legal settings, the type of offense (murder, first degree assault, etc.) represents qualitatively different types of failure events, and the different types of offenses are related to excuses and apologies communicated to parole boards and other relevant receivers (Carroll & Payne, 1977; Felson & Ribner, 1981; Henderson & Hewstone, 1984; Riordan, Marlin, & Kellogg, 1983; Rothman & Gandossy, 1982). In organizational settings, failure events include justifying questionable decisions, tardiness, accounting for performance errors, and the like (see Bies & Sitkin, this volume; Braaten et al., 1990). Nonetheless, failure events in different settings share common underlying variables: severity of the offense, causal attributions, guilt feelings, felt responsibility, and normative expectations.

Second, account episodes involve a three-part communication sequence involving a *reproach*, an *account*, and an *evaluation*. Each type of communication can be arrayed on a continuum of "politeness," or "preference," or along a "mitigation–aggravation" continuum. Some reproaches are polite, open-ended questions ("Edward," Mr. Winslow asks on the television show *Family Matters*, "can you please explain what happened to your grades this semester?"). Some accounts are requested only via nonverbal channels (reproaches are said to be "implicit") ("The mechanic looked so disgusted with the engine that I felt I owed him an explanation for why I never got around to changing the oil"). Some reproaches are hostile, or severe (see the following).

In our earlier work we coded accounts into four general categories: *apologies, excuses, justifications,* and *denials/refusals*. In interpersonal settings, apologies and excuses are perceived as more polite and more helpful in resolving a dispute, and in avoiding conflict, than justifications and refusals/denials. However, recent evidence indicates that certain forms of apologies and excuses are significantly more effective than other forms in performing remedial work. Specifically, Braaten et al. (1990), and Holtgraves (1989) found that "compensation" or "full blown" apologies are more effective than "perfunctory apologies" (i.e., "I am sorry."), excuses that contain elements of regret were more effective than excuses containing no regret (Holtgraves), or excuses involving "appeals to accident" were more frequently "honored" (i.e., rated or perceived as valid, credible accounts) than "denial of intent" (see Braaten et al.). Finally, the forms of evaluating accounts vary from polite or mitigating ("honoring") to more aggravating forms ("partial honoring," or "retreating" to "rejecting") (also see Schonbach, 1990, for types of accounts and forms of evaluations).

Are Reproaches Necessary?

Accounts are communicated when expectations are violated. However, either the reproacher or the account-giver can initiate the accounting process, and sometimes the account-giver knows implicitly to seek out and communicate an account without having to be asked. In medical settings, patients frequently offer accounts to medical advisers without being asked to do so: Dindia and Steele (1987) found that 13% of patients' accounts were unsolicited and that 31% of the accounts followed implicit reproaches. In a quasi-legal setting, traffic court, we found that judges often never "reproached" the defendant and relied on a range of utterances that served the function of cueing the defendant to tell his/her story: "Okay, what's your pleasure?" "Okay, let's keep this brief," "Okay, start" (Cody & McLaughlin, 1988). In both settings the fundamental *purpose* is to communicate an account, so it is not surprising that the reproach phase operates only at a perfunctory level.

We surveyed college students (in an unpublished project) and found that college students are not commonly reproached. Most of the failure events experienced by students involved missing classes, missing tests, and turning in late assignments. For events such as these the student is responsible for locating the professor and offering an explanation. Students were usually only *explicitly* reproached by professors and coaches for being late, turning in questionable work, and when accused of cheating—but these more severe types of failure events represented only 24% of the cases.

Additional projects indicated that reproaches are commonly employed in approximately 80% of the episodes (McLaughlin, Cody, & O'Hair, 1983; McLaughlin, Cody, & Rosenstein, 1983). For example, a survey of organizational members indicated that workers were reproached for failure events 84% of the time (Braaten et al., 1990). Most of the episodes that involved implicit reproaches involved the failure events of tardiness and performance errors, when workers probably (a) felt responsible for an action or at least perceived they would at some time be held responsible for an action, (b) believed that an explanation was expected, and, (c) believed that failing to provide an explanation was itself a "failure event" that could require further explanation. In yet another setting, traffic officers employed one of three forms of reproaches whenever (100% of the time) an offending driver was stopped: a *projected excuse*, a *projected justification*, or a *simple statement of offense* (see examples below) (Cody & McLaughlin, 1985).

Reproaches are not always necessary. In some settings (medical interviews, traffic court, explanations to parole boards, complaint departments), reproaches are not needed simply because the fundamental *purpose* of the communication exchange is to hear and evaluate accounts. In most settings, however, reproaches are frequently used, or at least implicit in that account-givers know that an explanation is required and that they will need to communicate the account at some time.

REPROACH FORMS
AND THE REPROACH-ACCOUNT PHASE

Two hypotheses concerning the reproach-account phase of the account episode have been advanced. First, a "reciprocity" expectation involved the prediction that reproach forms elicit similar kinds of accounts—polite reproaches elicit polite accounts, and hostile or aggravating forms of reproaches elicit hostile or aggravating accounts (Cody & McLaughlin, 1985; McLaughlin, Cody, & O'Hair, 1983; McLaughlin, Cody, & Rosenstein, 1983).

McLaughlin, Cody, and O'Hair, for example, found that reproachers generally employ one of six strategies for eliciting an account. Two implicit forms were labeled *silence* (the account-giver simply knew that s/he should offer an accounting) and *behavioral cues* (the reproachers' nonverbal behaviors, such as looks of disgust, disappointment). Four verbal tactics, however, mirrored four basic forms of accounts. When using a *projected concession* the reproacher clearly leads the account-giver toward the communication of a concession (admission of guilt, apology):

Aren't you sorry you did it?
Well, it sure was nice of you to have us come down so you could be gallivanting all over the country!

In *projected excuse*, the reproacher indicates that s/he expects the account-giver to deny responsibility for the failure event:

Were you stuck in traffic?
Did you forget to wind your watch again?

In a *projected justification*, the reproacher communicates that s/he anticipates hearing the account-giver minimize the severity of the failure event, or defend a questionable action:

I suppose you're going to try and tell me it was just a joke.
Did you have something more important to do?

Finally, in a *projected refusal*, the reproacher suggests that the account-giver will deny guilt, deny the failure event, or deny the reproacher's right to ask for an account:

Now, why haven't you been filling these out with the truth?
Don't try to pretend you didn't see me!

The McLaughlin, Cody, and O'Hair (1983) study found that (a) projected concessions do in fact lead to concessions, and, (b) that projected refusals lead to refusals, and projected refusals are negatively related to excuses. However, we also concluded that several of the reproach forms do not possess the same strength of implicature as the projected refusals and projected concessions. Projected excuses, for example, were not associated with the selection of any account type, and projected justifications did not lead to justifications. Instead, projected justifications led to the use of the more aggravating form of refusal. Finally, while projected concessions did in fact result in more frequent concessions, projected concessions also elicited more frequent reliance on refusals. It may be the case that when the account-giver is falsely accused of having committed an offense, a tactic that presupposes a concession is perceived to be quite *aggravating*.

McLaughlin, Cody, and Rosenstein (1983) coded reproaches that were employed by strangers involved in a "self-disclosure" half-hour discussion: surprise/disgust, moral/intellectual superiority, direct request (for an account), and direct rebuke. This study found that reproach forms are not related to the use of concessions, excuses, or justifications. However, use of more severe forms of reproaches (direct rebuke, moral/intellectual superiority reproaches, and direct requests) are related to the more aggravating forms of accounts: denials/refusals.

Cody and McLaughlin (1985) reported briefly on a survey of accounts drivers communicate to patrol officers. Three forms of reproaches were identified: projected excuses, projected justifications, and simple statement of the offense. The results indicate that apologies, admissions of guilt, and excuses are unrelated to forms of reproaches. Projected justifications ("Is there some emergency?" "What are you doing out this early in the morning?") elicited more explanations involving justifications (that there is an emergency, that the driver had good reasons for being out early). Further, refusals/denials were more likely to be associated with two reproach forms: simple statement of offense, and projected excuse. Some of these episodes may involve falsely accusing a driver of an offense, of an "apparent" exaggeration of a claim that would prompt a driver to deny the severity of the offense (e.g., "Son, I clocked you going 80 mph." "80!! No way. No way was I doing 80!").

We concluded from these studies that polite or mitigating forms of reproach are not consistently or strongly related to polite or mitigating forms of accounts. Generally speaking, polite or mitigating forms of reproaches allow the account-giver the freedom to communicate any account s/he desires. Determinants of accounts in such episodes are felt responsibility, guilt feelings, severity of the offense, the importance of interpersonal goals, and the nature of the reproacher/account-giver relationship (see Cody & McLaughlin, 1985). However, when an aggravating reproach form was used, the aggravating reproach form functioned as an interactional constraint that interfered with the account-giver's freedom to communicate an intended or preferred form of an account. Confronted with hostility, direct rebukes, expressions of moral superiority, projected refusals or reproaches that exaggerate the severity of the offense, account-givers become less conciliatory and more defensive.

A second hypothesis relies on psychological reactance theory (see Schonbach, 1986; Schonbach & Kleibaumhuter, 1990) and predicts that a severely phrased reproach form represents a threat to the account-giver's freedom and produces defensive reactions. This approach largely explains our earlier results.

Schonbach and Kleibaumhuter employed a scenario approach to studying account episodes and provided students with questionnaires that first asked them to imagine that they had been babysitting when the child in their care had sneaked into the kitchen and drunk from a bottle containing cleaning fluid. At the hospital the parents were described as using one of three types of reproaches:

1. *Neutral Question.* The parents only asked for an explanation.
2. *Derogation of Self-Esteem.* "How could that have happened to you? Apparently you were too much occupied with yourself!?"
3. *Derogation of Sense of Control.* "Why haven't you been able to prevent this? We wouldn't have thought that you would lose sight so easily!"

The central psychological reactance hypothesis is that threats to one's freedom will elicit a defensive reaction. In this study, reactions to the neutral question would be more conciliatory and less defensive (i.e., more apologies and excuses, fewer justifications and refusals/denials) than reactions to the two forms of reproaches. This central hypothesis was supported.

While scenario studies provide a high level of control over a limited number of behaviors in a survey, such projects tell us little about the range of reproaches that might be categorized as "severe" in everyday, real account episodes. Braaten et al. (1990) had the opportunity to collect survey data in a large financial institution, and 508 workers recalled and reported on account episodes that had recently occurred. Most of the account episodes were initiated via direct requests ($n = 241$, 47%), while a few episodes were initiated via polite requests ($n = 65$, 13%), or via implicit reproaches ($n = 72$, 14%). However, a fairly sizable number ($n = 119$, 23%) were initiated by what Braaten et al. had labeled rebukes.

Braaten et al. found that severe forms of reproach have a significant impact on accounts: rebukes frequently elicit refusals/denials, while polite requests and implicit reproaches rarely elicit refusals/denials. Further, both rebukes and direct requests elicit more "aggravating" forms of accounts (55.5% of rebukes were followed by justifications and refusals/denials, and 62.6% of direct requests were followed by justifications and refusals/denials).

A second hypothesis concerning reproach severity is that reproachers who employ rebukes are more likely to evaluate accounts negatively. Braaten et al. did in fact find that reproachers who used rebukes were significantly more likely to reject the account (in 73.1% of the cases) and were less likely to honor the account (in only 10.9% of the cases). Honoring was more likely to follow polite reproaches (which resulted in honoring 49.4% of the time) or implicit reproaches (which resulted in honoring 55.4% of the time).

A third hypothesis concerning reproach severity is that more severe reproaches are related to negative interpersonal and emotional consequences. Level of severity was in fact correlated with anger ($r = .392$), dissatisfaction ($r = .297$), ratings concerning a desire to complain about the episode ($r = .097$), and stress ($r =$

.150). Braaten et al. also found that "upward complaints" (i.e., filing complaints about the account episode) followed from the use of direct requests (40.2% of all upward complaints) and rebukes (36.1%). Upward complaints rarely occurred following polite requests (9.3%) or implicit reproaches (14.4% of upward complaints). Although the frequency of complaints is higher for direct requests than it is for the more hostile rebukes, the data indicate that at least some forms of rebuke and perhaps blunt reproaches are related to undesirable interpersonal and emotional consequences.

Different Types of Severe Reproaches

Little systematic research has focused on the question of the precise ways in which severe reproaches vary. A separate reading of the reproach forms labeled "severe" in the Braaten et al. data revealed that the severely phrased reproaches could be coded in certain ways. Two forms of severe reproaches include attack on esteem (see Table 12.1) and attack on commitment/dedication (see Table 12.2). Both of these forms of reproaches imply that the failure event was caused, in part, by causes that are personal, intentional, controllable, and stable. The attack on esteem reproach was used to claim that the account-giver was incompetent, stupid, racist or bigoted, slow, untrainable, or dumb. The attack on commitment/dedication reproaches involved the more specific claim that the account-giver was not putting much effort into his/her work.

Three other forms of severe reproaches include anger expressions, rude behavior, and threats/warnings (Tables 12.3, 12.4, & 12.5). Anger expressions reflect, in our opinion, a form of severe reproach that is qualitatively different from the other forms. Managers (or co-workers) who express anger by yelling, being aggressive, and screaming are engaging in behaviors that would be perceived as "failure events" in normal interpersonal settings. Anger should be an expression that individuals control, and once it is expressed, the reproacher (should be) obligated to account for his/her violation. What is used, then, to initiate an account episode for the account-giver's perceived failure may require an explanation (perhaps an

TABLE 12.1
Examples of Severe Reproaches: Attacks on Esteem

"Of course, the manager was so mad, and he told me that I was irresponsible, up to the extent that he accused me of doing it intentionally, but I explained . . ."

"Are you stupid, or what? You sent the wrong report to this customer!"

"He (over) acted by being emotional, rolling his eyes. He tried to make it seem like I was dumb. . . ."

"You've been abusing this nice supervisor for too long. I want you to be on time tomorrow."

"I was called up about a refused notification. She said: 'How long have you been working at the bank? How old are you? Are you a trainee?' She was *not* polite!"

"It's not fair to others that you are coming in late. There's some more smart people in that area, and they don't have a problem with time."

"I know there are certain racial overtones here . . . He tried to make me into a racist or something!"

TABLE 12.2
Examples of Severe Reproaches: Attacks on Commitment/Dedication

"Lady, this is your job. You gotta learn it!"

"I was told that I wasn't putt my 'all' into my work, that I was more involved with school. . . ."

"If I can do my half on time, why can't you?"

"You have to work *full time* when you are here."

"I don't understand this. Why are you leaving early? Again. The rules apply to everyone!"

"You had a meeting with _____ at 5 p.m. She waited for you, but you disappeared out the door. Is being the first out of the parking lot that important?"

"You have to start attending regular meetings. It's part of the job. Everyone does this."

"What is this I hear about leaving and going to a ball game?"

TABLE 12.3
Examples of Severe Reproaches: Expressions of Anger

"She yelled at me because (she thought) I was smoking in a nonsmoking section."

"He was mad. He said 'Where were you yesterday? How come you did not show up?' "

"[My manager] turned red and started yelling at me about not having a form available for a special client."

"Why the hell are you drinking beer here [at work]?" "How long has this been going on?"

"The manager was very upset, raised his voice and screamed about the importance of this deadline."

"I was asked in a challenging manner: *'What* is wrong with this form?' "

"The person said: 'Why in the hell are you so fucking late?' "

"My manager criticized one of her managers for the failure of his subordinates to attend my training sessions. He came to my office irate, and demanded to know why I had brought his absences to the attention of the supervisor. He was obviously angry in tone and in body language."

". . . Strongly, angrily: 'Well, you know we just have to get this done. We have no choice! And you are not going to make me look bad.' "

"The person was very aggressive in his tone of voice [about my absence]."

TABLE 12.4
Examples of Severe Reproaches: Rude Behavior

"She asked why I didn't try to edit the mistake. She was rude."

"This person was very persistent in asking me questions. Very rude, dominating. Not polite at all."

"My supervisor asked me why I wrote that person up. The supervisor was rude. It bothered me."

"The lady acted very rude, annoyed. 'You should ask me about picking up the mail-out log, not the secretary.' "

"As soon as I returned to my Department, my supervisor was standing waiting, and coldly asked why we went together to the bank when we were told not to do so. And that we left the Department short of help. She was kind of rude."

"He was rude, curt, short: 'Have you found the missing data yet?' "

TABLE 12.5
Examples of Severe Reproaches: Prejudged Guilt and Threats/Warnings

---

"You are late. Put it down (on the pay sheets)."

"The supervisor told me that this fellow employee stated that I threatened them. I was not allowed, at first, to deny the statement. When I tried, I was cut off."

"One worker is *constantly* asking my help. So, I told her to try harder. Later, I was confronted by three people and the supervisor about not helping others. The supervisor was already agreeing with her [the laggard] . . . "

"I attended a staff meeting and *I* was described as having made an error. *I* was the example! It just wasn't true."

"A co-worker and I had a conflict, and the co-worker told all sorts of stories about the episode. I was blamed . . . "

"The boss accused me of making a joke of his drug problem. It was all news to me, but he wrote me up. He was very defensive."

"My superior took his pencil and shook it at me and told me: 'If I *ever* see you, or hear of you, eating at your desk I will put you on written warning. This is a verbal warning.' "

"If you two don't stop chit-chatting there's going to be trouble. Every time I turn around you are talking. There will be a stop to this now — or I'll show you both to the front door."

"What is *your* reason this time? I feel this should be worked on or else some kind of action will have to take place!"

"You have absolutely no right to change my spreadsheet. Now you have completely ruined the whole thing. I don't want you to *EVER* touch any file again without my permission. What were you doing with my product files in the first place?"

---

apology) from the reproacher. Perhaps for this reason, reproachers who used anger outbursts were found to terminate the account sequence more leniently than when other severe reproaches were used (see later). Rude behaviors, however, can be more intentional, controllable, and manipulative, and were used with some frequency to assert dominance over the account-giver. On the other hand, threats/warnings involved a group of reproaches in which the account-giver was described as already guilty of having made an error and/or was written up for an offense.

The different forms of reproaches were used in different contexts and elicited different outcomes. Table 12.6 presents data from the Braaten et al. project indicating how four basic types of reproaches (pooling together attack on esteem and attack on commitment) differ in terms of how the account-giver perceived the account episodes. Table 12.7 displays how the severe forms of reproach affect the account episode and influence the evaluation of the account episode. All four of the forms of reproach were equal in eliciting anger from the account-giver (Ms = 2.06 to 2.26), and episodes involving severe forms of reproach elicited greater anger from the account-giver than other forms of reproach that were used (M = 3.56).

With the exception of anger, however, some noteworthy differences can be observed between the different forms of severe reproach:

1. Attack on esteem/commitment reproaches were rated as involving lower levels of perceived guilt and responsibility relative to other account episodes. Some

TABLE 12.6
Effects of Different Forms of Severe Reproaches

	Attacks on Esteem/ Commitment	Anger	Rudeness	Threats/ Warnings	All Other Reproaches
Guilt	3.86	4.50	4.52	4.31	3.97
Responsibility	3.24	3.50	3.63	3.62	2.78
Anger	2.07	2.23	2.26	2.06	3.56
Satisfaction	3.55	3.23	3.81	4.00	2.61
Friendly Relations	2.90	2.41	2.81	2.69	2.10
Stressful	2.35	2.41	2.81	2.12	3.18
Significant	2.48	3.63	2.56	2.69	3.33

Note: Larger numbers reflect greater guilt, responsibility, and stress; smaller numbers reflect increased anger, friendliness, significance and satisfaction.

TABLE 12.7
Effects of Severe Reproaches on Account Episodes

	Attacks on Esteem/ Commitment	Anger	Rudeness	Threats/ Warnings
Accounts				
Apology	46.2%	15.4%	23.1%	15.4%
Excuse	28.1	28.1	31.3	12.5
Justification	24.0	36.0	24.0	16.0
Refusal/denial	33.3	8.3	33.3	25.0
Evaluations				
Honoring	9.1	45.5	9.1	36.4
Retreat	33.3	33.3	22.2	11.1
Reject	33.8	16.9	33.8	15.4
Failure Event				
Tardy	30.4	30.4	21.7	17.4
Sociable	6.7	20.0	26.7	46.7
Judgement	42.9	23.8	19.0	14.3
Performance	34.3	20.0	40.0	5.7
Unprofessional	33.3	22.2	26.4	18.1
Complain	26.6	25.0	32.8	15.6

Note: Data included in this table represent all of the cases involving severe reproaches (i.e., *rebukes*) in the Braaten et al. (1990) study.

account-givers believed they were falsely accused, then, of these highly personal types of failure events.

2. Anger expressions were associated with relatively friendly relations as the norm between reproacher/account-giver (compared to the less friendly, more "cold and aloof," relationships with reproachers who used attack on esteem and rude behavior forms of reproaches). Also, episodes involving anger expressions were rated as less significant ($M = 3.63$) than attack on esteem and rude behavior reproaches ($Ms = 2.48, 2.56$).

3. Threats/warnings, along with rude behaviors, received extremely high ratings of dissatisfaction with one's employment position ($Ms = 4.00, 3.81$), and the threats/warnings forms of rebukes were associated with the highest levels of stress ($M = 2.12$).

The forms of severe reproach also were related to differences in the account episodes (see Table 12.7):

4. A significant number of claims of being treated unprofessionally and a significant number of complaints filed about the account episode were attributable to two of the reproach forms: Attack on esteem and rude behavior accounted for 59.7% of the claims of "unprofessional treatment" and 59.4% of the complaints. Account-givers did not frequently complain when threats/warnings were used, presumably because they were guilty and responsible for the failure events.

5. Most severe reproach forms in the Braaten et al. project elicited refusals/denials and justifications. However, a few apologies did occur when severe reproach forms were employed, and most of these occurred when the attack on esteem/commitment reproaches were used (see Table 12.7); however, these were later evaluated negatively (only 9.1% of the account episodes ended with the account being honored). Further, the most aggravating forms of accounts (refusals/denials) were more likely to follow from the use of two of the reproach forms: Two-thirds of all refusals/denials were elicited via attack on esteem and rude behavior reproaches.

6. Most of the account episodes in the Braaten et al. project that were initiated with a severe reproach form resulted in a negative evaluation. This effect was strongest for the two more personal forms of severe reproaches (attack on esteem and rude behaviors): Seventy per cent of all rejections followed from attack on esteem and rude behaviors, and the two reproach forms also accounted for 55.5% of all "retreats." Of the very few positive evaluations that occurred among the cases involving severe reproaches, most were due to the instances that were initiated with anger outbursts (see Table 12.7)—the types of reproaches that are themselves failure events that might require an accounting.

7. Failure events were significantly related to reproach forms. Threats/warnings were not (as one might suspect) substantially related to performance errors.

Rather, threats/warnings were frequently used when reproaching account-givers for failing to be sociable—that is, for failing to be a cooperative team player, obey norms and rules, and so on. Perhaps reproaches use threats/warnings in part because the account-giver is guilty and responsible (see Table 12.6) and because the failure event is public and affects other workers (hence, there is little choice but to write up or otherwise warn the worker). Almost all failure events involving performance errors prompted the use of attack esteem and rude behavior reproaches, and attack esteem reproaches were commonly used for failure events involving questionable judgment (when managers question the worker's commitment for spending time, leaving work early, and so forth).

What conclusions can be drawn from work on severe reproach forms? The three hypotheses offered in the literature linked severe forms of reproaches with defensive reactions, more frequently rejected accounts, and negative interpersonal and emotional consequences. We conclude that while polite reproaches are not consistently related to polite forms of accounting, a number of studies do, in fact, indicate that severely phrased reproaches appear to be related consistently to more defensive reactions. However, it is obvious that there are different types of severe reproaches. Threats/warnings are employed when the account-giver is guilty and responsible, and although the episodes are rated by account-givers as stressful and the communication as dissatisfying, account-givers engage in little complaining and do not frequently claim to be treated in an unprofessional manner.

Anger expressions, on the other hand, do not appear to harm interpersonal relations as drastically as do the attack esteem and rude behavior reproaches. Further, account episodes that were initiated via anger expression were rated as less significant compared to the three other forms of severe reproaches. Although events involving anger expressions were rated as stressful, account-givers responded with very few refusals/denials (relative to other severe reproaches) and relied on frequent justifications and excuses. Further, account-givers in such contexts found their accounts to be evaluated positively (frequent honoring and retreating) and had fewer complaints than they did with respect to two other forms of severe reproaches (see Table 12.7). Anger expressions appear, then, to be undesirable and negative encounters that are tolerated, perhaps because they are of a temporary nature.

As indicated above, more substantial and more significant consequences can be attributable to two of the severe forms of reproach: attack on esteem and rude behavior. As demonstrated earlier in the research on reproaches involving a "derogation of self-esteem" and a "derogation of sense of control" (Schonbach & Kleibaumhuter, 1990), certain forms of severe reproaches are better equipped than others at eliciting the defensive or negative reactions predictable from psychological reactance theory, or Schonbach's (1990) theory of conflict escalation. Severe forms of reproaches that attack the personal qualities of the account-giver and/or treat the account-giver rudely (specifically, acting superior to, or dominant over, the account-giver) elicit very strong reactions.

NEEDED RESEARCH

Theory

Although psychological reactance theory is used as the basis for predicting reactions to severe reproaches, much of the work in this area is largely descriptive. *Why* severe reproaches are used, and *how* they are evaluated should be studied more systematically from the framework of two relevant theories—attribution theory and impression management theory. Although attribution theory has been used for years in regard to the communication of accounts (especially excuses) (see Cody & McLaughlin, 1990; Mitchell, Green, & Wood, 1981; Weiner, this volume; Weiner, Figueroa-Muñoz, & Kakihara, 1991; Wood & Mitchell, 1981), research should focus on the attributions that account-givers assign for the causes of reproaches. Account-givers will have different reactions to reproaches depending on perceptions of distinctiveness, consistency, and consensus. Some managers may employ anger expressions for only one type of failure event (performance errors) consistently over time and direct their anger expressions at any and all workers who are judged as responsible for such failure events. Other managers may be perceived as employing anger expressions more frequently only with certain employees (but not all employees) and employing severe reproach forms for all types of failure events. In the latter case, some employees are likely to react negatively and complain about the use of severe reproach.

Impression management theorists have routinely argued that accounts are employed as part of the arsenal of tactics and strategies used to create and maintain desired public images (Braaten, et al., 1990; Jones & Pittman, 1982). Communication devices are used to foster impressions of intimidation, ingratiation, supplication, exemplification, and self-promotion. Some recent work (Braaten, et al., study 2) demonstrated a strong and predictable link between forms of apologies, excuses, justifications and denials/refusals with impressions of account-givers. However, reproachers are undoubtedly likely to phrase forms of reproach in order to foster particular goals. A manager, for example, may believe that adopting a confrontational style (using severe forms of reproach) would facilitate an image of being a strong, assertive, potent intimidator. A long-term goal is to increase the probability that his/her workers will not make many errors—out of concern for his/her reactions. On the other hand, ingratiating communicators, who desire liking, undoubtedly rely on more polite forms of reproach, while the "holier than thou" exemplifier would phrase and communicate (nonverbally) reproaches differently (the "moral superiority" form; see McLaughlin, Cody,

& Rosenstein, 1983) that may produce negative or defensive reactions (which was true in the McLaughlin et al. project, as was true of the "rude behavior" in the Braaten et al. project — see earlier).

Research Concerns

Can we claim that the effects of reproach severity are generalizable across situations? Not yet. However, the generalizability claim is somewhat bolstered by the fact that several different *types* of studies have found some consistent patterns. There are three approaches to the study of accounts: observational, scenario (or "vignette"), and survey (recalled episodes). Scenario studies provide strong support for the reproach-severity hypotheses (Schonbach, 1990; Schonbach & Kleibaumhuter, 1990), as do the surveys of recalled episodes (Braaten, et al., 1990; Cody & McLaughlin, 1985; McLaughlin, Cody, & O'Hair, 1983). One observational study found that certain forms of reproach elicited more aggravating forms of accounts (McLaughlin, Cody, & Rosenstein, 1983).

Unfortunately, it is difficult to say whether other observational studies employed or varied severe forms of reproaches. Gonzales, Pederson, Manning, and Wetter (1990) tricked students into believing that a cup of liquid in their charge had fallen into either a tote bag containing computer paper (a failure event Gonzales et al. labeled *low severity*) or into a tote bag containing computer paper and expensive film equipment (labeled *high severity* by Gonzales et al.). The following details were provided: "Immediately after the cup spilled, the confederate appeared in the doorway and exclaimed, 'Oh, shit. My stuff!' After approximately a three-second delay or after participants had fallen silent, whichever came first, the confederate asked, 'What happened?' " (Gonzales et al., p. 614). Given this brief description of the reproach, we have no way of knowing if the reproacher expressed anger, was upset (e.g., played the role of the distraught victim), or was merely using a direct request.

Improving Our Research by Avoiding Pitfalls

Three hypotheses involving severe reproach forms have been advanced that link severe reproaches to defensive reactions (aggravating accounts), negative evaluations, and negative interpersonal and emotional consequences. Another viable hypothesis appears, at first glance, to be obvious: *Reproachers are more likely to use severe reproach forms as the severity of the consequences of the failure event increase.* Reproachers are not likely to employ harsh rebukes if a friend yawns at a bridge party but could very well rebuke the friend for attempting to drive home drunk. The relationship, however, is untested.

Despite the fact that severity of consequences is an important underlying variable in the perception of failure events, considerable confusion exists concerning its role in the accounting process. A good deal of this confusion has surfaced, in part, because of a set of interrelated problems: a problem with the meaning of the term *severity*, and simplistic expectations concerning its operation; inadequate manipulation of variables in research; a problem of unmeasured variables and the related problem of uncovering "authentic" or "strategic" uses of accounts (i.e., "apologies" and "excuses" are often communicated merely for the sake of giving the receivers and experimenters what the account-givers think the receivers want to hear). Since these problems and concerns so profoundly affect the conclusions we draw about behavior and affect model-building, some attention is warranted.

Severity of Consequences

In the 1980s different hypotheses were offered concerning the operation of severity of the consequences associated with failure events. Schonbach (1986) predicted that more severe offenses would result in more *defensive* accounts, while we (see Cody & McLaughlin, 1985) argued that more severe offenses would result in more mitigating accounts (apologies and excuses). In reality, the central hypothesis is that as severity of the failure event increases the account-giver will be more motivated to construct and communicate elaborate forms of accounts of either a mitigating or aggravating form. Indeed, Schonbach's (1990) more recent framework includes two rival hypotheses:

Hypothesis A: The greater the severity of the failure event, the more defensive will be the actor's reaction during the account phase.

Hypothesis A': The greater the severity of the failure event, the more willing the actor will be to make concessions with respect to the failure event and his or her own involvement in it.

Hypothesis A is true if one of two conditions occur: A person is *wrongly* accused of a severe failure event, or a person is correctly accused of having caused a failure event, but the severity of the failure event has been exaggerated. Hypothesis A' is operative in any situation in which the account-giver expects that he or she will obtain lenient judgments by offering admissions of guilt, expressions of regret, compensation for damages, or by offering excuses to exonerate perceived responsibility. That is, account-givers legitimately offer apologies and elaborate forms of accounting when they experience feelings of guilt, when felt responsibility is high, and when there exists a strong desire to avoid being evaluated negatively.

In sum, higher levels of severity have predictable effects on accounting behavior when coupled with additional variables. One additional limitation must be noted, however. Some relational problems surface that are highly severe for which individuals claim there is no apparent solution (see Cody, Kersten, Braaten, & Dickson, in press). Some offenses are so inexcusable that offenders are not reproached and accounts are not communicated—the relationships simply decay. In sum, we see no reason to make any prediction concerning the form of reproach communicated (or the form of account that is communicated) based *solely* on operation of the variable of *severity*. Severity impacts on motivation—but motivation can result in elaborate forms of defenses, elaborate forms of apologies, or a determination to exit relationships.

Inadequate Manipulations

Some forms of severe failure events involve excessive speeding, drug use, cheating, and white collar crime (see review in Cody and McLaughlin, 1990). Severe failure events are ones in which the amount of harm done to a victim or to society is significant. Unfortunately, some studies employ the term *severity* when a different variable was in fact manipulated. For example, the Gonzales et al. study could have manipulated severity of *consequences* by tricking students into knocking (what appears to be) a fully functioning Pentax camera onto the ground in such a way that the camera breaks apart. Instead, the Gonzales (1990) project tricked students into dropping a liquid into various bags—failure events that were clearly *embarrassing*. However, one can raise the question as to whether or not the *consequences* between a wet tote bag with computer paper and a wet tote bag with a camera are significant or trivial.

In fact, Gonzales et al.'s manipulation check indicated that the manipulation of perceived severity failed: Even students in the *low severity* condition rated the offense as relatively severe ($M = 14.16$), at the same level as did the *high severity* condition students ($M = 14.34$). To salvage their study, Gonzales et al. argued that a greater portion of students in the high severity condition claimed levels of severity greater than 16 (on a scale of a maximum value of 20). It would seem that Gonzales et al. manipulated, then, high and moderate levels of embarrassment. But did they? Since the experimenter was the one who asked the manipulation check questions orally after the students were made to be embarrassed and prior to the debriefing, the students probably told the experimenter what they believed the experimenter (the one who designed the study) wanted to hear (that the experiment was a success).

Finally, there is an implicit assumption in the Gonzales et al. study that the tricked students would feel responsible for their action—although the cup of liquid was given to them, the liquid was resting on a table that someone else could have jarred (in fact, a trick wire was used to get the cup to fall), and the victim could have been criticized for being irresponsible for leaving his tote bag on the floor where it was in everyone's way. Even if the victim were blamed for placing his bag in a poor location, the appropriate course of action in a public setting (especially when there will be continued interaction—the "accident" occurred at the beginning of an experiment) is to apologize. However, Gonzales et al. found that the apologies by males were more perfunctory than the apologies by females, and Gonzales et al. spent a good deal of effort in explaining the results. If measures of perceived guilt and perceived responsibility were obtained, the results might have demonstrated that males were more likely than females to assign some of the blame to the victim; hence, feeling less guilty and less responsible, males used more perfunctory apologies. Gender differences can be "caused" by any number of variables, but researchers will have to measure relevant variables in order to provide support for one explanation over another.

CONCLUSION

Severely reproaching another has a significant effect on the accounting process. Severe forms of reproach that involve a personal attack, which derogates the self concept, elicit defensive reactions, result in negative evaluations, and cause negative interpersonal and emotional consequences. However, our report on the nature of reproaches is still preliminary at best, because so few studies to date have examined reproach forms from relevant theoretical frameworks, or even within a single, systematic, framework of reproach types. Since forms of reproach are so strongly linked to the escalation of conflict, we believe that a careful examination of reproach forms should be conducted in any setting where disputes are common, but where certain forms of conflict could be harmful—as in marriage counseling sessions, child custody mediation sessions, or appraisal interviews in organizational settings. Our expectation is that a careful examination of their impact will be attempted in those settings where conflict should be avoided—family therapy sessions and organizational settings.

REFERENCES

Braaten, D. O., Cody, M. J., & Bell, K. (1990, June). *Account episodes in organizations: Remedial work and impression management*. Paper presented at the annual meeting of the International Communication Association, Dublin, Ireland.

Carroll, J. S., & Payne, J. W. (1977). Judgments about crime and the criminal: A model and a method for investigating parole decisions. In B. D. Sales (Ed.), *Perspectives in law and psychology* (pp. 191-239). New York: Plenum Press.

Cody, M. J., Kersten, L., Braaten, D. O., & Dickson, R. (in press). Coping with relational dissolutions: Attributions, account-credibility, and plans for resolving conflicts. In J. H. Harvey, T. L. Orbuch, & A. L. Weber (Eds.), *Attribution, accounts, and close relationships*. New York: Springer-Verlag.

Cody, M. J., & McLaughlin, M. L. (1985). Models for the sequential construction of accounting episodes: Situational and interactional constraints on message selection and evaluation. In R. L. Street & J. N. Cappella (Eds.), *Sequence and pattern in communicative behaviour* (pp. 50-69). London: Edward Arnold.

Cody, M. J., & McLaughlin, M. L. (1988). Accounts on trial: Oral arguments in traffic court. In C. Antaki (Ed.), *Analyzing everyday explanation: A casebook of methods* (pp. 113-126). London: Sage.

Cody, M. J., & McLaughlin, M. L. (1990). Interpersonal accounting. In H. Giles & P. Robinson (Eds.), *Handbook of language and social psychology* (pp. 227-255). London: Wiley.

Dindia, K., & Steele, D. J. (1987, May). *Account sequences in medical encounters.* Paper presented at the annual meeting of the International Communication Association, Boston, MA.

Felson, R. B., & Ribner, S. A. (1981). An attributional approach to accounts and sanctions for criminal violence. *Social Psychology Quarterly, 44,* 137-142.

Gonzales, M. H., Pederson, J. H., Manning, D. J., & Wetter, D. W. (1990). Pardon my gaffe: Effects of sex, status, and consequence severity on accounts. *Journal of Personality and Social Psychology, 58,* 610-621.

Henderson, M., & Hewstone, M. (1984). Prison inmates' explanations for interpersonal violence: Accounts and attributions. *Journal of Consulting and Clinical Psychology, 52,* pp. 789-794.

Holtgraves, T. (1989). The form and function of remedial moves: Reported use, psychological reality, and perceived effectiveness. *Journal of Language and Social Psychology, 8,* 1-16.

Jones, E. E., & Pitman, T. S. (1982). Toward a general theory of strategic self-presentation. In J. Suls (Ed.), *Psychological perspectives on the self* (pp. 231-262). Hillsdale, NJ: Lawrence Erlbaum Associates.

McLaughlin, M. L., Cody, M. J., & O'Hair, H. D. (1983). The management of failure events: Some contextual determinants of accounting behavior. *Human Communication Research, 9,* 209-224.

McLaughlin, M. L., Cody, M. J., & Rosenstein, N. E. (1983). Account sequences in conversations between strangers. *Communication Monographs, 50,* 102-125.

Mitchell, T. R., Green, S. G., & Wood, R. (1981). An attributional model of leadership and the poor performing subordinate. In L. L. Cummings & B. M. Staw (Eds.), *Research in organizational behavior* (vol. 3, 151-198). Greenwich, CT: Aijai Press.

Riordan, C. A., Marlin, N. A., & Kellogg, R. T. (1983). The effectiveness of accounts following transgressions. *Social Psychology Quarterly, 46,* 213-219.

Rothman, M. L., & Gandossy, R. P. (1982). Sad tales: The accounts of white-collar defendants and the decision to sanction. *Pacific Sociological Review, 25,* 449-473.

Schonbach, P. (1986). *A theory of conflict escalation in account episodes.* Unpublished manuscript, Fakultat fur Psychologie, Ruhr-Universitat, Bochum, West Germany.

Schonbach, P. (1990). *Account episodes: The management or escalation of conflict.* New York: Cambridge University Press.

Schonbach, P., & Kleibaumhuter, P. (1990). Severity of reproach and defensiveness of accounts. In M. J. Cody & M. L. McLaughlin (Eds.), *The psychology of tactical communication* (pp. 229-243). Clevedon, England: Multilingual Matters, Ltd.

Weiner, B., Figueroa-Muñoz, A., & Kakihara, C. (1991). The goals of excuses and communication strategies related to causal perceptions. *Personality and Social Psychology Bulletin, 17,* 4-13.

Wood, R. E., & Mitchell, T. R. (1981). Manager behavior in a social context: The impact of impression management on attributions and disciplinary actions. *Organizational Behavior and Human Performance, 28,* 356-378.

13

▼▼▼▼▼▼▼

Storytelling as Collaborative Reasoning: Co-Narratives in Incest Case Accounts

Karin Aronsson
Claes Nilholm
Linköping University, Sweden

Story order in relation to the narrator's background information and perspective taking will be our focus in this chapter. Wittingly or unwittingly, narrators at times tend to relocate key events in their temporal ordering of failure-event accounts (Neisser, 1982). Presently, we will focus on collaborative constructions of false or veridical accounts in group decisionmaking in legal settings.

In line with an interactional philosophy of language, Ricoeur (1971) has argued that narration is basically dialogic, shaped by ongoing and past discourse. This emphasis on dialogue has also been articulated quite cogently in the work of Rorty (1979) and Rommetveit (1985,1990). Bakhtin (1981, 1986) (see also Wertsch, 1991) has demonstrated the multivoicedness of everyday narration, how social actors often speak both on their own behalf and (consciously or less consciously) as agents for other persons or institutions. Language as such is impregnated with social history, and in our everyday language, we recapitulate old attitudes and past thoughts. Everyday narratives reflect social history on the one hand, ongoing dialogue on the other. We hope to make a contribution to an empirical study of knowledge and dialogues by documenting how narratives are interactionally produced in legal settings.

Like human action in general, interactions may be "read" by an indefinite range of possible readers, and the interpretations of facts are linked to overriding story frameworks that in turn determine the interpretation of factual details (Cicourel, 1985; Ricoeur, 1971): "That means that, like a text, human action is an open work, the meaning of which is 'in suspense.' It is because it 'opens up' new references and receives fresh relevance from them, that human deeds are also waiting for fresh interpretations which decide their meaning" (p. 544).

Opposing interpretations may remain unresolved. Yet, such conflicts tend to come to an end in the course of social negotiations. Bennett (1978, 1979, 1991) has analyzed the role of opponent frameworks in legal storytelling practices and how "facts" are selected so as to provide the best fit to competing story versions. He based his theses on content analyses of legal argumentation, though, without detailing courtroom discourse as such. In a congenial study on courtroom discourse, Woodbury (1984) has, pointedly, described trials in terms of storytelling contests. Neither the prosecution lawyer, nor the defense lawyer may tell the story himself/herself, yet each party has to outperform the opposing party in telling the most convincing story. Successful lawyers employ strategic questioning techniques that tend to produce more plausible stories from defendants and witnesses. In a comprehensive review on legal interrogations, Aronsson (1991) has drawn on discourse studies, on the one hand, and witness psychology experiments, on the other, showing how legal evidence can become recycled through different types of questioning, and how legal evidence, in part, can be seen as the result of prior social interactions.

We would argue that co-participants also shape courtroom narratives in more subtle and, at times, less deliberate ways than through more or less coercive interrogation techniques (or through more or less leading questions). In a study of courtroom deliberations, Aronsson and Nilholm (1990) have shown how memories are co-constituted. Background facts are at times recycled into fabrications that fit into same-side versions of past realities. In this study of lay judges' discourse, twenty triads were presented with written background material from an authentic custody case (involving an incest accusation). In each triad, one participant, unknowingly, received a slightly different version of the background facts. Divergent background facts were often brought to the fore, but they were generally not challenged. Instead, co-participants would, unknowingly, integrate each other's "false" facts into collective memories as it were, combining information from the two different sets of information (pro-Mum (M)/pro-Dad (D) version). At times, the participants would themselves introduce new information that had not been included in either version of the background material. One case (Aronsson & Nilholm, 1990, Excerpt 2) concerns a discussion in which a pro-Mum discussant, Mona, emphatically stated that "before this happened, there were certainly no problems between D and M" and "They had not thought of divorce or anything like that. They had not been fighting" (before the incest incident). In this specific case, the two co-participants do challenge these radically false statements (according to both background versions, the parents did argue from the very outset of their marriage, in fact, even before they were married or had children).

In Aronsson and Nilholm, we discussed this recycling as a type of negation of "facts." We did not analyze story order. From the perspective of a narrative analysis, though, Mona's argumentation involves a reordering of story elements, the creation of a new story. Mona concedes that the parents did argue but she situates the arguing at a radically different point in time, which, in turn, means that the arguing assumes a completely different meaning:

Factual temporal sequence:	parents' arguing	$\longrightarrow$	incest/incest suspicion
New story: (invented sequence)	incest	$\longrightarrow$	parents' arguing

Since the parents had, indeed, argued for quite a while, this may implicate that the woman has motives for discrediting her husband, aside from the alleged incest and/or that she is also somewhat responsible for the collapse of her marriage (D is not exclusively to be blamed). In contrast, Mona's new (distorted) order of events implies a completely different story, which casts the woman (M) as more of a victim (someone who has not taken part in any rows).

In our study on collective remembering (Aronsson & Nilholm, 1990) we have primarily analyzed the recycling of "facts." Presently, we will explore in what ways different parties may also generate quite different—and at times quite distorted—temporal sequences of the same background facts. Actions primarily assume social meaning to the extent that they may be related to other actions in a meaningful causal order, and the same act may lead to radically different interpretations if the temporal order is altered (Read, 1987). Read, Druian, and Miller (1989) have experimented on story order and respondents' inferences (in a paper-and-pencil test tapping causal attributions). They have not studied participants' spontaneous distortions of story order or how such distortions are challenged or accepted in the course of human discourse.

Beach (1985) has shown how courtroom discourse involves extensive time travelling covering both future time and past events. Past events may refer to several different events, for instance different police interviews, several psychiatric interviews, and so on. For legal reasons, it may be important to pin-point at what specific encounter something was said or done (interview 1, 2, or N?). The court often asks for precise and exact dates and time references, whereas spoken discourse tends to be more vague and elusive. There is, thus, often a poor match between the written format of legal documents and the imprecision of spoken language, and it takes quite some work from prosecutors and defense lawyers before time and place references have been narrowed down to specific times and places.

As shown in Adelswärd, Aronsson and Linell (1988), inexperienced defendants are often taken aback by institutional (legal) requirements for exact references in that they frame intensive questioning as a type of "nagging" or distrust on the court's part. There is thus an inbuilt conflict between everyday framing of questioning and institutional (legal) framing. While exact time references are often important in courtroom interaction, temporal order is obviously often even more important. Did event x occur before event y?

In the present context, stories are defined as narrative accounts that provide causal explanations for social events, and failure events in particular. Accounts are discussed more fully in Cody and McLaughlin (1990). The present accounts are second-order accounts in that they concern how participants take sides, presenting accounts that explain one combative party's actions in a favorable light (thereby rendering competing accounts less credible). Our analyses thus concern "pro-Dad" or "pro-Mum" accounts in an incest case rather than the two parents' original accounts. The background material contains several different failure events. Presently, we will be particularly concerned with social explanations for why the target child (incest victim?) started to develop symptoms at a specific point of time. Our focus will be on temporal order and collaborative storytelling. To what extent can the deliberation interactions be described in terms of co-narration, and in what ways may this deepen our understanding of the various distortions of the background information?

METHOD

Lay Judges

In the Swedish judicial system, there are three or five lay judges who assist the judge in all aspects of the final decisionmaking in district court trials concerning criminal law. The lay judges are recruited among trusted citizens from the different political parties. The judge is to inform the lay judges about the legal aspects of the case. He or she may be more or less active during the deliberation. (The present simulations would obviously be most ecologically valid for an incest case with a professional judge who remains passive during the deliberation discussions).

Simulation Study Procedure

Participants were recruited among prospective nursery school teachers. Twenty groups (with three in each) discussed an authentic custody case involving a prior incest accusation. All discussions were audio-taped and transcribed. Each participant received a six-page document containing background information from the case in question. The participants could take their time reading, but they were not allowed to turn back pages. They were instructed to first tick their individual decisions on the custody question, as well as on the incest question. Participants were provided with four set alternatives for each question.

When all three participants had completed the individual task, they were instructed to try to reach a unanimous group decision (reservation could be formulated in writing). The experimenter left the group alone during the discussion, which lasted about 20 to 30 minutes.

Shared Background Information

A six-page document summarized information from an authentic custody case. Code names were used for the principal parties, the mother (M), the father (D), and the young girl (C), who was the alleged victim of sexual assault. The background material contained many references to exact times and places, and it was quite complex. For the purpose of the present discussion, the material can be summarized as follows:

D and M got married when C was 2 years old. The relationship between D and M was strained already before their marriage, and it continued to be marked by disagreements and rows. M claims that D is aggressive, abnormally jealous, and that he has problems holding his liquor. D, on his part, claims that M is overprotective, hysterical, and overly sensitive. D was on paternity leave when C was a baby. She was said to be "Daddy's girl" as a small child. When C was about 3 years old, she became withdrawn and seemed to be afraid of D (according to M). M suspected incest and consulted several experts. Some experts believed in her suspicions, whereas others did not. A police interrogation did not lead to official charges against D. On the advice of a psychologist, D moved away from home during the police investigation. D continued to visit his family almost daily, but when C was 4 years old, she became aggressive after seeing D. M again suspected incest. M and D got divorced sometime later, but D was allowed visitation rights. When C was about 5 years old, M obstructed D's visitation rights. At the time of the civil trial, M and D are divorced, and M claims that D should have no visitation rights whatsoever.

The temporal order of some of the key events is shown in Fig. 13.1.

Selective Background Information

There were two different versions of the background material. On a random basis, two persons in each group got an M-version modification of the case, while the third person got a D-modification. Background facts were withdrawn from the entire set of information in such a way that the M-version contained three unique facts favoring M's side (excluded in the D-version), and the D-version three unique facts favoring D's side (excluded in the M-version). The material was kept at an equal length but six background facts thus differed between the two differently abridged versions. Our main focus, however, will be on the temporal ordering of facts. A complete list of divergent background facts and other information on our method can be found in Aronsson and Nilholm (1990).

Coding

The whole set of background information was listed in terms of 30 argument data (six divergent and 24 shared "facts"). The discourse transcripts were coded for the presence of specific background data and for any distorted version of the same.

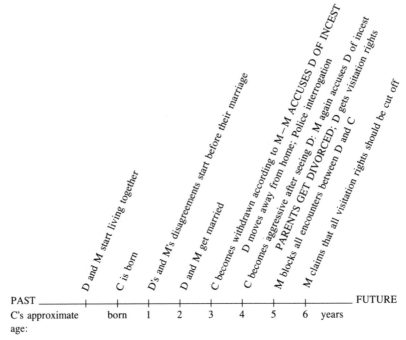

FIG. 13.1.   Time chart covering some key events in child custody case background
material.

Each argument was coded the first time it occurred (Who presented it? How was
it received? Was it challenged or ratified?) Two coders independently coded 1,290
turns (roughly 10% of the corpus) with respect to type of argument (1–30). Type
of argument yielded an 82% inter-rater reliability, whereas ratification/challenges
yielded an 86% reliability.

Participants who primarily favored D-claims in their individual ratings were
coded as pro-D (their fictionalized names begin with D in the excerpts), whereas
all those favoring M-claims on the custody and/or incest question were coded
as pro-M. Six groups happened to have consensus opinions (pro-D). In the remaining groups, there were always two persons with a majority and one with
a divergent minority opinion (pro-D or pro-M).

FINDINGS

Factual and Invented Story Sequences

In the present study, it can be seen how time order is sometimes quite crucial for
an understanding of the two parents' divergent accounts. However, factual time
sequences are occasionally supplanted by invented sequences that make narrative
sense in terms of, for instance, nonguilty frameworks (Table 13.1). The temporal
sequencing of events apparently becomes subordinate to overall story frameworks.

TABLE 13.1
Factual Story Sequences Versus Invented Story Sequences

Type of Sequence	Initial Event	Intermediate Event	Outcome Event
"Factual" Sequences[1]			
D as guilty	Incest	C's symptoms	Divorce
D as innocent	Parents' arguing/ D's drinking M's dislike of D	C's symptoms	Divorce
Invented Story Sequences			
D as innocent	Divorce	C's symptoms	Incest suspicion by M

[1]Possible scenarios that fit the temporal order of the background information.

This may, in part, be a result of the fact that time references are quite complex in the present background material (see also Fig. 13.1). The different groups of lay judges discuss future events (different custody scenarios) as well as events that predate the present conflict (e.g., questions concerning D's or M's moral character; M's previous marriage, etc.). The present conflict has developed during a period of several years; the parental conflict even predates the present marriage, whereas the incest accusation/incest has marred family life for some years.

In discussing the incest question, several participants claim that the child has become "withdrawn" after the parent's divorce. This story sequence is an inverted one in relation to the background information that indicates that the child became "withdrawn" (at the age of 3), and "aggressive" (at the age of 4) after the alleged incest incidents. The parents got divorced after these incidents (when the child was about 5 years old). The background information thus does not warrant a causal reasoning that states that the child has become withdrawn as an effect of the divorce. Yet, this invented story appears in several different groups (9/20 groups, Group 2, 6, 9, 10, 11, 12, 16, 17, 19).

As can be seen, there are two possible scenarios that would fit the background facts; one scenario would cast D as guilty of incest, and one scenario would cast him as innocent. In the invented story sequence, D is obviously also cast as non-guilty, and his innocence is perhaps more pronounced in that the casual sequence is now reversed; it is the divorce that causes the girl's symptoms and M's incest suspicions and not the other way round.

Altogether, nine different groups have thus produced at least one such invented story order (in relation to the factual events in the background material). However, these invented story sequences are only challenged in three cases.

Co-Narration and Challenges

In one case, the invented story order gets no support within the group. None of the co-participants ratifies the inverted story order (Excerpt 1):

Excerpt 1. Invented story sequence and co-participants' challenges. (Group 19, p. 2)[1]

Dotty: Well no, but she had a certain period. . . . when she was . . .

Daphne: Mmm, that was when

Melisse: Withdrawn and quite, yes

Dotty: Mmm

Daphne: /whispering/yes/normally/But that was er during the separation as I understood it to be

Melisse: /quietly/no

Dotty: No, that was before

Dotty challenges the false story order without any prefacing moves ("No, that was before"). Her response can be seen as an elaboration of the previous turn, though, that is the single word of protest ("no") by the previous speaker. Collaboration is characteristic for these encounters, and protests are often constructed in close cooperation with co-participants.

In our first example of a false story order (above), story order is immediately challenged. This is quite atypical for the present discussions. More typically, co-participants first tend to ratify the story or parts thereof. This can, for instance, be seen in Excerpt 2, where Desiree does not challenge Martina right away:

Excerpt 2. Invented story sequence and co-participant's challenges. (Group 10, p. 39)

Martina: Yes, I- as could be seen, I thought that er: one could see that before the separation she had had been in good rapport with, then there were some disturbances after that.

Desiree: Yes

Doris: Then it kind of- they- er if we- if incest had been going on during the marriage as well before they had separated then nothing could be seen, no disturbances in the daughter, right? The disturbances did appear in connection with the separation, didn't they.

---

[1]Transcription notations:
- :   Self-editing marker
:   Prolonged syllable
__   Demarcate overlapping utterances
/ /   Encloses description of how talk is delivered
. . .   Audible pause
CAPITALS   Relatively high amplitude

Martina:	Yes:
Desiree:	That was before. It must-
Doris:	Was that before?

Martina and Doris have construed a false story order in a type of co-narration, where Doris specifies (and thereby also ratifies) Martina's false story order. In her second contribution in this episode, Desiree ultimately challenges the false story order of her two co-participants ("That was before").

Typically, challenges tend to appear as the outcome of such more or less drawn out exchanges (e.g., Excerpt 3):

Excerpt 3. Invented story sequence and co-participant's challenges. (Group 16, p. 16)

Daisy:	Because the separation might, of course, have given the girl er: psychological: problems or er disturbances too
Dominique:	Mmm
Daisy:	The separation itself because that must have been very difficult
Minna:	But they ha- . . . she . . . er b- b- that she did say that the girl . . . had become . . . more quiet 'n' . . . so on
Daisy:	M:
Minna:	After that this had happened she did say
Daisy:	Yeah
Minna:	But this was before the separation, wasn't it?
Daisy:	Uhm it was when she er . . . threw out her suspicions that's when er
Minna:	Threw out?

This case illustrates Beach's (1985) analysis of natural language references and time complexities. Minna's first challenge is quite vague and tentative ("But they ha- . . . she . . . er b- b- . . .) Her pauses and hesitations seem to invite co-narrative support. In this initial (tentative?) protest, she does not explicitly voice any protest against the temporal order of events. She does not refer to when M had said that C had become more quiet. A little later, she clarifies her challenge ("But this was before the separation, wasn't it?"). In the ensuing discussion (not covered above), it could be seen that Daisy never accepted Minna's challenge. Instead, Daisy remarked that there is "always a danger that one reads too much

into the past" (referring not to her own but to M's difficulties in sorting out perceived reality and factual reality when looking back at past events). Daisy's invented story sequence is ratified by Dominique, who is not very active in the
discussion, but who does acknowledge Daisy's story, and who does not side with
Minna in connection with the discussion on story order (what happened before
what?). Obviously, the inverted story order makes good narrative sense in terms
of pro-D story frameworks.

Co-narration and Co-participants' Support

In the more typical cases, invented story order is not challenged, either by opponents or by same-side participants. In six groups out of nine, co-participants go
along with invented story sequences without voicing any protest (Excerpts 4–9).

Excerpt 4. Invented story order and co-participants' ratifications. (Group 2,
p. 19)

Matilda:	Of course, there can be problems due to the separation too.
Maria:	Mmm
Matilda:	It doesn't have to be the incest that makes her-
Dolly:	No, and then worry
Matilda:	Withdrawn and so on
Dolly:	No, and then the worries, then, because . . . They were so worried of course both parents like

As can be seen, no one challenges Matilda's false reasoning about the causal
chain. Similarly, Margit presents an uncontested false story in a different group
(Excerpt 5):

Excerpt 5. Invented story order and co-participants' ratifications. (Group 6,
pp. 10–11)

Margit:	But I find it difficult to remember properly, like how it was after-wards, if she ha-
Daga:	Mm
Margit:	Was a lot more difficult no and so on
Didi:	No, but er
Margit:	It cou- it could be due to the separation too

Didi: /whispering/yes

Daga: There wasn't anything about their sex-life directly . . . There wasn't, was there?

Margit: No

In this case, "afterwards" (Margit's first turn) refers to an alleged incest incident. The group had discussed the possibility that D had accosted his daughter in the course of drinking ("perhaps while being drunk" in Daga's words). Thus, "it" would refer to the alleged incest incident (in Margit's third turn). Reference is somewhat vague, which is quite typical for these discussions concerning sensitive topics. Participants are careful not to state their presuppositions very openly. Apparently, such vagueness opens up toward opposing interpretations or co-participants' support work. The exact reference of "it," "afterwards," and so on, may be negotiated during the deliberations, and participants may withdraw from their preliminary opinions without losing face. In Excerpt 5, it can be seen how no one contests the inverted story order. Daga inquires about the parents' sex-life, though (probably in order to find other mitigating circumstances for D's behavior). Parenthetically, it may be added that the background information, in fact, does indicate that M had reported that D had not shown any sexual aberrations before (or except for) the alleged incest incidents. Several groups do discuss this information (cf. Excerpt 9), but Daga does not retrieve this information.

Among the groups who rearrange the time order of the background information, the initiative may come from either a pro-D or a pro-M party. Participants who basically favor one type of story framework (pro-D/pro-M) have not always made up their minds entirely. They are open to negotiations, to new interpretations, and they may entertain more than one explanation at the same time (Excerpt 6).

Excerpt 6. Invented story order and co-participants' ratifications. (Group 9, pp. 6–7)

Mikaela: I mean the sort of behavior a child has when they get like her when they've bee- with- er <u>wound up and all that I mean</u>

Marta: <u>Mmm:</u>

Mikaela: On the whole it could be almost anything

Marta: Yes, of course it could <u>have been</u>

Dagny: <u>Yes</u>

Marta: The divorce itself <u>too</u>

Mikaela: <u>Yes</u>, but when the child starts talking about the father having done something <u>eh</u>

It can be seen that Mikaela perceives two rival (and incompatible) hypotheses: (a) that almost anything may have made the child withdrawn ("with-"), and (b) that C has to be taken seriously as she has been "talking." In the case of such competing stories, the final story is often the product of co-narration, that is, the type of explanation that the group majority will endorse.

It can, again, be seen how participants refer to "it" somewhat ambiguously (Mikaela, Marta above). In the opening sequence of the above episode, "it" could refer to the first and/or the second alleged incest incident or to some entirely different event. Ultimately, Mikaela's last statement clarifies that she is, in fact, referring to an alleged offense (which the child has started "talking about").

In a couple of cases, all the participants are pro-D, and everybody unhesitantly ratifies the idea that it is the separation that has caused the girl's symptoms (Excerpt 7, 8):

Excerpt 7. Invented story order and co-participants' ratifications. (Group 11, p. 6)

Drusilla:	The mother seems to influence the girl/Drusilla writes/ . . . or-
Dorit:	<u>Mm</u>
Drusilla:	What do you say?
Desideria:	Mm/they write/
Drusilla:	And the fact that the girl has become withdrawn may be an effect of the separation as such
Desideria:	/quietly/yes
Dorit:	It was the other girl that-?

In one of the other consensus groups, the co-participants' ratifications are even more explicit, e.g., "Yes, that's what I would say as well" (Excerpt 8):

Excerpt 8. Invented story order and co-participants' ratifications. (Group 12, p. 13)

Daniela:	In that case/if there had been incest/there certainly would have . . . been something even before the divorce, wouldn't there?
Delila:	M/quietly/
Donna:	Yes, that's what I would <u>say as well</u>
Daniela:	<u>It would have</u> shown in some way
Donna:	<u>Yes</u>

Daniela:	. . . in the girl
Donna:	And 'cos no one not even SHE
Delila:	M
Donna:	Not even the wife says that- . . . he . . . that she has-
Delila:	has shown
Donna:	seen any sexual
Delila:	/quietly/no:
Donna:	aberration in any way

This discussion illustrates a type of collective thinking aloud that is quite prototypical for consensus argumentation, where joint thinking is transformed into co-narratives. It can, for instance, be seen how the participants complete the prior utterances of their co-participants. Hence, Delila completes one of Donna's uncompleted sentences by adding "has shown." Reference is complex in this material, though, and she has confounded "he" and "she," which leads Delila to perform an other-repair, changing "shown" into "seen" (which fits better with a reference to "she").

In conflict opinion groups, it can be seen how minority opinion participants often maintain low-key profiles. They do not complete their opponents' sentences, nor do they contribute more actively in joint storytelling. On the other hand, they generally do not challenge the other two participants' co-narration (cf. Dagny in Excerpt 6 above or Maude in Excerpt 9, below).

Excerpt 9. Invented story sequence and co-participants' ratifications. (Group 17, p. 6)

Dorte:	Well, it was only . . . that the child was introverted and-
Dierdree:	Mmm
Dorte:	We- yes- this was-
Maude:	/quietly/yes
Dierdree:	And it's probably due to, what's it called- the actual separation of the parents and that
Dorte:	Yes
Dierdree:	The mother so clearly shows her dislike of the father
Dorte:	Yes, and their rows and so on, one can imagine eh

Maude provides but a minimal support to the other two participants' joint storytelling, but she does not challenge their story order. In contrast, the two pro-D participants, Dorte and Dierdree, mutually support each others' analyses to the point of creating a dialogical narrative (neatly linking background events to each other in an inverted order.)

CONCLUSIONS

Neisser (1985) has convincingly argued in terms of more ecologically oriented studies of human cognition. Recently, there has been a certain increase in ecologically oriented studies on discourse and narration in everyday life (Ochs, Smith, & Taylor, 1989) and in the legal arena (e.g., Adelswärd, Aronsson, & Linell, 1988; Conley & O'Barr, 1990; Jönsson & Linell, 1990; Liebes-Plesner, 1984; Maynard, 1982; O'Barr & Conley, 1985). The present study provides something of a bridge between experimentation on storytelling and cognition (Read, Druian, & Miller, 1989), on the one hand, and ecologically grounded discourse studies on the other.

As shown in our extensive presentation of individual discourse sequences, different groups of "lay judges" may, independently, arrive at related distortions of reality, inverting the temporal order of key events in such a way that specific social actions assume radically different meanings. Read, Druian, and Miller (1989) have shown related reinterpretations in an experimental setup, varying temporal order in the story structure. Our investigation shows how respondents spontaneously produce such story sequence variations in a quasi-natural setting.

The participants were presented with highly complex custody case material, dense with temporal references. The material also contained some important social questions (Should D be deprived of visitation rights? Was D guilty of incest?) Yet, the material contained many loose endings—being open to different readings—in that all participants had to take sides between two antagonistic (and mutually exclusive) accounts. In this complex situation, many respondents would make sense of socially puzzling accounts by integrating them into novel scenarios, thereby disambiguating complexities in the task as such. However, this also meant that they would (wittingly or unwittingly) distort the objective temporal order of the case, reinventing past reality.

The present data show how such story constructions may take place as a collaborative affair. Co-participants challenge or ratify "factual" and "invented" story sequences, thereby producing joint narratives. In a more direct sense, it could also be seen how participants would at times complete each other's sentences or expand each other's argumentation in ways that would produce truly dialogical narratives. Such co-narration thus goes beyond the type of interactional phenomena that can be found in experimental or natural variation of interrogation techniques and coerciveness. In line with Heider (1958) and Read (1987), it can be seen that human actors are storifying creatures, who make sense of complex actions by linking events into meaningful causal chains (be they factual or reinvented ones).

ACKNOWLEDGMENT

We thank the faculty and students at the Department of Preschool Teacher Training, Norrköping for their kind cooperation. Thanks are also extended to Professor Ulla Jacobsson, Department of Law, Lund University for helpful discussions at the outset of this project.

REFERENCES

Adelswärd, V., Aronsson, K., & Linell, P. (1988). Discourse of blame: Courtroom construction of social identity from the perspective of the defendant. *Semiotica, 71*, 261–284.

Aronsson, K. (1991). Social interaction and the recycling of legal evidence. In N. Coupland, J. M. Wiemann, & H. Giles (Eds.), *Problem talk and problem contexts. Handbook of miscommunication* (pp. 215–243). Newbury Park, CA: Sage.

Aronsson, K., & Nilholm, C. (1990). On memory and the collaborative construction and deconstruction of custody case arguments. *Human Communication Research, 12*, 289–314.

Bakhtin, M. (1981). *The dialogical imagination. Four essays by M. M. Bakhtin*. Austin, TX: University of Texas Press.

Bakhtin, M. (1986). *Speech genres and other late essays*. Austin, TX: University of Texas Press.

Beach, W. A. (1985). Temporal density in courtroom interaction. Constraints on the recovery of past events in legal discourse. *Communication Monographs, 52*, 1–19.

Bennett, W. L. (1978). Storytelling in criminal trials. *Quarterly Journal of Speech, 64*, 1–22.

Bennett, W. L. (1979). Rhetorical transformation of evidence in criminal trials: Creating grounds for legal judgment. *The Quarterly Journal of Speech, 65*, 232–311.

Bennett, W. L. (1991, June). *Legal fictions: Telling stories and doing justice*. Paper presented at the 40th Annual Conference of the International Communication Association, Trinity College, Dublin, Ireland.

Cicourel, A. V. (1985). Text and discourse. *Annual Review of Anthropology, 14*, 159–185.

Cody, M. J., & McLaughlin, M. (1990). Interpersonal accounting. In H. Giles & P. Robinson (Eds.), *The handbook of language and social psychology*. London: Wiley.

Conley, J. M., & O'Barr, W. M. (1990). Rules versus relationships in small claims disputes. In A. D. Grimshaw (Ed.), *Conflict talk* (pp. 178–196). Cambridge: Cambridge University Press.

Heider, F. (1958). *The psychology of interpersonal relations*. New York: Wiley.

Jönsson, L., & Linell P. (1990). Story generations: From dialogical interviews to written reports in police interrogations. *Text, 11*(3).

Liebes-Plesner, T. (1984). Rhetoric in the service of justice: The sociolinguistic construction of stereotypes in an Israeli rape trial. *Text, 4*, 173–192.

Maynard, D. W. (1982). Person-descriptions in plea bargaining. *Semiotica, 42*, 195–213.

Neisser, U. (1982). John Dean's memory. A case study. In U. Neisser (Ed.), *Memory observed: Remembering in natural contexts* (pp. 139–159). San Francisco: Freeman.

Neisser, U. (1985). Toward an ecologically oriented cognitive science. In T. M. Shlechter & M. P. Toglia (Eds.), *New directions in cognitive science* (pp. 17–32). Norwood, NJ: Ablex.

O'Barr, W. M., & Conley, J. M. (1985). Litigant satisfaction versus legal adequacy in small claims court narratives. *Law & Society Review, 19*, 661–701.

Ochs, E., Smith, R., & Taylor, C. (1989). Detective stories at dinnertime: Problem-solving through co-narratives. *Cultural Dynamics, II*(2), 238–257.

Read, S. J. (1987). Constructing causal scenarios: A knowledge structure approach to casual reasoning. *Journal of Personality and Social Psychology, 52*, 288–302.

Read, S. J., Druian, P. R., & Miller, L. C. (1989). The role of causal sequences in the meaning of actions. *British Journal of Social Psychology, 28*, 341–351.

Ricoeur, P. (1971). The model of the text: Meaningful action considered as text. *Social Research, 38*(3), 529–562.

Rommetveit, R. (1985). Language acquisition as increasing linguistic structuring of experience and symbolic behavior control. In J. V. Wertsch (Ed.), *Culture, communication and cognition: Vygotskian perspectives* (pp. 183–204). Cambridge: Cambridge University Press.

Rommetveit, R. (1990). *Outlines of a dialogically based social-cognitive approach to human cognition and communication.* Unpublished manuscript.

Rorty, R. (1979). *Philosophy and the mirror of nature.* Princeton: Princeton University Press.

Wertsch, J. V. (1991). *Voices of the mind: A sociocultural approach to mental action.* Cambridge: Cambridge University Press.

Woodbury, J. (1984). The strategic use of questions in court. *Semiotica, 48*, 197–228.

14
▼▼▼▼▼▼▼

What Went Wrong: Communicating Accounts of Relationship Conflict

Ann L. Weber
University of North Carolina at Asheville

John H. Harvey
University of Iowa

Terri L. Orbuch
University of Michigan

> *My college years changed me in ways I am still trying to understand. Somewhere else would have shaped me differently, but how? Better or worse? Keep asking yourself questions, I tell my students who are writing essays, until you know what you really think. Don't give up too quickly. Don't settle for easy answers. I don't always tell them how long one has to continue asking.*
>
> (Toth, 1984, p. xviii).

ACCOUNTS AND EXPLANATIONS

"Explaining oneself to others" suggests a prior acceptance of self-knowledge; first you figure yourself out, then you pass along this insider's information to interested others. But as Susan Allen Toth expressed above in the introduction to her college memoirs, *Ivy Days*, the self-questioning process may be unending and unrelenting. Self-understanding is more process than product, and so then is self-explanation to others. We reflect on our experiences and actions, deliberate or otherwise, deriving some essential form and lessons to distribute both to ourselves and to our significant others.

Our own work in recent years has focused on the this "essential form" of self-understanding and interpersonal meaning. From our beginnings in the study of attributional processes and causal analysis (Harvey, Weber, Galvin, Huszti, & Garnick, 1986; Harvey, Weber, Yarkin, & Stewart, 1982; Harvey, Wells, & Alvarez, 1978), we have become convinced that individuals seek to understand their own lives and their intimacy with others through a process of account

261

formation. Briefly, account-making refers to the construction of story-like understandings for events in our lives, and accounts are the products of this construction process (Harvey, Orbuch, & Fink, 1990; Harvey, Weber, & Orbuch, 1990). Accounts can be privately formulated and rehearsed, then publicly disclosed and negotiated with others. They contain attributions about the causes of important events (e.g., breakups) and usually have scripted markers for their beginnings, middles, and endings (see Gergen & Gergen, 1983). Simplified descriptions of the components of accounts belie the richness and complexity of their story-like quality and interwovenness with ideas of self, intimacy, fate, and justice. For example, an account for a marital breakup may summarize the plot leading up to terminal conflict, replay a critical exchange between the partners, present the account-relater in a sympathetic light, justify or wonder about the demise of the relationship thereafter, and conclude on a philosophical note about the relater's future expectations about intimacy. Consider some of those features in this near-comic excerpt from Nora Ephron's 1983 novel *Heartburn*, reputedly a fictionalized autobiographical account of her own marital experiences:

> My first husband was so neurotic he kept hamsters. They all had cute little names, like Arnold and Shirley, and he was very attached to them and was whipping up little salads for them with his Slice-o-Matic and buying them extremely small sweaters at a pet boutique in Rego Park . . . The reason my marriage to Charlie broke up — although by now you're probably astonished that it lasted even a minute — was not because he slept with my oldest friend Brenda or even that he got crabs from her. It was because Arnold died (p. 79).

This is only a sliver of one account, and admittedly fictional and presentation conscious. Nonetheless it rings familiar, recounting a complex experience in simplified terms (he was neurotic, he was immature, he overreacted when his hamster died) and exonerating the storyteller of blame. It has the added advantage of entertainment value. Accounts are not always "shared" with others, either intimates or in a public forum, but good accounts make good stories, and good stories make for good social exchange.

We argue that accounts are most often developed in the context of interpersonal relations. Accounts are often developed in response to others' questions and promptings, are withheld from or disclosed to others, are refined and negotiated through social interaction and communication, and are, essentially, *about* other people in individuals' lives and experiences. Accounts may well be the matrix of our identity concepts, especially in the broader sense that "an account is a narrative is a story." A central thesis remains, however, that accounts and account-making pervade our thoughts and feelings, in private ruminations and social behaviors, with powerful consequences for our personal and social lives (see Harvey, Orbuch, & Fink, 1990).

In previous discussions (e.g., Harvey, Weber, & Orbuch, 1990; Weber, Harvey, & Stanley, 1987) we have more directly explored the nature of the account-making process and its components. In the present chapter we shift our focus further along the social chain to examine the forms and uses of accounts in interactions with others. Specifically, why are accounts disclosed, or not disclosed, to others? What kinds of triggers or decisions precipitate account-relating? How do audience variables affect the process and the product? And how might the account itself affect the audience? In sum, we will explore the account as a vehicle of *communication*, from its formulation, through its relation to others, and to questions of the nature and motives of confidants. We have argued elsewhere (especially Weber et al., 1987) that accounts are a form of story*telling*, targeted at, presented to, and tailored for an audience. Here we extend this argument, in particular examining the role of accounts in understanding and explaining relationship conflict.

After a brief review of the attributional heritage of relationship accounts, we will focus on forms and dynamics of accounts about relationship conflict per se. We will next explore freely the issues involved in explaining "what went wrong" to others, and conclude with observations about the role of accounts in coping, comprehending, accepting, and planning for the intimate adventures of our lives. Our examples derive from widely varied literary and scholarly sources, a diversity that underscores the richness and ubiquity of the account in human discourse.

Relationship Accounts: Research and Theory

We define account-making as the process of constructing a story-like explanation of events and experiences. The account typically includes explanations, descriptions, predictions about relevant future events, recollections, justifications, and emotions. Accounts are likely to be formulated or resurrected when individuals are troubled by stressors or surprises, especially unpleasant ones. Sub-accounts for different episodes—for example, conflict experiences recalled about one's marriage—eventually comprise related "chapters" in an overarching master account of a person's life experiences.

Within the context of attribution theory, our initial work on accounts (e.g., Harvey, Wells, & Alvarez, 1978) began as a follow-up to Weiss's (1975) powerful analysis of marital separation. Weiss emphasized the organizing and energizing effect of accounts in the lives of persons adjusting to the loss of a close other. For Weiss, the account is vital in the chain of events by which a person achieves closure about the loss of a relationship and motivation to move on with his or her life. Our work on account-making was subsequently extended and now includes the role of accounts in other stressful circumstances, including Vietnam combat veterans' reactions to life after the war (Harvey, Agostinelli, & Weber, 1989) and elderly persons' reactions to the loss of loved ones through death, divorce, or relocation (Weber et al., 1987). Available evidence suggests that well-developed accounts play a salutary role in providing perspective, the will to carry on, hope for the future, and closure regarding such stressors (see Harvey, Weber, & Orbuch, 1990, for a general review).

In earlier work on attributions, Harvey, Wells, and Alvarez (1978) observed that the experience of relationship conflict is one for which people have few scripts or guidelines. Consistent with Weiss's (1975) description of the "obsessive review" that many newly separated individuals undertake, Harvey et al. (1978) suggested that "these vigilant, restless periods may be filled with incessant causal analyses. Further . . . continued causal analysis may make the difficulty of separation somewhat more palatable" (p. 256). In particular, Harvey et al. (1978) noted, such attributional analysis seems particularly important and intense *after* separation, although it might be argued that intimate partners are always interested in the whys and wherefores of their relationship experiences—especially when those experiences entail conflict.

Attribution is more active than mere curiosity, and account-making appears to be a major (if not always deliberate) cognitive undertaking. Relationship conflict is experienced as a stressor or trauma, and in this sense account-making develops as an attempt to cope or defend. In considering how account-making enters into people's reactions to severe stressors, we have borrowed and elaborated on Horowitz's (1986) sequential stage-model of reactions to stress. In our modification of this model (Harvey, Orbuch, & Weber, 1990), the stress response includes the following sequence of stages:

1. *Traumatic event*: involving shock (feeling overwhelmed, numb);
2. *Outcry*: involving emotional expression (panic, exhaustion, despair, hopelessness);
3. *Denial*: early stage of account-making, possibly involving escapism (avoidance, isolation);
4. *Intrusion*: continued or initial account-making, involving flooded states (distraction, obsessive review);
5. *Working through*: intensified account-making, confiding with close others;
6. *Completion*: completion of the "story," acceptance, possession of coping skills; and,
7. *Identity change*: behavioral expectations formulated in line with the account.

In this model we suggest that *failure* to engage in account-making will incur several negative consequences, including problems of failing to work through one's loss (e.g., psychosomatic illnesses related to denial), failing to complete the coping process (e.g., prolonged grief or anxiety), and failure to learn or adapt by developing a new identity in response to the loss (e.g., reiterated stress, exhaustion, or fixation of a maladaptive response pattern). In sum, we argue that account-making is a useful, healthy, adaptive strategy within the stress-response sequence. One's account, far from being an epiphenomenon or a kind of symptomatic imagery associated with grief or stress, is an essential process of coping with the stresses and losses inevitable in any life touched by intimacy and hope.

Understanding Conflict and Loss

Attribution can be described as the cognitive business of asking—and attempting to answer—the question, "Why?" The question is triggered by surprise or disappointment, not just "mystery." Not all mysterious events prompt causal analysis, and, ironically, many events that do not seem mysterious can prompt intense attributional activity: The loss of a loved one to disease may be medically "understood," but the process of acceptance and grief requires some questioning—"Why this person?" "Why me?" and "Why now?"

When a friend or an age-mate suffers a baffling fate, we defensively question the causes. "Could it happen to *me* if I am not careful?" When the inscrutable "Other" is one's own intimate partner, the questioning and obsessing are even more personal. We accept little and ask much when our own relationships are in trouble. Both the causes and the experience of relationship conflict can depend on the relationship's history and duration. One pattern of "conflict cognition" in close relationships was noted by Kyle and Falbo (1985), who have found that attributional discrepancy is related to the degree of marital stress that partners report. In their study, individuals in more stressed marriages were more likely to make situational attributions about their spouses' positive behavior ("She made a big deal about remembering my birthday, because my parents were visiting and she knew they expected to celebrate"), but dispositional attributions about their spouses' negative behavior ("He never remembers our anniversary; I guess it's just not important to him"). These misattributions may be tacit distortions of partners' roles in relationship satisfaction; people may assume that such interpretations are obvious, and not bother to share them, much less examine and question their validity. Thus Orvis, Kelley, and Butler (1976) warned that attributional conflicts will be unresolvable as long as they remain unspoken.

As silent as partners might choose to remain about sources of conflict in their relationships, they may nonetheless engage in a sort of "running attribution" throughout the course of their liaison (Harvey, 1987). This search for causes can be undertaken variously to smooth out a relationship's rough spots, identify salient issues, or justify the behavior of self or other. The running attribution may develop into a "master account" or story of the relationship we tell ourselves in the course of our accumulated experiences. This private story may set the tone for our attitudes toward relationship repair, breakup, or eventually getting over a loss.

However, we may not even realize we have been developing an attributional account until we experience stress or conflict in the relationship. With trouble comes a need for answers, prompting the search for explanations and interpretations. In a vicious circle, conflict may prompt both a need for honest attribution and a tendency to think in distorting, biased terms. Unfortunately, the stakes are high, as Harvey noted: "In a close relationship, this search for meaning takes on major significance to the individual because one is most vulnerable in such a relationship. It is in close relationships that humans' greatest jobs and, at the same time, greatest anguish are often experienced" (p. 431).

In his ingenious "map" of the terrain of relationship dissolution, Duck (1982) has proposed an inventive, comprehensive model of the stages of dissolution. In the first, *intrapsychic* phase, the decision to terminate is still more a temptation than a plan, although the aggrieved partner has crossed the threshold of tolerance for relationship dissatisfaction, and now collects ammunition—complaints, "proof" of the other's inadequacy, and attractions to alternative relationships— preparatory to withdrawing. In the second, *dyadic* phase, the temptation becomes a decision that is shared, or at least communicated in some sense to the till-now-unwitting other. Now the partners face or confront each other, engage in "our relationship" talks, perhaps attempt reconciliation, and consider the costs and benefits of changing or breaking up. In the third, *social* phase, other people—the network of friends, personal and mutual—become more important in shaping both partners' images of what Duck calls the "post-dissolution state" (1982, p. 16). In this social phase partners actively create publicly negotiable, face-saving and/or blame-placing stories and accounts. One's friends must be informed about the impending breakup, gossip must be spread, and attributions, to some slight extent, must be controlled. This may be each partner's last chance to influence the reputation that will follow him or her into the "pool of eligibles" outside the committed relationship.

In the fourth and final stage, which Duck calls the *grave-dressing* phase, one engages in various "getting over" activities, retrospects, shifts from constructive to postmortem attribution, and distributes his or her own version of the breakup story. By this time, the two ex-partners have somewhat separate audiences or clientele, and their accounts are freer to be discrepant and antagonistic. Are they accurate? Is *either* account accurate? Such questions assume that either partner had contact with the "real" relationship, and that distortions would be optional and deliberate. Our understanding of the account, however, accepts the likelihood that neither partner's story will resemble an "objective" rendering of the relationship's events, much less agree importantly with each other's. What is sought and revealed in these posttraumatic narratives is a psychological reality unassailable in terms of objectivity. Partners cannot be objective about each other; that is the nature of intimacy, whether now or once upon a time.

Interestingly, Duck's "topography" of relationship dissolution begins with an "intrapsychic" phase—a nonmutual, personally genuine experience of overwhelming doubt, dissatisfaction, and dilemma. Long before the breakup is real to the dyad, it is real to one partner, who may nurse or brood on it indefinitely before "breaking" it to the other, thus crossing the threshold to the dyadic phase. In her study of *Uncoupling*, Diane Vaughan (1986) noted that "Uncoupling begins with a secret. One of the partners starts to feel uncomfortable in the relationship. The world the two of them have built together no longer 'fits' " (p. 11). To some extent, then, conflict shakes the house-for-two and threatens to cast both partners back out into the street, where the price of admission—either to one's old or a new circle of support—is the story. "What went wrong? Why are you back out here (or there) among the uncoupled? It wasn't your fault, was it?"

To summarize, the attributional work of much of a relationship's maintenance is automatic, ongoing, even unconscious. When the unexpected occurs, or bad news is received, or one is tempted to invest in a replacement, the attribution becomes newly important. We scrutinize what we had barely noticed, analyze what was once thought to be obvious and honest. Attribution becomes deliberate, intense, and essential to self-justification. In terms of our "stress sequence" model of account-making (see earlier), conflict introduces a *traumatic event*. The distressed partner *cries out*, retreats and tries to *deny* the threat, brooding about the danger and its early warning signs. But the problem or loss does not go away; it *intrudes* into everyday life, reveals itself in errors, preoccupations, and altered affect. Nagging questions and curiosities explode into obsessive reviews: "Why did this happen? What could I have done to prevent it? Why couldn't we have been happy?" As each person *works through* the changes and transitions of coping, these account-making efforts forge and mature. Stories are repeated to oneself like litanies, then are shared with others, selectively or otherwise. In time, events suggest a *completion* to the story, one accepts the ending, the new state of self and the world, and moves on. One's *identity has changed*, the account continues to churn, alternately tugging and inspiring, suggesting how the future should and could be different.

But accounts are not forged in a vacuum. Few ex-partners ride out their anguish in lonely garrets until, paler and thinner, they again rejoin the social world. Essential to "working through" is *confiding* the account to others, hearing oneself think it out loud, confronting new information and insights, even using the story to gain or maintain membership in one's circle of friends. How does what was once intrapsychic anguish or irritation become translated into a social presentation? We turn our speculations to the process whereby one's private account becomes a public story.

Telling Our Stories

> We were trying to talk about love
> and blank pain that stays blank
> until music makes a shape for it
> so to know it, so to feel it out . . .
>   (From "Tanglewood," in Ryan, 1989, p. 74).

There is an essential skill in storytelling and in account-making: find a familiar form, a mundane example, a sympathetic lure for your tale. Invite your audience to give you more time, more grace, more idiosyncrasy credit. Anyone who has ever been invited to give a speech or keynote address understands the impossibility of coming up with something profound to say in the 35 minutes right after dinner. Instead, successful speakers start simple—and stay there. An essayist begins an abstract argument with a concrete example or personal anecdote. Aesop used fables to illustrate broader moral lessons. In time, one's account abbreviates a complex life experience into a form of self introduction: "As you can see from my story, I understand these things."

In our own work we have sometimes used the term "story" interchangeably with "account." But stories are colloquially assumed to be fiction ("Oh," we chide the liar, "now you're just telling me a story"), and social scientists are reluctant to welcome possible deceptions and distortions with open arms. The work of Cochran (1986, 1990) has made inroads in reassuring social psychologists that story offers more truth than otherwise. Cochran's concept of story itself is simple and familiar. A story has a *beginning* (introducing a *status quo* and an upset), a *middle* (when the gap is closed between the way things are and the way they ought to be), and an *end* (an opposition to the beginning, whether or not it is expected or desired). According to Cochran (1990), story mirrors and illumines human reality in at least four ways (pp. 73–74): (a) *we live in story*—we appreciate before and after, remembering the past as we anticipate the future; (b) *we represent life in story*—we dream, hope, plan, and despair in narrative form; (c) *we explain through story*—routes from one state or locus to another are related in terms of beginning-to-end changes; and (d) *we understand or comprehend through story*—we use narrative to synthesize the scattered parts of the now-meaningful pattern.

We cite Cochran here to support our argument that the story form is a friendly rather than alien form for our accounts. Because story, by definition, begins with a challenge or upset to existing order, *every* story is, in a sense, about conflict, and every conflict or loss lends itself to story. We now consider the factors that influence the early formation of a tellable story, a disclosable account: having something to tell; questioning and answering; giving narrative shape to amorphous thoughts and feelings; conjuring memories; constructing and construing meaning; and preparing, at last, to tell.

Something to Tell.   Conflict in close relationships lends itself readily to the narrative form. Several of Weiss's (1975) participants in Seminars for the Separated began their own accounts of life after loss with descriptions of the conflicts they believed had led to the separation. In her book *Necessary Losses* (1986), Judith Viorst cited examples of both "bad" and "not so bad" marital conflict, contrasting the cliches of "happily ever after" with the messier, complex tangles that more commonly describe intimate discord. Viorst's descriptions of "low-key" conflict may illustrate a healthier marital style, but they are not as dramatic—or entertaining—as *stories*. Harmony and compatibility make good relations but boring narratives; after all, "happily ever after" is how the story usually *ends*. As a consequence, we may not consider our own relationships accountworthy until and unless they are in trouble. Linguist Deborah Tannen (1990) grasped this irony with the following observation:

> I had a friend, a man, who had been single for many years and had developed a wide and strong network of women friends to whom he talked frequently. When he developed a stable relationship with a woman and they moved in together, his friends complained that he did not tell them anything anymore. "It's not that I'm keeping things from them," he told me. "It's just that Naomi and I get along fine and there's nothing to tell." (p. 99)

Part of the account-making process, then, must be the awareness of having "something to tell," a problem or challenge that is worthy of the story form.

Questions and Answers. Another aspect of account-making in the wake of conflict is the articulation of questions—usually *why* questions, as in *obsessive review* (Weiss, 1975)—and tentative answers or guesses. In a poignant and powerful memoir of his now long-ended marriage, Morris (1990) poured out his own account in response to such self-prompting and questioning:

> The anger, bafflement, jealousy, and sting threatened never to go away, and their scar tissue is probably on my heart forever. Yet whose *fault* was it? I ask myself now, hundreds of miles and a whole generation removed. And what did it say about ourselves? As with many strange and faraway things in one's life, did it ever mean anything at all? (p. 170)

Morris reconstructed a chronicle of events, beginning with their romance, early married days, early successes and divergent careers. He concluded: "It all happened too swiftly. . . . How to explain such things, or even to remember them and be honest about them, for memory itself selects and expurgates and diffuses. It was not as fun as it had been" (p. 172).

Morris's account, unusual in that it is admittedly autobiographical and very publicly presented, provides a neat example of Duck's (1982) placement of the attributional account in the social phase of his model of dissolution. In the social phase, the breakup account has at least two functions: it *recounts* (to others, the "social" audience) the events that led to the breakup; and it *charts a sequence* or sense (to oneself, the "intrapsychic" theater) of causes, effects, and agency. In this latter role, the account-maker, like Morris in the second excerpt above, can hear himself think. What begins as a convoluted and confused explanation is now summarized wryly, succinctly: "It was not as much fun as it had been."

Narrative Shape. Harvey, Orbuch, Chwalisz, and Garwood (1991) have observed that, during the Working Through and Completion stages of our stress-response model, account-making becomes more mature and takes on more narrative shape. Here, then, is another feature of account-making in its transition from private attribution to public distribution: It is given form and focus. Research on rumor-mongering and gossip (Rosnow & Fine, 1976) suggests three steps in the process of account-shaping: Irrelevant details are omitted (*leveling*), key points are exaggerated (*sharpening*), and one's values and world view are incorporated into the resulting lesson (*assimilation*). Presentation to and sharing with an audience are critical processes in account-shaping, as Duck and Pond (1989) described: "By means of accounts presented in public, whether as justification or as gossip with friends, humans structure for themselves the parts that they see as most significant and salient in their relationships, and this in turn constrains expectations" (p. 33). Duck and Pond explored the double meaning of "romance" as both falling in love and creating stories, suggesting they are equally noble human enterprises.

Remembering.   Among various indirect ways to collect others' accounts, one of the more straightforward and uncomplicated is to solicit people's relationship *memories*, with the safe assumption that the more available memories have significant status. Moreover, people who report their memories, we have found, seem to do so in a narrative form, rather than free-associating ideas or sensory impressions. In a cogent essay arguing for the use of stories in moral education, Vitz (1990) noted that narrative thought is one of two basic types of cognition, the other being propositional or paradigmatic (logical) thought. While propositional thinking relies on process or semantic memory (e.g., how to calculate 2 + 2, or the meaning of the word "reredos"), narrative thinking actively employs what Tulving (1983) called *episodic* memory (e.g., what was said the last time one argued with one's partner). Episodes may be fraught with meaning and yet far from simple to store or retrieve.

The historian David Thelen (1989) commented on the complex fabric of episodic memory in exploring the relationship between memory and history. If narrative is the most promising structure for solving problems of selection and interpretation in historical research, noted Thelen, then "the study of memory may provide the most promising entrance to the possibilities in narrative" (p. 1119). Ironically, Thelen chose a relationship example to illustrate the problem of reconstruction and divergent perspectives in social memory: "People are often surprised when they first learn that friends plan to get a divorce, but then they reconstruct their associations with the couple and create a new pattern in which the divorce seems a more logical outcome of what they remembered" (p. 1121). In the course of translating private attributions into public tale-spinning, we can expect much questing and construction of remembered details and negotiation with others for temporal landmarks: "We had a big argument, I remember, about the car. The car wouldn't start because it was too cold. So it must have still been winter at that time."

Meaning.   The sense-making dynamic of account-making pervades its route from private rumination to public presentation. Accounts have Gestalt properties (Weber, in press; Weber et al., 1987): they establish the account-maker's sense of *control*, and satisfy the search for *closure*. They are also subject to errors and illusions. In Michotte's (1946/1963) classic demonstration, participants who saw animated two-dimensional shapes move on a screen "interpreted" the movements in terms of entities and forces, causes and intentions. In our retrospective account-making, we "discover" connections of time or place that we had not previously seen, and this "explains" once-baffling events. Right or wrong, perceptive or paranoid, we look on all characters and events as possible symbols of something else or something more. From such exercises we construct a more meaningful story, and, for good or ill, our account gives us a new sense of identity, and of the world (Harvey, Orbuch, & Fink, 1990).

Preparation.   Finally, in the process of taking one's private account and retailing it in public, the account-maker prepares the account for its public "debut," so to speak. Vitz (1990) argued strongly that there exists in modern culture a "popular narrative need," perhaps engendered by the "abstract, juiceless quality of so much instruction in our contemporary schools" (pp. 716–717). In contrast, we infer, a good narrative, one that will satisfy and instruct its audience, has to be "juicy"—a word that can describe both fruit and gossip. To go public, one's account should offer high drama, tragic irony, or comic style. It should be *engaging* to the disclosee.

Aside from waiting until one's experiences have been tragic or absurd enough to warrant presentation, how else might the account-maker prepare material for public distribution? According to Sarbin (1986), a narrative or story has a temporal dimension: it has a beginning, a middle, and an end (or a sense of an ending). The ending may be the hardest contrivance for the account-maker to prepare—he or she may still be waiting for answers, feeling not at all "finished"—but in its public form the *account must conclude*, at least with a status report. For example, the hopeful account-maker could close by saying, "I never did get that phone call—at least, not yet." It has a cliffhanger quality that may work as an ending until the next installment.

Another preparation the account-maker may undertake is redefining the *role of self* in the story. The account may be born in questions and framed in guesses, but one must not keep one's listeners in the dark indefinitely. All must be revealed—eventually. If an account-maker at one point comments that "At the time I thought this meant . . ." then the listener will expect the later conclusion. "But I later found out what it really meant." Crites (1986) observed that the teller gains personal continuity from story-like narrative; separate (originally unrelated) episodes are all strung together with connective I's. This I-narrative may be distorted or illusory (e.g., autobiographers tend to recall events to their own advantage, what their critics call "lying," observed Crites), but its continuity be-comes real, and it relieves the "acute unease a human being can feel without a coherent story of a personal past" (p. 162). This self-meaning function of ready-ing one's account for relating exemplifies what Cochran (1990) termed the "bardic vision" of the story teller, who must interpret as well as report what happened. Indeed, we should take care, warned Shotter (1987), for as we tell our stories we come to believe them.

To review, the conflict account must summarize, in narrative form, what went wrong in the relationship. It must have something to tell, it must ask questions and pose answers, assembling fragments of obsessions and accusations into a fo-cused, highlighted, narrative shape. Within this shape the account-maker will resurrect and reconstruct old memories and plumb them for new meanings. To prepare it for public distribution or presentation, the account-maker must con-sider how to make the story engaging, finished, and self-descriptive. We have, up to now, examined the *inner* options of the account-maker, working alone and privately. But narratives are essentially *social* creations, subject to ongoing in-terpersonal checking (Robinson & Hawpe, 1986), constructed at least in part *for* social distribution, to fix blame and save face in the wake of relationship failure (Duck, 1982). Moreover, their very formulation involves others' input, or imag-inings of their inputs and responses: "Narrative construction can never be entire-ly a private matter. In the reliance on a symbol system for relating or connecting events, one is engaging in an implicit social act" (Gergen & Gergen, 1983, p. 268). The nature of the "audience," whether readers or listeners, supporters and defenders of the account-maker, or adversaries and critics, must influence the form and dynamics of the account. We now consider the strategies and dynamics of communicating the conflict account on the social level.

TELLING WHAT WENT WRONG

Secrecy and Confidence

To tell or not to tell? The question may come up at any point in the account-making/ stress-responding sequence. Harvey et al., (1991) pondered: "One of the most intriguing questions is for those who cope better, does private intensive account-making type activity occur before public confiding? Or vice versa? Or some com-bination of a little of each along the way?" (p. 17). We start by considering the oxymoron in quotation from Harvey et al.: "public confiding." To confide (liter-ally to communicate something "with faith" in its security) assumes selectivity— closer to the private end of the private–public continuum. "Public" seems too in-discriminate for most account communication. Just how public can an account-maker go? When is a message less a matter of "confiding" than of "broadcasting"?

The account-maker's alternative is, of course, secrecy. What Duck (1982) called the "intrapsychic stage" of relationship breakdown is necessarily one-sided but not necessarily silent. A dissatisfied partner need not suffer quietly. Even when the conflict escalates to the dyadic level, it need not be a surprise to either partner. By the time the account fragments are assembled in the social phase of breakdown, they consist largely of bits and pieces of affect, attribution, recrimination, and self-justification, with recurrent themes but little focus. The package has not yet been shaped into a narrative. Parts of the package may be familiar and oft-shared with others in one's network. Some of the "getting over" process will involve compiling reasons and rationalizations about why a breakup is "just as well," or a litany of the other's faults (Harvey et al., 1982). So much of what will become one's initial account may not have been secret, or kept as such.

In her provocative exploration of secrets, sociologist Sissela Bok (1983) noted that the word "secret" derives from the Latin *secernere*, meaning to sift apart as with a sieve. The etymology implies discernment (which shares a common root) and the ability to make distinctions. Another implication is of intimacy or privacy, a sense made clear in the German descriptor *heimlich* (pertaining to home, hearth, and family affairs). Bok observed that negative views of secrecy are common: "Why should you conceal something, many ask, if you are not afraid to have it known?" (Bok, p. 8). Thus the account-maker may consider it important to "tell all," then, in order to feel righteous and vindicated.

If secrecy depends on discernment, then the decision to confide depends on the nature of one's friendships. Linguist Deborah Tannen (1990) asserted that secrets in fact can *create* friendship, with a familiar gender effect: "Keeping friends up-to-date about the events in one's life is not only a privilege; for many women it is an obligation" (p. 98). Tannen has found that women are more likely than men to disclose confidential and personal information to their same-sex friends — and to expect that exchange as an aspect of friendship. Tannen commented that "many men resent their wives' or girlfriends' talking about their relationships to friends. To these men, talking about a personal relationship to others is an act of disloyalty" (pp. 109–110).

Tannen analyzed these gender differences in terms of power: To keep a secret is to hide vulnerabilities; to reveal it is to expose those vulnerabilities to attack, and thus to disarm the one whose trust has been betrayed. In traditional gender and power relationships, men are more fearful of "losing," and women are more likely to "talk." One consideration in favor of keeping one's account a secret, therefore, might involve fears of appearing to be the loser or the weak one in the conflicted or failed relationship.

Telling: Decisions and Deliberations

Benefits.   Why tell? There are surely benefits to crossing from the private anguish of "having" the story to the public release of "spilling" it. So many of our metaphors for self-disclosure convey this message of relief and unburdening:

getting it off one's chest; taking the lid off; letting others in on it; coming clean; making a clean breast of things; clearing the air. We can safely read in such idioms the promise that honesty and disclosure will ease the teller's tensions and invite support. Telling is also a simpler course than *not* telling. As a therapist we know has quipped, "The best thing about telling the truth is that you don't have to remember what you said."

In her extensive survey of adultery, Lawson (1988) discovered that access to a confidant was considered especially important to first-time participants in extramarital liaisons. Indeed, she observed, some may have all along been seeking a confidant more than a lover in the liaison itself! In confiding such a secret, the teller may be seeking approval, testing acceptance and friendship, or merely breaking the paralysis of the secrecy itself. A character in a short story by Laurie Colwin (1981) remarked about learning that her friend has begun an affair, that "I knew that if she needed to talk she would come to see me and eventually she did just that. . . . It is part of the nature of the secret that it needs to be shared. Without confession it is incomplete" (p. 129).

Finally, just as rumor-mongering has the benefit of conferring status on the monger ("I am in the know"), so also confiding one's account to another gives the account-maker control and status in that particular exchange and elevates the confidant to the level of *specially* trusted friend and intimate. The reward for disclosing a good story may include momentary status, fame, friendship, and appreciation. But the cost may be inclusion in the chain of gossip, with a resultant loss in control of who gets the story and how its characters are portrayed.

Risks.   Why not tell? One reason is the fear of having one's trust violated, being betrayed by having the account relayed beyond one's permitted circle. At some point the secret is lost, it is no longer one's own. Bok (1984) warned that "one cannot trust all who listen . . . to be either discreet or especially capable of bringing solace or help" (p. 80). Another risk is negative judgment by the recipient. Inette Miller (1987) waited almost a full year before revealing her extramarital affair to her brother, as she recounts in her diary:

> I confided to my brother by phone today the story of this affair. He and his daughters (had) visited here Thanksgiving, and he sensed then that something was very wrong. We had long private talks over that holiday visit, but I skirted the actual fact that I was involved with a man. . . . Already, talking to my brother and my friend Anna puts David and me into the category "people who have affairs"—a generic type, an academic classification. (p. 65)

The pain of this judgment, in Miller's interpretation, is that it oversimplifies her experience, labels her, and makes her a victim of prejudice by those who should know her best.

Harvey et al. (1991) noted that a bad or unhelpful response on the part of the confidant is a very real possibility, with painful consequences for the discloser.

One of Harvey et al.'s respondents commented that her early attempts to report sexual abuse by her brother were met with disbelief on the part of authorities and anger on the part of her parents: "Their reactions left me feeling totally isolated and alone. Forcing me to be victimized for another four years . . ." (p. 14). Perhaps in cases of undeniable tragedy and wrongdoing, like the assault and incest accounts Harvey et al. studied, it is reasonable to be anxious or cynical about outsiders' responses to a victim's confidences. But even in the cases of noncriminal or nonviolent tragedy, such as relationship loss, there are no clear guidelines or social scripts governing what victims might disclose or how their confidants can be expected to react. In Weiss's (1975) work with the recently separated, one man voiced the confusion of many would-be confidants:

> I remember when friends of ours separated, we were really awkward with them. We just didn't know how to talk to them. How do you talk to somebody who is so totally removed from your situation and so obviously miserable? What can you say? What can you do? . . . What the hell do you talk about? (Man, late twenties, separated). (p. 148)

Weiss further found that the newly separated are generally concerned about presenting themselves and explaining their new status to others. One decried the lack of script for announcing marital failure: "I've said, 'Well, there is something you ought to know,' and then told them. And then there is a short silence. And then they say, 'Oh, I'm really sorry.' And what do you say then? Thank you for being sorry?" (Man, about thirty) (p. 151). Another of Weiss's respondents even expressed feelings of responsibility toward her confidant, as if aware of the privilege of having someone to listen to her, and wary of abusing that privilege: "There's a person who knows me, my happy days and my sad days. I hate to think that every time I see her I have something sad to tell her. I'd like to think that I could tell her some of the happy things" (Woman, late thirties) (pp. 149–150).

Finally, even if one can overcome the fear of an unhelpful or awkward response on the part of caring and uncaring listeners alike, there is always the danger of outright contradiction. Gergen and Gergen (1983), commenting on the social essence of the narrative, noted that, especially when an account is justificatory, its content must be *negotiated* with others. One's confidant may take the side of one's ex-partner ("You must be wrong, I know So-and-so could never intentionally hurt your feelings!") or may more generally undercut the talker's emerging version of self ("I think you overreacted, just like you've done before").

Our brief examples here might create the unfortunate impression that the transition from private account to public story is accomplished in a moment's outburst, blurted out in its entirety, and frozen in form for all subsequent audiences. But this is far from the case. Harvey, Orbuch, and Fink (1990) argued that, for account relating to have positive consequences, the development and communication of the account takes time; it is not a short-term process providing instant relief: "We also believe that the confiding or account-making often requires much

work and many years in order for a sense of completion and tranquility to develop" (Harvey, Orbuch & Fink, 1990, p. 53). Although they note that writing
may be helpful as a supplement or occasional substitute for supportive interactions, a journal entry is no "quick fix," especially for more severe and enduring
stressors. Finally, work with elderly respondents has indicated that in cases of
loss through expected death (as a result of long-term illness), the bereaved person experienced less difficulty accepting the reality of the loss and reported less
need to develop accounts. Some were reluctant to "burden" others with their talk
or feelings, or at least felt that it was not an undue hardship not to talk about
the loss with others.

    In sum, there are often real costs and benefits to be considered in conveying
one's conflict account into social conversation. In addition, as we now examine,
the teller must consider, even choose, his or her audience.

Audience Considerations

In earlier work we have suggested that account-makers will consider characteristics of various audiences and "tailor" certain account presentations to fit the
listeners' expectations or roles (see Harvey, Weber, Galvin, Huszti, & Garnick,
1986; Weber et al., 1987). How might audience characteristics specifically affect the content and communication of the account?

Gossip management.   Duck (1982) summarized audience effects in terms
of a very practical problem:

> that relationship dissolution not only has to happen but has to be managed and dealt
> with in a teeming social context. Real friends, real relatives, real social institutions
> may have to be informed about the dissolution and, if the relationship was a signifi-
> cant one, these social entities will probably have a strong view about the whole
> thing. (p. 8)

McCall (1982) specified the terms of this "management" challenge, saying that,
after dissolution, one's reintegration of self depends on reintegration with the social network, answering personal questions for them as well as for self: "What
does Partner really mean to me and my life? Why me? What's wrong with me?
What's Partner really like? What am I really like? What really happened?" (p.
220). The social network provides active reconstructors of the accounts as well
as the more passive confidant role we have considered up till now, as McCall
continues: "Both partners find themselves called upon by others in their personal
networks to provide an account of the relationship's spoiling—some story of the
relationship that in some way answers the six key questions" [aforementioned]
(p. 224).

    Finally, LaGaipa (1982) proposed that audience considerations of account distribution might best be considered under the general rules of social gossip. LaGaipa said three criteria must be considered before telling one's disengagement story: (a) choose the right people to disclose to; (b) be selective about what and how much information to reveal; and (c) limit accountability by avoiding extreme forms of criticism or slander.

Social Sanctions.   Aside from matters of practical "rumor control," the account-maker is well advised to consider some aspects of old-fashioned human nature. Just as Rubin (1976) found, in her study of working class Americans, that "guys don't talk to other guys" about personal and marital issues, so also Komarovsky (1962) had earlier observed that intimate *talk*, even between women, might be a norm peculiar to middle-and upper-class relationships and households. The primarily middle-class researchers who speculate about responses to relationship conflict may transfer their (our) biases about the "talking cure" to our respondents by selectively sampling both our respondents and their problems. Even if an interviewer can manage to behave "blankly," not wishing to violate the prime directive against communicating value judgments to respondents, simply inviting talk can send a more accepting signal than would otherwise have been perceived. In her interviews with working class respondents, Rubin asked questions about marriage and sexual behavior for which many of her interviewees had no "public" language or scripts. One woman expressed relief at being able to discuss oral sex so "casually": "Jim keeps telling me and telling me it's okay, that it's not dirty. But I always worry about it, not really knowing if that's true or not. . . . I never talked to anyone but Jim about it before. . . . You're so cool about it; talking to you makes it seem not so bad" (p. 144). The story one tells may depend to no small degree on the reception one anticipates from the audience.

We thus rely on tacit rules of conversation and gossip in phrasing our accounts for distribution to others. The story itself may not seem finished or conclusive until we have had a chance to sound out our audience.

CONCLUSION: TALES OF FUTURE SELVES

The act—really a series of actions, a *process*—of communicating "what went wrong" in a relationship to others has important defining and reconstructing effects for self-concept and social identity. Elsewhere and consistently, we and our colleagues have argued that account-making has healthy, productive, positive consequences for the account-maker (Harvey et al., 1982, 1986, 1989, 1991; Harvey, Orbuch, & Weber, 1990; Harvey, Weber, & Orbuch, 1990; Weber et al., 1987). In terms of our stress-response model (Harvey, Orbuch, & Weber, 1990), sharing the account with others is important for working through the conflict or loss and pursuing another kind of completeness in its wake.

Ephron (1983) called on the social construction of account-sharing when her fictional alter-ego asks her nonfictional readers:

Is this inevitable, this moment when everything leads to irritation, when you become furious that he smokes, or that he coughs in the morning, or that he sheds crumbs, or that he exaggerates, or that he drives like a maniac, or that he says "Between you and I"? You fall in love with someone, and part of what you love about him are the differences between you; and then you get married and the differences start to drive you crazy. (p. 83)

Ephron's narrator uses the second person pronoun directly to *invite* her audience to agree with her, to commiserate, and to give social validation to her lament. A writer thus manipulates grammar and voice to establish what is more familiarly solicited between friends, speaking face-to-face: "Don't you know what I mean? Haven't you had the same experience as I?"

Finally, the account-maker forges a renewed identity by communicating the account and *being done with it*. Morrell (1988) explained to the reader in his preface that he *must* tell his painful story, "for like the Ancient Mariner, my heart surely burns to tell you—once and for all, to be done with my tale, to exorcise my demons, to gain and preserve my faith" (p. 5). To her surprise, when Rubin (1976) presented her completed manuscript to her interviewees for their perusal, they failed to recognize their own words, admitting they seemed familiar but attributing them to others. She commented, "These responses were typical—attempts to avoid re-experiencing the pain. If it can be externalized or denied, dealt with as a familiar experience but not one's own, it's easier to read about, easier to bear" (p. 214). Once the account is confided, part or all of it can be *let go*; the account-maker can get quit of it and move on with his or her life.

Ultimately, the sense of identity culled from account-making and sharing is one that is actively forged, achieved, composed. Harvey, Weber, & Orbuch (1990) likened this identity-shaping process in account-making to Erikson's adult life-goal of *generativity* (e.g., Erikson, 1963). Even when one's memories rise unbidden or one's account is confided with more impulse than discretion, this generative, shaping control is woven into its context. In concluding his sad retrospection of his marriage and divorce, Morris (1990) admitted this deliberate element:

In the course of an existence, people move in and out of one's life. Often we do not know the *whereabouts* of those once dear to us, much less what they are feeling or remembering. . . . There are a few small islands of warmth and belonging to sustain us if we are lucky. That is how I wish to think of her now, in the days of our happiness. (p. 175)

Wishing to think fondly, choosing to remember happily: these are examples of the ways accounts generate *hope*. Crites (1986) argued that hope for the future is implicit in weaving stories about the past, because the narrative form promises the power to reshape a future that is different from one's past. In a romantic sense—both as love and as story—Weber et al. (1987) commented that one's account is also an act of *faith*, because remembering and reconjuring one's account may be as close as it is possible to come to our past promises of "always." We hope the truths of our relationships will be more enduring than our mortal selves. In this endearing, doomed effort, each story told and heard gives breath to that hope.

REFERENCES

Bok, S. (1983). *Secrets: On the ethics of concealment and revelation*. New York: Vintage Books.

Cochran, L. R. (1986). *Portrait and story*. New York: Greenwood Press.

Cochran, L. R. (1990). Narrative as a paradigm for career research. In R. A. Young, & W. A. Borgen, (Eds.), *Methodological approaches to the study of career* (pp. 71–86). New York: Praeger.

Colwin, L. (1981). *The lone pilgrim*. New York: Aflred A. Knopf.

Crites, S. (1986). Storytime: Recollecting the past and projecting the future. In T. R. Sarbin (Ed.), *Narrative psychology: The storied nature of human conduct* (pp. 152–173). New York: Praeger.

Duck, S. (1982). A topography of relationship disengagement and dissolution. In S. Duck (Ed.), *Personal relationships 4: Dissolving personal relationships* (pp. 1–30). New York: Academic Press.

Duck, S., & Pond, K. (1989). Friends, Romans, countrymen, lend me your retrospections: Rhetoric and reality in personal relationships. In C. Hendrick (Ed.), *Close relationships* (pp. 17–38). Newbury Park, CA: Sage.

Ephron, N. (1983). *Heartburn*. New York: Alfred A. Knopf.

Erikson, E. (1963). *Childhood and Society*, 2nd edition. New York: W. W. Norton.

Gergen, K. J., & Gergen, M. M. (1983). Narratives of the self. In T. R. Sarbin & K. E. Scheibe (Eds.), *Studies in social identity* (pp. 254-273). New York: Praeger.

Harvey, J. H. (1987). Attributions in close relationships: Recent theoretical developments. *Journal of Social and Clinical Psychology, 5*, 420-434.

Harvey, J. H., Agostinelli, G., & Weber, A. L. (1989). Account-making and the formation of expectations about close relationships. In C. Hendrick (Ed.), *Close relationships* (pp. 39-62). Newbury Park, CA: Sage.

Harvey, J. H., Fink, K., & Orbuch, T. L. (1990, August). *Behavioral reactions to accounts*. Paper presented to the meeting of the New Zealand Psychological Society, Christ Church.

Harvey, J. H., Orbuch, T. L., Chwalisz, K. D., & Garwood, G. (1991). *Coping with sexual assault: The roles of account-making and confiding*. Unpublished manuscript.

Harvey, J. H., Orbuch, T. L., & Fink, K. (1990). The social psychology of account-making: Meaning, hope, and generativity. *New Zealand Journal of Psychology, 19*, 46-57.

Harvey, J. H., Orbuch, T. L, & Weber, A. L. (1990). A social psychological model of account-making in response to severe stress. *Journal of Language and Social Psychology, 9*, 191-207.

Harvey, J. H., Weber, A. L., Galvin, K. S., Huszti, H. C., & Garnick, N. N. (1986). Attribution and the termination of close relationships: A special focus on the account. In R. Gilmour, & S. Duck, (Eds.), *The emerging field of personal relationships* (pp. 189-201). Hillsdale, NJ: Lawrence Erlbaum Associates.

Harvey, J. H., Weber, A. L., & Orbuch, T. L. (1990). *Interpersonal accounts: A social psychological perspective*. Oxford: Basil Blackwell.

Harvey, J. H., Weber, A. L., Yarkin, K. L., & Stewart, B. E. (1982). An attributional approach to relationship breakdown. In S. Duck (Ed.), *Personal relationships 4: Dissolving personal relationships* (pp. 107-126). New York: Academic.

Harvey, J. H., Wells, G. L., & Alvarez, M. D. (1978). Attribution in the context of conflict and separation in close relationships. In J. H. Harvey, W. Ickes, & R. F. Kidd (Eds.), *New directions in attribution research, Vol. 2* (pp. 235-260). Hillsdale, NJ: Lawrence Erlbaum Associates.

Horowitz, M. J. (1986). *Stress response syndromes* (2nd ed.) Northvale, NJ: Jason Aronson.

Komarovsky, M. (1962). *Blue-collar marriage.* New York: Random House.

Kyle, S. O., & Falbo, T. (1985). Relationships between marital stress and attributional preferences for own and spouse behavior. *Journal of Social and Clinical Psychology, 3,* 339–351.

LaGaipa, J. (1982). Rules and rituals in disengaging from relationships. In S. Duck (Ed.), *Personal relationships 4: Dissolving personal relationships* (pp. 189–210). New York: Academic.

Lawson, A. (1988). *Adultery: An analysis of love and betrayal.* New York: Basic Books.

McCall, G. (1982). Becoming unrelated: The management of bond dissolution. In S. Duck (Ed.), *Personal relationships 4: Dissolving personal relationships* (pp. 211–232). New York: Academic.

Michotte, A. E. (1963). *The perception of causality.* London: Methuen. (Original work published 1946)

Miller, I. (1987). *Burning bridges: Diary of a mid-life affair.* New York: G. P. Putnam's Sons.

Morrell, D. (1988). *Fireflies.* New York: E. P. Dutton.

Morris, W. (1990, June). Here lies my heart. *Esquire,* 168–175.

Orvis. B. R., Kelley, H. H., & Butler, D. (1976). Attributional conflict in young couples. In J. H. Harvey, W. J. Ickes, & R. F. Kidd (Eds.), *New directions in attribution research, Vol. 1* (pp. 353–386). Hillsdale, NJ: Lawrence Erlbaum Associates.

Robinson, J. A., & Hawpe, L. (1986). Narrative thinking as a heuristic process. In T. R. Sarbin (Ed.), *Narrative psychology: The storied nature of human conduct* (pp. 111–125). New York: Praeger.

Rosnow, R. L., & Fine, G. A. (1976). *Rumor and gossip: The social psychology of hearsay.* New York: Elsevier.

Rubin, L. B. (1976). *Worlds of pain.* New York: Basic Books.

Ryan, M. (1989). *God hunger.* New York: Viking Books.

Sarbin, T. R. (1986). The narrative as root metaphor for psychology. In T. R. Sarbin (Ed.), *Narrative psychology: The storied nature of human conduct* (pp. 3–21). New York: Praeger.

Shotter, J. (1987). The social construction of an "us": Problems of accountability and narratology. In R. Burnett, P. McGhee, and D. D. Clarke (Eds.), *Accounting for relationships* (pp. 225–247). London: Methuen.

Tannen, D. (1990). *You just don't understand: Women and men in conversation.* New York: William Morrow & Co.

Thelen, D. (1989). Memory and American history. *Journal of American History, 75,* 1117–1129.

Toth, S. A. (1984). *Ivy days.* Boston: Little, Brown and Co.

Tulving, E. (1983). *Elements of episodic memory.* New York: Oxford University Press.

Vaughan, D. (1986). *Uncoupling: Turning points in intimate relationships.* New York: Oxford University Press.

Viorst, J. (1986). *Necessary losses.* New York: Ballantine Books.

Vitz, P. (1990). The use of stories in moral development. *American Psychologist, 45,* 709–720.

Weber, A. L. (in press). The account-making process: A phenomenological approach. In T. L. Orbuch (Ed.), *Close relationship loss: Interdisciplinary theoretical approaches.* New York: Springer-Verlag.

Weber, A. L., Harvey, J. H., & Stanley, M. A. (1987). The nature and motivations of accounts for failed relationships. In R. Burnett, P. McGhee, & D. D. Clarke (Eds.), *Accounting for relationships* (pp. 114–135). London: Methuen.

Weiss, R. S. (1975). *Marital separation.* New York: Basic Books.

15

▼▼▼▼▼▼▼

Accounting for Failure to Follow Advice: Real Reasons Versus Good Explanations

Margaret L. McLaughlin
Michael J. Cody
Risa Dickson
University of Southern California

Valerie Manusov
Rutgers University

Despite the recent proliferation of work on excuses and justifications, or more generally *accounts*, within the field of communication (see reviews in Cody & McLaughlin, 1990a, 1990b), such work has seemed to have little impact on social psychologists interested in ordinary explanation, with only a few notable exceptions (see for example Weiner, Amirkhan, Folkes, & Vereth, 1987; Weiner, Figueroa-Muñoz, & Kakihara, 1991), and at the same time communication researchers do not seem to have evidenced any interest in how causal reasoning and event comprehension might shape communicated explanations. The project reported here was designed in part to marry the insight gained from two largely independent research traditions, with the goal of furthering our understanding of the mutual interdependence of event comprehension and context.

Our project was influenced by four papers, which we will examine in some detail. The first was Weiner, Amirkhan, Folkes, & Vereth's (1987) attributional analysis of excuse-giving. The four experiments reported by Weiner et al. in the 1987 paper seemed to be motivated by a rather traditional perspective in attribution theory work: the notion that people explain events, to themselves and to others, in terms of dimensions like internal versus external causation (i.e., person versus situation), controllable versus uncontrollable, and intentional versus unintentional.

In a series of experiments on excuses given for a broken social contract, Weiner and his colleagues found that *communicated* explanations for failure events tended to be external to the person, uncontrollable, and unintentional, whereas *withheld* reasons (that is, the "real reasons") were apt to be internal, controllable, and either intentional (referring to lack of will or desire) or unintentional (e.g., forgetting). Weiner and his colleagues adduced data in support of the proposition that excuses that cite internal, controllable, intentional reasons for failing to perform as expected tend to create greater anger in those who hear them than do excuses that invoke external, uncontrollable, unintentional reasons. That is, pleading forgetfulness or lack of will could be expected to create less mitigation for the offender than citing factors beyond his or her control or conscious design.

We have also been influenced by current thinking about explanation coming out of cognitive psychology and cognitive science. In a 1987 paper, Stephen Read made a persuasive case for a knowledge-structure approach to causal reasoning. Read pointed out a number of shortcomings of classical approaches to attribution that focus heavily on such dimensions as internality versus externality in explaining causal reasoning. The case is made that the classic "covariation" principles of attribution, consistency, consensus, and distinctiveness, which are said to determine if the cause of an event lies in "something about the person," or "something about the event," fall far short of modeling the *concreteness* of most ordinary explanation. Read argued that classical approaches can't explain how people arrive at particular explanations; to do so requires that knowledge of specific stimulus domains be invoked. Other shortcomings of traditional approaches include their inability to account for *sequences* of behavior, multiple causes of behavior, or the role of the actor's plans and goals. It is to the latter factor that the current research project is addressed; that is, to the importance of plans and goals as *explanatory loci*.

In their 1986 paper on the nature of explanations, Leddo and Abelson contended that it "seems cognitively inefficient" that people possess specialized knowledge structures just for the explanation of events. Explanation is viewed as a specific application of the general process of event comprehension; thus the same knowledge structures involved in understanding should be sufficient to account for explanation. Like Read, Leddo and Abelson argued that most explanations are concrete; that rather than engaging an ANOVA-like process in which the actions of parties to some current explainable are compared to hypothetical parallel actions, most explanations derive from specific knowledge of the parties to the event and their relationship. Further, some explanations may be at a higher order of complexity and invoke an interaction effect between person and situation in order to provide a full and delimiting account.

In a 1988 paper by Abelson and Lalljee, the authors explicitly considered the knowledge structures available for the explanation of failed events—those episodes that do not "come off" as expected. Abelson and Lalljee contended that a good place to go for explanations for unsuccessful performances is to the sequence of actions, or script, for the successful performance of the action in question. For example, to explain why one's mate did not return from the market, as expected, with a carton of milk, one could search the conventional sequence of actions involved in making a purchase at a grocery store and look for possible steps at which the action could fail. These might include a failure of entry; a failure of initiation of instrumental action (for example, not being able to find the right item); a failure of "doing" (for instance, not having the wherewithal to complete the transaction); and so on (Leddo & Abelson, 1986). Abelson and Lalljee also developed the notion of an *explanation prototype*, a knowledge structure organized around the usual ways in which events fail.

In the Leddo and Abelson study, each respondent read ten failed scripts (Buying a Car, Riding a Roller Coaster, Cashing a Check at the Bank, etc.), and then for each script rated the likelihood of each of nine plan-based explanations for the failure event. They found that two plan categories, *entry* and *doing*, were rated as the most likely sources of script failure. Least likely were postcondition and exit failures.

In the project reported here, we were interested in applying a knowledge structure approach to the study of communicated explanations. Like Weiner, we wanted to look further into the perceived differences between the withheld, or real, reasons for failure events and the communicated reasons, or excuses. We took the study of Leddo and Abelson as a model, but extended it to include not only plan- or script-based explanations, but goal-based explanations as well. Given the importance of the internal–external dichotomy as a dimension for judging the plausibility and mitigativeness of excuses, it seemed important that respondents have available for judgment causes internal to the actor, such as characterizations of his/her inner state and motivations, as well as specific external obstacles to success, such as entry or implementation failures. Among the goal failures we included in our study were failures of will, forgetting, competing goals, and failures of understanding.

Briefly, we had respondents complete one of two forms of a questionnaire in which they provided both open-ended and scaled responses to questions about the likelihood of goal- and plan-based reasons for five failed event scenarios. In one form of the questionnaire, respondents were asked about *the reasons* for the failure event. On the other form, they were asked about *good explanations* for the failure event. Each of the scenarios represented a case in which someone failed to follow a friend's advice.

No main effect for Attribution Type was expected, but given the arguments for the concreteness of explanations, we anticipated a small within effect for Scenario and a strong Attribution Type × Scenario interaction effect.

METHOD

Preliminary Study

The preliminary study was designed to obtain independent assessments of advice-giving scenarios with respect to standard compliance-gaining situation factors (Cody & McLaughlin, 1985). Respondents were 50 students enrolled in undergraduate communication courses at two large universities in the western United States. Class credit was awarded for participation.

Respondents were asked to evaluate each of seven scenarios on seven-step rating scales measuring five dimensions of situation perception (Cody & McLaughlin, 1985). Advice-giving scenarios were developed from compliance-gaining goal prototypes obtained in Cody, Canary, & Smith (in press).

The seven scenarios were:

1. You advise your roommate to drop one English course in favor of another one which you had taken (DROP CLASS);
2. You advise your roommate against parking in a certain parking lot that you regard as unsafe (DON'T PARK);
3. You advise your roommate to call a doctor about his/her fever and cough (CALL DOCTOR);
4. You advise your roommate to watch a production of King Lear on TV (WATCH KING LEAR);
5. You advise your roommate to go to a suburban DMV office rather than the one downtown (GO TO DMV);
6. You advise your roommate to xerox the notes from the psychology class s/he's missed (COPY NOTES); and
7. You advise your roommate to be blunt in discouraging an unwanted admirer (BE BLUNT).

Respondents were asked to imagine giving the advice to a person who was their current, or a recent, roommate, and then to evaluate the advice with respect to five perceptual dimensions pertinent to compliance-gaining situations: (1) *personal benefit* ("I benefit" – "My roommate benefits"; "I am (am not) persuading my roommate to do something for his/her own benefit"); (2) *request size* ("My roommate would (would not) think this was too much to expect"; "It would (would not) take a lot of effort on the part of my roommate to do this"); (3) *right to request* ("I am justified (have no justification) in making this suggestion"; "I have (do not have) a right to make this suggestion"); (4) *relational consequences* ("This situation has (does not have) future consequences for the relationship between my roommate and me"; "The outcome of this situation could have (could not have) potentially harmed the relationship between me and my roommate"); and (5) anticipated *resistance* ("I think (do not think) my roommate would be very agreeable to doing this"; "I could (could not) talk my roommate into doing this very easily").

Five of the scenarios were selected for use in the main study. Ratings of the five advice-giving scenarios on the situation perception dimensions are presented in Table 15.1.

TABLE 15.1
Ratings of Advice-Giving Scenarios on Five Dimensions of Situation Perception

Scenario	Other-Benefit	Request Size	Right to Persuade	Relational Consequences	Resistance
(DROP CLASS) You advise your roommate to drop one English class in favor of another	5.66	2.78	5.70	3.46	2.84
(DON'T PARK) You advise your roommate against parking in a certain parking lot that you regard as unsafe	6.39	2.12	6.22	3.22	2.17
(CALL DOCTOR) You advise your roommate to call a doctor about his/her fever and cough	6.14	2.66	6.11	2.76	2.79
(WATCH KING LEAR) You advise your roommate to watch a production of *King Lear* on TV	6.18	2.57	5.69	1.89	2.65
(GO TO DMV) You advise your roommate to go to a suburban DMV office rather than the one downtown	6.20	2.75	5.98	2.62	2.76

MAIN STUDY

Respondents

Respondents were 215 undergraduates enrolled in introductory courses in communication at three large universities in the western United States. Class credit was awarded for participation.

The main task of respondents was to evaluate a series of explanations for a *compliance-gaining failure*. Compliance-gaining failure scenarios were constructed from the advice-giving scenarios developed for the preliminary study. For example:

> You advise your roommate to drop one English class in favor of another one that you had taken. Your roommate later returns with the same class schedule.

Approximately half of the respondents ($N = 110$) were asked to consider *the reason* why a roommate would not comply with the advice to drop a class, call a doctor, go to a different DMV office, and so on; the other half ($N = 105$)

were asked what might be a *good explanation* or acceptable excuse for the failure to comply.

In Part I of the questionnaire, respondents supplied open-ended answers, the analysis of which we will report elsewhere. In Part II respondents evaluated a series of candidate reasons (or good explanations) for each of five compliance-gaining failure scenarios on pairs of 7-step rating scales (probable explanation-improbable explanation and likely reason-unlikely reason, or, acceptable reason-unacceptable reason and good reason-not a good reason.

The explanations that respondents evaluated for each of the five scenarios were attributions of goal or planning failures modeled on items used in Leddo and Abelson (1986) in their study of attributions for script failure. Items were constructed for each of the following categories (definitions adapted from Leddo and Abelson):

GOAL FAILURES

Goal Absence (a): The action fails because the actor didn't recognize the importance of a goal.

Goal Absence (b): The action fails because the actor forgot the goal.

Goal Absence (c): The action fails because the actor lacked the will or desire to attain the goal.

Goal Conflict: The action fails because a competing goal takes precedence.

Goal Reversal: The action fails because the actor's goal is opposite that which ought to prevail in the situation.

Goal Dissolution: The action fails because of the actor's loss of interest in pursuing the goal.

Goal Satisfied: The action fails because the actor believes the goal has been/can be met by alternative means.

PLANNING FAILURES

Preparation Failure: The action fails because the actor did not undertake the necessary preliminaries (such as consulting a map).

Entry Failure: The action fails because the actor could not gain access to the main setting in which action was to occur (e.g., the parking lot is roped off).

Precondition Failure: The action fails because of the absence of normal input/output conditions or the unavailability of normal accompaniments to action (e.g., the doctor's telephone line was busy).

Instrumental Precondition Failure: The action fails because a preliminary or precursor action could not be undertaken (e.g., there was too much traffic).

Instrumental Initiation Failure: The action fails because the instrumental plan (main action) could not be completed (e.g., the doctor had no openings).

Instrumental Actualization Failure: The action fails because the instrumental plan (main action) could not be completed (e.g., the recommended class is already full).

Doing Failure: The action fails because the original goal which gave rise to the action cannot be achieved (Leddo & Abelson, 1986). (For example, the only parking spaces left were too small for the car.)

Sample items for the advice-giving scenario DROP CLASS are given in Table 15.2. Items were presented to respondents in random order, without category labels.

RESULTS

Reliabilities

Alpha reliabilities for the fourteen explanation items were computed using the SPSSX reliability routine. Reliabilities are reported in Table 15.3.

Multivariate Analysis of Variance

Data were subjected to a 2 (Attribution Type: Reason versus Good Explanation) × 5 (Scenarios) MANOVA with Scenarios as a within factor. The program used was BMDP4V.

Attribution Type: Reason versus Good Explanation: There was a significant main effect for Attribution Type, $F(14, 200) = 25.98, p < .0001$, with a general trend for the explanations to receive higher ratings as good explanations than as reasons for failure to comply with advice. Table 15.4 gives the cell means for each of the 14 explanations, for each of the five scenarios and attribution type. Higher numbers correspond to judgments of greater plausibility as a reason/a good (acceptable) explanation. All univariate main effects for attribution type were significant except those for preparation failure and for goal conflict.

Scenarios: There was a significant within-groups main effect for Scenario, $F(56, 158) = 12.81, p < .001$. The most apparent source of the effect for scenarios was a trend for respondents to give high ratings to goal failures both as reasons and good explanations (but particularly as reasons) in the KING LEAR failure scenario and to assign comparatively low ratings to planning failures as reasons for failure to comply. The WATCH KING LEAR scenario was the item with lowest ratings with respect to the relational consequences of failure to comply and rights of the advice-giver to persuade. Respondents may have reasoned

TABLE 15.2
Sample Items for DROP CLASS Scenario

You advise your roommate to drop one English class in favor of another one which you had taken. Your roommate later returns with the same class schedule. What do you think might be *the reason* for your roommate's not dropping the first course in favor of the one you had taken?

Goal Failures	*Planning Failures*
Goal Absence (a)	*Preparation Failure*
Your roommate didn't realize the importance of dropping the first course in favor of the one you had taken	Your roommate forgot to write down the number of the course to add
Goal Absence (b)	*Entry Failure*
Your roommate forgot to drop the first course in favor of the one you had taken	The hours for add/drop were over when your roommate arrived
Goal Absence (c)	*Precondition Failure*
Your roommate just didn't want to drop the first course in favor of the one you had taken	They were temporarily out of add/drop forms when your roommate went to make the schedule change
Goal Conflict	*Instrumental Prec. Failure*
Your roommate had something else to do and didn't have time to go to add/drop	The lines at add/drop were too long
Goal Reversal	*Instrumental Init. Failure*
Your roommate didn't want to take a class that you recommended	The course you recommended was not being offered this term
Goal Dissolution	*Instrumental Act. Failure*
Your roommate lost interest in dropping the first course in favor of the one you had taken	The class you recommended was already full
Goal Satisfied	*Doing Failure*
Your roommate knew s/he could sign up for the class next semester	Your roommate couldn't register because the computer showed a hold on the roommate's record for library fines

TABLE 15.3
Alpha Reliabilities for Fourteen Explanations, Across Scenario and Attribution Type

Explanations	*Alpha Reliabilities*
Goal Failures	
Goal Absence (a)	.85
Goal Absence (b)	.86
Goal Absence (c)	.89
Goal Conflict	.82
Goal Reversal	.85
Goal Dissolution	.86
Goal Satisfied	.89
Planning Failures	
Preparation Failure	.87
Entry Failure	.90
Precondition Failure	.91
Instrumental Prec. Failure	.85
Instrumental Init. Failure	.90
Instrumental Actual. Failure	.90
Doing Failure	.91

TABLE 15.4
Within-Cell Comparisons of Means for Fourteen Explanations
as a Function of Attribution Type

	DROP CLASS		DON'T PARK		CALL DOCTOR		WATCH KING LEAR		GO TO DMV	
	GE*	R**	GE	R	GE	R	GE	R	GE	R
Goal Failures										
Goal Absence (a)	4.18	4.03	3.67	4.49[b]	3.09	4.22[c]	3.90	4.10	4.07	4.56[a]
Goal Absence (b)	3.55	3.36	3.37	4.10[b]	3.19	4.06[c]	4.23	5.40[c]	4.03	3.94
Goal Absence (c)	5.66	5.40	3.87	4.99[c]	3.78	5.20[c]	5.58	5.99[a]	5.49	5.59
Goal Conflict	4.33	4.87[a]	5.40	5.86[a]	3.93	4.64[b]	6.06	6.06	6.20	5.33[c]
Goal Reversal	5.03	4.46[a]	2.28	1.88	2.15	1.98	3.99	3.62	2.74	2.04[b]
Goal Dissolution	5.07	4.71	3.26	4.00[b]	2.98	4.26[c]	4.91	5.01	4.44	4.63
Goal Satisfied	5.42	4.48[c]	4.85	5.26	4.58	5.27[b]	6.44	5.32[c]	5.97	5.53[a]
Planning Failures										
Preparation Failure	3.70	3.63	3.51	3.61	3.31	3.14	3.66	4.46[b]	4.37	3.58[b]
Entry Failure	5.49	4.10[c]	6.56	4.84[c]	4.64	3.74[c]	5.73	2.71[c]	5.89	3.31[c]
Precondition Failure	4.18	2.44[c]	6.49	4.89[c]	4.61	2.59[c]	6.39	3.25[c]	4.63	4.10[a]
Instr. Prec. Failure	3.52	5.30[c]	6.35	3.64[c]	3.91	3.67	5.68	4.76[c]	5.97	5.51[a]
Instr. Init. Failure	6.71	5.01[c]	6.48	5.52[c]	4.98	4.53	6.46	3.72[c]	4.89	3.46[c]
Instr. Actual. Failure	6.78	5.85[c]	5.19	5.27	6.04	4.65[c]	4.72	2.49[c]	5.07	3.45[c]
Doing Failure	5.56	3.25[c]	5.40	3.40[c]	5.60	4.04[c]	5.72	3.15[c]	5.69	2.97[c]

*GE = good explanation
**R = reason
[a] = within cell, significantly different at $p < .05$, two-tailed
[b] = within cell, significantly different at $p < .01$, two-tailed
[c] = within cell, significantly different at $p < .001$, two-tailed

that it was not plausible that failing to comply with a relatively inconsequential piece of advice was attributable to a breakdown in planning; rather, the event was attributed to such internal goal-related factors as forgetting, naivete, or lack of will, which are also more acceptable as excuses when the failure has relatively little relational import.

Attribution Type × *Scenario Interaction:*   There was a significant inter-action between Attribution Type (Reason versus Good Explanation) and Scenario, F (56, 158) = 6.24, p < .001. Within-cell comparisons of means for the 14 explanations are presented in Table 15.4.

There was a very strong tendency for the goal failure items to be rated higher as reasons than as good explanations, whereas the planning failure items were consistently rated higher as good explanations than as reasons in the DON'T PARK, CALL DOCTOR, and WATCH KING LEAR scenarios, but the trend was less evident or, to some extent, reversed in DROP CLASS and GO TO DMV (see Table 15.5).

Examination of the univariate statistics indicated that there was a significant interaction of attribution type and scenario for each of the 14 explanation types except Goal Reversal. Below we consider the interactions separately for the 13 explanations for which the interaction was significant.

Goal Failures

Goal Absence (a).   Differences between not recognizing the importance of the goal as reasons and as acceptable explanations were significant in DON'T PARK, CALL DOCTOR, and GO TO DMV. The differences were in the oppo-site direction, or not significant, in the DROP CLASS and WATCH KING LEAR scenarios, respectively.

Goal Absence (b).   Forgetting rated significantly higher as a reason than as a good explanation in three situations, DON'T PARK, CALL DOCTOR, and WATCH KING LEAR, but the trend was in the opposite direction for DROP CLASS and GO TO DMV.

Goal Absence (c).   "Not wanting to" was rated significantly higher as a rea-son than as a good explanation in DON'T PARK, CALL DOCTOR, and WATCH KING LEAR, but the differences were nonsignificant, or in the opposite direc-tion, in the GO TO DMV and DROP CLASS scenarios, respectively.

Instrumental Precondition Failure.   Instrumental Precondition failure was rated significantly higher as a good explanation than as a reason in the DON'T PARK, WATCH KING LEAR, and GO TO DMV scenarios, but a significant scenario effect in the opposite direction was obtained for DROP CLASS.

TABLE 15.5
Direction of Significant Within-Cell Differences as
a Function of Attribution Type for Fourteen Explanations

	DROP CLASS	DON'T PARK	CALL DOCTOR	WATCH KING LEAR	GO TO DMV
		Goal Failures			
Goal Absence (a)		Reason*	Reason		Reason
Goal Absence (b)		Reason	Reason	Reason	
Goal Absence (c)		Reason	Reason	Reason	
Goal Conflict	Reason	Reason	Reason		Good Ex.
Goal Reversal	Good Ex.				Good Ex.
Goal Dissolution		Reason	Reason		
Goal Satisfied	Good Ex.		Reason	Good Ex.	Good Ex.
		Planning Failures			
Preparation Failure				Reason	Good Ex.
Entry Failure	Good Ex.	Good Ex.	Good Ex.	Good Ex.	Good Ex.
Precondition Failure	Good Ex.	Good Ex.	Good Ex.	Good Ex.	Good Ex.
Instr. Prec. Failure	Reason	Good Ex.		Good Ex.	Good Ex.
Instr. Init. Failure	Good Ex.	Good Ex.		Good Ex.	Good Ex.
Instr. Actual. Failure	Good Ex.		Good Ex.	Good Ex.	Good Ex.
Doing Failure	Good Ex.	Good Ex.	Good Ex.	Good Ex.	Good Ex.

*Attribution type listed (Reason, Good Explanation) had higher mean rating within cell

Instrumental Initiation Failure. Instrumental Initiation failure was rated significantly higher as a good explanation than as a reason in the DROP CLASS, DON'T PARK, WATCH KING LEAR, and GO TO DMV scenarios.

Instrumental Actualization Failure. Instrumental Actualization failure was rated significantly higher as a good explanation than as a reason for failure to comply in DROP CLASS, CALL DOCTOR, WATCH KING LEAR, and GO TO DMV.

Doing Failure. Doing failures were rated significantly higher as good explanations than as reasons for failure to comply in all five scenarios.

CONCLUSIONS

Results of the multivariate analysis of the data on excuses for failing to comply were generally supportive of the following propositions:

1. Respondents clearly distinguished between the probable causes of a failure event, on the one hand, and mitigating excuses for the same event, on the other;
2. The peculiar characteristics of the failure event determine the extent to which goal-based, as opposed to plan-based, attributions are invoked;
3. The type of attribution (reason versus excuse) strongly interacts with scenario, resulting in a highly concrete pattern of explanation attributable to the particulars of the failure event itself.

As the main effects for Attribution Type and Scenario are complicated by an interaction effect, we shall not attempt to interpret them here. The most interesting of our findings has to do with the comparative utility of goal- and plan-based explanations as a function of attribution type and scenario (failure event) characteristics (see Tables 15.4, 15.5).

A very cursory examination of the data in Table 15.5 will give rise to the observation that, generally, goal failures such as forgetting or having competing obligations are regarded as good candidates for "real reasons," and plans are more attractive explanatory loci when providing excuses for failure to comply. This is consistent with the conclusions reached by Weiner and his colleagues that effective excuses invoke causes that are unstable, uncontrollable, and external to the person. Although some of the planning failures might be equally as "internal" as goal failures (e.g., forgetting to write down the number of the course to sign up for), most planning failures that might be invoked as excuses have to do with events or sub-events in the action setting that didn't go off as planned, owing to factors beyond the actor's control (the office was out of add/drop slips; the class was already full; etc.).

However, the preference for goal attributions as reasons and plan attributions as excuses was not consistent across scenarios. The pattern was most pronounced for goal attributions for the DON'T PARK and CALL DOCTOR scenarios. Our preliminary ratings of these two scenarios on dimensions of situation perception indicated that in both scenarios the person giving the advice (that the roommate should avoid an unsafe parking lot/contact a doctor about his or her illness) was regarded as having a more legitimate right to persuade than obtained in the other scenarios. Further, the DON'T PARK situation was lowest rated of the five scenarios with respect to anticipated *resistance* to taking the advice and to the degree of imposition (*request size*) associated with the suggested course of action. In the DON'T PARK and CALL DOCTOR scenarios the advice-giver is concerned with the roommate's well-being and safety, as opposed to his or her convenience (GO TO DMV) or educational enrichment (DROP CLASS/KING LEAR). This greater perceived legitimacy of the advice-giver's position in the DON'T PARK and CALL DOCTOR scenarios resulted in lower ratings of goal failure explanations like forgetting, obliviousness, or lack of interest as good excuses, as opposed to real reasons.

One departure from the pattern described (that greater advice-giver legitimacy resulted in lower ratings of goal failures as excuses) occurred with respect to attributions to Goal Reversal and Goal Satisfied. In the DROP CLASS and GO TO DMV scenarios, attributions to goal reversal and goal satisfaction were rated significantly higher as good excuses than as reasons. DROP CLASS was rated in the preliminary study as comparatively low on benefit to the advice recipient, high in request size (degree of imposition), high on anticipated resistance to complying, and low on the advice giver's right to persuade. In short, DROP CLASS would have the least normative pressure to comply of the five scenarios. GO TO DMV was also rated high on degree of imposition and anticipated resistance, and comparatively low on the advice-giver's right to persuade. In such circumstances, the advice recipient is freer to decline to comply, and may more easily invoke discrepancies between his/her own and the advice giver's goals as excuses for noncompliance. Attributing the rejection of the advice to goal satisfaction, for example, the advice recipient may say, "I know I could just sit in on the class if I wanted to"; "I know I could just go to the downtown DMV early," and so on. What we are hard pressed to explain is why respondents regarded goal reversal items ("I didn't want to take a class my roommate recommended") as better excuses than, say, forgetting or having a conflicting goal (see Table 15.4). Interestingly, Goal Satisfied was not regarded as a better excuse than a reason in the CALL DOCTOR scenario. Evidently, claiming that you knew you'd get better without medical attention is not as efficacious an excuse for failing to call the doctor when ill as is claiming alternative paths to the goal under less serious circumstances.

Planning failures were consistently given higher ratings as excuses than as reasons. And, in about two-thirds of the cases, planning failures were rated lower than goal failures as reasons for noncompliance with advice, although the differences were not always significant. In short, respondents were more likely to regard failure to follow advice as the result of internal factors such as failures of will rather than external, uncontrollable factors like the presence of obstacles to successful plan implementation.

Although failed plans were generally regarded as good material for excuses, there were some anomalies. For example, preparation failure (forgetting to check the TV guide to see what time the play began) was not regarded as a very good reason for not watching *King Lear* (although it might have been the real reason), and in fact ratings for preparation failures as excuses were generally quite low: a reflection, perhaps, of the extent to which they invoke goal-related constructs such as forgetting. Also, the instrumental precondition failure in the DROP CLASS scenario ("the lines were too long") was not regarded as a good excuse. Although the presence of others is an external obstacle, certain internal factors (not being motivated to get there early; being too lazy to stand in line; etc.) are also implicated in such an excuse.

We have given here only a brief gloss of the trends evident in our data, suggesting that specific situation factors such as request legitimacy, degree of imposition, right to persuade, and so on, determine the extent to which plans or goals should (or can) be invoked in excuses for noncompliance. However, the results obtained are of sufficient complexity to warrant a cell-by-cell examination of the means in our Table 15.4. We are convinced that accounting for one's conduct is governed by a set of highly specific contingencies and situational parameters.

REFERENCES

Abelson, R. P., & Lalljee, M. (1988). Knowledge structures and causal explanation. In D. J. Hilton (Ed.), *Contemporary science and natural explanation* (pp. 175–203). New York: New York University Press.

Cody, M. J., Canary, D., & Smith, S. W. (in press). Conceptualizing compliance-gaining goals. In J. Daly & J. Wiemann (Eds.), *Communicating strategically*. Hillsdale, NJ: Lawrence Erlbaum Associates.

Cody, M. J., & McLaughlin, M. L. (1985). Models for the sequential construction of accounting episodes: Situational and interactional constraints on message selection and evaluation. In R. L. Street & J. Cappella (Eds.), *Sequence and pattern in communicative behavior* (pp. 50–69). London: Edward Arnold.

Cody, M. J., & McLaughlin, M. L. (Eds.). (1990a). *The psychology of tactical communication*. Clevedon, UK: Multilingual Matters.

Cody, M. J., & McLaughlin, M. L. (1990b). Accounts. In H. Giles & P. Robinson (Eds.), *Handbook of language and social psychology* (pp. 227–255). London: Wiley.

Leddo, J., & Abelson, R. P. (1986). The nature of explanation. In J. A. Galambos, R. P. Abelson, & J. B. Black (Eds.), *Knowledge structures* (pp. 103–122). Hillsdale, NJ: Lawrence Erlbaum Associates.

Read, S. J. (1987). Constructing causal scenarios: A knowledge structure approach to causal reasoning. *Journal of Personality and Social Psychology, 52*, 288–302.

Weiner, B., Amirkhan, J., Folkes, V. S., & Vereth, J. A. (1987). An attributional analysis of excuse giving: Studies of a naive theory of emotion. *Journal of Personality and Social Psychology, 52*, 316–324.

Weiner, B., Figueroa-Muñoz, A., & Kakihara, C. (1991). The goal excuses and communication strategies related to causal perceptions. *Personality and Social Psychology Bulletin, 17*, 4–13.

Author Index

Subject Index